D0082806

# Anthropology of Aging

**Recent Titles in**
**Bibliographies and Indexes in Gerontology**

Elder Neglect and Abuse: An Annotated Bibliography
*Tanya F. Johnson, James G. O'Brien, and Margaret F. Hudson, compilers*

Retirement: An Annotated Bibliography
*John J. Miletich, compiler*

Suicide and the Elderly: An Annotated Bibliography and Review
*Nancy J. Osgood and John L. McIntosh, compilers*

Human Longevity from Antiquity to the Modern Lab: A Selected,
Annotated Bibliography
*William G. Bailey, compiler*

Federal Public Policy on Aging since 1960: An Annotated Bibliography
*William E. Oriol, compiler*

European American Elderly: An Annotated Bibliography
*David Guttmann, compiler*

Legal Aspects of Health Care for the Elderly: An Annotated Bibliography
*Marshall B. Kapp, compiler*

Crime and the Elderly: An Annotated Bibliography
*Ron H. Aday, compiler*

Jewish Elderly in the English-Speaking Countries
*David Guttmann, compiler*

Women and Aging: A Selected, Annotated Bibliography
*Jean M. Coyle, compiler*

Fundamentals of Geriatrics for Health Professionals: An Annotated Bibliography
*Jodi L. Teitelman and Iris A. Parham, compilers*

Geriatric Nursing Assistants: An Annotated Bibliography with Models to
Enhance Practice
*George H. Weber*

# ANTHROPOLOGY OF AGING

## A Partially Annotated Bibliography

MARJORIE M. SCHWEITZER,
General Editor

Prepared under the Auspices of the
Association for Anthropology and Gerontology

Bibliographies and Indexes in Gerontology,
Number 13

**GREENWOOD PRESS**
New York • Westport, Connecticut • London

**Library of Congress Cataloging-in-Publication Data**

Anthropology of aging : a partially annotated bibliography / Marjorie
  M. Schweitzer, general editor ; prepared under the auspices of the
  Association for Anthropology and Gerontology.
     p.    cm.—(Bibliographies and indexes in gerontology, ISSN
  0743-7560 ; no. 13)
    ISBN 0-313-26119-9 (alk. paper)
    1. Aged—Cross-cultural studies—Bibliography.  2. Aging—Cross-
cultural studies—Bibliography.  3. Gerontology—Bibliography.
I. Schweitzer, Marjorie M.  II. AAGE (Organization)  III. Series.
Z7164.O4A55  1991
[GN485]
016.30526—dc20      91-9707

British Library Cataloguing in Publication Data is available.

Copyright © by the Association for Anthropology and Gerontology

All rights reserved. No portion of this book may be
reproduced, by any process or technique, without the
express written consent of the publisher.

Library of Congress Catalog Card Number: 91-9707
ISBN: 0-313-26119-9
ISSN: 0743-7560

First published in 1991

Greenwood Press, 88 Post Road West, Westport, CT 06881
An imprint of Greenwood Publishing Group, Inc.

Printed in the United States of America

The paper used in this book complies with the
Permanent Paper Standard issued by the National
Information Standards Organization (Z39.48-1984).

10 9 8 7 6 5 4 3 2 1

GN
485
.Z926
1991

# Contents

# Preface

The 1970s saw the rise of a new specialty in the field of
anthropology called the "Anthropology of Aging" or
"Comparative Cultural Gerontology." The focus on aging from
a cross-cultural perspective found in Leo Simmons'
pioneering work on The Role of the Aged in Primitive Society
(1945) did not attract the attention of anthropologists
until the late 1960s. Scattered statements on aging could
be found prior to that date, but the publications by
Margaret Clark (1967, 1973), Donald Cowgill and Lowell D.
Holmes (1972)--among others--attracted anthropologists to a
new research area. Clark delineated the contributions that
cultural anthropology could make to the study of the aged
and the aging process and Cowgill and Holmes focused on the
issue of aging and modernization. As has been pointed out
in several publications, anthropologists often consulted the
elders of a society to gain a description of the ways of
life that could no longer be observed. But it was only in
the late 1960s to the mid-1970s that elderly people and the
process of aging became recognized as a bona fide research
topic for anthropologists.

By the late 1970s, courses on the anthropology of aging
were being taught in more than 40 colleges in the United
States. New publications presented the research of
anthropologists who were focusing on aging in different
cultures as a specific topic of research. Responding to the
increasing interest in the anthropological/cross-cultural
perspective on aging by anthropologists as well as by many
others from outside of the discipline, the Association for
Anthropology and Gerontology published a volume which could
be used in communicating that perspective.

Teaching the Anthropology of Aging and the Aged: A
Curriculum Guide and Topical Bibliography, prepared by Jay
Sokolovsky and printed in 1982, presented outlines of seven
different specific courses on Aging and the Aged, and a
Topical Bibliography. The volume, which focused on aging in
different cultural contexts and the use of anthropological
methodology (also referred to as qualitative methodology) to

present a broader perspective on aging, was used widely by teachers, students, researchers, social workers, service providers and administrators from many different disciplines.  However, since the appearance of this volume and the Supplement to the Topical Bibliography on the Anthropology of Aging by AAGE's Phil Silverman, research has continued unabated and many more publications have appeared. The number of courses being taught on different aspects of aging has also increased.  This growth in research, teaching and practical application resulted in AAGE's decision to produce separate volumes which could adequately encompass these changes.  In the mid-1980s plans were made to update the Topical Bibliography/Teaching Guide and publish two volumes.   Under the able editorship of Doris Francis, Dena Shenk and Jay Sokolovsky, AAGE published Teaching About Aging:  Interdisciplinary and Cross-Cultural Perspectives (1990).

The present book is an updated edition of the Topical Bibliography.  The focus of the bibliography is on citations which represent anthropological perspectives and/or cross-cultural data.  However, given the broad range of topics, data from other disciplines are included when contributors felt it was warranted.  The topical outline of the 1982 volume has been retained, with minor additions and changes. The most important feature to be added, besides the greatly expanded number of bibliographic references, is the inclusion of annotations for particularly important citations.

Since the early 1970s several books and articles appeared which presented, for the first time, a full discussion of the new focus of anthropologists on the cross-cultural/anthropological aspects of aging.  Many of these important contributions have been annotated.  Other annotated citations include those which address special issues, such as method and theory as it relates to aging, and those which provide the clearest treatment of a particular topic.  Other annotated citations include those that provide a useful summary of a particular topic.


Using the Bibliography

The bibliography is organized according to topic. These topics are of two kinds:  (1)  Subject topics (such as Modernization) and  (2)  Regional/Cultural Group topics (such as Great Britain/American Indian).  A quick glance at the Table of Contents will alert the user to the topical headings of the chapters as well as the section headings which appear in many of the chapters.

An example will show how best to use the bibliography. The chapter entitled Ethnic/Rural Segments of the United States contains several section headings, such as "General" and "American Indians."  The user can expect that each of the citations in the section on American Indians will refer to that topic heading.  Citations which make comparisons to American Indians and one or more other groups have been placed in the "General" section.  Subject sections such as

"Broad Cross-Cultural Comparison,"  "Health and Social
Services," "Modernization" and "Women" also may contain a
limited number of citations referring to American Indians.
Likewise, users looking for every citation in the
bibliography that has to do with "Health and Social
Services" should check each of the Regional/Cultural Group
topic sections.  However, they will find very few citations
referring to Health and Social Services not already listed
in Chapter 3.

# Acknowledgments

## The Contributors

An enterprise of this scope, encompassing many different content areas, could not have been done by one individual alone. As general editor, I contacted over 50 international scholars in the field of aging. Of this number more than 40 of the individuals agreed to volunteer their time and expertise to update the various sections of the original bibliography. These contributors worked under varying time and schedule constraints which determined the contribution that each individual could make. Some contributors researched and annotated one or more sections, while others contributed lists of publications with no annotations or simply provided lists of their own publications.

Professional contributions of this kind are seldom recognized to the extent that they should be, but I think I speak for AAGE when I say that, regardless of the type and amount of contribution made by each contributor, I as general editor, and AAGE, are grateful for a job well done.

Following is an alphabetical list of contributors and the sections in which they made contributions. Readers should also recognize that the lists are not necessarily discrete in the sense that some individuals sent citations which were ultimately placed in other sections.

Maria Cattell -- Africa
                  Age Sets and Age Group Systems

Jacob Climo -- People of Antiquity

Dorothy Counts -- Horticultural Peoples

Marcha Flint -- Women and Menopause

Nancy Foner -- Broad Cross-Cultural and Holocultural-
                Statistical Comparison

Christine Fry -- Life Cycle -- Life Course
                    Methods

Anthony Glascock -- Ireland

Jaber Gubrium -- General Reading, Theoretical Perspectives

Haim Hazan -- Israel, Jews Outside of Israel

Neil Henderson -- Hispanic Americans

Ellen Holmes and Lowell D. Holmes -- United States
                                    Other Asian/Pacific
                                        Americans
                                    Modernization

Barbara Hornum -- Great Britain

Charlotte Ikels -- China
                    Chinese Americans

Jennie Keith -- Community Organization and Age-Homogeneous
                    Residences
                Age-Sets and Age Group Formation

Mark Luborsky -- Retirement

Peter Mayer -- Demography, Biology and Longevity

Seamus Mettress -- Ireland

Robert L. Rubinstein -- General Gerontology Texts, Readers
                            and Handbooks
                        Horticultural Peoples
                        National Cultures/General Comparison
                        European Americans
                        Death and Dying
                        Bibliographies
                        Ethnic/Rural Segments of the
                            US/General

Marjorie M. Schweitzer -- American Indians
                          Israel -- Jews Outside of Israel
                          Other National/Regional Cultures
                          Other European Nations/Canada
                          Black Americans
                          Japanese Americans
                          Family -- Intergenerational
                              Relations -- Ancestors

Dena Shenk -- Rural/Appalachian Americans
              Women

Jay Sokolovsky -- Anthropology of Aging Texts and Cross-
                      Cultural Readers
                  Urban Aged, Social Networks, Support

                        Systems
                  Peasants/Non-Tribal Agrarian Peoples

Phil Stafford -- Institutionalization
                  Semiotics:   Communication and Aging

Barb Stucki -- Africa

Lenore Greenbaum Ucko -- USSR

Peter van Arsdale -- National Cultures--Other
                          National/Regional Cultures

Sylvia Vatuk -- India

Joan Weibel-Orlando -- American Indians

G. Clare Wenger -- Great Britain
                   Ireland

Darryl Wieland -- Health and Social Services
                  Institutionalization

     The following individuals either sent lists of their
own publications or allowed me to consult bibliographies
they had prepared for other publications.

        Gay Becker                Christie Kiefer
        Peter Coleman             Phillip Silverman
        J. Keven Eckert           Phil Stafford
        James J. Jackson          Joel Savishinsky
        Linda James-Boykins       Dennis Wiedman
        Sharon Kaufman            Peter Woolfson
        David Kertzer

     I would like to give special thanks to the following
individuals whose extraordinary efforts made my job go much
more smoothly.

        Charlotte Ikels          Peter Mayer
        Nancy Foner              Sylvia Vatuk
        Ellen Holmes


## The Project

     AAGE is indebted to Oklahoma State University,
Stillwater, Oklahoma, for initial funding of this project
through the Arts and Sciences Research Division, and for
continued financial support through the Department of
Sociology for the production of the manuscript on OSU's IBM
mainframe and laser printer.  The Department of Sociology
also contributed financial and secretarial support (for the
initial mailings and continued use of the Departmental
office and telephone), and supplied a graduate assistant,
Linda Curtis, in the initial stages of the project.

Otto von Mering, Director of the Center for Gerontological Studies at the University of Florida in Gainesville, provided funds to help with the cost of data entry.

The Association for Anthropology and Gerontology also provided funds to pay for data entry.

The scanning of the original bibliography, the format of the bibliography pages and one-half of the data entry were done by Jim Russell of Dimensional Concepts, Stillwater, Oklahoma.

During the final eighteen months of the project, I assumed the job of data entry.

## The Final Production

Thanks to Jan Fitzgerald, Jean Ryan and Behrooz Jahan of OSU's Department of Sociology for facilitating the production of this project.

Thanks to Tom Buttress, at OSU's Computer Center, who unscrambled the Index.

And a special thanks to the monitors of OSU's Microcomputer Lab for helping me unlock the mysterious ways of word processors, diskettes, and C:\ drives, and especially for their good cheer and enthusiasm for the world of computers. Although they might not believe it, I learned a great deal that I did not know when I started this project. Good luck to Allen Roller, Mohammad Ali, Wei Chao, Nalini Hosur and to Mark Reynolds (who did not work in the Lab, but should have).

The final credit for the production of this manuscript goes to Richard Dodder, Department of Sociology, OSU. His expert advice on the intricacies of using the main frame (Keep good notes!!) and his sage counsel were equaled only by his patience. Without him, I would never have completed this project.

Thanks to Ron and Thora duBois, John and Caryl Jobe, Rudy and Helen Miller, and Ken and Karen Bell who invited me to stay with them on my many trips from New Mexico to Stillwater where I worked for several weeks to complete the manuscript. They welcomed me as a member of their respective families (they never asked how long I was going to stay) and provided care, comfort, convenience and conversation--expressions of friendship I will not soon forget.

And a long over-due expression of appreciation to my husband, John, who offered love, support and good counsel, and kept the home fires burning.

After all is said and done, the final responsibility for the production of this bibliography lies with me. But I willing share accountability for the content and accuracy of each section with the contributors

# Anthropology
of Aging

# 1

# General, Theoretical and Comparative Works

ANTHROPOLOGY OF AGING TEXTS AND CROSS-CULTURAL READERS

Amoss, P. and S. Harrell (eds). Other Ways of Growing Old--Anthropological Perspectives. Stanford, CA: Stanford University Press, 1981.

Ethnographic studies describe aging among the !Kung hunter-gatherers of Botswana, the Chipewyan of northern Canada, the elderly Asmat of New Guinea, the Gwembe Tonga in Zambia, a Micronesian community on the Caroline Islands, the Kirghiz of Afghanistan, rural Taiwanese, Hindus of South India and the Coast Salish Indians of the Northwest Coast of North America. The descriptions focus on the balance between the contribution made by the elderly and the cost expended to keep them. One chapter deals with the behavior of aging female monkeys.

Cowgill, D. and L. Holmes (eds). Aging and Modernization. New York, NY: Appleton-Century-Crofts, 1972.

In the Introduction, the editors present a theory of modernization which lists universals and variations in aging among societies of varying degrees of modernization. Authors describe several groups in the United States and Africa as well as Thailand, the USSR and several countries of Europe. In the final chapter, the editors review the theory in light of the data presented in each chapter of the book. This book is an early and important contribution to the consideration of the effect of modernization and industrialization on the aging process.

Francis, D., D. Shenk, and J. Sokolovsky (eds). Teaching About Aging: Interdisciplinary and Cross-Cultural Perspectives. St. Cloud, MN: Association for Anthropology and Gerontology, St. Cloud, State University, 1990.

This publication is an expanded update of the original Teaching the Anthropology of Aging and the Aged: A

Curriculum Guide and Topical Bibliography published by AAGE
in 1982. Part 1 contains 30 syllabi for courses about
aging. Among the topics covered are the anthropology of
aging, biological aging, aging in cross-cultural
perspective, aging and caregiving; and death and dying in
crosscultural perspective. Syllabi include readings and
bibliographies. Part 2 provides teaching resources,
including bibliography and audiovisuals.

Fry, C. (ed). Aging in Culture and Society--Comparative
Viewpoints and Strategies. Brooklyn, NY: J. F. Bergin,
1980.

_____ Dimensions: Aging, Culture and Health. Brooklyn, NY:
J. F. Bergin, 1981.

Chapters describe aging in New Guinea, Canada, China,
England, Sudan, Germany and the United States, focusing on
support systems for the elderly, quality of care and
physician influence on the institutionalized and the
medicalization of old age.

Hendricks, J. In the Country of the Old. Farmingdale, NY:
Baywood, 1981.

This publication contains reprints of articles previously
published in the International Journal of Aging and Human
Development.

Holmes, L. Other Cultures, Elder Years: An Introduction to
Cultural Gerontology. Minneapolis, MN: Burgess, 1983.

A textbook in cross-cultural gerontology that includes
chapters on research interests in the anthropology of
aging; retirement, personality, and applied anthropology;
variations in longevity; the aging experience in Eskimo,
Samoan, and U. S. societies; aging among different American
minority groups; and the aged and cultural change.

Keith, J. Old People as People: Social and Cultural
Influences on Aging and Old Age. Boston, MA: Little,
Brown, 1982.

Morgan, J. (ed). Aging in Developing Societies: A Reader in
Third World Gerontology. Bristol, IN: Wyndham Hall, 1985.

Myerhoff, B. and A. Simic (eds). Life's Career--Aging:
Cultural Variations on Growing Old. Beverly Hills, CA:
Sage, 1978.

Silverman, P. The Elderly As Modern Pioneers. Bloomington,
IN: Indiana University Press, 1987.

This volume attempts to summarize contemporary research in
gerontology. It is ambitious in its combination of
interdisciplinary and cross-cultural perspectives. In
addition to an Introduction, there are 17 chapters on
various aspects of aging. Most of the contributors are

biological and cultural anthropologists.  The integrating theoretical approach is the life course perspective, which provides a framework for subsuming the diverse data from modern aging studies.  Specific chapters include the following topics:  biological theories, the life span, longevity, sensory functions, cognition, personality, sexuality, demography, family life, community studies, social class and ethnicity, ethnograhic studies, comparative studies, the old old, mental disorders, institutional settings, and death and dying.

Sokolovsky, J.  Growing Old in Different Cultures:  Cross-Cultural Perspectives.  Acton, MA:  Copley Press, 1987.  (Originally published in 1983 by Wadsworth.)

The book is divided into sections on Culture and Aging, Age Boundaries and Intergenerational Links, Aging and Modernization, the Ethnic Factor, Networks and Community Creation and Institutionalization.  The groups discussed are the Inuit, Yugoslavians, the people of Baganda, rural Irish, Japanese, the British in New Towns, and Italian Americans, American Indian communities, inner-city elderly, Jewish Americans and a nursing home in the United States.  The book is an important contribution to the study of the effect of culture on the aging process.

_____  The Cultural Context of Aging:  Worldwide Perspectives. Westport, CT:  Bergin & Garvey, 1990.

This collection of original, specially commissioned articles and a few reprinted pieces focuses on the multitude of cultural solutions societies have available for dealing with the challenges, problems and opportunities of growing old.  The book is designed for classroom use for advanced undergraduates and graduate students in a wide variety of disciplines such as anthropology, sociology, psychology, social work, geography and gerontology.  The six sections of the book integrate a world perspective on the topics of culture, intergenerational ties, modernization, ethnicity, community and health, along with studies of aging among the varied ethnic groups in the United States.  Eighteen articles describe aging in African hunter-gatherer communities, urban Nigeria, Japan, Yugoslavia, China, Sweden, a small South Pacific island, Israel and a variety of ethnic groups in the United States.

Stearns, P. (ed).  Old Age in Preindustrial Society.  New York, NY:  Holmes and Meier, 1982.

This volume compares the status of the elderly in several locations (Kenya, Tibet, India, Italy, western Europe and Russia) and finds that while industrialization was not uniformly detrimental for the elderly, in some countries, older people were particularly vulnerable.

Strange, H. and M. Teitelbaum (eds).  Aging and Cultural Diversity.  South Hadley, MA:  Bergin & Garvey, 1987.

Watson, W. and R. Maxwell (eds).  Human Aging and Dying, A
    Study in Sociocultural Gerontology.  New York, NY:   St.
    Martin's Press, 1977.

GENERAL GERONTOLOGY TEXTS, READERS AND HANDBOOKS

Atchley, R.  The Social Forces in Later Life (5th ed).
    Belmont, CA:  Wadsworth, 1988.

    One of the most widely-used college textbooks in social
    gerontology.  Sections center on the aging individual,
    situational contexts of aging (health, finances,
    retirement, leisure, death and dying) and the social
    response to older people (disengagement, economics,
    politics, and community life).

    _____  Aging:  Continuity and Conformity.  Belmont, CA:
    Wadsworth, 1983.

Barash, D. P.  Aging:  An Exploration.  Seattle, WA:
    University of Washington Press, 1983.

Barrow, G. M.  Aging, the Individual and Society (4th ed).
    St. Paul, MN:  West Publishing, 1989.

    A general text with a focus on social problems of the aged.
    These include ageism, stereotypes, the difficulties of
    older women, and the minority aged.  A wide-ranging text,
    it includes a chapter on aging in cross-cultural
    perspective.

Barry, J. R.  Let's Learn About Aging:  A Book of Readings.
    Boston, MA:  Little, Brown, 1977.

Bell, B. D.  Contemporary Social Gerontology:  Significant
    Developments in the Field of Aging.  Springfield, IL:  C.
    C. Thomas, 1976.

Bengtson, V. L.  The Social Psychology of Aging.
    Indianapolis, IN:  Bobbs-Merrill, 1973.

Berghorn, F. and D. Schafer, (eds).  The Dynamics of Aging.
    Boulder, CO:  Westview Press, 1981.

Binstock, R. and L. K. George (eds).  Handbook of Aging and
    the Social Sciences (3rd ed).  San Diego, CA:  Academic
    Press, 1990.

    A major guidebook to social aspects of aging.  Includes
    comprehensive articles on aging and social structure
    (includes chapters on mortality and morbidity,
    anthropological perspectives, and ethnicity); the life
    course (leisure and time use, social supports and
    relationships, aging and dying); aging and social
    institutions (comparative perspectives on housing, work and
    retirement, aging and politics); social intervention
    (economic status of elderly, income maintenance policies,

pensions, health care and social care).

Birren, J. and K. W. Schaie (eds). Handbook of the Psychology of Aging. San Diego, CA:  Academic Press, 1990.

A major resource on the psychology of aging.  Sections and chapters focus on general concepts and issues, theory and measurement (the history of the psycholgoy of aging, growth models for research, concepts of time and aging), behavioral sciences (including electrophysiology, vision and hearing, motivation and cognitive performance, models of learning, memory and language), and applications to the individual and society (psychological intervention, caregiving, special environments, ethical issues).

_____ Handbook of Mental Health and Aging. New York, NY: Van Nostrand Reinhold, 1980.

Botwinik, J.  We Are Aging. New York, NY:  Springer, 1981.

Breytspraak, L. M.  The Development of Self in Later Life. Boston, MA:  Little, Brown, 1984.

A general focus on the self in later life (rather than the usual focus on personality) and on social and psychological notions of selfhood.  Chapters review the self in gerontological theory, images of dynamic selfhood, and issues for the aging self, including the reconstruction of selfhood, the changing body, and social images of old age.

Bromley, D. B. Gerontology:  Social and Behavioral Perspectives. London, UK:  Croom Helm, 1984.

Busse, E. W. and D. G. Blazer.  The Handbook of Geriatric Psychiatry. New York, NY:  Van Nostrand Reinhold, 1980.

Chown, S. Human Aging:  Selected Readings. Baltimore, MD: Penguin, 1972.

Cole, T. R. and S. Gadow.  What Does It mean to Grow Old?: Reflections from the Humanities. Durham, NC:  Duke University Press, 1986.

Ten papers organized in sections on cultural meaning and subjectivity through literature. These focus, respectively, on the meaning of old age in relation to social problems and on aspects of subjectivity captured through literature on aging.  Each article has an editor's introduction.

Cox, H. Later Life:  The Realities of Aging. Englewood Cliffs, NJ:  Prentice-Hall, 1984.

Crandall, R. Gerontology:  A Behavioral Science Approach. Reading, MA:  Addison-Wesley, 1980.

A nineteen-chapter text.  Chapters include those on the history of gerontology, aging in preliterate societies and in the past, sexuality, the results of research, the environment, and minority group aging.

Datan, N. and N. Lohmann (eds). *Transitions of Aging*. New York, NY: Academic Press, 1980.

The proceedings of the first West Virginia University Gerontology Conference, focusing on the idea of aging as a transition. Chapter sections are on personal transitions (physical activity and competency), family transitions (widowhood and others), and environmental transitions (growing old "inside," environmental change and institutionalization).

Decker, D. *Social Gerontology: An Introduction to the Dynamics of Aging*. Boston, MA: Little, Brown, 1980.

Ferraro, K. (ed). *Gerontology: Perspectives and Issues*. New York, NY: Springer, 1990.

Fogel, R. W. (ed). *Aging: Stability and Change in the Family*. New York, NY: Academic Press, 1981.

Foner, A. *Aging and Old Age: New Perspectives*. Englewood Cliffs, NJ: Prentice-Hall, 1986.

Harris, D. K. *Sociology of Aging*. Boston, MA: Houghton-Mifflin, 1980.

Hendricks, J. and C. Hendricks (eds). *Dimensions of Aging: Readings*. Cambridge, MA: Winthrop, 1979.

_____ *Aging in Mass Society: Myths and Realities* (3rd ed). Boston, MA: Little, Brown, 1986.

Hess, B. B. and E. Markson (eds). *Growing Old in America: New Perspectives in Old Age* (3rd ed). New Brunswick, NJ: Transaction Books, 1985.

The third edition of a popular reader, containing 37 chapters in 9 sections. Of interest is the good coverage of cross-cultural perspectives (6 chapters) and cultural stereotypes. Also featured are sections on "bodies," "minds," the life-course and the family.

Holmes, M. B. *The Handbook of Human Service for Older People*. New York, NY: Human Sciences Press, 1979.

Johnson, E. S. and J. B. Williamson. *Growing Old: The Social Problems of Aging*. New York, NY: Holt, Rinehart and Winston, 1980.

Kalish, R. A. *The Later Years: The Social Applications of Gerontology*. Monterey, CA: Brooks/Cole, 1977.

Karp, D. A. and W. C. Yoels. *Experiencing the Life Cycle: A Social Psychology of Aging*. Springfield, IL: C. C. Thomas, 1982.

Kart, C.  The Realities of Aging:  An Introduction to
    Gerontology (3rd ed).  Boston, MA:  Allyn and Bacon, 1990.

    A nineteen-chapter text on social gerontology.  Easily
    written and widely cast, covering most standard aspects as
    well as minority aging, institutionalization and death and
    dying.  Includes an epilogue on careers in gerontology.

Kastenbaum, R. (ed).    Old Age on the New Scene.  New York,
    NY:  Springer, 1981.

Kiesler, S. B., J. N. Morgan, and V. Oppenheimer (eds).
    Aging:  Social Change.  New York, NY:  Academic Press,
    1981.

Koller, M. R.  Social Gerontology.  New York, NY:  Random
    House, 1968.

LeFevre, C. and P. LeFevre.  Aging and the Holy Spirit:  A
    Reader in Religion and Gerontology.  Chicago, IL:
    Exploration Press, 1985.

Lesnoff-Caravaglia, G.  Handbook of Applied Gerontology.  New
    York, NY:  Human Sciences Press, 1986.

Maddox, G. (ed).  The Encyclopedia of Aging.  New York, NY:
    Van Nostrand Reinhold, 1987.

    An all-inclusive overview of topics in aging from abilities
    to World Health Organization.  Of note, too, is the
    extensive bibliography.  Includes articles on the aging
    experience, research, and services.

Marshall, V. W.  Later Life:  The Social Psychology of Aging.
    Beverly Hills, CA:  Sage, 1985.

    Ten extraordinary chapters that treat aging from a
    nonquantitative point of view, through an examination of
    the subjective construction of self, symbolic interaction,
    friendships, the life course, and the older person as
    "stranger."

McPherson, B. D.  Aging as a Social Process:  An Introduction
    to Individual and Population Aging.  Toronto, Ontario:
    Butterworths 1983.

    An extremely comprehensive and fact-filled treatment of
    later life in eleven chapters.  Chapter 2 discusses
    cultural and subcultural variation and "the meaning of
    culture."  Also of note is the "microanalysis of aging"
    through a focus on the aging individual.

Monk, A. (ed).    The Age of Aging:  A Reader in Social
    Gerontology.  Buffalo, NY:  Prometheus Books, 1979.

    An edited volume of 27 chapters including several classics.
    Features sections on images and myths of aging, social
    theory, transitions, life styles and events, interventions

and policy, and the future.

_____ (ed).  The Handbook of Gerontological Services.  New York, NY:  Van Nostrand Reinhold, 1985.

Neugarten, B. (ed).  Middle Age and Aging.  Chicago, IL: University of Chicago Press, 1968.

An early classic, still fully relevant today.  Fifty-eight chapters on middle age and old age, primarily from social and psychological perspectives.  A clear focus throughout is on personality and personality change.  Also of note are the sections on theories of aging and on death and dying. Features a five-chapter section on aging in other societies.

Palmore, E. B.  Handbook of the Aged in the United States. Westport, CT:  Greenwood Press, 1984.

_____    International Handbook on Aging:  Contemporary Developments and Research.  Westport, CT:  Greenwood, 1980.

Features a wide variety of data on the aged cross-nationally.  Each of 28 chapters centers on a different (mostly developed) nation.  Each, too, develops information on the demography of the aged, the history of gerontology and geriatric organizations in the nation, clinical geriatrics, and the social contacts, employment, retirement, health and household status of the elderly. While the quality of the data varies, this is important as a source of international data and as an overview.

Perlmutter, M.  Human Development and Aging.  New York, NY: Wiley, 1985.

A general focus on adulthood.  Sections are on the biology of aging and health across adulthood, the psychology of aging, social aspects of adult development.  Includes information on cross-cultural perspectives (Chapter 15) and ethnicity.

Pifer, A. and D. Lydia (eds).  Our Aging Society:  Paradox and Promise.  New York, NY:  Norton, 1986.

Poon, L. W. (ed).  The Handbook for Clinical Memory Assessment of Older Adults.  Washington, DC:  American Psychological Association, 1986.

Poon, L. W., D. C. Rubin, and B. Wilson (eds).  Everyday Cognition in Adulthood and Later Life.  Cambridge, UK: Cambridge University Press, 1989.

Quandagno, J. (ed).  Aging, the Individual and Society: Readings in Social Gerontology.  New York, NY:  St. Martin's Press 1980.

Reinharz, S. and G. Rowles (eds).  Qualitative Gerontology. New York, NY:  Springer, 1987.

Schneider, E. L. and J. W. Rowe (eds). Handbook of the
   Biology of Aging (3rd ed). San Diego, CA: Academic Press,
   1990.

   A major resource on the biology of aging. Includes
   chapters on epidemiology of the older population;
   methodology for research on biological aging studies;
   molecular/cellular biology; physiology and neurobiology;
   human biology, nutrition and exercise.

Shanas, E., et al. Old People in Three Industrial Societies.
   New York, NY: Atherton, 1968.

   A classic in social gerontology. Compares aspects of the
   lives of the elderly in the U. S., the U. K., and Denmark.
   While all articles are first rate, focusing on health,
   psychology resources, and services, P. Townsend's on
   Isolation, Desolation, and Loneliness is a gem.

Seltzer, M. Social Problems of the Aging: Readings.
   Belmont, CA: Wadsworth, 1978.

Spicker, S. (ed). Aging and the Elderly: Humanistic
   Perspectives in Gerontology. New York, NY: Humanities
   Press, 1978.

   Twenty papers that focus on old age in historical
   perspective and as the object of cultural values and views.
   Features articles on paternalism, ethics, the origins of
   ageism, competency, and "gerontophobia," among others.

Tibbits, C. Handbook of Social Gerontology. Chicago, IL:
   University of Chicago Press, 1960.

Ward, R. A. The Aging Experience: An Introduction to Social
   Gerontology. New York, NY: Lippincott, 1979.

Watson, W. H. Aging and Social Behavior: An Introduction to
   Social Gerontology. Monterey, CA: Wadsworth, 1982.

Weeks, J. R. Aging: Concepts and Social Issues. Belmont,
   CA: Wadsworth, 1984.

Woodruff, D. S. and J. E. Birren. Aging: Scientific
   Perspectives and Social Issues (2nd ed). Belmont, CA:
   Brooks/Cole, 1983.

   Nineteen chapters authored by a variety of experts on
   aging, including pieces on social supports, ethnic and
   minority aging, demography and family life.


**GENERAL READING, THEORETICAL PERSPECTIVES**

Birren, J. and V. Clayton. History of Gerontology. Pp. 15-27
   in D. Woodruff and J. Birren (eds). Aging: Scientific
   Perspectives and Social Issues. New York, NY: Van
   Nostrand Reinhold, 1975.

12    ANTHROPOLOGY OF AGING

Carp, F. and C. Nydegger.  Recent Gerontological Developments
    in Psychology and the Social Sciences.  Gerontologist.
    15(4):368-70, 1975.

Cavan, R., et al.  Personal Adjustment in Old Age.  Chicago,
    IL:  Science Reasearch Associates, 1949.

    A pioneer study of the attitudes and activities of old
    people, using the "Chicago Attitudes and Activities
    Inventory."  A precursor of the activity theory of aging.

Cohen, R.  Age and Culture as Theory.  Pp. 234-49 in D. I.
    Kertzer and J. Keith (eds).  Age and Anthropological
    Theory.  Ithaca, NY:  Cornell University Press, 1984.

Cowgill, D. and L. Holmes.  Aging and Modernization.  New
    York:  NY:  Appleton-Century-Crofts, 1972.

    A collection of essays about aging in diverse cultural
    contexts framed by an evolutionary perspective on the
    status of the aged.

Cumming, E., L. Dean, and I. McCaffrey.  Disengagement:  A
    Tentative Theory of Aging.  Sociometry.  23:25-35, 1960.

Cumming, E. and W. Henry.  Growing Old:  The Process of
    Disengagement.  New York, NY:  Basic Books, 1961.

    Sets forth at length what came to be called the
    disengagement theory of aging, a functionalist approach.
    Empirical data and a set of propositions are provided.

Datan, N. and N. Lohman (eds).  Transitions of Aging.  New
    York, NY:  Academic Press, 1980.

Decker, D.  Sociological Theory and the Social Position of the
    Aged.  International Journal of Contemporary Sociology.
    15:303-17, 1978.

Dowd, J.  Aging As Exchange:  A Preface to Theory.  Journal of
    Gerontology.  30(5):584-95, 1975.

    Introduces a theoretical perspective based on exchange
    theory into the aging literature.  The approach draws
    together concerns with interpersonal contact and personal
    costs of sustained participation.

_____  Aging As Exchange, A Test of the Distributive Justice
    Proposition.  Pacific Sociological Review.  21(3):351-75,
    1978.

_____  Stratification Among the Aged.  Monterey, CA:
    Brooks/Cole, 1980.

_____  Social Exchange, Class and Old People.  Pp. 29-42 in J.
    Sokolovsky (ed).  Growing Old in Different Societies:
    Cross-Cultural Perspectives.  Acton, MA:  Copley Press,
    1987.

Eckert, P.  Age and Linguistic Change.  Pp. 219-33 in D. I.
    Kertzer and J. Keith (eds).  Age and Anthropological
    Theory.  Ithaca, NY:  Cornell University Press, 1984.

Estes, C.  The Social Construction of Reality:  A Framework
    for Inquiry.  Pp. 1-15 in C. Estes.  The Aging Enterprise.
    San Francisco, CA:  Jossey-Bass, 1979.

Fontana, A.  The Last Frontier:  The Social Meaning of Growing
    Old.  Beverly Hills, CA:  Sage, 1976.

    Treating the nature of old age as a social problem, Fontana
    describes three worlds of aging:  the senior center, the
    SRO and nursing homes.

Gubrium, J.  The Myth of the Golden Years:  A Socio-
    Environmental Theory of Aging.  Springfield, IL:  C. C.
    Thomas, 1973.

    A first attempt to integrate propositions of activity and
    disengagement theories into a general theory of life
    satisfaction.  Context or socio-environment and its
    relationship to personal resources is a major
    consideration.

    Oldtimers and Alzheimer's:  The Descriptive
    Organization of Senility.  Greenwich, CT:  JAI Press, 1986.

    Based on a field study of the Alzheimer's disease
    experience, consideration is given to the relationship
    between the disease and "normal aging" as a problem in the
    sociology of medical knowledge.

    Analyzing Field Reality.  Newbury Park, CA:  Sage,
    1988.

Gubrium, J. and D. Buckholdt.  Toward Maturity:  The Social
    Processing of Human Development.  San Francisco, CA:
    Jossey-Bass, 1977.

    A social phenomenological critique of developmentalism.
    The social construction of the life course is addressed and
    illustrated.  Aging is a way of thinking about getting old,
    not a chronology.

Gubrium, J. and J. Holstein.  What is Family.  Mountain View,
    CA:  Mayfield, 1990.

Halperin, R. H.  Age in Cross-Cultural Perspective:  An
    Evolutionary Approach.  Pp. 283-311 in P. Silverman (ed).
    The Elderly As Modern Pioneers.  Bloomington, IN:  Indiana
    University Press, 1987.

Hansen, P. F. (ed).  Age With a Future.  Copenhagen, Denmark:
    Munksgaard, 1964.

Havighurst, R., B. Neugarten, and S. Tobin.  Disengagement and
    Patterns of Aging.  Pp. 161-77 in B. Neugarten (ed).

*Middle Age and Aging*.  Chicago, IL:  University of Chicago Press, 1968.

Heenan, E.  The Sociology of Religion and the Aged.  *Journal for the Scientific Study of Religion*.  2(2):171-76, 1972.

Henthorn, B.  Disengagement and Reinforcement in the Elderly.  *Research in Nursing and Health*.  2:1-7, 1975.

Hobman, D. (ed).  *The Social Challenge of Aging*.  London, UK:  Croom Helm, 1978.

Hochschild, A.  Disengagement Theory:  A Critique and Proposal.  *American Sociological Review*.  40:553-69, 1975.

A sophisticated analytic critique of the main themes of disengagement theory.  In particular, the need to consider the place of meaning in any theory of aging is a challenge.

Jerrome, D. (ed).  *Ageing in Modern Society*.  New York, NY:  St. Martin's, 1983.

Contributors examine old age against a background of social change and cultural diversity.  Changing policies and practices in caring for the elderly are examined.

Kastenbaum, R.  Theories of Human Aging:  The Search for a Conceptual Framework.  *Journal of Social Issues*.  21:13-26, 1965.

Kertzer, D. and J. Keith, (eds).  *Age and Anthropological Theory*.  Ithaca, NY:  Cornell University Press, 1984.

Considers approaches based on the argument that the universal process of aging is an individual, social and cultural experience.  A first attempt to develop a systematic framework for the anthropological study of age.

Kleemeier, R. W. (ed).  *Aging and Leisure:  A Research Perspective into the Meaningful Use of Time*.  New York, NY:  Oxford University Press, 1961.

Kleemeier's book is an early and important contribution to the study of the use of "free" time and the meaning of activity in the later years of life.  In addition to an introduction which delineates the conceptual model, other chapters discuss time studies and activities in a variety of settings (such as family, work, commercial entertainment, hospitals).  The book's primary importance for the cross-cultural study of aging lies in the chapters where authors discuss cultural differences in the concept of time by presenting data from people of the Andes, the St.  Lawrence Island Eskimos, Japan, Burma and India.

Maas, H. and J. Kuyfers.  *From Thirty to Seventy*.  San Francisco, CA:  Jossey-Bass, 1977.

Maddox, G.  Fact and Artifact:  Evidence Bearing on

Disengagement Theory. Human Development. 8:117-30, 1965.

_____ Persistence of Life Style Among the Elderly. Pp.
181-83 in B. Neugarten (ed). Middle Age and Aging.
Chicago, IL: University of Chicago Press, 1968a.

_____ Themes and Issues in Sociological Theories in Human
Aging. Human Development. 13:17-27, 1970.

Malinchak, A. Crime and Gerontology. Englewood Cliffs, NJ:
Prentice-Hall, 1980.

Markson, E. and G. Batra (eds). Public Policies for an Aging
Population. Lexington, MA: Lexington Books, 1980.

Marshall, V. No Exit: A Symbolic Interactionist Perspective
on Aging. Aging and Human Development. 9(4):345-58,
1978/79.

The place of interpretation, role and self in the aging
process.

Matthews, S. The Social World of Old Women: Management of
Self-Identity. Beverly Hills, CA: Sage, 1979.

The approach taken is social constructivist. Considers
self-identity and stigma, and the maintenance of precarious
self-identity. The importance of setting is highlighted
for definitions of identity.

Moore, W. Aging and the Social System. Pp. 23-41 in J. C.
McKinney and T. DeVyver (eds). Aging and Social Policy.
New York, NY: Appleton-Century-Crofts, 1966.

Myles, J. Old Age in the Welfare State. Boston, MA: Little,
Brown, 1984.

Considers the social formation of old age in the welfare
state as a condition of the contradictory requirements of a
market economy on the one hand and a democratic polity on
the other.

National Council on Aging. Factbook on Aging: A Profile of
America's Older Population. Washington, DC: National
Council on Aging, 1979.

Neugarten, B. The Old and Young in Modern Societies. Pp.
13-24 in E. Shanas (ed). Aging in Contemporary Society.
Beverly Hills, CA: Sage, 1970.

_____ Aging in the Year 2000, A Look at the Future.
Gerontologist. 15(1):1-40, 1975.

Olson, L. K. The Political Economy of Aging. New York, NY:
Columbia University Press, 1982.

Examines the role of traditional American institutions in
fostering the social problems of old age in American

society.

Orbach, H.  Disengagement--Activity Controversy:  Underlying
   Theoretical Models of Aging.  Gerontologist.  13:72, 1973.

Ostor, A.  Chronology, Category, and Ritual.  Pp. 281-304 in
   D. I.  Kertzer and J. Keith (eds).  Age and Anthropological
   Theory.  Ithaca, NY:  Cornell University Press, 1984.

Paillat, P.  Bureaucratization of Old Age:  Determinants of
   the Process, Possible Safeguards, and Reorientation.  Pp.
   60-74 in E. Shanas and M. Sussman (eds).  Family,
   Bureaucracy, and the Elderly.  Durham, NC:  Duke University
   Press, 1973.

Palmore, E.  Facts on Aging:  A Short Quiz.  Gerontologist.
   17:315-20, 1977.

_____  The Social Factors in Aging.  Pp. 222-48 in E. Busse
   and D. Blazer (eds).  Handbook of Geriatric Psychiatry.
   New York, NY:  Van Nostrand Reinhold, 1980.

Palmore, E., et al.  Normal Aging III:  Reports from the Duke
   Longitudinal Studies, 1975-1984.  Durham, NC:  Duke
   University Press, 1985.

Parsons, T.  Old Age as a Consummatory Phase.  Gerontologist.
   3:53-54, 1963.

Peterson, W. A. and J. Quadagno (eds).  Social Bonds in Later
   Life.  Beverly Hills, CA:  Sage, 1985.

   Collection of papers focused on aging and interdependence.
   Various approaches to bonding, from intimate relations to
   support systems and service settings.

Pincus, A.  Toward a Developmental View of Aging For Social
   Work.  Social Work.  12:33-41, 1969.

Riley, M. (ed).  Aging From Birth to Death:
   Interdisciplinary Perspectives.  AAAS Selected Symposium,
   30.  Boulder, CO:  Westview Press, 1979.

Rose, A.  The Subculture of the Aged.  Pp. 3-16 in A. Rose and
   W.  Peterson.  Older People and Their Social World.
   Philadelphia, PA:  F. A. Davis, 1965.

_____  A Current Theoretical Issue in Social Gerontology.  Pp.
   184-89 in B. Neugarten (ed).  Middle Age and Aging.
   Chicago, IL:  University of Chicago Press, 1968.

Rosow, I.  Socialization to Old Age.  Berkeley, CA:
   University of California Press, 1974.

   Major variables of socialization are examined in
   demonstration of the roleless role of the elderly.
   Socialization alternatives are considered within the
   present institutional structure of American society.

Ross, J. K.  Social Borders:  Definitions of Diversity.
    Current Anthropology.  16(1):53-61, 1975.

Rowles, G.  Toward a Geography of Growing Old.  Pp. 55-72 in
    A.  Buttimer and D. Seamon (eds).  The Human Experience of
    Space and Place.  London, UK:  Croom Helm, 1980.

Rubinstein, R. L. (ed).  Anthropology and Aging:
    Comprehensive Reviews.  Norwell, MA:  Kluwer, 1990.

    The papers in this volume present up-to-date reviews in
    three main areas of the anthropology of aging:  Biological
    and Health Issues, Cultural Issues, and Areal Studies.  The
    areal studies focus on Japan and China while the cultural
    issues section focuses on nature, culture and gender and
    the life course perspective.  The Biology/Health section
    includes a chapter on nursing and aging.

Schultz, J.  The Economic Status of the Aged.  Pp. 14-48 in J.
    Schultz (ed).  The Economics of Aging.  Belmont, CA:
    Wadsworth, 1980.

Seltzer, M., S. Corbett, and R. Atchley.  Social Problems of
    the Aging.  Belmont, CA:  Wadsworth, 1978.

Shanas E. and M. B. Sussman (eds).  Family, Bureaucracy, and
    the Elderly.  Durhamm NC:  Duke University Press, 1977.

    This collection of individually-authored chapters focuses
    on the linkage of elderly people with bureaucratic
    organizations in complex societies and the role of family
    networks in these linkages.

Sill, J.  Disengagement Reconsidered:  Awareness of Finitude.
    Gerontologist.  20:457-62, 1980.

Stennett, R. and M. Thurlow.  Cultural Symbolism:  The Age
    Variable.  Journal of Consulting Psychology.  22:496, 1958.

Talmon, Y.  Aging:  Social Aspects.  Pp. 186-96 in
    International Encyclopedia of the Social Sciences.  1968.

Tibbitts, C. and W. Donahue (eds).  Aging Around the World:
    Social and Psychological Aspects of Aging.  New York, NY:
    Columbia University Press, 1962.

Townsend, P.  The Structured Dependency of the Elderly.  Aging
    and Society.  1(1):5-28, 1981.

Unruh, D. R.  Invisible Lives:  Social Worlds of the Aged.
    Beverly Hills, CA:  Sage, 1983.

    The concept of social worlds is applied to the lives of the
    aged.  Social integration is a major consideration with a
    discussion of types and social invisibility.

Usdin, G. and C. Hofling (eds).  Ageing:  The Process and the
    People.  New York, NY:  Bruner/Mazel, 1978.

Youmans, E.  Some Views on Human Aging.  Pp. 17-26 in R. Boyd and C. Oakes (eds).  Foundations of Practical Gerontology (2nd ed).  Columbia, SC:  University of South Carolina Press, 1973.

## BROAD CROSS-CULTURAL AND HOLOCULTURAL-STATISTICAL COMPARISONS

Altergott, K.  Daily Life in Later Life:  Personal Conditions in a Comparative Perspective.  Newbury Park, CA:  Sage, 1988.

_____ Qualities of Daily Life and Suicide in Old Age:  A Comparative Perspective.  Journal of Cross-Cultural Gerontology.  3(4):361-76, 1988.

Amoss, P. and S. Harrell.  Introduction:  An Anthropological Perspective on Aging.  Pp. 1-24 in P. Amoss and S. Harrell (eds).  Other Ways of Growing Old:  Anthropological Perspectives.  Stanford, CA:  Stanford University Press, 1981.

This introduction to a volume of essays on aging in different societies seeks to define those aspects of aging that are human universals as well as the nature and extent of cultural variation.  The authors hypothesize that the relative success of old people in a particular society depends on:  1) the balance between the costs they represent to the group and the contributions they make and, 2) the degree of control the aged maintain over resources necessary to the fulfillment of the needs or wants of younger members of the group.

Arnhoff, F., H. Leon, and I. Lorge.  Cross-Cultural Acceptance of Stereotypes Towards Aging.  Journal of Social Psychology.  63:41-58, 1964.

Arth, M.  Ageing:  A Cross-Cultural Perspective.  Pp. 352-64 in D. Kent, R. Kastenbaum, and S. Sherwood (eds).  Research Planning and Action for the Elderly.  New York, NY:  Behaviorial Publications, 1972.

Beall, C. and J. K. Eckert.  Approaches to Measuring Functional Capacity Cross-Culturally.  Pp. 21-55 in C. Fry and J. Keith (eds).  New Methods for Old Age Research.  South Hadley, MA:  Bergin and Garvey, 1980.

Beatte, W.  The Place of Older People in Different Societies.  Pp. 44-47 in Age With a Future.  Proceedings of the 6th International Congress of Gerontology, Copenhagen, Denmark, 1963.  Philadelphia, PA:  F. A. Davis, 1964.

Bergener, M., et al.  Aging in the Eighties and Beyond:  Highlights of the Twelfth International Congress of Gerontology.  New York, NY:  Springer, 1983.

Binstock, R.  Drawing Cross-Cultural "Implications for Policy":  Some Caveats.  Journal of Cross-Cultural

Gerontology.  1:331-37, 1986.

Boyd, R.  Preliterate Prologues to Modern Aging Roles.  Pp.
35-46 in R.  Boyd and C. Oakes (eds).  Foundations of
Practical Gerontology (2nd ed).  Columbia, SC:  University
of South Carolina Press, 1973.

Brown, J. K.  Introduction.  Pp. 1-11 in J. K. Brown and V.
Kerns (eds).  In Her Prime:  A New View of Middle-Aged
Women.  South Hadley, MA:  Bergin and Garvey, 1985.

Clark, M.  The Anthropology of Aging:  A New Area for Studies
of Culture and Personality.  Gerontologist.  7:55-64, 1967.

_____  Contributions of Cultural Anthropology to the Study of
the  Aged.  Pp. 78-88 in L. Nader and T. Maretzki (eds).
Cultural Illness and Health:  Essays in Human Adaptation.
Washington, DC:  American Anthropological Association,
1973.

Clark, R. L.  Economic Well-Being of the Elderly:  Theory and
Measurement.  Journal of Cross-Cultural Gerontology.
4(1):1-18, 1989.

Cowgill, D.  A Theory of Aging in Cross-Cultural Perspective.
Pp. 1-13 in D. Cowgill and L. Holmes (eds).  Aging and
Modernization.  New York, NY:  Appleton-Century-Crofts,
1972.

Cowgill sets forth several hypotheses which attempt to
derive generalizations about aging that can be considered
universals as well as those which are considered systematic
variations.  These propositions form the hypotheses around
which the chapters in the book are ordered.

_____  Aging Around the World.  Belmont, CA:  Wadsworth, 1986.

Examines the commonalities and varieties of the aging
experience around the world.  Focuses on a comparative
demography of aging; value systems pertinent to aging in
different cultures; the relationship between kinship and
economic systems and the aged; and political, religious and
economic roles of the elderly.  A major emphasis throughout
is on the role of modernization in undermining the
privileges and powers of the elderly.  The author discusses
the modernization theory in detail in the concluding
chapter.

Cowgill, D. and L. Holmes.  Summary and Conclusions.  Pp.
305-24 in D.  Cowgill and L. Holmes (ed).  Aging and
Modernization.  New York, NY:  Appleton-Century-Crofts,
1972.

Evaluates the hypotheses set forth in the Introduction in
light of the ethnographic studies presented in the book.
Best-known is the proposition that the status of the aged
varies with the degree of modernization of society and that
modernization tends to decrease the relative status of the

aged.

de Beauvoir, S.  The Coming of Age.  New York, NY:  Putnam, 1972.

Department of International Economic and Social Affairs.  The World Aging Situation:  Strategies and Policies.  New York, NY:  United Nations, 1985.

By bringing together relevant data from the abundance of new national, regional, and internationally oriented literature stimulated by the World Assembly on Aging, this report provides a comprehensive picture of the world aging situation--including current and project demographic trends, estimates of their socio-economic and humanitarian implications and present and proposed policy responses.

Foner, N.  Some Consequences of Age Inequality in Nonindustrial Societies.  Pp. 71-85 in M. W. Riley, R. P. Abeles, and M. S. Teitelbaum (eds).  Aging From Birth to Death.  Vol. 2.  Sociotemporal Perspectives.  Boulder, CO: Westview, 1982.

_____  Ages in Conflict:  A Cross-Cultural Perspective on Inequality Between Old and Young.  New York, NY:  Columbia University Press, 1984a.

Pulls together the ethnographic literature to analyze the implications of age inequality for old and young in nonindustrial societies.  Several chapters explore the bases--and consequences--of inequality between old and young, focusing on strains that arise when the old are at the top of the age hierarchy as well as when they experience social losses.  Privileged older women receive special investigation.  Two chapters consider the ways conflict between old and young is openly expressed in different cultures, including witchcraft, and the factors encouraging cooperation and accommodation between the privileged and deprived.  The analysis of social change in chapter 7 challenges the premise of the modernization model that all people's status inevitably deteriorates in the changing nonindustrial world.

_____  Age and Social Change.  Pp. 195-216 in D. I. Kertzer and J. Keith (eds).  Age and Anthropological Theory.  Ithaca, NY:  Cornell University Press, 1984b.

From a cross-cultural perspective, Foner examines the premises of the modernization model regarding the inevitable deterioration of the status of the aged.  It also argues that the concept of cohort succession, developed by age stratification theorists, provides insights into the processes of change in nonindustrial societies.

_____  Caring for the Elderly:  A Cross-Cultural View.  Pp. 387-400 in B. Hess and E. Markson (eds).  Growing Old in America (3rd ed).  New Brunswick, NY:  Transaction Books,

1985a.

Explores relations between old people in need of custodial care and younger ones who care for them in nonindustrial societies.  The article examines factors motivating younger adults to support the frail elderly as well as the sources of strain between themn, and it looks at how the young feel about caring for the aged as well as how the aged feel about their treatment.

_____ Old and Frail and Everywhere Unequal.  The Hastings Center Report.  15(2):27-31, 1985b.

_____ Older Women in Nonindustrial Cultures:  Consequences of Power and Privilege.  Pp. 227-37 in L. Grau (ed).  Women in Later Years.  Binghamton, NY:  Harrington Park Press, 1989.

Examines the strains between privileged old women and disadvantaged younger women in non-Western cultures as well as the way change affects the position of old women.  It is argued that older women have a strong interest in maintaining young women's subordinate position.

Fortes, M.  Age, Generation and Social Structure.  Pp. 99-122 in D. I. Kertzer and J. Keith (eds).  Age and Anthropological Theory.  Ithaca, NY:  Cornell University Press, 1984.

Fry, C.  Toward an Anthropology of Aging.  Pp. 1-20 in C. Fry (ed).  Aging in Culture and Society:  Comparative Viewpoints and Strategies.  Brooklyn, NY:  J. F. Bergin, 1980.

This introduction to a collection of anthropological papers on aging reviews the field of gerontological anthropology, including a brief discussion of cross-cultural comparisons.

_____ Culture, Behavior and Aging in the Comparative Perspective.  In J. Birren and K. W. Schaie (eds).  Handbook of Aging and Psychology (2nd ed).  New York, NY:  Reinhold, 1985.

Fry, C. and J. Keith.  The Life Course As a Cultural Unit.  Pp. 51-70 in M. W. Riley, R. P. Abeles, and M. S. Teitelbaum.  Aging From Birth to Death.  Vol. 2. Sociotemporal Perspectives.  Boulder, CO:  Westview, 1982.

Examines variation in cultural conceptions of the life course and suggests four general patterns of age differentiation for cross-cultural research.

Glascock, A.  Decrepitude and Death-Hastening:  The Nature of Old Age in Third World Societies.  J. Sokolovsky (ed).  Aging and the Aged in the Third World:  Part 1.  Studies in Third World Societies.  22:43-66, 1982.

_____ By Any Other Name, It Is Still Killing:  A Comparison of "Death Hastening" of the Elderly in America and Other

Societies.  Pp.  43-56 in J. Sokolovsky (ed).  The Cultural
Context of Aging:  Worldwide Perspectives.  Westport, CT:
Bergin and Garvey, 1990.

A comparison of the treatment of the elderly in Western and
non-Western societies.  Special emphasis is placed on a
comparison of death-hastening behavior found in a large
number of non-Western societies and the type of care given
to the elderly in American society.

Glascock, A. and S. Feinman.  Holocultural Analysis of Old
Age.  Comparative Social Research.  3:311-32, 1980.

A preliminary analysis of the treatment of old people in
nonindustrial societies utilizing the 60 societies within
the Probability Sample Files.  A consideration of
supportive, non-supportive and death-hastening behavior is
undertaken and the attempt is made to determine in what
type of society each of these behaviors is found.

_____ Social Asset or Social Burden:  Treatment of the Aged
in Non-Industrial Societies.  Pp. 13-31 in C. Fry (ed).
Dimensions:  Aging, Culture, and Health.  Brooklyn, NY:  J.
F.  Bergin, 1981.

An examination of the type of behavior directed toward
different types of the elderly in non-industrial societies.
In particular, the differential treatment of the intact and
decrepit elderly is undertaken.

Goody, J.  Aging in Non-Industrial Societies.  Pp. 117-29 in
R. Binstock and E. Shanas (eds).  The Handbook of Aging
and the Social Sciences.  New York, NY:  Van Nostrand
Rheinhold, 1976.

Looks at how the positions of the aged in nonindustrial
societies are affected by the control as well as transfer
of economic resources.  Also discussed are ways the elderly
maintain their patterns of consumption, control of women by
older men, and the role of the aged in the kinship,
political and religious spheres.

Gutmann, D.  The Cross-Cultural Perspective:  Notes Toward a
Comparative Psychology of Aging.  Pp. 302-26 in J. Birren
and K. W. Schaie (eds).  Handbook of the Psychology of
Aging.  New York, NY:  Van Nostrand Reinhold, 1977.

_____ Reclaimed Powers:  Toward a New Psychology of Men and
Women in Later Life.  New York, NY:  Basic Books, 1987.

Hallowell, A.  Review of Leo Simmons' The Role of the Aged In
Primitive Society.  Annals, American Academy of Political
and Social Sciences.  244:229, 1946.

Halperin, R.  Age in Cultural Economics:  An Evolutionary
Approach.  Pp. 159-94 in D. I. Kertzer and J. Keith (eds).
Age and Anthropological Theory.  Ithaca, NY:  Cornell
University Press, 1984.

A cross-cultural analysis of the relationship between age
and economic organization, focusing on the way roles in
production processes are allocated according to age among
hunter-gatherers, egalitarian and ranked horticulturalists,
and state-level societies.

_____ Age in Cross-Cultural Perspective:  An Evolutionary
Approach.  Pp. 283-311 in P. Silverman (ed).  The Elderly
as Modern Pioneers.  Bloomington, IN:  Indiana University
Press, 1987.

Heath, A.  The Aged in the Developing Countries:  A Review of
the Literature.  Washington, DC:  International Federation
on Ageing, 1981.

Holmes, E.  Aging in Modern and Traditional Societies.  The
World and I.  9:170-83, 1986.

Holmes, L.  Trends in Anthropological Gerontology:  From
Simmons to the Seventies.  International Journal of Aging
and Human Development.  7:211-20, 1976.

_____ Anthropology and Age:  An Assessment.  Pp. 272-84 in
Fry, C. (ed).  Aging in Culture and Society:  Comparative
Viewpoints and Strategies.  Brooklyn, NY:  J. F. Bergin,
1980.

Johnson, D. P. and L. C. Mullins.  Growind Old and Lonely in
Different Societies:  Toward a Comparative Perspective.
Journal of Cross-Cultural Gerontology.  2(3)257-76, 1987.

Keith, J.  The Best is Yet to Be:  Toward an Anthropology of
Age.  Annual Review of Anthropology.  9:339-64, 1980a.

_____ The 'Back to Anthropology' Movement in Gerontology.  Pp.
285-91 in C. Fry (ed).  Aging In Culture and Society:
Comparative Viewpoints and Strategies.  Brooklyn, NY:  J.
F.  Bergin, 1980b.

_____ Old People As People:  Social and Cultural Influences
On Aging and Old Age.  Boston, MA:  Little, Brown, 1982.

A comparative examination of various dimensions of age and
aging.  The introductory chapter outlines the development
of cross-cultural research on old age.  Subsequent chapters
examine the way people in different societies think about
age and use age as a basis of categorization, the
conditions and consequences of age-related norms, factors
promoting age ideology, conditions under which age peers
become members of informal social networks, and age as a
basis for formal associations.

_____ Age and Anthropological Research.  Pp. 213-63 in R.
Binstock and E. Shanas (eds).  Handbook of Aging and Social
Sciences (2nd ed).  New York, NY:  Van Nostrand Reinhold,
1985.

Reviews the questions, strategies and results of an

anthropological/ cross-cultural approach to aging and old age.  It examines the status and treatment of old people in different cultures and the consequences of social change for their participation in society; discusses questions about cultural definitions of the life course, including rituals and symbols associated with age and the impact of cultural values on the aging experience; and it considers the conditions and consequences of various uses of age as a principle of social organization.

Keith, J. and D. Kertzer.  Introduction.  Pp. 19-61 in D. Kertzer and J. Keith (eds).  Age and Anthropological Theory.  Ithaca, NY:  Cornell University Press, 1984.

Reviews previous anthropological research on age and the life course as well as theoretical perspectives in psychology and sociology.  It raises theoretical questions for the cross-cultural study of aging in a number of areas: age stratification; the acquisition, maintenance and transmission of norms; symbol and ritual; marriage, kinship and the family; and power and conflict.

Kertzer, D.  Generation and Age in Cross-Cultural Perspective. Pp.  27-50 in M. W. Riley, R. Abeles, and M. Teitelbaum (eds).  Aging From Birth To Death.  Vol 2.  Sociotemporal Perspectives.  Boulder, CO:  Westview, 1982.

Examines the conceptual confusion often found in social science discussions of generation, arguing for a more limited definition of generation.  It also considers the relationship between generation and age in other cultures, especially conflicts that arise, and looks at societies where generation is a principle of social grouping.

Kertzer, D, J. Meyer, and K. W. Schaie (eds).  Social Structure and Aging:  Comparative Perspectives in Age Structuring in Modern Societies.  Hillsdale, NJ:  Erlbaum Associates, 1988.

Kimball, S.  Review of L. Simmons' The Role of the Aged in Primitive Society.  American Journal of Sociology.  52:287, 1946.

Kinsella, K. G.  Aging in the World.  Washington, DC:  Center for International Research, U. S. Bureau of the Census, 1988.

Little V.  Open Care for the Aged.  Social Work.  23:282-87, 1978.

_____  Open Care for the Aging:  Comparative International Approaches.  New York, NY:  Springer, 1982.

_____  Introduction:  Cross-National Reports on Elderly Care in Developing Countries.  Gerontologist.  23(6):573-75, 1983.

Maxwell, E.  Fading Out:  Resource Control and Cross-Cultural

Patterns of Deference.  _Journal of Cross-Cultural Gerontology_.  1:73-90, 1986.

Using a sample of 95 societies, the author identifies four patterns of deference interaction, which generally include displays of influence by elders and displays of respect by younger people.  It is shown that as the aged deploy their resources differently, patterns of deference toward them are recast.

Maxwell, E. and R. Maxwell.  Contempt for the Elderly:  A Cross-Cultural Analysis.  _Current Anthropology_.  21:569-70, 1980.

Maxwell, R. and P. Silverman.  Information and Esteem: Cultural Considerations in the Treatment of the Aged. _International Journal of Aging and Human Development_. 1:361-92, 1970.

Analyzing a sample of 26 societies from the Human Relations Area Files, the article shows that high informational control among the aged is associated with their being held in esteem.

Maxwell, R., P. Silverman, and E. Maxwell.  The Motive for Gerontocide.  J. Sokolovsky (ed).  Aging and the Aged in the Third World.  Part 1.  _Studies in Third World Societies_.  22:67-84, 1982.

Using a cross-cultural sample of 95 societies, the frequency of abandonment and/or killing of the aged is identified and the factors leading to gerontocide analyzed.

Mead, M.  Ethnological Aspects of Aging.  _Psychosomatics_. 8(4):33-7, 1967.

Myerhoff, B.  Aging and the Aged in Other Cultures:  An Anthropological Perspective.  Pp. 151-66 in E. Bauwens (ed).  _The Anthropology of Health_.  St. Louis, MO:  C. V. Mosby, 1978.

_____ Rites and Signs of Ripening:  The Intertwining of Ritual, Time and Growing Older.  Pp. 305-30 in D. Kertzer and J. Keith eds).  _Age and Anthropological Theory_. Ithaca, NY:  Cornell University Press, 1984.

Nusberg, C, with M. J. Gibson and S. Peace.  _Innovative Aging Programs Abroad:  Implications for the US_.  Westport, CT: Greenwood Press, 1984.

Nydegger, C.  Gerontology and Anthropology:  Challenge and Opportunity.  Pp. 293-302 in C. Fry (ed).  _Dimensions: Aging, Culture and Health_.  New York, NY:  J. F. Bergin, 1981.

_____ Family Ties of the Aged in Cross-Cultural Perspective. _Gerontologist_.  23:26-32, 1983.

Argues that a cross-cultural perspective dispels certain
widely-held myths about "golden times and places for the
aged."  Sets out hypotheses concerning sources of
variability in the status of the elderly within and among
societies.  Stresses that there are unpleasant as well as
positive aspects of family relations in all societies.

O'Donnell, C.  Aging in Preindustrial and Contemporary
Industrial Societies.  Pp. 3-13 in W. Bier (ed).  Aging:
Its Challenges to the Individual and to Society.  New York,
NY:  Fordham University Press, 1974.

Ostor, A.  Chronology, Category and Ritual.  Pp. 281-304 in D.
Kertzer and J. Keith (eds).  Age and Anthropological
Theory.  Ithaca, NY:  Cornell University Press, 1984

Press, I. and M. McKool, Jr.  Social Structure and Status of
the Aged:  Toward Some Valid Cross-Cultural
Generalizations.  Aging and Human Development.  3:297-306,
1972.

Preston, C.  Cross-National Comparison of Subjective Agedness.
International Journal of Comparative Sociology.  11:54-8,
1971.

Rubinstein, R. L.  What Is 'Social Integration of the Elderly'
in Small-Scale Society?  Journal of Cross-Cultural
Gerontology.  1:391-409, 1986.

Raises questions about how to best use the concept of
social integration in cross-cultural studies of the
elderly, with particular reference to old age in one small-
scale Melanesian society, Malo, Vanuatu.

Rubinstein, R. L. and P. Johnson.  Toward a Comparative
Perspective on Filial Response to Aging Populations.  J.
Sokolovsky (ed).  Aging and the Aged in the Third World.
Part 1.  Studies in Third World Societies.  22:115-71,
1982.

Discusses some issues in the cross-cultural study of filial
caregiving and examines factors affecting caregiving to the
elderly in Malo, Vanuatu, in Melanesia.

Sahud, A. R., W. H. Bruvold, and E. A. Merino.  An Initial
Cross-Cultural Assessment of Attitudes Toward the Elderly.
Journal of Cross-Cultural Gerontology.  5(4):333-44, 1990.

Sheehan, T.  Senior Esteem as a Factor of Societal Economic
Complexity.  Gerontologist.  16(5):433-40, 1976.

Silverman, P.  Comparative Studies.  Pp. 312-44 in P.
Silverman (ed).  The Elderly as Modern Pioneers.
Bloomington, IN:  Indiana University Press, 1987.

Reviews the findings of some of the more recent cross-
cultural studies of the aged.  Among the subjects discussed
are:  the modernization hypothesis, resource control and

the elderly, aging men and women, grandparents, and death and dying.

Silverman, P.  The Significance of Information and Power in the Comparative Study of the Aged.  Pp. 43-55 in J. Sokolovsky (ed).  Growing Old in Different Societies: Cross-Cultural Perpectives.  Acton, MA:  Copley Press, 1987.

Based on a statistical analysis of variables from a cross-cultural sample of 95 societies, the authors conclude that information processing is positively related to the social esteem enjoyed by the elderly; that the elderly tend to have an increasing role as relevant sources of information until, perhaps, the more advanced stages of modernization; and that various internal barriers to communication in a community tend to maximize old people's participation.

Silverman, P. and R. J. Maxwell.  How Do I Respect Thee?  Let Me Count the Ways:  Deference Towards Elderly Men and Women.  Behavior Science Research.  13:91-108, 1978.

An analysis of the role and status of the elderly in non-industrial societies utilizing a sub-set of the Standard Cross-Cultural Sample.  Emphasis is placed on the relationship between high status of the elderly and the possession on their part of important societal knowledge.

_____  Cross-Cultural Variation in the Status of Old People.  Pp. 46-69 in P. Stearns (ed).  Old Age in Preindustrial Society.  New York, NY:  Holmes and Meier, 1982.

Simic, A.  Introduction:  Aging and the Aged in Cultural Perspective.  Pp. 9-22 in B. Myerhoff and A. Simic (eds).  Life's Career-- Aging:  Cultural Variations on Growing Old.  Beverly Hills, CA:  Sage 1978.

A review of the literature on the anthropology of aging that raises some theoretical and methodological questions involved in cross-cultural comparisons.

Simic, A. and B. Myerhoff.  Conclusion.  Pp. 231-46 in B. Myerhoff and A. Simic (eds).  Life's Career--Aging:  Cultural Variations On Growing Old.  Beverly Hills, CA:  Sage, 1978.

This concluding chapter analyzes three themes in cross-cultural comparisons of aging:  continuity/discontinuity, the sexual dichotomy, and aging as a career.  Examples are drawn from the five groups (Chagga of Kilimanjaro in Tanzania, a village in Yugoslavia, a Jewish community in California, a Chicano settlement in Los Angeles and a settlement of rural Mexicans living in Mexico City) portrayed in the volume.

Simmons, L.  The Role of the Aged in Primitive Society.  New Haven, CT:  Yale University Press, 1945.  Reprint.  Archon Books, 1970.

In this classic study of aging in cross-cultural perspective, Simmons draws on data from 71 noninudstrial societies to analyze the relationship between 109 physical and cultural characteristics (pertaining to habitat and economy, social and political organization, and religious beliefs and practices) and the status and treatment of the elderly. The eight chapters deal with the following themes: the assurance of food, mainly by communal sharing; property rights which may be used by the aged; the safeguarding of prestige of the aged; routine activities of the aged which are mainly related to economic functions and personal services; civil and political functions of the aged; the use of magic, knowledge, and religion; the aged's adjustments to family life and treatment of the aged with respect to death.

_____ Position and Treatment of the Aged in Primitive and Other Societies. Pp. 26-31 in R. Havighurst (ed). Social Adjustment in Old Age. New York, NY: Social Science Research Council, 1946a.

_____ Attitudes Toward Aging and the Aged: Primitive Societies. Journal of Gerontology. 1:72-95, 1946b.

_____ Social Participation of the Aged in Different Cultures. Annals, American Academy of Political and Social Science. 279:43-51, 1953.

_____ An Anthropologist Views Old Age. Public Health Reports. 72:290-94, 1957.

_____ Aging in Pre-industrial Cultures. Pp. 65-74 in C. Tibbitts and W. Donahue (eds). Aging in Today's Society. New York, NY: Columbia University Press, 1960a.

_____ Aging in Preindustrial Societies. Pp. 62-91 in C. Tibbitts (ed). Handbook of Social Gerontology. Chicago, IL: University of Chicago Press, 1960b.

Examines a broad range of issues concerning old people's needs and interests--and solutions to meeting these needs--in preindustrial societies. Topics include: security in food sharing; old people's economic activities, skills and rights; the aged in the family and polity; the use of knowledge, magic and religion; respect for the aged; and death.

_____ Aging in Primitive Societies: A Comparative Survey of Family Life and Relationships. Law and Contemporary Problems. 27:36-51, 1962.

Slater, P. Cultural Attitudes Toward the Aged. Geriatrics. 18:308-314, 1963.

_____ Cross-Cultural Views of the Elderly. In R. Kastenbaum (ed). New Thoughts On Old Age. New York, NY: Springer, 1964.

Sokolovsky, J.  Perspective on Aging in the Third World.  J.
    Sokolovsky (ed).  Aging and the Aged in the Third World.
    Part 1.  Studies in the Third World.  22:1-21, 1982.

    Introduces a collection of articles on aging with a
    discussion of demographic changes in the Third world;
    modernization, development and the aged; and treatment and
    care for the aged in different societies.

_____ Background To Comparative Sociocultural Gerontology.
    Pp. 1-8 in J. Sokolovsky (ed).  Growing Old In Different
    Societies:  Cross-Cultural Perspectives.  Acton, MA:
    Copley Press, 1987.

    Introduction to a collection of articles on cross-cultural
    aging that briefly reviews the anthropology of aging.

_____ Introduction.  Pp. 1-11 in J. Sokolovsky (ed).  The
    Cultural Context of Aging:  Worldwide Perspectives.
    Westport, CT:  Bergin and Garvey, 1990.

Teski, M.  The Evolution of Aging, Ecology and the Elderly in
    the Modern World.  Pp. 14-23 in J. Sokolovsky (ed).
    Growing Old in Different Societies:  Cross-Cultural
    Perspectives.  Acton, MA:  Copley Press, 1987.

Togonu-Bickersteth, F. and E. O. Akinnawo.  Filial
    Responsibility Expectations of Nigerian and Indian
    University Students.  Journal of Cross-Cultural
    Gerontology.  5(4):315-32, 1990.

Tout, K.  Aging in Developing Countries.  Oxford, UK:  Oxford
    University Press, 1989.

Tripp-Reimer, T.  Cultural Perspectives on Aging.  Pp. 18-50
    in M.  Schrock (ed).  Holistic Assessment of the Healthy
    Aged.  New York, NY:  John Wiley, 1980.

Tuckman, J. and I. Lorge.  Attitudes Toward Old People.
    Journal of Social Psychology.  37:249-60, 1953.

United Nations.  The World Aging Situation:  Strategies and
    Policies.  New York, NY:  United Nations, 1985.

van den Berghe, P.  Age Differentiation in Human Societies.
    Pp. 72-81 in J. Sokolovsky (ed).  Growing Old in Different
    Societies:  Cross-Cultural Perspectives.  Acton, MA:
    Copley Press, 1987.

Warnes, T.  The Elderly in Less Developed Countries.  Ageing
    and Society.  6:373-80, 1986.

# 2

# Demography, Biology and Longevity

Acsadi, G. and J. Nemeskeri. History of Human Lifespan and Mortality. Translated by K. Balas. Budapest, Hungary: Akademiai Kiado, 1970.

This volume is a primary source of methods and data in historical- and paleo-demography. Includes discussion of life span and mortality, methods of paleodemography, determination of age and sex from skeletal material, and history of the human lifespan from the Paleolithic to historical times.

Adelman, R. C. and G. S. Roth (eds). Testing the Theories of Aging. Boca Raton, FL: CRC Press, 1982.

Critically reviews theories of aging and use of cell cultures as a model system. Includes chapters on longevity-determining genes, free radical theory, error theories of aging, autoimmunity, and genetic alterations and pathology of aging.

Anderson, A. Ageing in Japan: Riches Make for Longevity. Nature. 310:92, 1984.

Andres, R. Mortality and Obesity: The Rationale for Age-Specific Height-Weight Tables. Pp. 311-18 in R. Andres, E. L. Bierman, and W. R. Hazzard (eds). Principles of Geriatric Medicine. New York, NY: McGraw-Hill, 1985.

Anisimov, V. N. Dependence of Susceptibility to Carcinogenesis on Species Life Span. Archiv fur Geschwulstforschung. 59:205-13, 1989.

Araki, S. and K. Murata. Factors Affecting the Longevity of Total Japanese Population. Tohoku Journal of Experimental Medicine. 3(2):237-52, 1987.

Arriaga, E. E. Measuring and Explaining the Change in Life Expectancies. Demography. 21:83-96, 1984.

Baird, P. A. and A. D. Sadovnick. Life Table for Down
     Syndrome. Human Genetics. 82:291-92, 1989.

Bayliss, R., C. Clarke, and A. G. Whitfield. Problems in
     Comparative Longevity. Journal of the Royal College of
     Physicians of London. 21:134-39, 1987.

Beall, C. M. Theoretical Dimensions of a Focus on Age in
     Physical Anthropology. Pp. 82-95 in D. I. Kertzer and J.
     Keith (eds). Age and Anthropological Theory. New York,
     NY: Cornell University Press, 1984.

_____ Studies of Longevity. Pp. 73-93 in P. Silverman (ed).
     The Elderly as Modern Pioneers. Bloomington, IN: Indiana
     University Press, 1987.

Beall C. M. and J. K. Eckert. Measuring Functional Capacity
     Cross-Culturally. Pp. 21-55 in C. L. Fry and J. Keith
     (eds). New Methods for Old Age Research. South Hadley,
     MA: Bergin and Garvey, 1986.

Beall, C. M. and M. Goldstein. Biological Function, Activity
     and Dependency Among Elderly Sherpa in the Nepal Himalayas.
     Social Science and Medicine. 16(2):135-41, 1982a.

Beall, C. M., M. C Goldstein, and E. S. Feldman (eds). Cross-
     Cultural Studies of Biological Aging. Special Issue.
     Social Science and Medicine. 16(2), 1982a.

     This special issue contains twelve essays in the biological
     and physical anthropology of aging in diverse sociocultural
     groups, ranging from Sherpas and Tibetan migrants in Nepal
     to Samoans in California.

_____ Work, Aging and Dependency in a Sherpa Population in
     Nepal. Social Science and Medicine. 16(2):141-48, 1982b.

_____ The Physical Fitness of Elderly Nepalese Farmers
     Residing in Rugged Mountain and Flat Terrain. Journal of
     Gerontology. 40:529-35, 1985a.

_____ Social Structure and Intracohort Variation in Physical
     Fitness Among Elderly Males in a Traditional Third World
     Society. Journal of the American Geriatrics Society.
     33:406-12, 1985b.

Beaubier, J. High Life Expectancy on the Island of Paros,
     Greece. New York, NY: Philosophical Library, 1976.

_____ Biological Factors in Aging. Pp. 21-41 in C. Fry (ed).
     Aging in Culture and Society: Comparative Viewpoints and
     Strategies. Brooklyn, N.Y.: J. F. Bergin, 1980.

Beller, S. and E. Palmore. Longevity in Turkey.
     Gerontologist. 14:373-76, 1974.

Benet, S. Abkhasians: The Long-Living People of the
     Caucasus. New York, NY: Holt, Rinehart and Winston, 1974.

An ethnography which helps to place one presumed "long-lived" people in their environmental and sociocultural context.  Includes chapters on kinship, family living, religion and folklore, "life on the land" and speculations as to "why the Abkhasians are long-living."

Bennett, N. G. and L. K. Garson.  Extraordinary Longevity in the Soviet Union:  Fact or Artifact?  Gerontologist. 26(4):358-61, 1986.

Berard, J. D.  Life Histories of Male Cayo Santiago Macaques. Puerto Rico Health Sciences Journal.  8:121-27, 1989.

Bergener, M., et al. (eds).  Aging in the Eighties and Beyond: Highlights of the Twelfth International Congress of Gerontology.  New York, NY:  Springer, 1983.

Berkel, J. and F. de Waard.  Mortality Pattern and Life Expectancy of Seventh-Day Adventists in the Netherlands. International Journal of Epidemiology.  12:455-59, 1983.

Berkman, L. F.  The Changing and Heterogenous Nature of Aging and Longevity:  A Social and Biomedical Perspective. Annual Review of Gerontology and Geriatrics.  8:37-68, 1988.

Bittles, A. H. and K. J. Collins (eds).  The Biology of Human Ageing.  Cambridge, MA:  Cambridge University Press, 1986.

Contributions include discussions of:  Evolution; rodent dietary restriction; tissue culture systems; biological, biochemical and skeletal age asessment; demography of UK, USA, and USSR; human homeostasis; and physical activity. From a symposium held in April, 1984.

Borkan, G. A.  Biological Age Assessment in Adulthood.  Pp. 81-93 in A. H. Bittles and K. J. Collins (eds).  The Biology of Human Ageing.  Cambridge:  Cambridge University Press, 1986.

Borkan, G. A., D. E. Hults, and P. J. Mayer.  Physical Anthropological Approaches to Aging.  Yearbook of Physical Anthropology.  25:181-202, 1982.

This review article summarizes research in prehistoric and nonhuman primate aging, size and body composition, genetics, demography, evolution, experimental modification of rates of aging, and human aging rates.

Borkan, G. A., et al.  Body Weight and Coronary Disease Risk; Patterns of Risk Factor Change Associated With Long-Term Weight Change.  American Journal of Epidemiology. 124:410-19, 1986.

Bornstein, R. and M. T. Smircina.  The Status of the Empirical Support for the Hypothesis of Increased Variability in Aging Populations.  Gerontologist.  22:258-60, 1982.

Bouliere, F.  The Assessment of Biological Age in Man.
    Geneva, Switzerland:  World Health Organization Paper No.
    37, 1970.

_____ Ecology of Human Senescence.  Pp. 71-85 in J. C.
    Brocklehurst (ed).  Textbook of Geriatric Medicine and
    Gerontology (2nd ed).  Edinburgh, Scotland:  Churchill
    Livingstone, 1978.

Bowden, D. M. (ed).  Aging in Nonhuman Primates.  New York,
    NY:  Van Nostrand Reinhold, 1979.

    Contains chapters on:  nervous system, immune system and
    behavior; endocrine system (reproduction and stress);
    cardiovascular, pulmonary and renal systems; skeletal
    system.  All data refer to crosssectional study of Macaca
    nemestrina (pigtail macaque) individually housed in cages.

Bowden, D. M., R. Short and D. D. Williams.  Constructing an
    Instrument to Measure the Rate of Aging in Female Pigtailed
    Macaques (Macaca nemestrina).  Journal of Gerontology.
    45:B59-66, 1990.

Bramblett, C. A.  Non-Metric Skeletal Age Changes in the
    Darajani Baboon.  American Journal of Physical
    Anthropology.  30:161-72, 1969.

Brennan, E. R.  Secular Changes in Age-Specific Cause of Death
    in Sanday, Orkney Islands.  Social Science and Medicine.
    16:155-64, 1982.

Brody, J. A.  Chronic Diseases and Disorders.  Pp. 137-42 in
    A. L. Goldstein (ed).  Biomedical Advances in Aging.  New
    York, NY:  Plenum, 1990.

Busse, E. W. and G. L. Maddox (eds).  The Duke Longitudinal
    Studies of Normal Aging:  1955-1980.  New York, NY:
    Springer, 1985.

Callow, P.  Life Cycles:  An Evolutionary Approach to the
    Physiology of Reproduction, Development and Ageing.
    London:  Chapman and Hall, 1978.

    One of the few texts to adopt a perspective on biological
    aging which emphasizes a continuum from conception to
    senescence.

Charlesworth, B.  Evolution in Age-structured Populations.
    Cambridge:  Cambridge University Press, 1980.

    Sophisticated mathematical treatment of models where
    fertility and survival are functions of age.  Discusses
    demography, ecology, selection, genetic drift and life
    history evolution.

Chandra, R. K. (ed).  Nutrition, Immunity and Illness in the
    Elderly.  New York, NY:  Pergamon, 1985.

Chandra, R. K., et al.  Nutrition and Immunocompetence of the Elderly.  Effect of Short Term Nutritional Supplementation on Cell-Mediated Immunity and Lymphocyte Subsets. Nutrition Research.  2:223-32, 1982.

Clark, G. A., et al.  Poor Growth Prior to Early Childhood: Decreased Health and Life-span in the Adult.  American Journal of Physical Anthropology.  70:145-60, 1986.

_____ Poor Early Growth and Adult Mental and Somatic Health. Pp. 331-46 in A. L. Goldstein (ed).  Biomedical Advances in Aging.  New York, NY:  Plenum, 1990.

Clarke, C.  Increased Longevity in Man.  Journal of the Royal College of Physicians.  20:145-60, 1986.

Cole L. C.  The Population Consequences of Life History Phenomena.  Quarterly Review of Biology.  29(2):103-37, 1954.

Comfort, A.  The Biology of Senescence (3rd ed).  New York, NY:  Elsevier, 1979.

     The most comprehensive and readable textbook on the biology of aging.  Includes chapters on distribution of senescence, genetic factors in longevity, growth and senescence, mechanisms of senescence, physiology and homeostasis, measurement of human aging rate, and critical evaluation of theories.

Cook, S. F.  Aging of and in Populations.  Pp. 581-606 in P. Timiras (ed).  Developmental Physiology and Aging.  New York, NY:  MacMillan, 1972.

Corruccini, R. S. and S. S. Kaul.  The Epidemiological Transition and Anthropology of Minor Chronic Non-Infectious Diseases.  Medical Anthropology.  7(3):36-50, 1983.

Crawford, M. and L. Rogers.  Population Genetic Models in the Study of Aging and Longevity in a Mennonite Community. Social Science and Medicine.  16(2):149-53, 1982.

Crews, D. E. (ed).  Symposium:  Evolutionary, Biosocial, and CrossCultural Perspectives on Aging.  American Journal of Human Biology.  1:303-82, 1989.

     This 1987 symposium includes 8 papers on aspects of morbidity and mortality (hypertension, chronic diseases, amyotrophic lateral sclerosis), and on diet and dietary restriction, as these factors vary with age among diverse human populations.

Cutler, R. G.  Evolution of Longevity in Primates.  Journal of Human Evolution.  5:169-202, 1976.

_____ Evolution of Human Longevity:  A Critical Overview. Mechanisms of Ageing and Development.  9:337-91, 1979.

_____    Antioxidants and Longevity of Mammalian Species.    Basic
Life Sciences.    35:15-73, 1985.

Das-Gupta, P.    A Note on the Consistency of Life Tables for
Total Populations with Those for Their Subpopulations.
Social Biology.    35:158-63, 1988.

Davies, A. M.    Epidemiology and the Challenge of Aging.
International Journal of Epidemiology.    14(1):9-21, 1985.

Davies, D.    The Centenarians of the Andes.    Garden City, NY:
Anchor Press, 1975.

Dolhinow, P.    The Primates:  Age, Behavior and Evolution.    Pp.
65-81 in D. I. Kertzer and J. Keith (eds).    Age and
Anthropological Theory.    New York, NY:  Cornell University
Press, 1984.             .

Dublin, L. I., A. J. Lotka, and M. Speigelman.    Length of
Life.    New York, NY:  Ronald Press, 1949.

A detailed historical and analytical discussion of the life
table.    Considers such variables as geography, genetics,
occupation, medicine and economics.

Dunbar, R. I. M.    Demographic and Life History Variables of a
Population of Gelada Baboons (Theropithecus gelada).
Journal of Animal Ecology.    49:485-506, 1980.

Farhat, Y.    Demography of Muslims in Australia.    Journal of
Biosocial Science    22:77-84, 1990.

Finch, C. E. and E. L. Schneider (eds).    Handbook of the
Biology of Aging (2nd ed).    New York, NY:  Van Nostrand
Reinhold, 1985.

Valuable source of review articles and references in:
epidemiology, cross-species comparisons, interventions in
longevity, lower eukaryotes, molecular biology, cellular
biology, physiology, neurobiology, and human biology and
pathology.

Forster, L. E. and J. Lynn.    The Use of Physiological Measures
and Demographic Variables to Predict Longevity Among
Inpatient Hospice Applicants.    American Journal of Hospice
Care.    6:31-34, 1989.

Foster, D., L. Klinger-Vartabedian, and L. Wispe.    Male
Longevity and Age Differences between Spouses.    Journal of
Gerontology.    39:117-20, 1984.

Fries, J. F.    The Compression of Morbidity.    Milbank Memorial
Fund Quarterly.    61:397-419, 1983.

Fries, J. and L. Crapo.    Vitality and Aging.    San Fransisco,
CA:  W. H. Freeman, 1981.

This book presents the hypothesis and consequences of the

"rectangularization" of the human survivorship curve.  The central idea, that the duration of infirmity in the elderly will decrease in the future, and many of its implications are controversial.

Fries, J. F., L. W. Green, and S. Levine.  Health Promotion and the Compression of Morbidity.  <u>Lancet</u>.  1(8636):481-83, 1989.

Frisancho, A. R.  New Standards of Weight and Body Composition by Frame Size and Height for Assessment of Nutritional Status of Adults and the Elderly.  <u>American Journal of Clinical Nutrition</u>.  40:808-19, 1984.

Gage, T. B.  Bio-Mathematical Approaches to the Study of Human Variation in Mortality.  <u>Yearbook of Physical Anthropology</u>. 32:185-214, 1989.

Garruto, R. M.  Disease Patterns of Isolated Groups.  Pp. 557-97 in H.  Rothschild (ed).  <u>Biocultural Aspects of Disease</u>.  New York, NY:  Academic Press, 1981.

Garruto, R. M. and D. C. Gajdusek.  Pacific Cultures:  A Paradigm for the Study of Late Onset Neurological Disorders.  Pp. 71-98 in H.  Rothschild (ed).  <u>Risk Factors for Senility</u>.  New York, NY:  Oxford University Press, 1983.

Gavrilov, L. A., N. S. Gavrilova, and V. N. Nosov.  Human Life Span Stopped Increasing:  Why?  <u>Gerontology</u>.  29:176-80, 1983.

Gerber, L. M.  The Influence of Environmental Factors on Mortality and Coronary Disease Among Filipinos in Hawaii. <u>Human Biology</u>.  52:269-78, 1980.

_____  Gains in Life Expectancies If Heart Disease and Stroke Were Eliminated Among Caucasians, Filipinos and Japanese in Hawaii.  <u>Social Science and Medicine</u>.  17(6):349-53, 1983.

Goldstein A. and S. Goldstein.  The Challenge of an Aging Population:  The Case of the People's Republic of China. <u>Research Aging</u>.  8(2):179-200, 1986.

Gould, S. J.  <u>Ontogeny and Phylogeny</u>.  Cambridge, MA:  Harvard University Press, 1977.

Historical tracing of development and critical analysis of the biogenetic law "ontogeny recapitulates phylogeny". Suggests clarification of heterochronic processes and applies concepts of neoteny and paedomorphosis to human evolution.

Graham, C. E., O. R. Kling, and R. A. Steiner.  Reproductive Senescence in Female Nonhuman Primates.  Pp, 183-202 in D. M. Bowden (ed).  <u>Aging in Nonhuman Primates</u>.  New York, NY: Van Nostrand Reinhold, 1979.

Gruman, G. J.  A History of Ideas about the Prolongation of
    Life. New York, NY:  Arno Press, 1977.

    The author provides a lengthy review of the comparative
    history of ideas regarding interventions to extend the
    human life span.  A large bibliography is provided.

Guthrie, R. O.  Senescence as an Adaptive Trait.  Perspectives
    in Biology and Medicine.  12:313-24, 1969.

Halsell, G.  Los Viejos:  Secrets of Long Life from the Sacred
    Valley.  Emmaus, PA:  Rodale Press, 1976.

Hamilton, W.  The Moulding of Senescence by Natural Selection.
    Journal of Theoretical Biology.  12:12-45, 1966.

Haug, M. R. and S. J. Folmar.  Longevity, Gender, and Life
    Quality.  Journal of Health and Social Behavior.
    27(4):332-45, 1986.

Hayflick, L.  Biological Aspects of Aging.  Pp. 26-49 in S. H.
    Preston (ed).  Biological and Social Aspects of Mortality
    and the Length of Life.  Liege, Belgium:  Ordina Editions,
    1982.

_____  Why Do We Live So Long?  Geriatrics.  43:77-9, 1988.

Haynes, S. G. and M. Feinleib (eds).  Second Conference on
    the Epidemiology of Aging.  Bethesda, MD:  USDHHS, National
    Institute of Health Publication No. 80-969, 1980.

    Proceedings of a 1977 conference which considered:
    biological, genetic, immunological and functional measures
    of age; biomedical correlates of aging; social,
    psychological and functional correlates of aging; and
    demographic trends and health care implications.

Hazzard, W. R.  Biological Basis of the Sex Differential in
    Longevity.  Journal of the American Geriatric Society.
    34:455-71, 1986.

_____  Why Do Women Live Longer Than Men?  Biologic
    Differences That Influence Longevity.  Postgraduate
    Medicine.  85:271-83, 1989.

Heyden, S. and G. J. Fodor.  Does Regular Exercise Prolong
    Life Expectancy?  Sports Medicine.  6:63-71, 1988.

Holliday, R.  MINIREVIEW:  The Limited Proliferation of
    Cultured Human Diploid Cells:  Regulation or Senescence?
    Journal of Gerontology.  45:B36-41, 1990.

Horowitz, A., et al (eds).  Nutrition of the Elderly.  Oxford:
    Oxford University Press, 1989.

Horowitz, S., G. Armelagos, and K. Wachter.  On Generating
    Birth Rates from Skeletal Populations.  American Journal of
    Physical Anthropology.  76:189-96, 1988.

Horrocks, J. A.  Life History Characteristics of a Wild
    Population of Vervets (Cercopithecus aethiops sabaeus) in
    Barbados, West Indies.  International Journal of
    Primatology.  7:31-47, 1986.

Howell, N.  Toward a Uniformitarian Theory of Human
    Paleodemography.  Pp. 25-40 in R. Ward and K. Weiss (eds).
    The Demographic Evolution of Human Population.  New York,
    NY:  Academic Press, 1976.

_____  The Demography of the Dobe !Kung.  New York, NY:
    Academic Press, 1979.

    Among other aspects of !Kung demography, this book
    discusses mortality, longevity and life table analysis.

Hrdy, S.  'Nepotists' and 'Altruists':  The Behavior of Old
    Females Among Macaques and Langur Monkeys.  Pp. 59-76 in P.
    T. Amoss and S.  Harrel (eds).   Other Ways of Growing Old.
    Stanford, CA:  Stanford University Press, 1981.

Hunt, E., Jr.  Evolutionary Comparisons of the Demography,
    Life Cycles, and Health Care of Chimpanzee and Human
    Populations.  Pp. 52-57 in M. Logan and E. Hunt (eds).
    Health and the Human Condition.  North Scituate, MA:
    Duxbury Press, 1978.

Jensen, G. D. and A. H. Polloi.  Health and Life-Style of
    Longevous Palauans:  Implications for Development Theory.
    International Journal of Aging and Human Development.
    19(4):271-86, 1984.

Johnston, F., A. Roche, and C. Suzanne (eds).   Human Physical
    Growth and Maturation.  New York, NY:  Plenum Press, 1980.

Jones, E. C.  The Post-fertile Life of Non-human Primates and
    Other Mammals.  Pp. 13-39 in A. A. Haspels and H. Musaph
    (eds).  Psychosomatics in Peri-Menopause.  Baltimore, MD:
    University Park Press, 1979.

Jurmain, R.  Paleoepidemiology of a Central California
    Prehistoric Population from CA-ALA-329:  2.  Degenerative
    Disease.  American Journal of Physical Anthropology.
    83:83-94, 1990.

Kaprio, J., M. Koskenuuo, and H. Rita.  Mortality After
    Bereavement:  A Prospective Study of 95,647 Widowed
    Persons.  American Journal of Public Health.  77(3):283-87,
    1987.

    An incidence study of bereavement mortality using a
    population register in Finland.

Katz, S.  Anthropological Perspectives on Aging.  Annals,
    American Academy of Political and Social Sciences.
    438:1-12, 1978.

Katz, S., et al.  Active Life Expectancy.  New England Journal of Medicine. 309(20):1218-24, 1983.

Kaufert, P. A. Anthropology and the Menopause: The
Development of a Theoretical Framework. Maturitas.
4(3):181-94, 1982.

Kent, S. The Evolution of Longevity. Geriatrics. 35:98-104,
1980.

_____ Body Weight and Life Expectancy. Geriatrics.
37:149-57, 1982.

Keys, A. B. Seven Countries: A Multivariate Analysis of
Death and Coronary Heart Disease. Cambridge, MA: Harvard
University Press, 1980.

_____ Longevity of Man: Relative Weight and Fatness in
Middle Age. Annals of Medicine. 21:163-68, 1989.

Kirkwood, T. B. L. Comparative and Evolutionary Aspects of
Longevity. Pp. 27-44 in C. E. Finch and E. L. Schneider
(eds). Handbook of the Biology of Aging (2nd ed). New
York, NY: Van Nostrand Reinhold, 1985.

_____ DNA, Mutations, and Aging. Mutation Research.
219:1-7, 1989.

Kirkwood, T. B. L. and R. Holliday. Aging as a Consequence of
Natural Selection. Pp. 3-22 in A. H. Bittles and K. J.
Collins (eds). The Biology of Human Ageing. Cambridge,
MA: Cambridge University Press, 1986.

Koslov, V. Longevity in Abkhasia. Gerontologist. 24:446,
1984.

Kuznetsova, S. M. Polymorphism of Heterochromatin Areas on
Chromosomes 1,9,16 and Y in Long-Lived Subjects and Persons
of Different Ages in Two Regions of the Soviet Union.
Archives of Gerontology and Geriatrics. 6:177-86, 1987.

Leaf, A. Getting Old. Pp. 291-99 in S. Katz (ed).
Biological Anthropology. San Francisco, CA: W. H.
Freeman, 1979.

_____ Long-lived Populations: Extreme Old Age. Journal of
the American Geriatric Society. 30(8):485-87, 1982.

_____ Unusual Longevity: The Common Denominators. Hospital
Practice. 8:75-86, 1983.

Lelashvili, N. G. and S. M. Dalakishvili. Genetic Study of
High Longevity Index Populations. Mechanisms of Ageing and
Development. 28:261-71, 1984.

Leviatan, U., J. Cohen, and A. Jaffe-Katz. Life Expectancy of
Kibbutz Members. International Journal of Aging and Human
Development. 23(3):195-206, 1986.

Lieber, M. and H. T. Blumenthal.  Lifespan Changes in the
    Index of Cephalization.  Experimental Ageing Research.
    10:127-35, 1984.

Lovejoy, O. C., et al.  Paleodemography of Libben Site, Ottawa
    County, Ohio.  Science.  198:291-93, 1977.

Mahoney, M. C., et al.  Years of Potential Life Lost Among a
    Native American Population.  Public Health Reports.
    104:279-85, 1989.

Mann, A. E.  Paleodemographic Aspects of the South African
    Australopithecines.  Philadelphia, PA:  University of
    Pennsylvania Publications in Anthropology, No. 1, 1975.

Manson, J. E., et al.  Body Weight and Longevity:  A
    Reassessment.  Journal of the American Medical Association.
    257:353-58, 1987.

Manton, K. G.  Sex and Race Specific Mortality Differentials
    in Multiple Causes of Death Data.  Gerontologist.
    20:480-93, 1980.

_____  Past and Future Life Expectancy Increases At Later
    Ages:  Their Implications for the Linkage of Chronic
    Morbidity, Disability and Mortality.  Journal of
    Gerontology.  41(5):672-81, 1986.

Manton, K. G., S. S. Poss, and S. Wing.  The Black/White
    Mortality Crossover.  Gerontologist.  19:291-300, 1979.

Markides, K. S. and R. Machalek.  Selective Survival, Aging
    and Society.  Archives of Gerontology and Geriatrics.
    3:207-22, 1984.

Martin, G. M.  Genetic Syndromes in Man with Potential
    Relevance to the Pathobiology of Aging.  Birth Defects:
    Original Articles Series.  14(1):5-39, 1978.

    Lists and discusses Mendelian traits which best model
    biological aging processes in human beings.

_____  Genetics of Human Disease, Longevity and Aging.  Pp.
    415-44 in R. Andres, E. L. Bierman, and W. R. Hazzard
    (eds).  Principles of Geriatric Medicine.  New York, NY:
    McGraw-Hill, 1985.

Masoro, E. J.  Biology of Aging:  Current State of Knowledge.
    Archives of Internal Medicine.  147:166-69, 1987.

_____  Life Span Extension and Food Restriction.
    Comprehensive Therapy.  14:9-13, 1988.

Mayer, P. J.  Evolutionary Advantage of the Menopause.  Human
    Ecology.  10(4):477-94, 1982.

_____  Biological Theories of Aging.  Pp. 17-53 in P.
    Silverman (ed).  The Elderly as Modern Pioneers.

Bloomington, IN:   Indiana University Press, 1987.

_____ Age-dependent Decline in Rejoining of X-ray-induced DNA Double Strand Breaks in Normal Human Lymphocytes.  Mutation Research.  219:95-100, 1989.

Mazess, R.  Health and Longevity in Vilcabamba, Ecuador. Journal of the American Medical Association.  240:1781, 1978.

Mazess, R. and S. Forman.  Longevity and Age Exaggeration in Vilcabamba, Ecuador.  Journal of Gerontology.  34:94-98, 1979.

Mazess, R. and R. W. Mathisen.  Lack of Unusual Longevity in Vilcabamba, Ecuador.  Human Biology.  54:517-24, 1982.

McEvoy, A. W. and O. F. James.  Anthropometric Indices in Normal Elderly Subjects.  Age and Ageing.  11(2):97-100, 1982.

Medvedev, A.  Aging and Longevity:  New Approaches and New Perspectives.  Gerontologist.  15:196-201, 1975.

_____ Negative Trends in Life Expectancy in the USSR, 1964- 1983.  Gerontologist.  25(2):201-08, 1985.

Meindl, R. S.  Components of Longevity:  Developmental and Genetic Responses to Differential Childhood Mortality. Social Science and Medicine.  16:165-74, 1982.

Mellstrom, D., A. Rundgren, and A. Svanborg.  Tobacco Smoking, Ageing and Health Among the Elderly:  A Longitudinal Population Study of 70-Year-Old Men and An Age Cohort Comparison.  Age and Ageing.  11(1):45-58, 1982.

Mendenhall, C. L., et al.  Longevity Among Ethnic Groups in Alcoholic Liver Disease.  Alcohol and Alcoholism. 24:11-19, 1989.

Metropolitan Insurance Company.  Recent International Changes in Longevity.  Statistical Bulletin of the Metropolitan Insurance Company.  67:16-21, 1986.

_____ Profile of Centenarians.  Statistical Bulletin of the Metropolitan Insurance Company.  68:2-9, 1987a.

_____ Trends in Longevity after Age 65.  Statistical Bulletin of the Metropolitan Insurance Company.  68:10-17, 1987b.

Micozzi, M. S. and T. M. Harris.  Age Variations in the Relation of Body Mass Indices to Estimates of Body Fat and Muscle Mass.  American Journal of Physical Anthropology. 81:375-80, 1990.

Miller, G.  Male-Female Longevity:  Comparisons Among the Amish.  Journal of the Indiana State Medical Association. 73:471-73, 1980.

Miller, G. and D. Gerstein.  The Life Expectancy of Non-
smoking Men and Women.  Public Health Reports.  98:343-49,
1983.

Milner, G. R., D. A. Humpf, and H. C. Harpending.  Pattern
Matching of Age-at-Death Distributions in Paleodemographic
Analysis.  American Journal of Physical Anthropology.
80:49-58, 1989.

Molleson, T. I.  Skeletal Age and Paleodemography.  Pp. 95-118
in A. H.  Bittles and K. J. Collins (eds).  The Biology of
Human Ageing.  Cambridge:  Cambridge University Press,
1986.

Moore, M.  Physical Aging:  A Cross-Cultural Perspective.  Pp.
27-40 in F. Berghorn and D. Schafer (eds).  The Dynamics
of Aging.  Boulder, CO:  Westview Press, 1981.

_____  The Human Life Span.  Pp. 54-72 in P. Silverman (ed).
The Elderly as Modern Pioneers.  Bloomington, IN:  Indiana
University Press, 1987.

Morrison, S. D.  Nutrition and Longevity.  Nutrition Reviews.
41:133-42, 1983.

Mulder, M. B.  Menarche, Menopause and Reproduction in the
Kipsigis of Kenya.  Journal of Biosocial Science.
21:179-92, 1989.

Murphy, E. A.  Genetics of Longevity in Man.  Pp. 261-301 in
E. L.  Schneider (ed).  The Genetics of Aging.  New York,
NY:  Plenum,

Ohtsuka, R.  Hunting Activity and Aging Among the Gidra
Papuans:  A Biobehavioral Analysis.  American Journal of
Physical Anthropology.  80:31-40, 1989.

Onishi, N., S. Sato, and K. Kimotuki.  Follow-up Study of Life
Span of Farmers in Relation to Physical Fitness Data in
1963.  Journal of Human Ergology.  17:43-56, 1988.

Osness, W.  Biological Aspects of the Aging Process.  Pp.
41-60 in F.  Berghorn and D. Schafer (eds).  Dynamics of
Aging.  Boulder, CO:  Westview Press, 1981.

Paffenbarger, R. S., Jr., et al.  Physical Activity, Other
Life-Style Patterns, Cardiovascular Disease and Longevity.
Supplement.  Acta Medica Scandinavica.  711:85-91, 1986.

Paine, R. R.  Model Life Table Fitting by Maximum Likelihood
Estimation:  A Procedure to Reconstruct Paleodemographic
Characteristics from Skeletal Age Distributions.  American
Journal of Physical Anthropology.  79:51-61, 1989.

Palmore, E. B.  Predictors of the Longevity Difference:  A
25-year Follow-up.  Gerontologist.  22:513-18, 1982.

_____  Longevity in Abkhazia:  A Reevaluation.  Gerontologist.

24:95-96, 1984.

———— Trends in the Health of the Aged.  Gerontologist.
26:298-302, 1986.

Pawson, G. and G. Janes.  Biocultural Risks in Longevity:
Samoans in California.  Social Science & Medicine.
16:183-90, 1982.

Pearl, R.  The Inheritance of Longevity.  Human Biology.
3:245-69, 1931.

Pearl, R. and H. D. Pearl.  The Ancestry of the Long-Lived.
Baltimore, MD:  Johns Hopkins University Press, 1934.

Peterson, M. and C. L. Rose.  Historical Antecedents of
Normative vs. Pathologic Perspectives in Aging.  Journal of
the American Geriatric Society.  30(4):289-94, 1982.

Pitskhelauari, G.  The Long-Living of Soviet Georgia.
Translated and edited by G. Lesnoff-Caravaglia.  New York,
NY:  Human Sciences Press, 1981.

Uncritical presentation of "extraordinary" longevity,
including brief discussions of diet, lifestyle, health,
work, sex, and "prevention and treatment of premature
aging."

Plato, C. C., R. M. Garruto, and D. C. Gajdusek.  Aging and
Chronic Degenerative Diseases of the Central Nervous
System.  2.  Utilization of Patient Control Registries in
Studying Late Onset Disorders.  American Journal of
Physical Anthropology.  54:263-64, 1981.

Plato, C. C., et al.  Amyotrophic Lateral Sclerosis and
Parkinsonian-Dementia on Guam:  a 25-year Prospective Case-
Control Study.  American Journal of Epidemiology.
124:643-56, 1986.

Plude, D. J.  Sensory, Perceptual, and Motor Function in Human
Aging.  Pp. 94-113 in P. Silverman (ed).  The Elderly as
Modern Pioneers.  Bloomington, IN:  Indiana University
Press, 1987.

Reff, M. E. and E. L. Schneider (eds).  Biological Markers of
Aging.  Bethesda,MD:  USDHHS, National Institute of Health
Publication No. 82-2221, 1982.

This report from a conference convened by NIA includes
discussion of animal markers (rodents) and biochemical,
physiological, and behavioral indices in human beings.

Richardson, A. (ed).  Molecular Interactions in Aging and
Cancer.  Journal of Gerontology.  44:3-80, 1989.

This special section (evolved from a symposium at the 39th
Annual Meeting of the Gerontological Society of America)
provides a recent update and overview of biochemical,

cellular, physiological and epidemiological studies as well
as molecular investigations.

Robbins, R. A.  Objective and Subjective Factors in Estimates
     of Life Expectancy.  Psychological Reports.  63:47-53,
     1988.

Rockstein, M., J. Chesky, and M. Sussman.  Comparative Biology
     and Evolution of Aging.  Pp. 3-34 in C. E. Finch and L.
     Hayflick (eds).  Handbook of the Biology of Aging.  New
     York, NY:  Van Nostrand Reinhold, 1977.

Rockstein, M. and M. Sussman.  Biology of Aging.  Belmont, NY:
     Wadsworth, 1979.

Rogers, R. G. and S. Wofford.  Life Expectancy in Less
     Developed Countries:  Socioeconomic Development or Public
     Health?  Journal of Biosocial Science.  21:245-52, 1989.

Rorick, M. H., et al.  Comparative Tolerance of Elderly from
     Differing Backgrounds to Lactose-containing and Lactose-
     free Dairy Drinks:  A Double-Blind Study.  Journal of
     Gerontology.  34(2):191-96, 1979.

Rose, M. R. and P. M. Service.  Evolution of Aging.  Review of
     Biological Research in Aging.  2:85-98, 1985.

Rose, M. R. and J. L. Graves, Jr.  Minireview:  What
     Evolutionary Biology Can Do for Gerontology.  Journal of
     Gerontology. · 44:B27-29, 1989.

Rosenwaike, I.  A Demographic Portrait of the Oldest Old.
     Milbank Memorial Fund Quarterly.  63:187-205, 1983.

Rosenwaike, I. and S. H. Preston.  Age Overstatement and
     Puerto Rican Longevity.  Human Biology.  56:503-25, 1984.

Rubin, V. (ed).  Proceedings of the First Joint US-USSR
     Symposium on Aging and Longevity.  New York, NY:
     International Research and Exchange Program, 1982.

Rushton, J. P.  An Evolutionary Theory of Health, Longevity
     and Personality:  Sociobiology and r/K Reproductive
     Strategies.  Psychological Reports.  60:539-49, 1987.

Rykken, D. E.  Sex in the Later Years.  Pp. 158-82 in P.
     Silverman (ed).  The Elderly as Modern Pioneers.
     Bloomington, IN:  Indiana University Press, 1987.

Sacher, G.  Maturation and Longevity in Relation to Cranial
     Capacity in Hominid Evolution.  Pp. 417-42 in R. Tuttle
     (ed).  Primate Functional Morphology and Evolution.  The
     Hague, The Netherlands:  Mouton, 1975.

_____  Life Table Modification and Life Prolongation.  Pp.
     582-638 in C. E. Finch and E. L. Schneider (eds).
     Handbook of the Biology of Aging.  New York, NY:  Van
     Nostrand Reinhold, 1977.

_____ Longevity, Aging and Death:  An Evolutionary
Perspective.  Gerontologist.  18(2):112-19, 1978.

Samuelsson, G. and O. Dehlin.  Social Class and Social
Mobility-- Effects on Survival.  A Study of an Entire Birth
Cohort During an 80-Year Life Span.  Zeitschrift fur
Gerontologie.  22:156-61, 1989.

Schneider, E. L. and J. D. Reed, Jr.  Life Extension.  New
England Journal of Medicine.  312:1159-68, 1985.

Schimke, R. T. (ed).  Biological Mechanisms in Aging.
Bethesda, MD:  USDHHS.  National Institute of Health
Publication No. 81-2194, 1981.

These proceedings of a 1980 conference discuss:  mechanisms
of aging and the human condition; dynamical aspects of
senescence; pathology of DNA and the biology of aging; the
influences of aging on protein synthesis; post-
translational changes in cells and tissues; immunological
aspects of aging; neural and endocrine mechanisms in aging;
and senescence in plants.

Shea, B. T.  Heterochrony in Human Evolution:  The Case for
Neoteny Reconsidered.  Yearbook of Physical Anthropology.
32:69-101, 1989.

A critical reappraisal of the role neoteny has played in
hominoid evolution with specific emphasis on human growth
and development.

Shock, N.  Biological Theories of Aging.  Pp. 103-15 in J.
Birren and N. Schaie (eds).  Handbook of the Psychology of
Aging.  New York, NY:  Van Nostrand Reinhold, 1977.

Siegel, J. S. and S. L. Hoover.  Demographic Aspects of the
Health of the Elderly to the Year 2000 and Beyond.  Geneva,
Switzerland:  World Health Organization, 1982.

Population projections from the United Nations for more
developed regions and less developed regions assess
distribution of older people and factors affecting
mortality and morbidity.

Siler, W.  Parameters of Mortality in Human Populations with
Widely Varying Life Spans.  Statistics in Medicine.
2(3):373-80, 1983.

Simopoules, A. and T. Van Itallie.  Body Weight, Health and
Longevity.  Annals of Internal Medicine.  100:285-95, 1984.

Sinclair, D.  Human Growth After Birth (4th ed).  New York,
NY:  Oxford University Press, 1985.

Short textbook on ontogeny which includes a chapter on
aging and the elderly.

Smith, D. W.  Variablility in Life Span Functional Capacity.

Basic Life Sciences.   43:177-82, 1988.

_____ Is Greater Female Longevity a General Finding Among
Animals?  Biological Reviews of the Cambridge Philosophical
Society.   64:1-12, 1989.

Smith, J. R.  MINIREVIEW:  DNA Synthesis Inibitors in Cellular
Senescence.  Journal of Gerontology.  45:B32-35, 1990.

Smith, J. R., A. L. Spiering, and O. M. Pereira-Smith.  Is
Cellular Senescence Genetically Programmed?  Basic Life
Sciences.  42:283-94, 1987.

Soules, M. R. and W. H. Bremner.  The Menopause and
Climacteric:  Endocrinological Basis and Associated
Symptomology.  Journal of the American Geriatric Society.
30(9):547-61, 1982.

Steen, B. (ed).  Nutrition and Ageing:  An Interdisciplinary
Symposium.  Age and Ageing.  19:S3-52, 1990.

     A collection of six contributions which discuss
     biochemistry, immunology, dementia and cross-cultural
     studies.

Stevens, M. E.  Longevity Factor in Hominoid Social
Organization.  American Journal of Physical Anthropology.
81:357-62, 1990.

Stini, W.  Early Nutrition, Growth, Disease and Human
Longevity.  Nutrition and Cancer.  1(1):31-41, 1978.

_____ Growth Rates and Sexual Dimorphism in Evolutionary
Perspective.  Pp. 121-38 in R. I. Gilbert and J. H. Mielke
(eds).  The Analysis of Prehistoric Diets.  New York, NY:
Academic Press, 1985.

Svanborg, A., et al.  Comparison of Ecology, Ageing and State
of Health in Japan and Sweden, the Present and Previous
Leaders in Longevity.  Acta Medica Scandinavica.  218:5-17,
1985.

Swedlund, A. C., et al.  Family Patterns in Longevity and
Longevity Patterns of the Family.  Human Biology.
55:115-19, 1983.

Takata, H., et al.  Influence of Major Histocompatibility
Complex Region Genes On Human Longevity Among Okinawan-
Japanese Centenarians and Nonagenarians.  Lancet.
2(8563):824-26, 1987.

Trinkhaus, E. and D. D. Thompson.  Femoral Diaphyseal
Histomorphometric Age Determinations for the Shanidar
3,4,5, and 6 Neandertals and Neandertal Longevity.
American Journal of Physical Anthropology.  72:123-29,
1987.

Turnbridge, R.  Life Span and Life Expectancy of Elderly

People Under Different Conditions and Cultures.  Pp. 32-43 in P. Hansen (ed).  Age With a Future.  Proceedings of the 6th International Congress of Gerontology, Copenhagen, 1963.  Philadelphia, PA:  F. A. Davis Company, 1964.

Uhlenberg, P.  A Demographic Perspective on Aging.  Pp. 183-204 in P.  Silverman (ed).  The Elderly as Modern Pioneers.  Bloomington, IN:  Indiana University Press, 1987.

Vaupel, J. W.  Inherited Frailty and Longevity.  Demography. 25:277-87, 1988.

Vaupel, J. W. and A. E. Gowan.  Passage to Methuselah:  Some Demographic Consequences of Continued Progress Against Mortality.  American Journal of Public Health.  76:430-43, 1986.

Verbrugge, L. M.  Longer Life But Worsening Health?  Trends in Health and Mortality of Middle-aged and Older Persons. Milbank Memorial Fund Quarterly.  62:475-519, 1984.

Verbrugge, L. M. and D. L. Wingard.  Sex Differentials in Health and Mortality.  Women and Health.  12:103-45, 1987.

Vijg, J.  DNA Sequence Changes in Ageing:  How Frequent, How Important?  Ageing.  2:105-23, 1990.

Vir, S. H. and A. H. G. Love.  Anthropometric Measurements in the Elderly.  Gerontology.  26:1-8, 1980.

Walford, R.  Maximum Life Span.  New York, NY:  W. W. Norton, 1983.

    Popular account of biology of aging research with an emphasis on the multiple effects of dietary restriction. Practical suggestions on how to apply principle of "undernutrition without malnutrition" to daily living.

Warner, H. R., et al (eds).  Modern Biological Theories of Aging.  New York, NY:  Raven Press, 1987.

    From a conference held in June, 1986, these papers review and critically evaluate current theories of aging (developmental program, free-radical damage, error catastrophe, DNA damage and repair, and organ systems as pacemakers of aging) and suggest avenues for future research.

Waser, P. M.  Postreproductive Survival and Behavior in a Free-ranging Female Mangabey.  Folia Primatologica. 29:142-60, 1978.

Washburn, S. L.  Longevity in Primates.  Pp. 11-29 in J. L. McGaugh and S. B. Kiesler (eds).  Aging:  Biology and Behavior.  New York, NY:  Academic Press, 1981.

Weale, R. A.  Evolution, Age and Ocular Focus.  Mechanisms of

Ageing and Development. 53:85-89, 1990.

Weindruch, R. and R. L. Walford. The Retardation of Aging and Disease by Dietary Restriction. Springfield, IL:  C. C. Thomas, 1988.

Thorough review of results from the only experimental regimen which reproducibly increases the maximum lifespan of mammals (rodents).

Weiss, K. Demographic Models for Anthropology. Memoirs of the Society for American Archeology. 27:1-186, 1973.

Available as a paperback, this text presents model life tables for anthropological populations and explains how to use them. Also briefly discusses history of human life span and stationary population theory.

_____ Evolutionary Perspectives on Human Aging. Pp. 25-58 in P. Amoss and S. Harrell, (eds). Other Ways of Growing Old. Stanford, CA:  Stanford University Press, 1981.

_____ On the Number of Members of the Genus Homo Who Have Ever Lived, and Some Evolutionary Implications. Human Biology. 56:637-49, 1984.

Weitz, C. A. Effects of Acculturation and Age on the Exercise Capacities of Solomon Islanders. American Journal of Physical Anthropology. 81:513-25, 1990.

West, R. R. High Death Rates:  More Deaths or Earlier Deaths? Journal of the Royal College of Physicians. 21:73-76, 1987.

White, L. R., et al. Geriatric Epidemiology. Annual Review of Gerontology and Geriatrics. 6:215-311, 1986.

Useful compendium of recent studies of:  arthritis, osteoporosis, fractures, heart disease and hypertension, stroke, hearing, vision, brain aging, cancer and physical disability.

Wiedman, D. W. Adiposity or Longevity:  Which Factor Accounts for the Increase in Type II Diabetes Mellitus When Populations Acculturate to an Industrial Technology? Medical Anthropology. 11:237-53, 1989.

Williams, G. C. Pleiotropy, Selection and the Evolution of Senescence. Evolution. 11:398-411, 1957.

Williams, G. C. and P. D. Taylor. Demographic Consequences of Natural Selection. Basic Life Sciences. 42:235-45, 1987.

Wingard, D. L. The Sex Differential in Mortality Rates:  Demographic and Behavioral Factors. American Journal of Epidemiology. 115:205-16, 1982.

Wolanski, N. Urbanization and the Life Span. Current

Anthropology.  23(5):579-80, 1982.

Woodhead, A. D. and K. H. Thompson (eds).  Evolution of
    Longevity in Animals:  A Comparative Approach.  New York,
    NY:  Plenum, 1987.

Xi, H. and A. F. Roche.  Differences Between the Hand-Wrist
    and the Knee in Assigned Skeletal Ages.  American Journal
    of Physical Anthropology.  83:95-102, 1990.

Zubrow, E. B. W. (ed).    Anthropological Demography.
    Albuquerque, NM:  University of New Mexico Press, 1976.

# 3

# Medical Aspects
# of Aging

## HEALTH AND SOCIAL SERVICES

Albert, S. M.  Caregiving as a Cultural System:  Conceptions
of Filial Obligation and Parental Dependency in Urban
America.  American Anthropologist.  92(2):319-31, 1990.

Alexander, L.  Illness Maintenance and the New American Sick
Role.  Pp. 351-67 in N. J. Crisman and T. W. Maretski
(eds).  Clinically Applied Anthropology:  Anthropologists
in Health Science Settings.  Dordrecht, The Netherlands:
Reidel, 1982.

Altman, I., J. Wohwill, and M. P. Lawton (eds).  Human
Behavior and the Environment:  The Elderly and the Physical
Environment.  New York, NY:  Plenum Press, 1984.

Ammundsen, E.  The Future of Health-Related Care for the
Elderly in Europe.  Pp. 259-79 in B. Herzog (ed).  Aging
and Income:  Programs and Prospects for the Elderly.  New
York, NY:  Human Sciences Press, 1978.

Anderson, B. G.  Love and Sex After Sixty.  Pp. 163-86 in A.
Kolker and P. I. Ahmed (eds).  Aging:  Coping with Medical
Issues.  New York, NY:  Elsevier Science, 1982.

Arluke, A. and J. Peterson.  Accidental Medicalization of Old
Age.  Pp. 271-84 in C. Fry (ed).  Dimensions:  Aging,
Culture, and Health.  New York, NY:  Bergin, Praeger, 1981.

Atkinson, J. H.  and M. A. Schuckit.  Alcoholism and Over-the-
Counter and Prescription Drug Misuse in the Elderly.
Annual Review of Gerontology and Geriatrics.  2:255-84,
1981.

Atwood, J.  The Phenomenon of Selective Neglect.  Pp. 192-200
in E.  Bauwens (ed).  The Anthropology of Health.  St.
Louis, MO:  C. V. Mosby, 1978.

Barker, J.  Between Humans and Ghosts:  The Decrepit Elderly
in a Polynesian Society.  Pp. 295-314 in J. Sokolovsky

(ed). The Cultural Context of Aging: Worldwide Perspective. Westport, CT: Bergin and Garvey, 1990.

Barker, W. H. Adding Life to Years: Organized Geriatric Services in Great Britain and Implications for the United States. Baltimore, MD: Johns Hopkins University Press, 1987.

An interesting review of the divergent development of health services for elderly people in the U.K. and U.S. Highlights national institutional and political preoccupations and concerns in geriatric service delivery.

Barrow, C. and L. Roeder. Nutrition. Pp. 561-81 in C. Finch and L. Hayflick (eds). Handbook of the Biology of Aging. New York, : NY: Van Nostrand Reinhold, 1977.

Becker, G. and G. Nadler. The Aged Deaf: Integration of a Disabled Group into an Agency Serving Elderly People. Gerontologist. 20:214-21, 1980.

Bell, D. and G. Zellman. Issues in Service Delivery to Ethnic Elderly. Santa Monica, CA: The Rand Corporation, 1976.

Bell, D., P. Kasschau, and G. Zellman. Delivery of Services to Elderly Members of Minority Groups: A Critical Review of the Literature. Santa Monica, CA: The Rand Corporation, 1976.

Bergener, M., et al (eds). Aging in the Eighties and Beyond: Highlights of the Twelfth International Congress of Gerontology. New York, NY: Springer, 1983.

Berkman, L. F. Physical Health and the Social Environment: A Social Epidemiological Perspective. Pp. 51-75 in L. Eisenberg and A. Kleinman (eds). The Relevance of Social Science for Medicine. Dordrecht, The Netherlands: D. Reidel, 1981.

Bicknell, W. J. and C. L. Parks. As Children Survive: Dilemmas of Aging in the Developing World. Journal of Social Science and Medicine. 29(1):59-67, 1989.

The authors describe the emergence of several chronic diseases in the developing world against the background of the decline in infant mortality and an increasing burden of morbidity.

Blumhagen, D. The Meaning of Hypertension. Pp. 297-323 in N. J. Crisman and T. W. Maretski (eds). Clinically Applied Anthropology: Anthropologists in Health Science Settings. Dordrecht, The Netherlands: D. Reidel, 1982.

Blust, E. P. and R. J. Scheidt. Perceptions of Filial Responsibility by Filipino Widows and Their Primary Caregivers. Intergenerational Journal of Aging and Human Development. 26(2):91-106, 1988.

This study examines the relationship among filial and parental perceptions of responsibility, expectations of support, and actual support received and given in a town near Manila.

Bock, E.  Aging and Suicide:  The Significance of Marital Kinship and Alternative Relations.  The Family Coordinator. 21:71-79, 1972.

Bock, E. and I. Webber.  Suicide Among the Elderly:  Isolating Widowhood and Mitigating Alternatives.  Journal of Marriage and the Family.  34:24-31, 1972.

Boyer, E.  Health Perception in the Elderly:  Its Cultural and Social Aspects.  Pp. 198-216 in C. Fry (ed).  Aging in Culture and Society:  Comparative Viewpoints and Strategies.  Brooklyn, NY:  J. F. Bergin, 1980.

Brocklehurst, J. (ed).  Geriatric Care in Advanced Societies. Baltimore, MD:  University Park Press, 1975.

Edited volume includes national studies of Australia, U.K., Netherlands, Sweden, the U. S., and U.S.S.R.

Butler, R.  Why Survive? Being Old in America.  New York, NY: Harper and Row, 1970:.

An oft-cited and comprehensive view of the status and treatment of dependent elderly in the U.S.  The author is the former Director of the National Institute on Aging.

Cantor, M. and M. Mayer.  Health and the Inner-City Elderly. Gerontologist.  16:17-25, 1976.

Carboni, D. K.  Geriatric Medicine in the United States and Great Britain.  Westport, CT:  Greenwood Press, 1982.

Explores development of geriatric medicine in Great Britain and the United States.  Great Britain's state mediation system is viewed as more successful than the United States system.  Bibliography included.

Carter, J.  Psychiatry, Racism and Aging.  Journal of the American Geriatrics Society.  20:343-46, 1972a.

_____ Differential Treatment of the Elderly Black, Victims of Stereotyping.  Postgraduate Medicine.  52(5):211-13, 1972b.

_____ Recognizing Psychiatric Symptoms in Black Americans. Geriatrics.  29:96-99, 1974.

_____ Racism in the Psychiatric Care of Older Blacks.  Pp. 304-06 in B. Hess (ed).  Growing Old in America.  New Brunswick, NJ:  Transaction Books, 1976.

_____ The Black Aged:  A Strategy for Future Mental Health Services.  Journal of the American Geriatrics Society. 26:553-56, 1978.

Cervantes, R.  Urban Chicanos, Failure of Comprehensive Health
    Services.  Health Service Reports.  87:932-40, 1972.

Chebotarev, D. and N. Sachuk.  A Social Policy Directed Toward
    the Health and Welfare of the Aged in the Soviet Union.
    Journal of the American Geriatrics Society.  27(2):49-53,
    1979.

Chen, P. C. Y.  Family Support and the Health of the Elderly
    Malaysian.  Journal of Cross-Cultural Gerontology.
    2(2):187-93, 1987.

Chovan, M. J. and W. Chovan.  Stressful Events and Coping
    Responses Among Older Adults in Two Sociocultural Groups.
    Journal of Psychology.  119(3):253-60, 1984.

Ciliberto, D. J., J. Levin, and A. Arluke.  Nurses' Diagnostic
    Stereotyping of the Elderly.  Research on Aging.
    3(3):299-310, 1981.

Clark, Margaret.  Health in the Mexican-American Culture.
    Berkeley, CA:  University of California Press, 1959.

_____    Cultural Values and Dependency in Later Life.  Pp.
    263-74 in D. Cowgill and L. Holmes (eds).  Aging and
    Modernization.  New York, NY:  Appleton-Century Crofts,
    1972.

Cohen, C. and J. Sokolovsky.  Clinical Use of Network Analysis
    for Psychiatric and Aged Populations.  Community Mental
    Health Journal.  15:2-3
    213, 1979a.

_____    Health Seeking Behavior and Social Networks of the Aged
    Living in Single Room Occupancy Hotels.  Journal of the
    American Geriatric Society.  37(6):270-78, 1979b.

Colen, J. M. and D. Soto.  Service Delivery to Aged
    Minorities:  Techniques of Successful Programs.
    Sacramento, CA:  School of Social Work, California State
    University, 1979.

Curtin, S.  Nobody Ever Died of Old Age.  Boston, MA:  Little
    Brown & Company, 1972.

Dalgaard, O. Z.  Care of the Elderly in Denmark:  Special
    Aspects Including Geriatrics and Long-Term Care Medicine.
    Danish Medical Bulletin.  29(3):131-34, 1982.

Dennis, R.  Social Stress and Mortality Among Nonwhite Males.
    Phylon.  38(3):315-27, 1977.

Dougherty, M. C.  An Anthropological Perspective on Aging and
    Women in the Middle Years.  Pp. 167-76 in E. E. Bauwens
    (ed).  The Anthropology of Health.  St. Louis, MO:  C. V.
    Mosby, 1978.

Dowd, J. J.  Mental Illness and the Aged Stranger.

International Journal of Health Services. 14(1):69-87, 1984.

A critical review of dominant mental health programs within social gerontology.

Dunham, A., C. Nusberg, and S. Sengupta. Toward Planning for the Aging in Local Communities: An International Perspective. Washington, DC: International Federation on Ageing, 1978.

Earley, L. W. and O. Von Mering. Growing Old the Outpatient Way. American Journal of Psychiatry. 125:968-77, 1969.

Ebersole, P. and P. Hess (eds). Toward Healthy Aging. St. Louis, MO: C. V. Mosby, 1981.

Eckert, J. K. (ed). Introduction to Special Section: Extra-Familial Care Arrangements for the Elderly. Journal of Cross-Cultural Gerontology. 2(4):343-44, 1987.

Eckert, J. K. and S. S. Galazka. An Anthropological Approach to a Community Diagnosis in Family Practice. Journal of Family Medicine. 18(5):274-77, 1986.

Eckert, J. K., K. H. Namazi, and E. Kahana. Unlicensed Board and Care Homes: An Extra-Familial Living Arrangement for the Elderly. Journal of Cross-Cultural Gerontology. 2(4):377-93, 1987.

Estes, C. L. Austerity and Ageing in the U. S.: 1980 and Beyond. International Journal of Health Services. 12(4) 573-84, 1982.

Evers, J. The Frail Elderly Woman: Emergent Questions in Aging and Women's Health. In E. Lewin and V. Oleson (eds). Women, Health and Healing. New York, NY: Tavistock, 1985.

Eve, S. and H. Friedsam. Ethnic Differences in the Use of Health Care Services Among Older Texans. The Journal of Minority Aging. 4:62-75, 1979.

Fandetti, D. and D. Gelfand. Care of the Aged: Attitudes of White Ethnic Families. Gerontologist. 16(6):544-49, 1976.

Faulkner, A., M. Heisel, and P. Simms. Life Strengths and Life Stresses: Explorations in the Measurement of Mental Health of the Black Aged. American Journal of Orthopsychiatry. 45:102-10, 1975.

Fenton. S. Race, Health and Welfare: Afro-Caribbean and South Asian People in Central Bristol: Health and Social Services. Bristol, UK: Department of Sociology, University of Bristol, 1985.

A service study based upon interviews with middle-aged and elderly residents of Bristol.

Ferraro, K. F.  The Health Consequences of Relocation Among
    the Aged in the Community.  Journal of Gerontology.
    38(1):90-96, 1982.

_____  The Effect of Widowhood on the Health Status of Older
    Persons.  International Journal of Aging and Development.
    21(1):9-25, 1985.

Figa-Talamanca, I.  The Health Status and the Health Care
    Problems of the Aged in an Italian Community.  Aging and
    Human Development.  7:39-48, 1976.

Ford, C. V. and R. J. Sbordone.  Attitudes of Psychiatrists
    Toward Elderly Patients.  American Journal of Psychiatry.
    137:571-75, 1980.

Frankfather, D. L., M. J. Smith, and F. G. Caro.  Family Care
    of the Elderly.  Lexington, MA:  Lexington Books, 1981.

Freeman, J. T.  Aging:  Its History and Literature.  New York,
    NY:  Human Sciences Press, 1979.

    The author provides a history of Western ideas on aging and
    geriatrics, as well as a review and guide to other
    historians of aging and aging interventions.  An extensive
    reference list is provided.

French, J. and D. Schwartz.  Terminal Care at Home in Two
    Cultures.  American Journal of Nursing.  73:502-05, 1973.

Fuji, S.  Elderly Asian Americans and Use of Public Services.
    Social Casework.  57(3):202-07, 1976.

Galazka, S. S. and J. K. Eckert.  Diabetes Mellitus from the
    Inside Out:  Ecological Perspectives on a Chronic Disease.
    Journal of Family Systems Medicine.  2(1):28-36, 1984.

_____  Clinically Applied Anthropology:  Concepts for the
    Family Physician.  Journal of Family Practice.
    22(2):159-65, 1986.

Garcia-Alvarez, A.  The Contribution of Social Security to the
    Adequacy of Income of Elderly Chicanos.  Waltham, MA:
    Garcia, 1979.

Gelfand, D.  The Aging Network--Programs and Services.  New
    York, NY:  Springer, 1980.

George. V and A. Dundes.  The Gomer.  Journal of American
    Folklore.  91:568-81, 1978.

Gerber, L. and S. Madhaven.  Epidemiology of Coronary Heart
    Disease in Migrant Chinese Populations.  Medical
    Anthropology.  Winter:3307-20, 1980.

German, P., et al.  Health Care of the Elderly in a Changing
    Inner City Community.  Black Aging.  3:122-32, 1978a.

_____ Health Care of the Elderly in Medically Disadvantaged
   Populations. Gerontologist. 18:547-55, 1978b.

Glendennning, F. (ed). Care in the Community: Recent
   Research and Current Prospects. Stoke-on-Trent, England:
   Beth Johnson Foundation Publications, 1982.

Goldberg, E. M. and N. Connely. The Effectiveness of Social
   Care for the Elderly: An Overview of Recent Evaluative
   Research. London, UK: Heinemann Educational Books, 1982.

Gray, D. "Arthritis": Variations in Beliefs About Joint
   Disease. Medical Anthropology. 7(4):29-46, 1983.

Gui, S. X., et al. Status and Needs of the Elderly in Urban
   Shanghai: Analysis of Some Preliminary Statistics.
   Journal of Cross-Cultural Gerontology. 2(2):171-86, 1987.

Gurland, B. J., et al. A Comparison of the Outcomes of
   Hospitalization of Geriatric Patients in Public Psychiatric
   Wards in New York and London. Canadian Psychiatric
   Association Journal. 21:421-31, 1976.

Gurland, B. J., et al. Personal Time Dependency in the
   Elderly of New York City: Findings from the US-UK Cross-
   National Geriatric Community Study. Pp. 9-45 in B. Gurland
   (ed). Dependency in the Elderly of New York City. New
   York, NY: Community Council of Greater New York, 1978.

Gurland, B. J., et al. The Mind and Mood of Aging: Mental
   Health Problems of Community Elderly in New York and
   London. London, UK: Croom Helm, 1983.

   Report summarizing the US-UK Cross-National Project (which
   produced more than 100 papers). Focus of this project was
   to describe cross-national differences in psychiatric
   morbidity prevalence and their interrelationship to other
   health and social problems, differences in health care, and
   long-term differences in course and outcome.

Haavisto, M., et al. A Health Survey of the Very Aged in
   Tampere, Finland. Age and Ageing. 13(5)266-72, 1984.

Hale, W. D. Locus of Control and Psychological Distress Among
   the Aged. International Journal of Aging and Human
   Development. 21(1):1-8, 1985.

Hall, A. and P. Bourne. Indigenous Therapists in a Southern
   Black Urban Community. Archives of General Psychiatry.
   28:137-42, 1973.

Hampson, J. Elderly People and Social Welfare in Zimbabwe.
   Ageing and Society. 5(1):39-67, 1985.

Hartford, J. T. and T. Samorajski (eds). Alcoholism in the
   Elderly: Social and Biomedical Issues. New York, NY:
   Raven Press, 1984.

58    ANTHROPOLOGY OF AGING

Harvey, D. and O. Cap.  Elderly Service Workers' Training
Project.  Block B:  Cultural Gerontology.  Module B.3:
French Culture.  Winnipeg, Canada:  Faculty of Education,
Manitoba University, 1987.

Haug, M. (ed).  Elderly Patients and Their Doctors.  New York,
NY:  Springer, 1981.

Haug, M., A. Ford, and M. Sheafor (eds).  The Physical and
Mental Health of Aged Women.  New York, NY:  Springer,
1985.

Hawkins, B.  Mental Health of the Black Aged.  Pp. 166-79 in
L. Gary (ed).  Mental Health:  A Challenge to the Black
Community.  Philadelphia, PA:  Dorrance, 1978.

Henderson, G. and M. Primeaux.  Transcultural Health Care.
Menlo Park, CA:  Addison-Wesley, 1981.

Hickey, T.  Health and Aging:  An Overview.  Pp. 1-30 in T.
Hickey.  Health and Aging.  Monterey, CA:  Brooks/Cole,
1980a.

_____    The Long-Term Care Person.  Pp. 33-53 in T. Hickey.
Health and Aging.  Monterey, CA:  Brooks/Cole, 1980b.

Hill, C. E.  Differential Perceptions of the Rehabilitation
Process:  A Comparison of Client and Personnel Incongruity
in Two Categories of Chronic Illness.  Social Science and
Medicine.  12(1):57-63, 1978.

Henderson, J. N.  Alzheimer's Disease in Cultural Context.
Pp. 315-30 in J. Sokolovsky, ed.  The Cultural Context of
Aging:  Worldwide Perspectives.  Westport, CT:  Bergin and
Garvey, 1990.

Hokenstad, M. C. and K. A. Kendall (eds).  Gerontological
Social Work:  International Perspectives.  New York, NY:
Haworth Press, 1988.

Hollander, C. F and H. A. Becker (eds).  Growing Old in the
Future:  Scenarios on Health and Ageing.  Dordrecht, The
Netherlands:  Nijhoff, 1987.

Holmes, D., et al.  The Use of Community-Based Services in
Long-Term Care by Older Minority Persons.  Gerontologist.
19:4, 1979.

Hurowitz, E. R.  Preventive Geriatric Care on the Kibbutz.
Journal of American Geriatric Society.  33(11):788-89,
1985.

Ikels, C.  Non-Institutional Alternatives in Long-Term Care:
Establishment of a Geriatric Foster Care Program.  Boston,
MA:  Intercollegiate Case Clearinghouse, 1980.

International Federation on Ageing.  Home Help Services for
the Ageing Around the World.  Washington, DC:

International Federation on Ageing, 1975.

Provides basic cross-national data on home service
provision, including information from developing countries.

Jonas K. and E. Wellin. Dependency and Reciprocity: Home
    Health Aid in an Elderly Population. Pp. 217-38 in C. Fry
    (ed). Aging in Culture and Society: Comparative
    Viewpoints and Strategies. Brooklyn, NY: J. F. Bergin,
    1980.

Justice, J. Policies, Plans and People: Culture and Health
    Development in Nepal: Comparative Studies of Health
    Systems and Medical Care. Berkeley, CA: University of
    California Press, 1986.

Kahn, A. and S. Kamerman. Social Services in International
    Perspective. Washington, DC: US Government Printing
    Office 1976.

Kalish, R. (ed). The Dependencies of Old People. Occasional
    Papers on Gerontology. No. 6. Ann Arbor, MI: Institute
    of of Gerontology, University of Michigan, 1969.

Kamerman, S. Community Services for the Aged: The View from
    Eight Countries. Gerontologist. 16:529-37, 1976.

Provides cross-national comparisons of services, rates of
utilization, and policies in eight industrialized nations.

Kane, R. L. and R. A. Kane. Long-Term Care in Six Countries:
    Implications for the United States. DHEW Publication No.
    (NIH) 76-1207. Washington, D. C.: Government Printing
    Office, 1976.

Kaufman, S. K. and G. Becker. Stroke: Health Care on the
    Periphery. Social Science and Medicine. 22:983-89, 1986.

Kelman, H. R. The Underdevelopment of Evaluative Research on
    Health Services for the Elderly in the United States.
    International Journal of Health Services. 10(3):501-11,
    1980.

Khan, N. Mental Health Services to the Aged of Minority
    Groups. Psychiatric Opinion. 11:20-23, 1974.

Kim, S. S. Ethnic Elders and American Health Care--A
    Physicians's Perspective. M. M. Clark (ed). Cross-
    Cultural Medicine. Special Issue. Western Journal of
    Medicine. 139(6):885-91, 1983.

The author discusses the differing culture-bound
perceptions of health, illness and healing held by
providers and consumers of American health care services.
The essay is part of a special issue on cross-cultural
medicine.

Kitano, H. Mental Illness in Four Cultures. The Journal of

Social Psychology. 80:121-34, 1970.

Koo, J. and D. O. Cowgill. Health Care of the Aged in Korea.
Social Science and Medicine. 23(12):1347-52, 1986.

Changes in the social and health status of Korean elderly
are described through Korea's period of modernization. The
demographic transition and organization and financing of
modern medical care are discussed, as well as the ongoing
role of the family and traditional medical practices.

Kutzik, A. American Social Provision for the Aged: A
Historical Perspective. Pp. 32-65 in D. Gelfand and A.
Kutzik (eds). Ethnicity and Aging: Theory, Research and
Policy. New York, NY: Springer, 1979.

Lang A. and E. M. Brody. Characteristics of Middle-Aged
Daughters and Help to Their Elderly Mothers. Journal of
Marriage and the Family. 45:193-202, 1983.

Langness, L. L. and H. G. Levine (ed). Culture and
Retardation: Life Histories of Mildly Mentally Retarded
Persons in American Society. Norwell, MA: D. Reidel,
1986.

Lawson, I. R. Community-Based Care in Three Settings. Pp.
373-92 in S. R. Ingman and A. E. Thomas (eds). Topias and
Utopias in Health: Policy Studies. Chicago, IL: Aldine,
1975.

A geriatrician offers his experience with attempts to
deliver comprehensive geriatric care in Scotland, the U.S.
and India.

Lawton, M. P. The Impact of the Environment on Aging and
Behavior. Pp. 276-301 in J. Birren and K. Schaie (eds)
Handbook of the Psychology of Aging. New York, NY: Van
Nostrand Reinhold, 1977.

_____ Environment and Aging. Monterey, CA: Brooks/Cole,
1980.

Lawton, M. P., P. G. Windley, and T. O. Byerts (eds). Aging
and the Environment: Theroretical Approaches. New York,
NY: Springer, 1982.

Lee, G. R. Kinship and Social Support of the Elderly: The
Case of the United States. Ageing and Society.
5(1):19-38, 1985.

Leininger, M. (ed). Transcultural Nursing Care of the
Elderly. Salt Lake City, UT: University of Utah Press,
1977.

Lesnoff-Caravaglia, G. Attitudes and Aging: U.S./U.S.S.R.
Contrasted. In G. Lesnoff-Caravaglia, (ed). Health Care
of the Elderly. New York, NY: Human Sciences Press, 1980.

Linn, M., K. Hunter, and B. Linn.  Self-Assessed Health,
    Impairment and Disability in Anglo, Black and Cuban
    Elderly.  Medical Care.  18(3):282-88, 1980.

Linn, M., K. Hunter, and P. Perry.  Differences by Sex and
    Ethnicity in the Psychosocial Adjustment of the Elderly.
    Journal of Health and Social Behavior.  20:273-81, 1979.

Linn, M. W. and B. S. Linn.  Objective and Self-Assessed
    Health in the Old and Very Old.  Social Science and
    Medicine.  14:311-15, 1980.

Little, V.  Open Care for the Aged:  Swedish Model.  Social
    Work.  July:282-87, 1978.

_____  Open Care for the Aging:  Comparative International
    Approaches.  New York, NY:  Springer, 1982.

    Examines community-based (open) care in Samoa, Hong Kong,
    Japan and Sweden; focuses on family as unit of care.

Liu, W. T.  Culture and Social Support.  Research on Aging.
    8(1):57-83, 1986a.

    Introduction to a special journal section dealing with
    immigrant Asian elderly in the U.S. and their use and need
    for formal and informal social and health services.

_____  Health Services for Asian Elderly.  Research on Aging.
    8(1):156-75, 1986b.

Lock, M.  Licorice in Leviathan:  The Medicalization of Care
    for the Japanese Elderly.  Culture, Medicine and
    Psychiatry.  8:121-39, 1984.

_____  Models and Practice in Medicine:  Menopause as Syndrome
    or Life Transition?  Pp. 115-39 in R. A. Hahn and A. D.
    Gaines (eds).  Physicians of Western Medicine:
    Anthropological Approaches to Theory and Practice.
    Dordrecht, The Netherlands:  D. Reidel, 1985.

_____  Ambiguities of Aging:  Japanese Experience and the
    Perception of Menopause.  Culture, Medicine and Psychiatry.
    10:22-46, 1986.

Lurie, E., et al.  On Lok Senior Day Health Center:  A Case
    Study.  Gerontologist.  16:39-46, 1976.

Margulec, I.  The Care of the Aged in Israel.  Gerontologist.
    3:61-66, 1965.

Manton, K. and B. J. Soldo.  Dynamics of Health Changes in the
    Oldest Old:  New Perspectives and Evidence.  Milbank
    Memorial Fund Quarterly:  Health and Society.
    63(2):206-85, 1985.

Manton, K. G., J. E. Dowd, and M. A. Woodbury.  Conceptual and
    Measurement Issues in Assessing Disability Cross-

Nationally: Analysis of a WHO-Sponsored Survey of the Disablement Process in Indonesia. Journal of Cross-Cultural Gerontology. 1(4):339-62, 1986.

Manton, K. G., G. C. Myers, and G. R. Andrews. Morbidity and Disability Patterns in Four Developing Nations: Their Implications for Social and Economic Integration of the Elderly. Journal of Cross-Cultural Gerontology. 2(2):115-29, 1987.

Reports an epidemiological analysis of chronic disease and disability patterns in four Western Pacific nations: the Republic of Korea, the Philippines, Malaysia and Fiji. Implications of chronic morbidity/ disability for elders' social and economic status are discussed.

Markides, K. S. Minority Status, Aging and Mental Health. International Journal of Aging and Human Development. 23(4):285-300, 1986.

McKeown, T. Planning for Geriatric Services in Britain. Gerontologist. 4:18-24, 1964.

McMahon, M., et al. Life Situations, Health Beliefs and Medical Regimen Adherence of Patients with Myocardial Infarction. Heart and Lung. 15(1):82-86, 1986.

Metress, S. Nutrition in Old Age. Pp. 176-88 in C. Kart and B. Manard (eds). Aging in America (2nd ed). Sherman Oaks, CA: Alfred Publishing Company, 1981.

Meyers, J. M. and C. Drayer. Support Systems and Mental Illness in the Elderly. Community Mental Health Journal. 4:277-86, 1979.

Moskowitz, R. W. and M. R. Haug. Arthritis and the Elderly. New York, NY: Springer, 1986.

Neal, M. But I'm Not Dead Yet: Self-Help and Terminal Illness. Papers in Anthropology. 22(2):101-14, 1981.

Neugarten, B. and R. Havighurst (eds). Social Policy, Social Ethics and the Aging Society. Washington, DC: National Science Foundation, 1976.

Newman, S. J. Worlds Apart? Long Term Care in Australia and the United States. New York, NY: Haworth Press, 1987.

Nobles, W. and G. Nobles. African Roots in Black Families: The Social-Psychological Dynamics of Black Family Life and the Implications for Nursing Care. Pp. 6-11 in D. Luckraft (ed). Black Awareness: Implications for Black Patient Care. New York, NY: American Journal of Nursing Company, 1976.

Nusberg, C. (ed). Self-Determination by the Elderly. Washington, DC: International Federation on Ageing, 1981.

_____ Innovative Aging Programs Abroad:  Implications for the United States.  Westport, CT:  Greenwood Press, 1984.

Nuttbrock, L.  Socialization to the Chronic Sick Role in Later Life:  An Interactionist View.  Research on Aging. 8(3):368-87, 1986.

   Applies the symbolic interactionist viewpoint to sick role identification and retention in a group of ill elderly patients.

Orgel, G.  Self-Concept and the Use of Community Service: Activity and Dignity in Aging.  Pp. 13-28 in E. Markson and G. Batra (ed).  Public Policies for an Aging Population. Lexington, MA:  Lexington Books, 1980.

Paganni-Hill, A., R. K. Ross, and B. E. Henderson.  Prevalence of Chronic Disease and Health Practices in a Retirement Community.  Journal of Chronic Disease.  39(9):699-707, 1986.

Palmore E.  Health Care Needs of the Rural Elderly. International Journal of Aging and Human Development. 18(1):39-46, 1983.

Palmore, E. B., J. B. Nowlin, and H. S. Wang.  Predictors of Function Among the Old-Old:  A Ten-Year Follow-Up.  Journal of Gerontology.  40(2):244-50, 1985.

Quinn, P. K. and M. Reznikoff.  The Relationship Between Death Anxiety and the Subjective Experience of Time in the Elderly.  International Journal of Aging and Human Development.  21(3):197-210, 1985.

Raffel, N. K. and M. W. Raffel.  Elderly Care:  Similarities and Solutions in Denmark and the United States.  Public Health Reports.  102(5):494-99, 1987.

Raffoul, P. R., J. K. Cooper, and D. W. Love.  Drug Misuse in Older People.  Gerontologist.  21:147-50, 1981.

Reif, L. and B. Trager (eds).  International Perspectives on Long-Term Care.  New York, NY:  Haworth Press, 1985.

Reynolds, D. K. and R. A. Kalish.  Anticipation  of Futurity as a Function of Ethnicity and Age.  Journal of Gerontology.  29:224-31, 1974.

Rodin J., C. Timko, and S. Harris.  The Construct of Control: Biological and Psychosocial Correlates.  Annual Review of Gerontology and Geriatrics.  5:3-55, 1985.

Ruther, M. and A. Dobson.  Equal Treatment and Unequal Benefits:  A Re-Examination of the Use of Medicare Services by Race:  1967-1976.  Health Care Financing Review. 3:55-83, 1981.

Sanjek, R.  Anthropological Work at a Gray Panther Health

Clinic:  Academic, Applied and Advocacy Goals.  Pp. 148-75
in L. Mullings (ed).  Cities of the United States:  Studies
in Urban Anthropology.  New York, NY:  Columbia University
Press, 1987.

Sankar, A.  "It's Just Old Age":  Old Age as a Diagnosis in
American and Chinese Medicine.  Pp. 250-80 in D. I. Kertzer
and J. Keith (eds).  Age and Anthropological Theory.
Ithaca, NY:  Cornell University Press, 1984.

Sauer, W. J. and R. T. Coward.  Social Support Networks and
the Care of the Elderly:  Theory, Research and Practice.
New York, NY:  Springer, 1985.

Savishinsky, J.  Dementia Sufferers and Their Carers:  A Study
of Family Experiences and Supportive Services in the London
Borough of Islington.  A Report Prepared for the Working
Party on Dementia Sufferers and Their Carers.  London:
Islington Age Concern, 1989a.

Describes the experiences of families in the London Borough
of Islington who are caring for a demented, elderly
relative at home; examines the community services available
to support them; identifies problems facing caregivers and
service deliverers, and offers recommendations for
improving support systems.

_____ Families, Dementia Sufferers, and Community Services:
An Assessment of Programs in a London Borough.  Association
for Anthropology and Gerontology Newsletter.  10(1):5-7,
1989b.

A short report on the above-cited (1989) report by
Savishinsky.

Scharf, W. A.  The Implementation of European Shelter and
Services Programs for the Elderly:  An Analysis of
Innovations for Use in Lehigh County, Pennsylvania.
Allentown, PA:  Progress Associates, 1980.

Describes European social service programs (Denmark,
Sweden, Holland, Belgium, England, Scotland and West
Germany) which might be transferable to communities in the
U. S.

Schrock, M. (ed).   Holistic Assessment of the Healthy Aged.
New York, NY:  John Wiley, 1980.

Seeman, M. and T. E. Seeman.  Health Behavior and Personal
Autonomy:  A Longitudinal Study of the Sense of Control in
Illness.  Journal of Health and Social Behavior.
24:144-160, 1983.

Shanas, E.  The Health of Older People:  A Social Survey.
Cambridge, MA:  Harvard University Press, 1962.

_____ Measuring the Home Health Needs of the Aged in Five
Countries.  Journal of Gerontology.  26:37-40, 1971.

_____ Health Status of Older People:  Cross-National
Implications. American Journal of Public Health.
64:261-64, 1974.

Shield, R.  Liminality in an American Nursing Home:  The
Endless Transition.  Pp. 331-52 in J. Sokolovsky (ed).  The
Cultural Context of Aging:  Worldwide Perspectives.
Westport, CT:  Bergin and Garvey, 1990.

Shlewet, L.  Application of Modern Social Services for the
Aged in Israeli-Arab Villages. Gerontologist. 15:560-61,
1975.

Siemaszko, M.  Kin Relations of the Aged:  Possible
Consequences to Social Service Planning.  Pp. 253-71 in C.
Fry (ed). Aging in Culture and Society:  Comparative
Viewpoints and Strategies.  Brooklyn, NY:  J. F. Bergin,
1980.

Simon, R. J., et al.  Pathways to the Hospital for the
Geriatric Psychiatric Patient in New York and London.
American Journal of Public Health.  66:1074-77, 1976.

Simons, R. L. and G. E. West.  Life Changes, Coping Resources
and Health Among the Elderly.  International Journal of
Aging and Human Development.  20(3):173-89, 1985.

Slivinske, L. R.  Assessing the Effect of a Personal Health
Management System Within Retirement Communities:  A
Preliminary Investigation. Gerontologist.  24(3)280-85,
1984.

Snider, E.  The Role of Kin in Meeting Health Care Needs of
the Elderly. Canadian Journal of Sociology.  6:325-36,
1981.

Solomon, B. Ethnicity, Mental Health and the Older Black
Aged.  Los Angeles, CA:  Gerontology Center, University of
Southern California, 1970.

Stall, R.  Respondent-Identified Reasons for Change and
Stability in Alcohol Consumption as a Concomitant of the
Aging Process.  Pp. 275-301 in C. R. Janes, R. Stall, and
S. M. Gifford (eds). Anthropology and Epidemiology.
Dordrecht, The Netherlands:  D. Reidel, 1986.

Stein, H.  Rehabilitation and Chronic Illness in American
Culture:  The Cultural Psychodynamics of a Medical and
Social Problem. Ethos:  Journal of Psychological
Anthropology.  2(2):153-76, 1979.

Strauss, A., et al. (eds). Chronic Illness and the Quality of
Life.  St. Louis, MO:  C. V. Mosby, 1975.

Sullivan, T.  Some Values, Beliefs, and Practices of the
Elderly in the United States:  Implications for Health and
Nursing Care. Transcultural Nursing Care.  2:13-26, 1977.

Svanborg, A., G. Bergstrom, and D. Mellstrom. Survey of
    Epidemiological Studies on Social and Medical Conditions of
    the Elderly. Geneva, Switzerland: World Health
    Organization, 1984.

Synak, B. The Elderly in Poland: An Overview of Selected
    Problems and Changes. Ageing and Society. 7(1):19-35,
    1987.

    Outlines demographic and socio-economic changes in Poland
    since the Second World War with respect to the position and
    service needs of the elderly.

Tanaka, Y. The Pathology of the Extremely Aged. Tokyo,
    Japan: Ishiyaku Euro American, 1984.

Teicher, M., D. Thurz, and J. Vigilante (eds). Reaching the
    Aged: Social Services in Forty-Four Countries. Beverly
    Hills, CA: Sage, 1979.

    Reviews programs for the aged from the perspective of
    changing demographic and international factors:
    innovations in services in Israel, New York and Florida;
    interrelationships between family and service in People's
    Republic of China, Italy and India.

Thursz, D. and J. Vigilante (eds). Meeting Human Needs. 2.
    Additional Perspectives from Thirteen Countries. Beverly
    Hills, CA: Sage, 1976.

Togonu-Bickersteth, F. Self-Assessed Health as Predictor of
    Objective Health Status Among the Rural Aged in Nigeria.
    Journal of Cross-Cultural Gerontology. 2(1):79-91, 1987.

Tropman, J. E. Public Policy Opinion and the Elderly,
    1952-1978: A Kaleidoscope of Culture. New York, NY:
    Greenwood Press, 1987.

US Congress. Older Americans Act Amendments of 1987. Public
    Law 100-175. 1987.

US Congress. Senate. Committee on Labor and Human Resources.
    Older Americans Act of 1987. Washington, DC: Government
    Printing Office, 1987.

US Congress. House. Report by the National Council on Aging.
    The Senior Community Service Employment Program: Its
    History and Evolution. Washington, DC: Government
    Printing Office, 1988.

Verbrugge, L. M. A Health Profile of Older Women with
    Comparisons to Older Men. Research on Aging.
    6(3):291-322, 1984.

von Mering, O. An Anthropomedical Profile of Aging:
    Retirement from Life into Active Ill Health. Journal of
    Geriatric Psychiatry. 3:61-81, 1969.

von Mering, O. and A. O'Rand.  Illness and the Organization of
    Health Care:  A Sociocultural Perspective.  Pp. 255-70 in
    C. Fry (ed).  Dimensions:  Aging, Culture and Health.  New
    York, NY:  Bergin, 1981.

Walker, A.  Community Care and the Elderly in Great Britain:
    Theory and Practice.  International Journal of Health
    Services.  11(4):541-57, 1981.

    Critical review of the post-war development of community-
    and family-based geriatric care.  Implications of policies
    for the status and role of women are discussed.

Wan, T. T. H.  Health Consequences of Major Role Losses in
    Later Life.  Research on Aging.  6(4):469-89, 1984.

Ward, R. A.  Informal Networks and Well-Being in Later Life:
    A Research Agenda.  Gerontologist.  25(1):55-61, 1985.

Watson, W., J. Skinner, and I. Lewis.  Health and the Black
    Aged.  Washington, DC:  National Center on Black Aged,
    1978.

Weaver, J.  National Health Policy and the Under-Served Ethnic
    Minorities, Women, and the Elderly.  St. Louis, MO:  C. V.
    Mosby, 1976.

Weeks, H. and B. Darsky.  The Urban Aged:  Race and Medical
    Care.  School of Public Health.  Bureau of Public Health
    Economic Research Series, No. 14.  Ann Arbor, MI:
    University of Michigan, 1968.

Weinberger, M., et al.  Self-Rated Health As a Predictor of
    Hospital Admission and Nursing Home Placement in Elderly
    Public Housing Tenants.  American Journal of Public Health.
    76(4):457-59, 1984a.

Weinberger, M., et al.  The Effects of Positive and Negative
    Life Changes on the Self-Reported Health Status of Elderly
    Adults.  Journal of Gerontology.  4(1):114-19, 1984b.

Wellman, B. and A. Hall.  Social Networks and Social Support:
    Implications for Later Life.  Pp. 191-231 in V. W. Marshall
    (ed).  Later Life:  The Social Psychology of Aging.
    Beverly Hills, CA:  Sage, 1986.

    The authors relate basic aspects of network theory to
    analysis of social support systems in particular relation
    to health care of elderly people.

Wieland, G. D. and D. Palsdottir.  The Development of Health
    and Social Services for the Elderly in Iceland:  An
    Overview.  Social Sciences and Medicine.  23(12):1333-46,
    1986.

    The authors provide an overview of the condition of elderly
    Icelanders and geriatric health and social services from
    medieval times.  Demographic, economic and public health

changes are described as they have affected the health and
welfare of older Icelanders.

Wilkinson, S. J., et al. Rating Reliability for Life Events
and Difficulties in the Elderly. _Psychology and Medicine_.
16(1):101-05, 1986.

Written in the context of service provision, this piece
broaches a subject of interest to ethnographers as well as
service providers-- assessment of the validity of self-
reported information concerning older people's personal
history and functioning.

Williams, I. _The Care of the Elderly in the Community_.
Ottowa, Canada: Barnes and Noble, 1979.

World Health Organization. _The Uses of Epidemiology in the
Study of the Elderly_. Geneva, Switzerland: World Health
Organization, 1984.

World Health Organization. _Drugs for the Elderly_. Geneva,
Switzerland: World Health Organization, 1985.

World Health Organization. _Health of the Elderly: Report of
a WHO Expert Committee_. Technical Report Series, 779.
Geneva, Switzerland: World Health Organization, 1989.

Wright, R., Jr., et al. _Transcultural Perspective in the
Human Services: Organizational Issues and Trends_.
Springfield, IL: C. C. Thomas, 1983.

Yu, E. S. H. Health of the Chinese Elderly in America.
_Research on Aging_. 8(1):84-109, 1986.

Zambrana, R. E., R. Merino, and S. Santana. Health Services
and the Puerto Rican Elderly. Pp. 308-19 in D. E. Gelfand
and A. J. Kutzik (eds). _Ethnicity and Aging: Theory,
Research and Policy_. New York, NY: Springer, 1979.


**INSTITUTIONALIZATION**

Arling, G., E. B. Harkins, and J. A. Capitman.
Institutionalization and Personal Control: A Panel Study
of Impaired Older People. _Research on Aging_. 8(1):38-56,
1986

Article reports on a longitudinal panel study of the effect
of institutionalization on perceived personal control in
151 impaired elderly residents. Authors report that
personal control declines independent of functional status.

Bagshaw, M. and M. Adams. Nursing Home Nurses' Attitudes,
Empathy, and Ideological Orientation. _International
Journal of Aging and Human Development_. 22(3):235-46,
1985-1986.

Bjelland, A. K. Aging and Identity Management in a Norwegian

Elderly Home.  Human Relations.  38:151-65, 1985.

An ethnographic study of residents in a Norwegian
institution.  Strategies for establishing and maintaining
social identities in this environment are described and
analyzed.

Bourestom, N. and S. Tars.  Alterations in Life Patterns
    Following Nursing Home Relocation.  Gerontologist.
    14:506-10, 1974.

Caringer, B.  Caring for the Institutionalized Filipino.
    Journal of Gerontological Nursing.  3:5, 1977.

Chee, P. and R. L. Kane.  Cultural Factors Affecting Nursing
    Home Care for Minorities:  A Study of Black-American and
    Japanese-American Groups.  Journal of the American
    Geriatrics Society.  31(2):109-12, 1983.

Coe, E.  Self-conception and Institutionalization.  Pp. 225-44
    in A.  Rose and W. Peterson (eds).  Older People and Their
    Social World.  Philadelphia, PA:  F. A. Davis, 1965.

Crandall, W. H.  Border of Time:  Life in a Nursing Home.  New
    York, NY:  Springer, 1990.

    This narrative describes social conditions in an Oregon
    skilled nursing facility from a resident's viewpoint.

Diamond, T.  Social Policy and Everyday Life in Nursing Homes:
    A Critical Ethnography.  Social Science and Medicine.
    23(12):  1287-95, 1986.

    The author reports on his fieldwork as a nursing assistant
    trainee and subsequent employment in U. S. nursing homes.
    The training, role, and perceptions of nurses' aides are
    extensively described, and linked to social and economic
    policies, and the comodification of care.  The impact of
    nursing home organization on patient care and the patient
    role is discussed.

Dominick, J.  Mental Patients in Nursing Homes:  Four Ethnic
    Influences.  Journal of the American Geriatric Society.
    17:63-4, 1969.

Dominick, J. and B. Stotsky.  Mental Patients in Nursing
    Homes:  4.  Ethnic Influences.  Journal of the American
    Geriatrics Society.  17:63-4, 1969.

_____  The Growth of Nursing Home Care.  Lexington, MA:
    Lexington Books, 1979.

Eribes, R. and M. Bradley-Rawls.  The Underutilization of
    Nursing Home Facilities by Mexican-American Elderly in the
    Southwest.  Gerontologist.  18:(4):363-71, 1978.

Faulwell, M. and R. S. Pomerantz.  Physician Influence in the
    Selection of Institutionalization of the Elderly.  Pp.

219-32 in C. L. Fry (ed). Dimensions: Aging, Culture, and Health. Brooklyn, NY:  J. F.  Bergin, Praeger, 1981.

The authors describe two studies of physician-level factors which are associated with relatively higher rates of institutionalizing elderly patients from acute-care hospitals.  Three factors are important to physicians' decisions:  the dissimilarity of personal characteristics with the patient, the length of association with the patient, and the mode of patient's referral to the physician.

Garen, W., et al.  Alternatives to Institutionalization:  An Annotated Research Bibliography on Housing and Services for the Aged.  Urbana, IL:  Housing Research and Development, University of Illinois at Urbana, Champaign, 1976.

George, L., et al.  Quality of Care in Nursing Homes: Attitudinal and Environmental Factors.  Durham, NC:  Center for the Study of Aging and Human Development, 1979.

Glasscote, R. M., et al.  Old Folks at Home:  A Field Study of Nursing and Board and Care Homes.  Washington, DC:  Joint Information Service of the American Psychiatric Association and the National Association for Mental Health, 1976.

Golander, H. and M. Hirschfeld.  Nursing Care of the Aged in Israel.  Journal of Gerontological Nursing.  7(11):677-80, 1981.

Greene, V. L. and D. Monahan.  The Impact of Visitation on Patient Well-Being in Nursing Homes.  Gerontologist. 22(4):418-23, 1982.

Grundy, E. and T. Arie.  Institutionalization of the Elderly: International Comparisons.  Age and Ageing.  13(3):129-37, 1984.

Gubrium, J.  Death Worlds in a Nursing Home.  Urban Life. 4:317-38, 1975.

_____  Notes on the Social Organization of Senility.  Urban Life.  7:23-44, 1978.

Gurdin, B.  A Report from a Swedish Old Folks Home. Anthropologiska Studies.  No. 1, 1971.

Hanson, B. G.  Negotiation of Self and Setting to Advantage: An Interactionist Consideration of Nursing Home Data. Sociology of Health and Illness.  7:21-25, 1985.

Participant observation of a Toronto facility contributed to this analysis of interaction patterns and social control.

Hay, D.  Profile of Three Nursing Homes and a Long-Term Hospital in Scandinavia.  Gerontologist.  15:297-303, 1975.

Hendel-Sebestyn, G.   Role Diversity:   Toward the Development
   of Community in a Total Institutional Setting.   J. Keith
   (ed).   The Ethnography of Old Age.   Special Issue.
   Anthropological Quarterly.   52:19-28, 1979.

Henderson, J.   Nursing Home Housekeepers:   Indigenous Agents
   of Psychosocial Support.   Human Organization.   40:300-05,
   1981.

Hendricks, J. (ed).   Institutionalization and Alternative
   Futures.   Farmington, NY:   Baywood, 1980.

Henry, J.   Human Obsolescence.   Pp. 391-474 in J. Henry.
   Culture Against Man.   New York, NY:   Random House, 1956.

Horowitz, M. J. and R. Schulz.   The Relocation Controversy:
   Criticism and Commentary on Five Recent Studies.
   Gerontologist.   23:229-34, 1983.

Hutchinson, S. and R. B. Webb.   Intergeneratinal Geriatric
   Remotivation:   Elders' Perspectives.   Journal of Cross-
   Cultural Gerontology.   3(3):273-98, 1988.

Ito, A.   Keiro Nursing Home, A Study of Japanese Cultural
   Adaptation.   Pp. 80-85 in E. Stanford (ed).   Minority
   Aging:   Proceedings.   San Diego, CA:   Center on Aging, San
   Diego University, 1974.

Johnson, C. L.   The Institutional Segregation of the Aged.
   Pp. 375-88 in P. Silverman (ed).   The Elderly as Modern
   Pioneers.   Bloomington, IN:   Indiana University Press,
   1987.

Johnson, C. L. and L. A. Grant (eds).   The Nursing Home in
   American Society.   Baltimore, MD:   The Johns Hopkins
   University Press, 1985.

Johnson, C. and F. Johnson.   A Micro-Analysis of Senility:
   The Responses of the Family and the Health Professionals.
   Culture, Medicine and Psychiatry.   7:77-96, 1983.

Jones, C. C.   Caring for the Aged:   An Appraisal of Nursing
   Homes and Alternatives.   Chicago, IL:   Nelson-Hall, 1982.

Kane, R. L., R. M. Bell, and S. Z. Riegler.   Value Preferences
   for Nursing Home Outcomes.   Gerontologist.   26(3):303-08,
   1986.

Kart, C. and B. Beckham.   Black-White Differentials in the
   Institutionalization of the Elderly:   A Temporal Analysis.
   Social Forces.   54:901-10, 1976.

Kastenbaum, R. and S. Candy.   The 4% Fallacy:   A
   Methodological and Empirical Critique of Extended Care
   Facility Population Statistics.   International Journal of
   Aging and Human Development.   4(1):15-21, 1973.

Kayser-Jones, J.   Care of the Institutionalized Aged in

Scotland and the United States:  A Comparative Study.
_Western Journal of Nursing Research_.  1(3):190-99, 1979.

_____ Review of Limbo:  A Memoir About Life in a Nursing Home
by a Survivor (by Carobeth Laird).  _Medical Anthropology
Newsletter_.  2:30, 1980.

_____ Quality of Care for the Institutionalized Aged:  A
Scottish-American Comparison.  Pp. 233-54 in C. L. Fry
(ed).  _Dimensions:  Aging, Culture and Health_.  Brooklyn,
NY:  J. F.  Bergin, 1981a.

The study compares one long-term care facility in Scotland
with an American nursing home.  Each institution was
examined using an ethnographic method over three- and four-
month periods.  Staff-patient interactions are described,
and systemic determinants of the organization of care are
considered.

_____ A Comparison of Care in a Scottish and a U. S.
Facility.  _Geriatric Nursing_.  2:44-50, 1981b.

_____ Gerontological Nursing Research Revisited.  _Journal of
Gerontological Nursing_.  7:217-23, 1981c.

_____ _Old, Alone and Neglected:  Care of the Aged in Scotland
and the United States_.  Berkeley, CA:  University of
California Press, 1981d.

_____ Institutional Structures:  Catalysts of or Barriers to
Quality Care for the Institutionalized Aged in Scotland and
the US.  _Social Science and Medicine_.  16(9):935-44, 1982.

_____ Distributive Justice and the Treatment of Acute Illness
in Nursing Homes.  _Social Science and Medicine_.  23(12):
1279-86, 1986.

This is an ethnographic study of social and cultural
factors influencing decision-making in the assessment and
treatment of acute conditions arising among nursing home
residents.  The author found that judgments of the
residents or their families regarding residents' quality of
life were routinely not considered in acute management.
Physicians' assessments of mental status and costs of care
were the most important factors.

Kayser-Jones, J. S. and F. A. Minnigerode.  Increasing Nursing
Students' Interest in Working with Aged Patients.  _Nursing
Research_.  24(1):23-26, 1975.

Knapp, M. and S. Missiakoulis.  Predicting Turnover Rates
Among the Staff of English and Welsh Old People's Homes.
_Social Science and Medicine_.  17(1):29-36, 1983.

Koemig, R., et al.  Ideas About Illness of Elderly Black and
White In An Urban Hospital.  _Aging and Human Development_.
2:217-25, 1971.

Laird, C.  Limbo:  A Memoir About Life in a Nursing Home By a
     Survivor.  Novato, CA:  Chandler and Sharp, 1979.

Lawrence, T. L.  Health Care Facilities for the Elderly in
     Japan.  International Journal of Health Services.
     15(4):677-97, 1985.

Lella, J. W.  The Perils of Patient Government:  Professionals
     and Patients in a Chronic-Care Hospital.  Waterloo,
     Ontario:  Wilfred Laurier University Press, 1986.

Maluccio, A. N.  Alternatives to Institutionalization:  A
     Selective Review of the Literature.  Saratoga, CA:  Century
     Twenty-One, 1980.

Markson, E.  Ethnicity as a Factor in the Institutionalization
     of the Ethnic Elderly.  Pp. 341-56 in D. Gelfand and A.
     Kutzik (eds).  Ethnicity and Aging:  Theory, Research and
     Policy.  New York, NY:  Springer, 1979.

_____  Institutionalization:  Sin, Cure, or Sinecure for the
     Impaired Elderly.  Pp. 105-20 in E. Markson and G. Batra
     (eds).  Public Policies for an Aging Population.
     Lexington, MA:  Lexington Books, 1980.

Matthews, S. H.  The Social World of Old Women:  Management of
     Self-Identity.  Beverly Hills, CA:  Sage Publications,
     1979.

     This monograph contains much material of ethnographic
     nature, including a chapter on the negotiation of social
     identities for elderly residents in institutional settings
     in the U. S.

Mendelson, M.  Tender Loving Greed.  New York, NY:  Alfred
     Knopf, 1974.

Miller, D. B., et al.  Nurse-Physician Communication in a
     Nursing Home Setting.  Gerontologist.  12(3):225-29, 1972.

Monk, A. and L. W. Kaye.  The Ombudsman Volunteer in the
     Nursing Home:  Differential Role Perceptions of Patient
     Representatives for the Institutionalized Aged.
     Gerontologist.  22(2):194-99, 1982.

Moss, F. and V. Halamandaris.  Too Old, Too Sick, Too Bad:
     Nursing Homes in America.  Germantown, MD:  Aspen Systems
     Corporation, 1979.

Mummah, H.  Group Work With the Aged Blind Japanese in the
     Nursing Home and in the Community.  New Outlook for the
     Blind.  69:160-67, 1975.

McConnel, C. E.  A Note on the Lifetime Risk of Nursing Home
     Residency.  Gerontologist.  24(2):193-98, 1984.

Noelker, L. S. and S. W. Poulshock.  Intimacy:  Factors
     Affecting Its Development Among Members of a Home for the

Aged. International Journal of Aging and Human Development. 19(3):177-90, 1984.

Reif, L. and B. Trager (eds). International Perspectives on Long-Term Care. New York, NY: Haworth Press, 1985.

Powers, B. A. Self-Perceived Health of Elderly Institutionalized People. Journal of Cross-Cultural Gerontology. 3(3):299-321, 1988.

Rodstein, M. Initial Adjustment to a Long-Term Care Institution: Behavioral Aspects. Journal of the American Geriatrics Society. 2:65-71, 1976

Sager, A. P. Planning Home Care with the Elderly: Patient, Family, and Professional Views of an Alternative to Institutionalization. Cambridge, MA: Ballinger, 1982.

Samuelsson, G. and G. Sundstrom. Ending One's Life in a Nursing Home: A Note on Swedish Findings. International Journal of Aging and Human Development. 27(2):81-88, 1988.

Savishinsky, J. S. In the Company of Animals: An Anthropological Study of Pets and People in Three Nursing Homes. The Latham Letter. 5(1)1, 9-10, 21-22, 1983-84.

    Describes the organization and operation of pet therapy programs in three American nursing homes, comparing the consequences of using different kinds of visiting formats and techniques.

_____ Staying in Touch: A Report on Pet Therapy Programs in Four Geriatric Facilities. Ithaca, NY: Department of Anthropology, Ithaca College, 1984a.

    Report on the second year of operation of pet therapy programs in four upstate New York geriatric facilities; focus is on the social and institutional effects of visiting animals and volunteers.

_____ What Cornell Has Discovered About Volunteer Experiences. People--Animals--Environment. 2(1)14-18, 1984b.

    Analyzes the roles of nursing home volunteers, and their reflections on their work: motivations, guilt, unexpected forms of intimacy; recommendations for improving volunteer experiences are discussed.

_____ Pets and Family Relationships Among Nursing Home Residents. Marriage and Family Review. 8(3-4):109-34, 1985.

    Examines the way nursing home residents interpret their relationships with pets and family members: issues considered include domesticity, morality, mortality, the narrative styles of residents, and the symbolism of pets in family reminiscences.

_____ The Human Impact of a Pet Therapy Program in Three
Geriatric Facilities. Central Issues in Anthropology.
6(2):31-41, 1986.

Describes pet therapy programs in three geriatric
institutions, with a focus on several of their unintended
consequences: ties between community volunteers and
residents, the stimulation of reminiscences, the creation
of domestic imagery, the effect of different program
formats on outcomes, and the roles of institutional staff,
are considered.

_____ The Meanings of Loss: Human and Pet Death in the Lives
of the Elderly. Pp. 138-47 in W. Kay, et al (eds).
Euthanasia, Veterinary Medicine, and the Human Companion
Animal Bond. Philadelphia, PA: The Charles Press, 1988a.

Considers how elderly nursing home residents respond to
death and loss by comparing their reactions to the death of
pets, kin, and friends: issues of longevity, intimacy,
kinship metaphors, humor, moral meanings, and mourning are
dealt with.

_____ Stigma, Silence, Contact: Responses to Alzheimer's
Sufferers in Two Nursing Homes. Pp. 49-65 in R. Mayeux, et
al (eds). Alzheimer's Disease and Related Disorders.
Springfield, IL: C. C. Thomas, 1988b.

Considers the reactions to Alzheimer's Disease by nursing
home residents, staff, and volunteers, as well as the
response by sufferers themselves; compares American
attitudes towards silence, stigma, and randomness with the
responses to these experiences found in other societies;
examines the use of non-verbal and other forms of
communication with demented individuals.

Savishinsky, J. S., et al. The Life of the Hour: A Study of
People and Pets in Three Nursing Homes. Ithaca, NY:
Department of Anthropology, Ithaca College, 1983.

Research report, describing and evaluating a series of pet
therapy programs in upstate New York geriatric facilities.

Schafft, G. Long-Term Care for Minorities: An Unfinished
Agenda. Pp. 73-76 in P. Stanford (ed). Minority Aging:
Policy Issues for the 80's. San Diego, CA: Center on
Aging, San Diego State University, 1980a.

_____ Nursing Homes and the Minority Elderly. The Journal of
Long-Term Care Administration. 8(4):1-31, 1980b.

Shield, R. R. Uneasy Endings: Daily Life in an American
Nursing Home. Ithaca, NY: Cornell University Press, 1988.

_____ Liminality in an American Nursing Home: The Endless
Transition. Pp. 331-52 in J . Sokolovsky, ed. The
Cultural Context of Aging: Worldwide Perspectives.
Westport, CT: Bergin and Garvey, 1990.

Sigman, S. J.  The Applicability of the Concept of Recruitment to the Communications Study of a Nursing Home:  An Ethnographic Case Study.  International Journal of Aging and Human Development.  22(3):215-34, 1985-86.

Author describes and analyzes institutional procedures for assigning incoming patients to wards and for interward transfer.  Ethnographic observations of staff-patient and patient-patient interactions are outlined.

Silberstein, J., et al.  Causes of Admissions to Nursing Homes in Israel.  Medical Care.  8:221-33, 1970.

Stannard, C.  Old Folks and Dirty Work:  The Social Conditions for Patient Abuse in a Nursing Home.  Social Problems. 20(3):329-42, 1973.

Stotsky, B. A.  Unacceptable Behavior in Nursing Homes. Nursing Homes.  15:30-33, 1965.

Tellis-Nayak, V and M. Tellis-Nayak.  Quality of Care and the Burden of Two Cultures:  When the World of the Nurse's Aide Enters the World of the Nursing Home.  Gerontologist. 29(7):307-13, 1989.

This study contains some ethnographic information on the movement of nursing assistant into and out of the world of nursing home employment from their social positions within a largely deprived underclass.  The pattern of movement and its causes are described.

Tibbett, L. R.  An Evaluation of Institutional Care of the Aged in South Africa.  South Africa Medical Journal. 64(7):241-45, 1983.

Tobin, S.  The Mystique of Deinstitutionalization.  Society. 15:73-75, 1978.

_____  Institutionalization of the Aged.  Pp. 195-211 in N. Datan and N. Lohmann (eds).  Transitions of Aging.  New York, NY:  Academic Press, 1980.

Tobin, S. and M. Lieberman.  Last Home for the Aged.  San Francisco, CA:  Jossey Bass, 1976.

Townsend, C.  Old Age:  The Last Segregation.  New York, NY: Grossman, 1971.

Uyehara, B.  Context and Environment:  The Physical and Social Influences on the Design of a Hawaiian Elderly Community. Berkeley, CA:  University of California, Department of Architecture, 1982.

Van Tassel, D. and P. N. Stearns (eds).  Old Age in Bureaucratic Society:  The Elderly, the Experts, and the State in American History.  Westport, CT:  Greenwood Press, 1986.

Contains a chapter on the history of institutionalization
of elderly people in American Society.

Vesperi, M.  The Reluctant Consumer:  Nursing Home Residents
in the Post-Bergman Era.  Pp. 225-37 in J. Sokolvsky (ed).
Growing Old in Different Societies:  Cross-Cultural
Perspectives.  Acton, MA:  Copley Press, 1987.

Vicente, L., J. A. Wiley, and R. A. Carrington.  The Risk of
Institutionalization Before Death.  Gerontologist.
19:361-67, 1979.

Wells, L. and G. MacDonald.  Interpersonal Networks and Post-
Relocation Adjustment of the Institutionalized Elderly.
Gerontologist.  21(2):177-83, 1983.

York, J. and R. Caslyn.  Family Involvement in Nursing Homes.
Gerontologist.  17(6):500-05, 1977.

# 4

# Non-Industrialized
# Societies

## AFRICA--SMALL SCALE TRADITIONAL SOCIETIES--AGRARIAN

Adeokun, L.  Social Aging in Yoruba Women.  Pp. 29-34 in
    Proceedings of 9th International Conference of Social
    Gerontology, Quebec, Canada.  Adaptability and Aging.  Vol.
    2.  Paris:  International Center on Social Gerontology,
    1988.

Arth, M.  Ideals and Behavior:  A Comment on Ibo Respect
    Patterns.  Gerontologist.  8:242-44, 1968.

_____  Aging:  A Cross-Cultural Perspective.  Pp. 352-64 in
    D. Kent, R. Kastenbaum, and S. Sherwood (eds).  Research
    Planning and Action for the Elderly.  New York, NY:
    Behavioral Publications, 1972.

    Ibo [Ibgo] values and customs in the aging process.

Bledsoe, C. and U. C. Isiugo-Abanihe.  Strategies of Child
    Fosterage Among Mende Grannies in Sierra Leone.  Pp. 442-74
    in R. Lesthaeghe (ed).  African Reproduction and Social
    Organization.  Berkeley, CA:  University of California
    Press, 1989.

Brain, J.  Ancestors as Elders in Africa--Further Thoughts.
    Africa.  43:122-33, 1973.

Brown, E.  Hehe Grandmothers.  Journal of the Royal
    Anthropological Institute.  65:82-96, 1935.

Drucker-Brown, S.  Joking at Death:  The Mamprusi Grandparent-
    Grandchild Joking Relationship.  Man.  (n.s.)  17:714-27,
    1982.

Gracia, M.  Research Findings in Cameroon:  Older Persons in
    Villages in the District of Dibombari.  African
    Gerontology.  No. 3:25-40, 1985.

Kopytoff, I.  Ancestors as Elders in Africa.  Africa.
    41:129-42,  1971.

A classic paper. See Brain 1973 and Sangree 1974 for responses.

LeVine, R. Intergenerational Tensions and Extended Family Structures in Africa. Pp. 188-92 in E. Shanas and G. Streib (eds). Social Structure and the Family: Generational Relations. Englewood Cliffs, NJ: Prentice-Hall, 1965.

MacCormack, C. Dying as Transformation to Elderhood: The Sherbro Coast of Sierra Leone. Curare. 4:117-26, 1985.

Sangree, W. Youths as Elders and Infants as Ancestors: The Complementarity of Alternate Generations, Both Living and Dead, in Tiriki, Kenya, and Irigwe, Nigeria. Africa. 44: 65-70, 1974.

_____ The Childless Elderly in Tiriki, Kenya, and Irigwe, Nigeria: A Comparative Analysis of the Relationship Between Beliefs About Childlessness and the Social Status of the Childless Elderly. Journal of Cross-Cultural Gerontology. 2:201-24, 1987.

_____ Age and Power: Life-Course Trajectories and Age Structuring of Power Relations in East and West Africa. Pp. 23-46 in D. Kertzer and K. Schaie (eds). Age Structuring in Comparative Perspective. Hillsdale, NY: Lawrence Erlbaum Associates, 1989.

Shelton, A. Ibo Aging and Eldership: Notes for Gerontologists and Others. Gerontologist. 5:20-23, 1965.

Discussion of ways that Ibo [Igbo] elders replace physical labor with responsibilities for social order and teaching the young, thereby earning respect.

_____ Igbo Child-Raising, Eldership and Dependence: Further Notes for Gerontologists and Others. Gerontologist. 8:236-41, 1968.

Teitelbaum, M. Old Age, Midwifery and Good Talk: Paths to Power in a West African Gerontocracy. Pp. 39-60 in H. Strange and M. Teitelbaum (eds). Aging and Cultural Diversity: New Directions and Annotated Bibliography. South Hadley, MA: Bergin and Garvey, 1987.

Togonu-Bickersteth, F. Self-Assessed Health as Predictor of Objective Health Status Among Rural Aged in Nigeria. Journal of Cross-Cultural Gerontology. 2:79-93, 1987.

**AFRICA--SMALL SCALE TRADITIONAL SOCIETIES--PASTORALISTS**

Andretta, E. H. Aging, Power and Status in an East African Pastoral Society. J. Sokolovsky and J. Sokolovsky (eds). Aging and the Aged in the Third World. Part 2. Regional and Ethnographic Perspectives. Studies in Third World Societies. 23:83-110, 1982.

Glascock, A. P.  Old Rules Are Made To Be Broken:  Resource
    Transfer Among Agro-Pastoralists in Somalia.  Pp. 61-76 in
    J. Morgan (ed).  Aging in Developing Societies:  A Reader
    in Third World Gerontology.  Bristol, IN:  Wyndham Hall
    Press, 1985.

_____ Resource Control Among Older Males in Southern Somalia.
    Journal of Cross-Cultural Gerontology.  1:51-72, 1986a.

_____ Broken Rules and Broken Promises:  Status and Role of
    Widows in Southern Somalia.  Pp. 104-18 in A. Sontz (ed).
    Compendium Series:  Cultural Gerontology, A Folio of the
    Brunswick Institute.  Jersey City, NJ, 1986b.

Hamer, J.  Myth, Ritual and the Authority of Elders in an
    Ethiopian Society.  Africa.  46:327-39, 1976.

Nadel, S.  Witchcraft in Four African Societies.  American
    Anthropologist.  54:18-29, 1949.

    This classic study correlates patterns of intergenerational
    witchcraft accusations, age grades and individuals'
    physical capability.

## AFRICA--SMALL SCALE TRADITIONAL SOCIETIES--GATHERER-HUNTERS

Biesele, M. and N. Howell.  The Old People Give You Life:
    Aging Among !Kung Hunter-Gatherers.  Pp. 77-98 in P. Amoss
    and S. Harrell (eds).  Other Ways of Growing Old:
    Anthropological Perspectives.  Stanford, CA:  Stanford
    University Press, 1981.

Lee, R.  Work, Sexuality and Aging Among !Kung Women.  Pp.
    23-35 in J. Brown and V. Kerns (eds).  In Her Prime:  A New
    View of Middle-Aged Women.  South Hadley, MA:  Bergin and
    Garvey, 1985.

Rosenberg, H.  Complaint Discourse, Aging, and Caregiving
    Among the !Kung San of Botswana.  Pp. 19-41 in J.
    Sokolovsky (ed).  The Cultural Context of Aging:  Worldwide
    Perspectives.  Westport, CT:  Bergin & Garvey, 1990.

## AFRICA--MODERNIZATION AND SOCIAL CHANGE--AGRARIAN SOCIETIES

Arth, M.  An Interdisciplinary View of the Aged in Ibo
    Culture.  Journal of Geriatric Psychology.  2:33-39, 1968.

    This article deals with intergenerational relationships,
    traditional values, modernization and social change.

Cattell, M.  Old Age in Rural Kenya:  Gender, the Life Course
    and Social Change.  Ann Arbor, MI:  University Microfilms,
    1989a.

    Ethnographic study of aging and old age among the Samia of
    western Kenya.

_____ Knowledge and Social Change in Samia, Western Kenya.
Journal of Cross-Cultural Gerontology. 4:225-44, 1989b.

_____ Models of Old Age Among the Samia of Kenya:  Family
Support of the Elderly. Journal of Cross-Cultural
Gerontology. 5(4):375-94, 1990.

Cohen, D. W.  Doing Social History from Pim's Doorway.  Pp.
191-235 in O. Zunz (ed). Reliving the Past: The Worlds of
Social History. Chapel Hill, NC:  University of North
Carolina Press, 1985.

Historical perspective on older women as teachers of Kenyan
Luo children and shapers of Luo culture and society.

Colson, E. and T. Scudder.  Old Age in Gwembe District,
Zambia.  Pp. 125-53 in P. Amoss and S. Harrell (eds).
Other Ways of Growing Old. Stanford, CA:  Stanford
University Press, 1981.

Based on research done from 1949 to 1976, this paper deals
with the impacts of socioeconomic change and forced
relocation on elderly Gwembe Tonga, including vivid
portraits of 7 elderly persons.

Cox, F. with N. Mberia. Aging in a Changing Village Society:
A Kenyan Experience. Washington, DC:  International
Federation on Ageing, 1977.

Description of the elderly in a Kikuyu village and also a
home for the aged destitute in that village, including the
voices of some old people on their experiences of social
change.

Davison, J. with the Women of Mutira. Voices from Mutira:
Lives of Rural Gikuyu Women. Boulder, CO:  L. Riener
Publisher, 1989.

The life stories of 5 older Gikuyu women and 2 young women
organized around the theme of learning and change.

Folta, J. and E. Deck.  Elderly Black Widows in Rural
Zimbabwe. Journal of Cross-Cultural Gerontology.
2:321-42, 1987.

Moore, S.  Old Age in a Life-Term Social Arena:  Some Chagga
of Kilimanjaro in 1974.  Pp. 23-76 in B. Myerhoff and A.
Simic (eds). Life's Career--Aging: Cultural Variations on
Growing Old. Beverly Hills, CA:  Sage, 1978.

Extended case studies of two elderly Chagga, a woman and a
man, based on life history interviews.

Nahemow, N.  Residence, Kinship and Social Isolation Among the
Aged Baganda. Journal of Marriage and the Family.
41:171-83, 1979.

_____ Grandparenthood Among the Baganda:  Role Option in Old

Age?  Pp. 104-15 in J. Sokolovsky (ed).  Growing Old in
Different Societies.  Acton, MA:  Copley Press, 1987.

Nahemow, N. and B. Adams.  Old Age Among the Baganda:
Continuity and Change.  Pp. 147-66 In J. Gubrium (ed).
Late Life:  Communities and Environmental Policy.
Springfield, IL:  C. C. Thomas, 1974.

Rosenmayr, L.  More Than Wisdom:  A Field Study of the Old in
an African Village.  Journal of Cross-Cultural Gerontology.
3:21-41, 1988.

Sangree, W.  Role Flexibility and Status Continuity:  Tiriki
(Kenya) Age Groups Today.  Journal of Cross-Cultural
Gerontology.  1:117-38, 1986.

Shelton, A.  The Aged and Eldership Among the Igbo.  Pp. 31-49
in D. Cowgill and L. Holmes (eds).  Aging and
Modernization.  New York, NY:  Appleton-Century-Crofts,
1972.

Ssenkoloto, G.  Status Report of Selected African Countries on
Conditions and Philosophies Toward Old Age Care.  Buea,
South West Province, Cameroon:  Regional Pan African
Institute for Development, 1981.

    Report on conditions of the elderly in 5 Cameroonian
    villages including data from a census of the elderly and
    discussion of services needed by rural elderly.

_____  Examples of Contributions Made by the Aging to Rural
Development.  Aging Well Through Living Better.
Proceedings of 10th International Conference of Social
Gerontology, Deauville, France.  2:17-32.  Paris:
International Center on Social Gerontology, 1982.

Teitelbaum, M.  Singing for Their Supper and Other Productive
Work of African Elderly.  Pp. 61-68 in E. Gort (ed).  Aging
in Cross-Cultural Perspective:  Africa and the Americas.
New York, NY:  Phelps-Stokes Fund, 1988.

Wanjala, C.  Twilight Years Are the Years of Counsel and
Wisdom.  Pp. 78-91 in S. Wandibba (ed).  History and
Culture in Western Kenya:  The People of Bungoma District
Through Time.  Nairobi, Kenya:  Gideon S. Were Press, 1985.

Wilson, M.  For Men and Elders:  Change in the Relations of
Generations of Men and Women Among the Nyakyusa-Ngonde
People, 1945-1961.  New York, NY:  Africana, 1977.

## AFRICA--MODERNIZATION AND SOCIAL CHANGE--PASTORALISTS

Deng, F.  The Dinka of the Sudan.  Prospect Heights, IL:
Waveland Press, 1986.

    Deng organizes his ethnography by life stages, including a
    chapter on old age, with data from his own experiences

growing up as a Dinka.  This edition is a reissue and
includes "Postscript 1986," updating the original edition
of 1972.

Hamer, J.  Aging in a Gerontocratic Society:  The Sidamo of
Southwest Ethiopia.  Pp. 15-30 in D. Cowgill and L. Holmes
(eds).  Aging and Modernization.  New York, NY:  Appleton-
Century-Crofts, 1972.

_____  The Generation Gap in an Ethiopian Society.  Pp. 264-77
in J. Gubrium (ed).  Time, Roles and Self in Old Age.  New
York, NY:  Human Sciences Press, 1976.

## AFRICA--MODERNIZATION AND SOCIAL CHANGE--GATHERER-HUNTERS

Shostak, M.  Nisa:  The Life and Words of a !Kung Woman.
Cambridge, MA:  Harvard University Press, 1984.

Vivid autobiography arranged by life stages, including old
age.

## AFRICA--MODERNIZATION AND SOCIAL CHANGE--URBAN AND NATIONAL PERSPECTIVES

Adeokun, L.  Urban/Rural Differentials in Age and Professional
Activity.  Aging Well Through Living Better.  Proceedings
of 10th International Conference of Social Gerontology,
Deauville, France.  1:790-96.  Paris:  International Center
on Social Gerontology, 1982.

_____  The Elderly All Over the World:  Nigeria.  Paris:
International Center of Social Gerontology, 1984.

Demographic characteristics of the elderly in Nigeria
(national data) and other descriptive material based on
inadequately specified survey research in Ile-Ife.

Apt, N.  A Survey of the Socio-Economic Conditions of the Aged
in Ghana.  Legon, Ghana:  Department of Social Welfare and
Community Development Monograph, 1971.

Aspects of this study are discussed in Apt 1975.

_____  Urbanization and the Aged.  Pp. 177-83 in C. Oppong
(ed).  Changing Family Studies.  Legon Family Research
Reports, No. 3.  Legon, Ghana:  Institute of African
Studies, 1975.

This paper discusses care for the elderly, with special
emphasis on the conditions and characteristics of destitute
elderly in urban centers of Ghana.  Specific topics include
living conditions, physical and mental conditions, and use
of leisure time.

_____  Aging in Africa.  Pp. 17-32 in E. Gort (ed).  Aging in
Cross-Cultural Perspective:  Africa and the Americas.  New

York, NY:  Phelps-Stokes Fund, 1988.

Overview based primarily on West African materials, with
discussion of demographic changes, traditional roles of
elderly, and effects of modernization.

Brown, C. K.  Research Findings in Ghana:  A Survey on the
Elderly in the Accra Region.  African Gerontology.  No.
4:11-33, 1985.

Report on characteristics of the elderly, their attitudes,
and family roles and relationships, including a few rural-
urban comparisons.

Caldwell, J.  The Erosion of the Family:  A Study of the Fate
of the Family in Ghana.  Population Studies.  20:5-26,
1966.

Report of findings from survey research on relationship
between fertility and family support of elderly Ghanaians
in both urban and rural areas.

Carre, P.  From Old to New in Algeria.  African Gerontology.
No. 4:3-10, 1985.

Clarke, D. G.  The Economics of African Old Age Subsistence in
Rhodesia.  Gwelo, Zimbabwe:  Mambo Press, 1977.

This volume discusses the financial condition of retired
and elderly workers in Rhodesia (Zimbabwe) from pre-
colonial times until 1977.  The focus of the study is on
post-retirement subsistence with a description of formal
pension provisions and kin-based social security systems.
Characteristics of the aged are outlined, including who is
classified as 'old,' accommodations, ethnic origin,
educational status, and dependency ratios.  The author also
examines government policies affecting social security
provisions for the elderly.

Cohen, R.  Age and Culture as Theory.  Pp. 234-49 in D.
Kertzer and J. Keith (eds).  Age and Anthropological
Theory.  Ithaca, NY:  Cornell University Press, 1984.

Perceptions and experiences of aging among Muslim Bura,
Nigeria.

Coles, C.  The Older Woman in Hausa Society:  Power and
Authority in Urban Nigeria.  Pp. 57-81 in J. Sokolovsky
(ed).  The Cultural Context of Aging:  Worldwide
Perspectives.  Westport, CT:  Bergin and Garvey, 1990.

Cowgill, D.  Aging in Cross-Cultural Perspective:  Africa and
the Americas.  Pp. 7-16 in E. Gort (ed).  Aging in Cross-
Cultural Perspective:  Africa and the Americas.  New York,
NY:  Phelps-Stokes Fund, 1988.

Brief summary of current and future research trends and
discussion of aging and modernization.

Dorjahn, V.  Where Do the Old Folks Live?  The Residence of
the Elderly Among the Temne of Sierra Leone.  Journal of
Cross-Cultural Gerontology.  4:257-78, 1989.

Edington, G. and A. Odebiyi.  Cancer and Aging in Ibadan.
Social Science and Medicine.  11:477-81, 1976.

Socioeconomic factors, traditional medicine and cancer
treatment among elderly Nigerians.

Ekpenyong, S., O. Oyeneye, and M. Peil.  Nigerian Elderly:  A
Rural, Urban and Interstate Comparison.  African
Gerontology.  No. 5:5-19, 1986.

Survey findings on migration, retirement, income, housing,
health, attitudes of old people toward their roles in
contemporary Nigerian society in both urban and rural
areas.

_____ Health Problems of Elderly Nigerians.  Social Science
and Medicine.  24:885-88, 1987.

Health problems and family care of elderly Nigerians.

Ferreira, M., L. Gillis, and V. Moller (eds).  Ageing in South
Africa:  Social Research Papers.  Pretoria, South Africa:
Human Sciences Research Council, 1989.

Articles and research reports about South Africans (mostly
black) in rural and urban areas on themes of social welfare
and well-being, housing, health care, and attitudes toward
care of the aged.

Fosu, G. B.  Aging in Ghana.  Pp. 23-38 in J. Morgan (ed).
Aging in Developing Societies:  A Reader in Third World
Gerontology.  Vol. 2.  Bristol, IN:  Wyndham Hall Press,
1985.

Fuller, C.  Aging Among Southern African Bantu.  Pp. 51-72 in
D. Cowgill and L. Holmes (eds).  Aging and Modernization.
New York, NY:  Appleton-Century-Crofts, 1972.

Guillette, E. A.  Socio-Economic Change and Cultural
Continuity in the Lives of the Older Tswana.  Journal of
Cross-Cultural Gerontology.  5(3):191-204, 1990.

Hampson, J.  Old Age:  A Study of Aging in Zimbabwe.  Gweru,
Zimbabwe:  Mambo Press; Northampton, UK:  Leishman and
Taussig, 1982.

This volume presents a broad overview of the conditions of
the elderly in Zimbabwe.  The author and his assistants
interviewed 117 individuals aged 60 and older from the city
of Harare.  The focus of this study was to examine the
experiences of the elderly and their feelings about old
age.  Topics include accommodation, employment status,
impact of migration, feelings of respect, loneliness,
availability of social services and coping behavior.

_____ Elderly People and Social Welfare in Zimbabwe. _Ageing and Society_. 5:39-67, 1985.

History of social welfare in Zimbabwe and recommendations for alternative, non-pension-based social security systems in rural areas.

Harare School of Social Work. _Zimbabwe Action Plan on Elderly_. Harare, Zimbabwe:  School of Social Work, 1987.

Presents a report and conclusions of a workshop held at the School of Social Work, Harare, December 15-18, 1986.

International Center of Social Gerontology. _Recommendations Adopted by the African Conference of Gerontology, Dakar, December 10-14, 1984_. Paris, France, 1984.

This booklet provides a summary of views and recommendations of experts and government officials on a variety of issues concerning the elderly in Africa.  Areas of concern discussed include medical and economic features, the need for better demographic data, traditional versus Western health care, and social welfare.  A list of participants from the 25 African nations represented at the conference is also included.

Jack, D., L. Adeokun, and S. Jaiyesimi.  The Image of the Elderly in Nigeria. _African Gerontology_. No. 2:15-32, 1984.

The elderly in traditional society and characteristics of today's elderly, especially new images of old people in the mass media and among young people.

Kabwasa, N. and A. Kawata.  The Elderly and the Media:  The Case of Zaire. _African Gerontology_. No. 3:41-44, 1985.

Kenya NGO Organizing Committee. _Women and Ageing_. Nairobi, Kenya, 1985.

Prepared for Forum '85 in conjunction with UN Decade for Women Conference.  Includes articles on biological and medical aspects of aging, women and aging in Kenya, social work with elderly, economic security, and modernization.

Khasiani, S. _The Effectiveness of the Family and Other Organizations in Meeting the Social and Economic Needs of the Aging Population in Kenya_. Nairobi, Kenya:  Kenya National Council of Social Service, 1983.  (Reprinted in _Genus_. 43:103-18, 1987.)

Kivnick, H.  Adulthood and Old Age Under Apartheid:  A Psychosocial Consideration. _Ageing and Society_. 8:425-40, 1988.

LeVine, S. and R. LeVine.  Age, Gender, and the Demographic Transition:  The Life Course in Agrarian Societies.  Pp. 29-42 in A. S. Rossi (ed). _Gender and the Life Course_.

New York, NY:  Aldine, 1985.

Includes comparative material from the authors' research in
Kenya and Mexico.

Masamba ma Mpolo.  Older Persons and Their Families in a
     Changing Village Society:  A Perspective from Zaire.
     Washington, DC:  The International Federation on Ageing and
     the World Council of Churches, 1984.

     Rural-urban differences and personal experiences of the
     author and his parents.

Menya, M.  Medical and Social Welfare of the Elderly in Kenya.
     African Gerontology.  No. 4:35-47, 1985.

Moller, V. and G. J. Welch.  Polygamy, Economic Security and
     Well-Being of Retired Zulu Migrant Workers.  Journal of
     Cross-Cultural Gerontology.  5(3):205-16, 1990.

Muchena, O. N.  The African Aged in Town.  Harare, Zimbabwe:
     Harare School of Social Work, 1978.

     This paper examines the problems faced by elderly, urban
     Africans in Harare.  The author discusses the
     characteristics of the urban elderly, the type and extent
     of problems they face, and the attitudes of community
     leaders concerning care for the elderly.  Problems
     mentioned include accommodations, food, clothing, medical
     and finances.  The author describes social services
     available to the elderly.

Nyanguru, A.  Residential Care for the Destitute Elderly:  A
     Comparative Study of Two Institutions in Zimbabwe.  Journal
     of Cross-Cultural Gerontology.  2:345-58, 1987.

Okojie, F.  Aging in Sub-Saharan Africa:  Toward Redefinition
     of Needs Research and Policy Directions.  Journal of Cross-
     Cultural Gerontology.  3:3-20, 1988.

Peil, M.  Old Age in West Africa:  Social Support and Quality
     of Life.  Pp. 1-22 in J. Morgan (ed).  Aging in Developing
     Societies:  A Reader in Third World Gerontology.  Vol. 2.
     Bristol, IN:  Wyndham Hall Press, 1985.

_____  Studies of Ageing in Africa.  Ageing and Society.
     7:459-66, 1987.

     Review of Cowgill (1986) Aging Around the World and Morgan
     (1985) Aging in Developing Societies, and discussion of
     other research on aging in Africa.

Peil, M., A. Bamisaiye, and S. Ekpenyong.  Health and Physical
     Support for the Elderly in Nigeria.  Journal of Cross-
     Cultural Gerontology.  4:89-106, 1989.

Peil, M., S. Ekpenyong, and O. Oyeneye.  Retirement in
     Nigeria.  Cultures et Developpement.  17:665-82, 1985.

_____ Going Home:  Migration Careers of Southern Nigerians.
International Migration Review.  22:563-85, 1988.

Robertson, C. C.  Sharing the Same Bowl:  A Socioeconomic
History of Women and Class in Accra, Ghana.  Bloomington,
IN:  Indiana University Press, 1984.

      This volume discusses the impact of changing socioeconomic
      conditions on women's access to the means of production in
      the late nineteenth and twentieth centuries.  It provides a
      context within which to understand the impact of past
      events and present conditions on the lives of elderly and
      other urban women in Ghana.  Topics discussed include
      changes in residence, marriage, inheritance, employment,
      education, fertility and support of dependents.  Four life
      histories of elderly women are presented, and a section on
      old age support and dependency.

Rwezaura, B.  Changing Community Obligations to the Elderly in
Contemporary Africa.  Journal of Social Development in
Africa.  4:5-24, 1989.

Togonu-Bickersteth, F.  Age Identification Among Yoruba Aged.
Journal of Gerontology.  41:110-13, 1986.

_____ Chronological Definitions and Expectations of Old Age
Among Young Adults in Nigeria.  Journal of Aging Studies.
1(2):113-24, 1987.

_____ Aging in Nigeria:  Current and Future Policy Issues in
Caring for the Elderly.  Journal of Applied Gerontology.
7:474-84, 1988.

_____ Conflicts Over Caregiving:  A Discussion of Filial
Obligations Among Adult Nigerian Children.  Journal of
Cross-Cultural Gerontology.  4(1):35-48, 1989.

Twumasi, P.  Ageing and Problems of Old Age in Africa:  A
Study in Social Change and a Model for Its Solution.  Pp.
94-100 in L. Levi (ed).  Society, Stress and Disease.  Vol.
5.  New York, NY:  Oxford University Press, 1987.

Ware, H.  Female and Male Life-Cycles.  Pp. 6-31 in C. Oppong
(ed).  Female and Male in West Africe.  London, UK:  George
Allen and Unwin, 1984.

Warnes, T.  The Elderly in Less-Developed World Regions.
Ageing and Society.  6:373-80, 1986.

      Review of several United Nations publications on aging and
      also some by the International Center of Social
      Gerontology.

## AUSTRALIA--GATHERER-HUNTERS

Bell, D.  Daughters of the Dreaming.  Melbourne, Australia:
McPhee Gribble/George Allen and Unwin, 1983.

Bell describes sexual politics and social change among
Kaytej (Aranda) of central Australia by focusing on the
process by which Kaytej women learn to be adult ("old") or
boss women through the acquisition of ritual knowledge and
conducting women's rituals.

Birdsell, J.  How Do Those Old Men Get All the Girls?  Pp.
364-46 in J. Birdsell.  Human Evolution.  Chicago, IL:
Rand McNally, 1972.

Goodale, J.  Tiwi Wives:  A Study of the Women of Melville
Island, North Australia.  Seattle, WA:  University of
Washington Press, 1971.

This is an ethnography of Tiwi women from a life cycle
perspective.

Hart, C. W. M., A. A. Pilling, and J. C. Goodale.  The Tiwi of
North Australia (3rd ed).  New York, NY:  Holt, Rinehart
and Winston, 1988.

Earlier editions of this monograph reported research done
by Hart in 1928-29 and Pilling in 1953-54.  They emphasized
the male perspective, including an account of the marriage
system through which men accumulate wives, prestige and
power over their lifetimes.  This newest edition includes a
chapter on cultural change by Goodale, who did research
among the Tiwi in 1954, 1962, 1980-81 and 1986-87.

Kaberry, P.  Aboriginal Women:  Sacred and Profane.  London:
George Routledge and Sons, 1939.

A detailed examination of Aboriginal women's lives in the
Kimberleys, including their development of greater
authority, assertiveness and advisory roles as they age.
Kaberry uses a Durkheimian sacred-profane framework and a
life cycle approach.

Reid, J.  "Going Up or Going Down":  The Status of Old People
in an Australian Aboriginal Society.  Ageing and Society.
5:69-95, 1985.

The author discusses aging among the Yolngu (Murngin), the
social roles of older people, and determinants of their
treatment and status:  personal characteristics, kin
network, colonization and social change, and other
situational and structural factors.

Warner, L.  A Black Civilization:  A Social Study of an
Australian Tribe.  1937.  Reprint.  New York, NY:  Harper
Torchbook, 1958.

This monograph uses a Durkheimian framework in describing

the progression of male Murngin from a profane to a sacred
existence.  It includes a short chapter on male age-grading
and a personal account of the life of one Murngin man who
was Warner's good friend.

PACIFIC RIM--HORTICULTURAL/GATHERER-HUNTER PEOPLES

Counts, D. A.  Sweeping Men and Harmless Women:
Responsibility and Gender Identity in Later Life.  J.
Sokolovsky and J. Sokolovsky (eds).  Aging and the Aged in
the Third World:  Part 2.  Regional and Ethnographic
Perspectives.  Studies in Third World Societies.  23:1-16,
1983.

Counts, D. A. and D. R. Counts.  The Cultural Construction of
Aging and Dying in a Melanesian Community.  International
Journal of Aging and Human Development.  20:229-40, 1985a.

The notion of a substantive contrast between premodern and
modern societies in respect to aging and dying is debunked.
The authors conclude that aging and dying are cultural
constructs.

_____  Aging and Its Transformations:  Moving Towards Death in
Pacific Societies.  ASAO Monograph No. 10.  Lanham, MD:
University Press of America, 1985b.

This is a highly significant work of interest to all social
scientists.  It features situated, detailed accounts of
aging and old age in Pulap and Ujelang, in Micronesia; New
Zealand (the Maori and Pakeha) and the Marquesas in
Polynesia and in New Britain and several societies in New
Guinea, in Melanesia.  Also of tremendous interest is the
important introduction which discusses aging and death as
cultural constructions, and their relationship to gender
constructs in Pacific cultures.  The conclusion, by Victor
Marshall, attempts a synthesis of the diverse ethnographic
materials presented in the book with concepts from the
anthropology of aging and from mainstream social
gerontology.

Delaney, Bill.  Is Uncle Sen Insane?:  Pride, Humor and Clique
Formation in a Northern Thai Home for the Elderly.
International Journal of Aging and Human Development.
13:137-50, 1981.

Behind the question of whether or not Uncle Sen, a resident
of the home, is insane, are two adaptive styles of northern
Thai elderly to changes in the traditional social system.

Donner, W.  Compassion, Kinship and Fosterage:  Contexts for
Care of the Childless Elderly in a Polynesian Community.
Journal of Cross-Cultural Gerontology.  2:43-60, 1987.

Conditions of childless elderly in Sikiana, Solomon
Islands, are analyzed.  Given the local kinship idiom, it
is relatively easy to remain cared for.

Holmes, L.   The Role and Status of the Aged in a Changing
    Samoa.   Pp.   73-90 in D. Cowgill and L. Holmes (eds).
    Aging and Modernization.  New York, NY:  Appleton-Century-
    Crofts, 1972.

_____    Samoan Village.  New York, NY:  Holt, Rinehart and
    Winston, 1974.

Holmes, L. and E. C. Rhoads.  Aging and Change in Modern
    Samoa.  Pp. 119-29 in J. Sokolovsky (ed).  Growing Old in
    Different Societies:  Cross-Cultural Perspectives.  Acton,
    MA:  Copley Press, 1987.

Jensen, G. D. and A. H. Polloi.  Health and Lifestyle of
    Longevous Palauans:  Implications for Development Theory.
    International Journal of Aging and Human Development.
    19:271-85, 1984.

    Examines the lives of 38 Palauans, 86-111 years old.
    Discusses how limits to physical usefulness engender a
    crisis for older individuals.

Maxwell, R.   The Changing Status of Elderly in Polynesian
    Society.  Aging and Human Development.  1:127-46, 1970.

Meigs, A. S.  Male Pregnancy and the Reduction of Sexual
    Opposition in a New Guinea Highlands Society.  Ethnology.
    15:393-407, 1976.

    Because they exchange vital substances over a lifetime of
    reproductive activity, the gender roles of elderly Hua
    women and men are reversed.  Post-menopausal women who have
    borne three or more children lose their polluting power and
    become as vulnerable as young men, while elderly men
    acquire the ability to contaminate.

_____    Food, Sex and Pollution.  Baltimore, MD:  Rutgers
    University Press, 1983.

Nason, J.   Respected Elder or Old Person:  Aging in a
    Micronesian Community.  Pp. 155-74 in P. Amoss and S.
    Harrell (ed).  Other Ways of Growing Old:  Anthropological
    Perspectives.  Stanford, CA:  Stanford University Press,
    1981.

Poole, F. J. P.   Transforming 'Natural' Woman:  Female Ritual
    Leaders and Gender Ideology Among Bimin-Kuskusmin.  Pp.
    116-65 in S. B. Ortner and H. Whitehead (eds).  Sexual
    Meanings:  The Cultural Construction of Gender and
    Sexuality.  Cambridge, UK:  Cambridge University Press,
    1981.

    This is a fascinating account of the changing gender role
    and identity of elderly women in a Papua New Guinea
    society.

Rhoads, E. C.   Reevaluation of the Aging and Modernization
    Theory:  The Samoan Evidence.  Gerontologist.  24:243-50,

1984.

The author suggests that the rapid and extensive social change of recent years has not eroded the status of elders, contrary to the predictions of modernization theory.

Rhoads, E. C. and L. D. Holmes. Mapuifagalele, Western Samoa's Home for the Aged: A Cultural Enigma. International Journal of Aging and Human Development. 13:121-35, 1981.

This is a discussion of Polynesia's first home for the aged. Despite the fact that Samoans insist that they provide for their elderly, the institution is filled. The authors discuss changes in life style as well as economic patterns and world view as significant for understanding the existence of the home.

Rubinstein, R. L. What is "The Social Integration of the Elderly" in Small-Scale Society? The Journal of Cross-Cultural Gerontology. 1(4):391-409, 1986.

The author discusses aspects of social integration in Malo, Vanuatu, suggesting that this comparative concept requires a good deal of local tailoring.

Rubinstein, R. L. and P. T. Johnsen. Toward a Comparative Perspective on Filial Response to Aging Populations. J. Sokolovsky (ed). Aging and the Aged in the Third World: Pt. 1. Studies in Third World Societies. 22:115-72, 1982.

Strange, H. Rural Malay Aged in Contrasting Developmental Contexts. Pp. 14-38 in H. Strange and M. Teitelbaum (eds). Aging and Cultural Diversity: New Directions and Annotated Bibliography. South Hadley, MA: Bergin and Garvey, 1987.

van Arsdale, P. The Elderly Asmat of New Guinea. Pp. 111-23 in P. T. Amoss and S. Harrell (eds). Other Ways of Growing Old: Anthropological Perspectives. Stanford, CA: Stanford University Press, 1981a.

_____ Disintegration of the Ritual Support Network Among Aged Asmat Hunter-Gatherers of New Guinea. Pp. 33-45 in C. Fry (ed ). Dimensions: Aging, Culture, and Health. Brooklyn, NY: J. F. Bergin, 1981b.

Zimmer, L. "Who Will Bury Me?" The Plight of Childless Elderly Among the Gende. Journal of Cross-Cultural Gerontology. 2(1):61-77, 1987

Among the consequences of being old and childless in this New Guinea group is that one is considered to be like a child and non-productive. There is also a status of de facto childlessness due to the outmigration of younger wage earners. There is competition among older adults for the support of the young who are financially secure.

## ASIA--PASTORALISTS

Shahrani, N.  Growing in Respect:  Aging Among the Khirghiz of
    Afghanistan.  Pp. 175-92 in P. Amoss and S. Harrell (eds).
    Other Ways of Growing Old:  Anthropoloical Perspectives.
    Stanford, CA:  Stanford University Press, 1981.

## LATIN AMERICAN/CARIBBEAN HORTICULTURAL/GATHERER-HUNTER PEOPLES

Brathwaite, F. (ed).  The Elderly in Barbados.  Bridgetown,
    Barbados:  Carib Research and Publications, 1986.

    Seven substantive articles, an introduction, and a
    conclusion, on economic conditions, social and
    psychological characteristics, social relations,
    retirement, health, and policy programs of the elderly in
    Barbados.

Grell, G.  The Elderly in the Carribbean.  Kingston, Jamaica:
    University of the West Indies, 1987.

Holmberg, A.  Nomads of the Long Bow:  The Siriono of Eastern
    Bolivia.  New York, NY:  American Museum Science Books,
    1969.

Kerns, V.  Aging and Mutual Support Relations Among the Black
    Carib.  Pp. 112-25 in C. Fry (ed).  Aging in Culture and
    Society:  Comparative Viewpoints and Strategies.  Brooklyn,
    NY:  Bergin, 1980.

Priest, P.  Provision for the Aged Among the Siriono Indians
    of Bolivia.  American Anthropologist.  69:1245-7, 1966.

Tout, K. and J. Tout.  Perspectives on Aging in Belize.
    London, UK:  Help Age International, 1985.

Werner, D.  Gerontocracy Among the Mekranoti of Central
    Brazil.  Anthropological Quarterly.  54(1):15-27, 1981.

Wolk, R. L., R. B. Wolk, and A. Sholk.  The Kuna Indians:
    Their Attitudes Toward the Aged.  Journal of the American
    Geriatric Society.  19:406-16, 1971.

## LATIN AMERICAN PEASANTS

Adams, F.  The Role of Old People in Santo Tomas Mazaltepec.
    Pp.  103-26 in D. Cowgill and L. Holmes (eds).  Aging and
    Modernization.  New York, NY:  Appleton-Century-Crofts,
    1972.

De Tichaues, R.  Old People No Problem Among the Aymara
    Indians of Bolivia.  Woman Physician.  25:295-96, 1971.

Edmonson, M.  Los Manitos:  A Study of Institutional Values.
    Middle American Research Institute, Publication 25.  New

Orleans, LA:  Tulane University, 1957.

Gutmann, D.  Mayan Aging--A Comparative TAT Study. Psychiatry.
29:246-59, 1966.

_____ Aging Among the Highland-Maya:  A Comparative Study.
Journal of Personality and Social Psychology.  7:28-35,
1967.

Holmberg, A.  Age in the Andes.  Pp. 86-90 in R. Kleemeier.
Aging and Leisure.  New York, NY:  Oxford University, 1961.

Kagan, D.  Activity and Aging in a Colombian Peasant Village.
Pp. 65-79 in C. Fry (ed).  Aging in Culture and Society:
Comparative Viewpoints and Strategies.  Brooklyn, NY:  J.
F.  Bergin, 1980.

McElroy, J. L., P. A. Quinn, and M. M. McCarthy.  The Economic
Condition of the Aged in the Caribbean:  Evidence from the
United States Virgin Islands.  Pp. 53-75 in J. Morgan (ed).
Aging in Developing Societies:  A Reader in Third World
Gerontology.  Bristol, IN:  Wyndham Hall, 1985.

Moore, A.  Life Cycles in Atchalan:  The Diverse Careers of
Certain Guatemalans.  New York, NY:  Teachers College,
Columbia University, 1973.

O'Nell, C.  Aging in a Zapotec Community.  Human Development.
15:294-309, 1972.

Press, I.  Maya Aging:  Cross-Cultural Projective Techniques
and the Dilemma of Interpretation.  Psychiatry.
30:197-202, 1967.

Reina, R.  The Law of the Saints:  A Pokomam Pueblo and Its
Community Culture.  Indianapolis, IN:  Bobbs Merrill, 1966.

Sokolovsky, J. and J. Sokolovsky.  Familial and Public Context
for Aging:  Growing Old in a Rapidly Changing Mexican
Village.  J.  Sokolovsky (ed).  Aging and the Aged in the
Third World:  Part 2.  Regional and Ethnographic
Perspectives.  Studies in Third World Society.  23:111-38,
1983.

Taggart, J.  'Ideal' and 'Real' Behavior in the Mesoamerican
Nonresidential Extended Family.  American Ethnologist.
2:347-57, 1975.

Velez, C.  Youth and Aging in Central Mexico:  One Day in the
Life of Four Families of Migrants.  Pp. 107-62 in B.
Myerhoff and A. Simic (eds).  Life's Career--Aging:
Cultural Variations on Growing Old.  Beverly Hills, CA:
Sage, 1978.

Vogt, E.  The Zinacantecos of Mexico:  A Modern Way of Life.
New York, NY:  Holt, Rinehart and Winston, 1970.

## OTHER PEASANTS/AGRARIAN PEOPLES

Benet, S.  Abkhasians:  The Long-Living People of the
   Caucasus.  New York, NY:  Holt, Rinehart and Winston, 1974.

Fel, E. and T. Hofer.  Proper Peasants:  Traditional Life in a
   Hungarian Village.  Chicago, IL:  Aldine, 1969.

Groger, L.  Peasants and Policy:  Comparative Perspectives on
   Aging.  In C. Stack and R. Hall (eds).  Holding on to the
   Land and the Lord.  Southern Anthropological Society
   Proceedings 15.  Athens, GA:  University of Georgia Press,
   1982.

Gutmann, D.  Alternatives to Disengagement:  The Old Man of
   the Highland Druze.  Pp. 232-45 in R. LeVine (ed).
   Culture and Personality:  Contemporary Readings.  Chicago,
   IL:  Aldine, 1974.

Halpern, J. M. and B. Kerewsky-Halpern.  A Serbian Village in
   Historical Perspective.  Prospect Heights, IL:  Waveland
   Press, 1986.

Harrell, S.  Growing Old in Rural Taiwan.  Pp. 193-210 in P.
   Amoss and S. Harrell (eds).  Other Ways of Growing
   Old--Anthropological Perspectives.  Stanford, CA:  Stanford
   University Press, 1981.

Lansing, J. S.  Cycles of Time.  Parabola.  5(1):34-37, 1980.


## PEOPLE OF ANTIQUITY

Ben-Sassoon, H.  Old Age in the Jewish Structure of the Ages
   of Man.  Gerontology.  1(4):4-8, 1975.

Chang, G.  The Village Elder System of the Early Ming Dynasty.
   Ming Studies.  7:53-62, 1978.

   The early Ming Dynasty (late 14th century) granted those
   over fifty significant controls over village life, taking
   away judicial powers from local officials.  The village
   elderly system had four main functions:  first, to handle
   judicial cases such as marriage, land disputes, adultery,
   robbery, and homicide; second, to oversee agriculture by
   supervising farming, managing irrigation ditches, and
   operating granaries; third, to maintain local peace by
   organizing village police to arrest local villains,
   drafting replacements for the military, watching the
   performance of local officials and arresting corrupt
   officials; and fourth, but foremost, to instill state
   ideology in the minds of the populace by supervising
   community schools, maintaining local religious temples and
   shrines, assisting the needy, and recognizing exemplary
   filial conduct.

Haynes, M.  The Supposedly Golden Age for the Aged in Ancient
   Greece.  A Study of Literary Concepts of Old Age.

Gerontologist.  2:93-98, 1962.

In The Republic, Plato joined Homer and the succeeding long line of famous men in Greek literature in describing the life of aging men and women as they wished to be:  wise, attractive to the younger generation, honored, and held in high esteem.  But in Laws, Plato revealed in a highly realistic manner a profound concern with the miseries many old people suffered in ancient Greece.  This latter brought him very close to Aristotle's view that old age was not a golden age but a time of physical and mental decay requiring laws to protect the aged from filial abuses.

_____  The Supposedly Golden Age for the Aged in Ancient Rome. Gerontologist.  3:26-35, 1963.

Roman writers on the predominant concepts of old age first reveal that in general, old age was felt to be a burdensome stage rather than a blessing, for it brought not only the loss of health but also, very often, a weakening of man's mental powers.  These writers further inform us of the extraordinary show of reverence the aged in Rome enjoyed because their position of "paterfamilias" necessitated reverence from the young since they held the strings of the money purse until their last breath.  Despite the generally negative view, a small upper class of elite old men lived a comfortable, pleasant life in villas surrounded by servants and friends.  If life became too wearisome, suicide was considered an admirable end though natural death was preferred.

Petersen, M. and C. L. Rose.  Historical Antecedents of Normative vs.  Pathological Perspectives in Aging.  Journal of the American Geriatrics Society.  39(4):289-94, 1982.

Concepts of aging, traced through selected writings from ancient China, India, Egypt, Greece and modern times, are described and analyzed in terms of the weight they give to "normal" vs. "pathological" causes of the process.

Piovesana, G.  The Aged in Chinese and Japanese Cultures.  Pp. 14-25 in Aging:  Its Challenge to the Individual and Society.  New York, NY:  Fordham University Press, 1974.

Japanese Confucianists cultivated filial piety as much as their Chinese colleagues.  Chinese and Japanese societies were, however, quite different, which explains why filial piety took different forms.  Differences considered include aging and Confucianism, ancestor worship and aging, the Confucian tradition in Japan, and aging and family in Chinese and Japanese societies.

Spector, S.  Old Age and the Sages.  International Journal of Aging and Human Development.  4(3):199-209, 1973.

In Jewish law, concepts and definitions of old age and the problems of the status of the aged and death are considered in the Talmud.  Both positive and negative images are

reviewed as well as prescriptions for attaining old age and
deriving satisfactions from long life.  Many of the
psychological insights from Talmudic times remain fresh and
meaningful for contemporary life.

Suolahti, J.  The Attitude of People in Antiquity Towards Old
    Age.  Gerontologist.  19:19-18, 1969-1970.

# 5

# National Cultures

**GENERAL COMPARISON**

Ageing International.

   This journal is published four times a year in English and
   Spanish by the International Federation on Ageing.  It
   features reports on international trends and policy and
   program innovations.

Amann, A.  Open Care for the Elderly in Seven European
   Countries:  A Pilot Study in the Possibilities and Limits
   of Care.  Oxford, UK:  Pergamon, 1980.

_____  The Status and Prospects of the Aging in Western
   Europe.  Eurosocial.  Occasional Papers No. 8, 1981.

_____  Social Gerontology Research in European Countries:
   History and Current Trends.  West Berlin, Germany and
   Vienna, Austria:  German Center of Gerontology and Ludwig-
   Boltzman Institute of Social Gerontology, 1984.

Binstock, R. H.  Drawing Cross-Cultural "Implications for
   Policy":  Some Caveats.  Journal of Cross-Cultural
   Gerontology.  1(4):331-38, 1986.

Binstock, R. H., W-S. Chow, and J. H. Schulz (eds).
   International Perspectives on Aging:  Population and Policy
   Challenges.  New York, NY:  United Nations Fund for
   Population Activities, 1982.

   This collection of papers was prepared for the World
   Assembly on Aging held in 1982 and reexamines and compares
   data from developed and developing countries:  aging of
   populations, challenges for health policy and planning,
   environments and living arrangements, employment, family
   and social networks, income, and issues of social service
   policy.

Blakemore, K.  Ageing in the Inner City--A Comparison of Old
   Black and Whites.  Pp. 81-102 in D. Jerrome, ed.  Ageing in

Modern Society. London, UK:  Croom Helm, 1983.

Deaton, R. L.  The Political Economy of Pensions:  Power,
    Politics and Social Change in Canada, Britain and the
    United States. Vancouver, British Columbia:  University of
    British Columbia Press, 1989.

Diessenbacher, H.  The Generation Contract, Pension Schemes,
    Birth Control and Economic Growth:  A European Model for
    the Third World? Journal of Cross-Cultural Gerontology.
    4(4):357-76, 1989.

Friis, H.  Living Conditions of the Aged in Three Industrial
    Societies. Bulletin of the International Social Security
    Association. July-August:277-85, 1966.

Ginzberg, E.  The Elderly :  An International Policy
    Perspective. Milbank Memorial Fund Quarterly:  Health and
    Society. 61(3):473-88, 1983.

    The author surveys problems (slow economic growth, high
    inflation, high unemployment) faced by people 60 and older
    in advanced industrial and less-developed countries.

Havighurst, R.  Ageing in Western Society. Pp. 15-44 in D.
    Hobman (ed).  The Social Challenge of Ageing. London, UK:
    Croom Helms, 1973.

Hawkins, C. H.  Residents' Power in Retirement Homes.  Special
    Issue.  The Retirement Community Movement:  Contemporary
    Issues.  Journal of Housing for the Elderly.  5(2):51-63,
    1989.

Hoover, S. L. and J. B. Siegel.  International Demographic
    Trends and Perspectives on Aging. Journal of Cross-
    Cultural Gerontology. 1:5-30, 1986.

    In the year 2000, there will be 600 million persons aged 60
    and over in the world.  Sixty percent of these will be in
    the lesser-developed nations.  The authors discuss the far-
    reaching consequences of this fact, including national
    resources and health consequences.

Keith, J., C. L. Fry, and C. Ikels.  Community as Context for
    Successful Aging. Pp. 245-61 in J. Sokolovsky (ed).  The
    Cultural Context Of Aging:  Worldwide Perspectives.
    Westport, CT:  Bergin and Garvey, 1990.

    Analyzes the bases for subjective well-being in three
    sites:  Hong Kong; Momence, Illinois; and Swarthmore,
    Pennsylvania.  Based on fieldwork carried out over a one-
    year period in each site.

Kleiman, M. B.  Social Gerontology. Interdisciplinary Topics
    in Gerontology. Vol 17.  Basel, Switzerland:  Karger,
    1983.

    This volume focuses on behavioral and social-psychological

aspects of aging, housing and environmental design, service
provision and support systems, aging and the political
system, and theoretical and methodological issues.

Lee, R. D., W. B. Arthur, and G. Rodgers. Economics of
Changing Age Distribution in Developed Countries. Oxford,
UK: Clarendon Press, 1985.

Manton, K. G., J. E. Dowd, and M. A. Woodbury. Conceptual and
Measurement Issues in Assessing Disability Cross-
Nationally: Analysis of a WHO-Sponsored Survey of the
Disablement Process in Indonesia. Journal of Cross-
Cultural Gerontology. 1:339-62, 1986.

Manton, K. G., G. C. Myers, and G. R. Andrews. Morbidity and
Disability Patterns in Four Developing Nations: Their
Implications for Social and Economic Integration of the
Elderly. Journal of Cross-Cultural Gerontology. 2:115-30,
1987.

A discussion of comparative aspects of chronic morbidity
and disability in Korea, the Philippines, Malaysia, and
Fiji.

Morgan, J. H. Aging in Developing Societies: A Reader in
Third World Gerontology. 2 vols. Bristol, IN: Wyndham
Hall Press, 1985.

Mullins, L. C. and R. D. Tucker (eds). Snowbirds in the
Sunbelt: Older Canadians in Florida. Tampa, FL:
International Exchange Center on Gerontology, 1988.

Myers, G. Cross-National Trends in Mortality Rates Among the
Elderly. Gerontologist. 18(5):441-8, 1978.

Nissinen, A., et al. Comparison of Health Status Between
Portuguese and Finnish Elderly People. Journal of Cross-
Cultural Gerontology. 2(3):277-92, 1987.

Noin, D. and Warnes, A. M. (eds). The Geography of Ageing in
Great Britain and France. Proceedings of a Franco-British
Symposium, July, 1986. Special Issue. Espaces,
Populations et Societes. 1987.

Twenty papers from French and British demographers and
geographers dealing with the process of demographic ageing,
migration and residential mobility, innovations in health
and social service distributions and the changing household
arrangements of elderly people.

Nugent, J. B. Old Age Security and the Defense of Social
Norms. Journal of Cross-Cultural Gerontology.
5(3):243-54, 1990.

Nusberg, C. The Situation in Western Industrialized
Countries. Pp. 23-50 in C. Nusberg and M. Osako (eds).
The Situation of the Asian/Pacific Elderly. Washington,
DC: International Federation on Ageing, 1981.

Nusberg, C., M. J. Gibson, and S. Peace. Innovative Aging Programs Abroad: Implications for the US. Westport, CT: Greenwood Press, 1984.

Eleven chapters on program and policy issues in thirty nations, including mostly the industrialized West, but also China and eastern Europe. No developing nations are included.

Nusberg, C. and M. Osako (eds). The Situation of the Asian/Pacific Elderly. Washington, DC: International Federation on Ageing, 1981.

This volume contains papers from two symposia which focused on the changing role of family and government in providing for Asian/Pacific elderly. "Economic Security for the Elderly in Hard Times" addressed the issue of economic constraints; "Cultural, Economic, Political Factors and Social Policy for the Aged in China, Japan, and India" examined the effects of modernization on public policies for the aged.

Oriol, W. E. Aging in All Nations: A Special Report on the UN World Assembly on Aging. Washington, DC: National Council on Aging, 1982.

Osako, O. Increase of Elderly Poor in Developing Nations: The Implications of Dependency Theory and Modernization Theory for the Aging of the World Population. Special Issue on Aging and the Aged in the Third World. Studies in Third World Societies. 22:85-114, 1982.

Paillat, P. Europe is Ageing: Causes, Aspects, and Repercussions of Demographic Ageing. International Social Security Review. 29:152-66, 1976.

Palmore, E. Cross-Cultural Perspectives on Widowhood. Journal of Cross-Cultural Gerontology. 2:93-106, 1987.

No matter here that the author means cross-national and not cross-cultural, this important paper presents comparative statistics on the occurrence of later-life widowhood in several dozen nations, and focuses on several structural problems (remarriage, widow inheritance, economic solvency and living arrangements) as options in different societies.

Peterson, C. Middle Age in Urban Australia and an Israeli Kibbutz. Journal of Social Psuchology. 127(4):405-06, 1987.

Rathbone-McCuan, E. and B. Havens (eds). North American Elders: United States and Canadian Perspectives. New York, NY: Greenwood Press, 1988.

Salmon, D. P., et al. Cross-Cultural Studies of Dementia: A Comparison of Mini-Mental State Examination Performance in Finland and China. Archives of Neurology. 46(7):769-72, 1989.

Savishinsky, J. and H. Wimberley.  The Living and the Dead:  A
    Cross-Cultural Perspective on Jewish Memorial Observances.
    Jewish Social Studies.  36(4):304-23, 1974.

    Compares attitudes towards death and mourning among
    Japanese and East European Jews:  special attention is
    given to the impact of ancestral images, family dynamics,
    and parental roles on how younger generations deal with the
    death of elders.

Selby, P., et al.  Aging 2000:  A Challenge for Society.
    Boston, MA:  MTP Press, 1982.

    An international survey identifies problems of elderly in
    sixteen countries, examines measures for dealing with
    problems and suggests ideas for the future.

Teski, M.  What Can the Industrialized World Teach the Third
    World About Aging?  Aging and the Aged in Third World
    Societies.  Part 1.  Studies in Third World Societies.
    22:23-42, 1982.

Thomae, H. and G. L. Maddox (eds).  New Perspectives on Old
    Age:  A Message to Decision Makers.  New York, NY:
    Springer, 1982.

    Directed to United Nations member countries, this message
    prepared on behalf of the International Association of
    Gerontology outlines policy for the 1980s and beyond;
    discusses issues in health care, in biological science and
    the behavioral and social science research.

Thomas, L. E. and K. O. Chambers.  Phenomenology of Life
    Satisfaction Among Elderly Men:  Quantitative and
    Qualitative Views.  Psychology and Aging.  4(3):284-89,
    1989.

Tien-Hyatt, J. L.  Self-Perceptions of Aging Across Cultures:
    Myth or Reality?  International Journal of Aging and Human
    Development.  24(2):129-48,1986-1987.

Tout, K.  Ageing in Developing Countries.  Oxford:  Oxford
    University Press, 1989.

United Nations.  Aging in Slums and Uncontrolled Settlements.
    Department of Economic and Social Affairs.  New York, NY:
    United Nations, 1977.

_____  The World Aging Situation:  Strategies and Policies.
    Department of International Economic and Social Affairs.
    New York, NY:  United Nations, 1985.

Warnes, A. M (ed).  Geographical Perspectives on the Elderly.
    Chichester, UK:  Wiley, 1982.

    A collection of original papers dealing with the
    distribution, migration, housing, mobility and activity
    patterns of elderly people in Britain (with some papers on

France and the United States).

Woolfson, P.  Non-Verbal Interaction of Anglo-Canadian,
    Jewish-Canadian, and French-Canadian Physicians with Their
    Young, Middle-Aged, and Elderly Patients.  Visual
    Anthropology.  1:401-14, 1988.

    The study investigates the role of non-verbal communication
    in the interaction (establishing and maintaining rapport)
    between physicians and their patients.

Young, M. and H. Geertz.  Old Age in London and San Francisco:
    Some Families Compared.  British Journal of Sociology.
    12:124-41, 1961.


## CHINA, TAIWAN, HONG KONG AND SINGAPORE

Ahern, E.  The Cult of the Dead in a Chinese Village.
    Stanford, CA:  Stanford University Press, 1973.

    Describes and analyzes the variations in the practice of
    ancestor worship in a Taiwan community.

Aimei, J.  New Experiments with Elderly Care in Rural China.
    Journal of Cross-Cultural Gerontology.  3(2):139-48, 1988.

Baker, H. D. R.  Chinese Family and Kinship.  London, UK:
    Macmillan, 1979.

Brower, H. T.  A Look at China's Eldercare.  Geriatric
    Nursing.  5(6):250-53, 1984.

    Short article describing mortality and morbidity patterns
    as well as availability of beds and health care workers.

Chan, K. B.  Coping with Aging and Managing Self-Identity:
    The Social World of the Elderly Chinese Woman.  Canadian
    Ethnic Studies.  15:36-50, 1983.

Chandler, A.  The Traditional Chinese Attitude Towards Old
    Age.  Journal of Gerontology.  5:239-44, 1950.

Chang, J. L. H.  Reflections from the Field:  Community
    Services for the Aged in Taipei.  Social Development
    Issues.  10(2):84-88, 1986.

    Extended life expectancy and increasing urbanization and
    industrializaton have reduced traditional family support of
    the elderly in Taipei, Taiwan.  Over the last 20 years the
    Taipei City Government and the Taiwan government have
    responded to this decline with increased community, medical
    and housing services for the elderly.  Author argues for an
    integrated welfare service system to strengthen programs
    with a greater variety of specialized services and more
    volunteer involvement.

Chang, R. H. and R. A. Dodder.  The Modified Purpose in Life

Scale:  A Cross-National Validity Study.  International Journal of Aging and Human Development.  18(3)207-17, 1984.

Analyzes the utility of a modified version of the twenty-item Purpose-in-Life Test as an alternative measure for comparing the psychological well-being of the elderly cross-nationally.  The sample consisted of 17 retired teachers in Oklahoma and 202 retired teachers in Taipei, Taiwan.

Chen, A. J. and P. Cheung.  The Elderly in Singapore.  ASEAN Populatin Project, Singapore, 1988.

Chen, T. H. E. and W. C. Chen.  Changing Attitudes Towards Parents In Communist China.  Sociology and Social Research. 43:175-82, 1959.

Describes the Communist Party attempt to break the authority of the older generation over the younger while at the same time insisting that young people could not use this break as a justification for neglecting their elders.

Chen, X.  The One-Child Population Policy, Modernization, and the Extended Chinese Family.  Journal of Marriage and the Family.  47(1):193-202, 1985.

Considers the impact of the one-child policy, restrictions on mobility, cohort differences in wage-earning potential, and a housing shortage on intergenerational aid flows within the Chinese family.

Cherry, R. and S. Magnuson-Martinson.  Modernization and the Status of the Aged in China:  Decline or Equalization?  The Sociological Quarterly.  22(2):253-61, 1981.

Discusses the limitations of modernization theory in explaining the changed status of the elderly in China. Argues that government policies explicitly aimed at reducing age inqualities interact with changes in levels of education and the demographic transition to alter the age stratification system.

Cheung, F. C. H.  Implications of the One-Child Family Policy on the Development of the Welfare State in the People's Republic of China.  Journal of Sociology and Social Welfare.  15(1):5-25, 1988.

Based on demographic trends, the author argues that families will face additional responsibilities as they continue to be the primary sources of care for the elderly. Recommends that the Chinese government develop a universal social security system and improve occupational welfare, child care, health services, and higher education in the near future in order to achieve the goals of modernization as well as population control.

Chow, N.  The Hong Kong Situation.  Pp. 5-8 in C. Nusberg and M. Osako (eds).  The Situation of the Asian/Pacific

Elderly. Washington, DC:  International Federation on Ageing, 1981.

_____ The Chinese Family and Support of the Elderly in Hong Kong. Gerontologist. 23:584-88, 1983.

_____ The Administration and Financing of Social Security in China. Hong Kong:  University of Hong Kong, 1988.

The best comprehensive review of social security policies in China. Explains regulations and coverage of workers, retirees, and dependents. Relates the proposals to revamp regulations in the context of the economic reforms of the mid-1980s.

Cowart, M. E. and G. F. Streib. Taiwan and Its Elderly:  Taxi Nurses and Home Care. Journal of Applied Gerontology. 6(2):156-62, 1987.

This health care service has some of the features of home care services in the United States, but also has developed some qualities that make it unique to the local culture. While services provided and the role of the nurse are similar, payment mechanisms and transportation differ.

Davis, D. Chinese Social Welfare:  Policies and Outcomes. The China Quarterly. 119:577-97, 1989.

This article addresses the apparent contradiction of increasing welfare inequality during years of declining income inequality, arguing that the negative impact of decollectivization on social welfare programs is the logical outcome of  (1)  specific principles behind Chinese welfare policies since 1950 and  (2) a generally disadvantaged position for all welfare organizations in centrally planned economies.

Davis-Friedmann, D. Strategies for Aging:  Interdependence between Generations in the Transition to Socialism. Contemporary China in Developmental, Comparative and Global Perspective. 1(6):35-42, 1977.

_____ Welfare Practices in Rural China. World Development. 6:609-19, 1978.

_____ Retirement and Social Welfare Programs for Chinese Elderly:  A Minimal Role for the State. Pp. 52-65 in C. Nusberg and M. Osako (eds). The Situation of the Asian/Pacific Elderly. Washington, DC:  International Federation on Ageing, 1981.

_____ Long Lives:  Chinese Elderly and the Communist Revolution. Cambridge, MA:  Harvard University Press, 1983.

Drawing on news reports and literature published by the Chinese government between 1949 and 1982, interviews with emigrants from China to Hong Kong in 1976, and interviews with Chinese citizens in the People's Republic of China in 1979, Davis-Friedmann analyses the impact of Chinese Communist Party policies on the circumstances of the elderly.  Attitudes towards the elderly, work and retirement, living arrangements, relations with children, funerals and filial piety, intergenerational conflict and the childless elderly are examined.

_____ Granny Cheung.  Pp. 71-75 in Mary Sheridan and Janet Salaff (eds).  Lives:  Chinese Working Women.  Bloomington, IN:  Indiana University Press, 1984.

_____ Chinese Retirement:  Policy and Practice.  Pp. 295-313 in Z. Blau (ed).  Current Perspectives on Aging and the Life Cycle.  Greenwich, CT:  JAI Press, 1985a.

_____ Intergenerational Inequalities and the Chinese Revolution.  Modern China.  11(2):177-201, 1985b.

The primary hypothesis of this article is that the fundamental explanation for the existence of age-related inequalities in China lies not in any particular policies to favor one age group over another but in a fundamental structural characteristic of the post-1949 Party-state to rely on bureaucratic procedures to allocate jobs, wages, salary increments and fringe benefits.

_____ Old Age Security and the One-Child Campaign.  Pp. 149-61 in E. Croll, D. Davin, and P. Kane (eds).  China's One-Child Family Policy.  New York, NY:  St. Martin's Press, 1985c.

Analyzes the differential acceptance of the One-Child family campaign by China's rural and urban populations. Points out the likely consequences of the one-child option and the fact that recent economic reforms provide incentives for larger family size.

Dixon, J.  The Aged.  Pp. 247-63 in The Chinese Welfare System 1949-1979.  New York, NY: Praeger, 1981.

Reviews changes over a thirty-year period in the forms of welfare and retirement benefits available to the elderly. Appendix includes various reforms to the Labor Insurance regulations.

Gallin, R. S.  Mothers-in-law and Daughters-in-law: Intergenerational Relations within the Chinese Family in Taiwan.  Journal of Cross-Cultural Gerontology.  1:31-49, 1986.

Using ethnographic data, this paper explores the proposition that the position of old people is a function of a "cost/contribution" balance compounded by resources controlled.

Ganschow, T.  The Aged in a Revolutionary Milieu:  China.  Pp. 305-20 in S. Spicker, K. Woodward, and D. van Tassel (eds).

Aging and the Elderly:  Humanistic Perspectives in
Gerontology.  Atlantic Highlands, NJ:  Humanities Press,
1978.

Goldstein, A. and S. Goldstein.  The Challenge of an Aging
Population:  The Case of the People's Republic of China.
Research on Aging.  8(2):179-99, 1986.

Explores the changes in the magnitude of the aged
population and then discusses current policies, e.g., the
One-Child Family policy, assignment of jobs, the new
economic responsibility system, the retirement and pension
systems, that affect the elderly and their implications for
the future.

Goldstein, M. C., Y. Ku, and C. Ikels.  Household Composition
of the Elderly in Two Rural Villages in the People's
Republic of China.  Journal of Cross-Cultural Gerontology.
5(2):119-30, 1990.

Considers three forms of household composition:  one
generation, multigeneration, and "by-turns" households.
By-turns households include several subtypes but have in
common the fact that the elder neither lives alone nor
lives with others, but rotates among the households of
descendants.

Grigsby, J. S. and S. J. Olshansky.  The Demographic Component
of Population Aging in China.  Journal of Cross-Cultural
Gerontology.  4(4):307-34, 1989.

The authors examine meeasures of population aging in China
from 1953 to 1982 and project population aging to the year
2050 using a cohort-component methodology.  The analysis
provides a demographic basis for evaluating the possible
effects of population aging on health care, social
security, and other social and economic issues.

Gui, S-X.  A Report from Mainland China:  Status and Needs of
Rural Elderly in the Suburbs of Shanghai.  Journal of
Cross-Cultural Gerontology.  3(2):149-67, 1988.

A 1986 survey of 1581 respondents 60 years or older living
in 9 counties at varying distances from Shangahi.  Focuses
on income and health issues.

Gui, S-X., et al.  Status and Needs of the Elderly in Urban
Shanghai:  Analysis of Some Preliminary Statistics.
Journal of Cross-Cultural Gerontology.  2(2):171-86, 1987.

Describes the results of a 1985 four-per-1000 sample survey
of males age 55 and older and females age 50 and older in
the urban areas of Shanghai.  Living arrangements,
employment, economic status, ability to manage daily
routines, and life satisfaction are among the topics
covered.

Harrell, S.  Growing Old in Rural Taiwan.  Pp. 193-210 in P.

Amoss and S. Harrell (eds). Other Ways of Growing Old: Anthropological Perspectives. Stanford, CA: Stanford University Press, 1981.

Based on ten months of fieldwork in a rural community, the author examines gender differences in the experience of aging (women improve their position relative to men as they age). Although the elderly are shown respect and deference, they nevertheless appear to have very little real power in the family.

Hsu, F. L. K. Under the Ancestors' Shadow. Reprint. Stanford, CA: Stanford University Press, 1971.

This study is based on fieldwork during the Second World War in Yunnan Province. The author uses a psychological framework to interpret the significance of ancestors in the daily lives of their descendants.

Hu, R., L. Wang, and Y. Zhang. The Roles of the Chinese Urban Elderly in Social Development: Direct and Indirect Participation. Pp. 271-80 in J. Schulz and D. Davis-Friedmann (eds). Aging China: Family, Economics and Government Policies in Transition. Washington, DC: The Gerontological Society of America, 1987.

Looks at the factors facilitating or hindering the participation of the elderly in social development and at how the changing nature of the elderly population will lead to different kinds of participation in the future.

Ikels, C. Old Age in Hong Kong. Gerontologist. 15:230-35, 1975.

Describes the backgrounds and characteristics of the minority of elderly who inhabit homes for the aged in Hong Kong. The residents are largely those without any children (or without any children in Hong Kong) who lived alone, with more distant relatives, or with employers before entering the homes for the aged.

_____ The Coming of Age in Chinese Society: Traditional Patterns and Contemporary Hong Kong. Pp. 80-100 in C. Fry (ed). Aging in Culture and Society: Comparative Viewpoints and Strategies. Brooklyn, NY: J. F. Bergin, 1980.

_____ Aging and Adaptation: Chinese in Hong Kong and the United States. Hamden, CT: Archon Books, 1983.

Reviews the historical and cultural antecedents which shaped the expectations of Chinese elders for their later years. Through interviews and participant observation carried out over a two-year period in both Hong Kong and the United States, the author describes and analyzes the diverse strategies the elderly have created in order to find security in old age.

_____ Becoming a Human Being in Theory and in Practice:
Chinese Views of Human Development. Pp. 109-34 in D.
Kertzer and K. Warner Schaie (eds). Social Structure and
Aging: Comparative Perspectives on Age Structuring in
Modern Societies. Hillsdale, NJ: Erlbaum, 1989.

A 1983 study of the views of 204 Hong Kong residents (aged
from 18 to the mid-80s) from four neighborhoods on the
characteristics of the adult life course. Relates these
views to the traditional Confucian ethos and to
contemporary views of human development in the People's
Republic of China.

_____ Family Caregivers and the Elderly in China. Pp. 270-84
in D. E. Biegal and A. Blum (eds). Aging and Caregiving:
Theory, Research, and Policy. Newbury Park, CA: Sage,
1990a.

Looks at structural factors promoting the availability of
family members to provide care for the elderly. Compares
the commune period with the post-commune period as well as
urban and rural settings during both periods.

_____ The Resolution of Intergenerational Conflict:
Perspectives of Elders and Their Family Members. Modern
China. 16(4):379-406, 1990b.

Jia, A. New Experiments with Elderly Care in Rural China.
Journal of Cross-Cultural Gerontology. 3(2):139-48, 1988.

Describes the reasons behind the development of social
security programs for the rural elderly and the regulations
of the programs in a particular locality which implemented
its program in 1987.

Kwan, A. Y. H. Caregiving Among Middle and Low Income Aged in
Hong Kong. Tampa, FL: International Exchange Center on
Gerontology, 1988a.

_____ Suicide Among the Elderly: Hong Kong. Journal of
Applied Gerontology. 7(2):248-59, 1988b.

Reports on the sociodemographic aspects of elderly suicides
in Hong Kong from 1983 to 1986 based on analysis of 385
cases reported in a major Chinese newspaper, the Oriental
Daily News. Recommendations for intervention and
prevention are offered.

Lee, S. M. Dimensions of Aging in Singapore. Journal of
Cross-Cultural Gerontology 1(3):239-54, 1986.

Describes some of the major findings of research on the
elderly population in Singapore (the vast majority of which
is of Chinese ancestry), discusses the role of political
authorities in defining and shaping the problems of aging
in the country, and identifies the implications that the
Singapore case may hold for further cross-cultural research
on aging.

Lewis, M.  Aging in the People's Republic of China.
    International Journal of Aging and Human Development.
    15(2):79-105, 1982.

    General description of life of old people in China as it
    was circa 1980, i.e., before the impact of the post-1978
    reforms and dismantling of the commune system.  Topics
    covered include:  retirement, community life, daily life
    and health care.

Liang, J., E. J.-C. Tu, and X. Chen.  Population Aging in the
    People's Republic of China.  Social Science and Medicine.
    23(12):1353-62, 1986.

    This paper provides a factual assessment of China's
    population aging and its social and economic consequences.
    Major policy implications concerning old age support and
    health care are examined.

Liu, B. and H. Li.  General Situation and Features of
    Geriatric Epidemiologic Study in China.  Chinese Medical
    Journal.  99(8):619-27, 1986.

    Describes mortality from and prevalence rates of various
    common diseases of the elderly in different parts of the
    country.  Pinpoints areas with high numbers of centenarians
    and attempts to account for their longevity.

Liu, L.  Mandatory Retirement and Other Reforms Pose New
    Challenges for China's Government.  Aging and Work.
    5:119-33, 1982.

    An excellent review of retirement and pension policies in
    the first years under the new economic reforms.  Points out
    that the policies were developed at a time when the number
    of retirees was small, but that the state now faces an
    enormous economic responsibility for large numbers of
    retirees.

Martin, L. G.  The Aging of Asia.  Journal of Gerontology:
    Social Sciences.  43(4):S99-113, 1988.

    This article reviews some of the demographic
    characteristics of population aging and the elderly
    population in 14 Asian countries, including China, Hong
    Kong and Singapore.  It also focuses on current programs
    for the elderly in Asia and discusses three general issues
    of importance in the development of aging policies:  (a)
    to what extent should the West be used as a model;  (b)
    what should be the role of the family versus the government
    in caring for elderly people who cannot care for
    themsleves, and  (c)  should the eligibility for programs
    be based on age or need?

Mok, B-H.  Social Welfare in China in an Era of Economic
    Reform.  International Social Work.  30:237-50, 1987.

    Discusses the impact of the economic reforms on three

populations:  the poor, the disabled, and the elderly.  The
paper looks at the issue from a policy perspective; it is
not an empirical work.

Morrisey, S.  Attitudes on Aging in China.  Journal of
    Gerontological Nursing.  9(11):589-93, 1983.

    Based on a three-week visit to China, the author describes
    the health care, housing and retirement pensions for the
    elderly.

Olson, P.  A Model of Eldercare in the People's Republic of
    China.  International Journal of Aging and Human
    Development.  24(4):279-300, 1987.

    Describes a wide range of programs for the elderly that
    have developed in the wake of the post-1978 economic
    reforms.  Analysis reveals that the future of the elderly
    in the PRC will be greatly influenced by the nature of the
    political economy which the author views as the critical
    variable in mediating the impact of modernization on the
    elderly.

_____  Modernization in the People's Republic of China:    The
    Politicization of the Elderly.  Sociological Quarterly.
    29(2):241-62, 1988.

    Applies a model of bureaucratic politics to explain both
    increases and decreases in the elderly's economic and
    social status that occur with modernization.  Documents an
    increased concern with the elderly in terms of policies,
    publications, programs devoted to their retirement pensions
    and medical care, housing, and special educational and
    social activities.

_____  The Elderly in the People's Republic of China.  Pp.
    143-61 in J. Sokolovsky (ed).  The Cultural Context of
    Aging:  Worldwide Perspectives.  Westport, CT:    Bergin and
    Garvey, 1990.

    Describes the situation of the elderly in the context of
    modernization theory and the post-1978 economic reforms.
    Argues that the state and its agenda are often missing
    variables in modernization theory, and that in a highly
    centralized state such as China, the state policy plays a
    crucial role in affecting the status of the elderly.

Parish, W. L. and M. K. Whyte.  Village and Family in
    Contemporary China.  Chicago, IL:  University of Chicago
    Press, 1978.

Phillips, D. R.  Accommodation for Elderly Persons in Newly
    Industrializing Countries:  The Hong Kong Experience.
    International Journal of Health Services.  18(2):255-79,
    1988.

    A review of public and private housing types especially for
    the elderly as they have developed over the past few

decades in Hong Kong.  Discusses the shift from shelter for the well elderly to housing with a health care orientation.

Prybyla, J.  Growing Old in China.  Current History. 71:56-59, 80, 1976.

Sando, R.  Doing the Work of Two Generations:  The Impact of Out-Migration on the Elderly in Rural Taiwan.  Journal of Cross-Cultural Gerontology.  1:163-75, 1986.

Describes the role of the elderly in actively promoting out-migration of the young which then necessitates their own adaptation to the consequent depopulation of the community.

Sankar, A.  The Conquest of Solitude:  Singlehood and Old Age in Traditional Chinese Society.  Pp. 65-83 in C. Fry (ed). Dimensions:  Aging, Culture and Health.  South Hadley, MA: J. F.  Bergin, 1981.

The focus is on single Chinese adults (especially women) in the traditional (pre-revolutionary) context.  The exigencies of dependency are covered, as are the difficulties in dealing with the contraints of a society where the failure to produce heirs was considered an affront to one's ancestors.  Comparisons are offered with the problems that confronted childless couples.  Of particular interest is the section on the spinsters of Kwangtung, followed by a discussion of "secular sisterhoods."

_____ Gerontological Research in China:  The Role of Anthropological Inquiry.  Journal of Cross-Cultural Gerontology.  4(3):199-224, 1989.

This paper provides an overview of recent research findings primarily by Western scholars and of ethnographic research in progress in the areas of demography, state policy, age stratification, family planning, residence patterns, intergenerational transfers, patrilineality, health, illness, long-term care, social welfare, and mortuary ritual.

Schulz, J. and D. Davis-Friedmann (eds).  Aging China: Family, Economics, and Government Policies in Transition. Washington, DC:  The Gerontological Society of America, 1987.

This 330-page volume contains the proceedings of the International Forum on Aging held in Beijing, China, May 20-23, 1986.  Papers from Chinese authors are organized around three themes:  "Population Aging in China and Its Impact," "Economic and Social Development in China:  The Role of the Aged," and "Health and the Aged in China." Papers from American authors focus on "Patterns of Support in Other Countries" and "The Role of Government Programs."

Sheppard, H. L. and G. F. Streib.  Aging in China.  Tampa, FL:

International Exchange Center on Gerontology, 1985.

General impressions gathered in an eighteen-day visit to the PRC by a team of epidemiologists and gerontologists.

Sher, A. E. Aging in Post-Mao China: The Politics of Veneration. Boulder, CO: Westview, 1984.

Deals with the quality of life of the elderly in Shenyang, an industrial city in northeast China with a high proportion of state workers (and well-developed retirement programs). Based largely on interviews arranged by the Chinese for the author as well as on informal interviews and essays derived from younger people attending English-language classes in Shenyang.

Streib, G. P. Old Age in Socio-Cultural Context: China and the United States. Journal of Aging Studies. 1(2):95-112, 1987.

Available data from a variety of social science sources are utilized to compare how the socio-cultural context of China and the United States have different impacts upon the older population in each society. Three major determinants specify the theoretical context: economic development, traditional cultural patterns, and social control mechanisms.

Su, W. (ed). From Youth to Retirement. Beijing, China: Beijing Review, 1982.

This is volume 4 in the China Today series published by Beijing Review. Of particular interest is chapter 4: Growing Older, Gaining Respect.

Tien, H. How China Treats its Old People. Asian Profile. 5:1-7, 1977.

Treas, J. Socialist Organization and Economic Development in China: Latent Consequences for the Aged. Gerontologist. 19:34-43, 1979.

Tsai, W.-H. Life After Retirement: Elderly Welfare in China. Asian Survey. 27(5):566-76, 1987.

General article based on secondary sources describing retirement life in the context of the current push to remove over-aged party and government officials from their posts.

Tu, E. J.-C., J. Liang, and S. Li. Mortality Decline and Chinese Family Structure: Implications for Old Age Support. Journal of Gerontology: Social Sciences. 44(4):S157-68, 1989.

Compares national level statistics for Taiwan and the Chinese mainland with regard to changes in family structure. Notes that major increases in life expectancy over the past 60 years have led to the doubling of the average number of person years an individual spends as a grandparent.

Ward, C.  Stereotypes of Old Persons in Singapore.  Journal of Cross-Cultural Gerontology.  3(2):95, 1988.

Wei, H.  Growth of the Aged Population in China:  Trends and Policies.  Pp. 10-18 in J. Schulz and D. Davis-Friedmann (eds).  Aging China:  Family, Economics and Government Policies in Transition.  Washington, DC:  The Gerontological Society of America, 1987.

Describes the characteristics and effects of an aging population in China and indicates the kinds of policy measures necessary to respond to it.

Wilhelm, H.  The Image of Youth and Age in Chinese Communist Literature.  The China Quarterly.  13:180-94, 1963.

Woon, Y.-F.  Growing Old in a Modernizing China.  Journal of Comparative Family Studies.  12(2):245-57, 1981.

As China puts her emphasis on the Four Modernizations Program, on her young workers and farmers and on her sent-down youth, the author sees the elderly losing their leadership roles in society and predicts that they will be pushed more and more to the task of performing supportive roles in service activities.

Wu, C.  Family Planning and Population Aging in China.  Pp. 47-56 in J. Schulz and D. Davis-Friedmann (eds).  Aging China:  Family, Economics and Government Policies in Transition.  Washington, DC:  The Gerontological Society of America, 1987.

Discusses the linkage between family planning and population aging in a new way.  Rather than focussing on the impact of the one-child family campaign, the author implicates the lack of a family planning program in the 1950s and 1960s when the drop in the death rate was not balanced by a drop in the birth rate.

Wu, C.-I., et al.  Evaluation of the Family System and Its Influence on the Mental Health of the Aged in China.  Pp. 147-56 in T.-Y. Lin and L. Eisenberg (eds).  Mental Health Planning for One Billion People:  A Chinese Perspective.  Vancouver, BC:  University of British Columbia Press, 1985.

An optimistic assessment of the role of the cultural heritage, social system and family structure in promoting the mental health of the elderly.  Data are derived from a 1980 study of depression conducted on a sample of 403 Beijing residents over the age of 65.

Wu, Y. and Q. Xu.  The Impact of an Aging Population on Socio-economic Development and Families in China.  Pp. 29-35 in J. Schulz and D. Davis-Friedmann (eds).  Aging China:

Family, Economics and Government Policies in Transition.
Washington, DC:  The Gerontological Society of America,
1987.

Describes the changing nature of the labor force, shifts in
the dependency ratio and its composition, and new
consumption needs of the elderly (i.e., more services) as
the population ages and advocates increased productivity
and material resources as the basis for dealing with these
changes.

Yang, C.  The Decline of Importance of Age.  Pp. 415-23 in W.
Liu (ed).  Chinese Society Under Communism.  New York, NY:
John Wiley, 1967.

_____    The Chinese Family:  The Young and the Old.  Pp. 306-30
in R. Coser (ed).  The Family:  Its Structures and
Functions.  New York, NY:  St. Martin's Press, 1964.

Yang, Q.  The Aging of China's Population:  Perspectives and
Implications.  Asia-Pacific Population Journal.
3(1):55-74, 1988.

Yin, P. and H. L. Kwok.  A Reconceptualization of Age
Stratification in China.  Journal of Gerontology.
38(5):608-13, 1983.

The authors argue that the most important change in the age
stratification system in China during the Maoist years was
the change in the criterion from age differences to cohort
and subcohort differences.  Furthermore, the subcohort of
elderly adults who suffered the most status decline during
the Maoist years--the bougeoisie--may actually enjoy an
increase in status with the recent modernization drive.

Yu, E. S. H., et al.  Cognitive Impairment Among Elderly
Adults in Shanghai, China.  Journal of Gerontology:  Social
Sciences.  44(3):S97-106, 1989.

This study provides prevalence rates for cognitive
impairment among more than 5,000 non-institutionalized
persons 55 years or older living in Shanghai.  The research
was carried out in 1987 and represents the first phase of a
large-scale longitudinal psychiatric epidemiologic
investigation of Alzheimer's disease and dementia.

Yuan, F.  The Status and Role of the Chinese Elderly in
Families and Society.  Pp. 36-46 in J. Schulz and D. Davis-
Friedmann (eds).  Aging China:  Family, Economics and
Government Policies in Transition.  Washington, DC:  The
Gerontological Society of America, 1987.

Describes changing living arrangements and authority
patterns within families as well as the roles elderly can
play in the community even after retirement.

Yuan, J.  The Reform of the Social Security System for the
Aged in China.  Pp. 243-51 in J. Schulz and D. Davis-

Friedmann (eds).  Aging China:  Family, Economics and Government Policies in Transition.  Washington, DC:  The Gerontological Society of America, 1987.

Discusses the impact of the unequal distribution of retirees among enterprises on the ability of these enterprises to contribute to China's modernization. Advocates a more equal distribution of the pension burden as well as maintenance of the current budgetary decentralization of services for the elderly.

Zhang, C.  Welfare Provision for the Aged in Rural China.  The Australian Journal of Chinese Affairs.  15:113-24, 1986.

A detailed breakdown of the means by which the rural childless elderly are provided the "Five (Welfare) Guarantees," the significance of old age pensions for agricultural workers, and recommendations for the future of welfare services for the aged in the countryside.

Zhang, K. and X. Chen.  Economic Development and Population Aging.  Pp. 252-63 in J. Schulz and D. Davis-Friedmann (eds).  Aging China:  Family, Economics and Government Policies in Transition.  Washington, DC:  The Gerontological Society of America, 1987.

Considers the relationship between economic development and population aging by a detailed consideration of the case of Shanghai, the metropolis with the highest proportion of the aged in all of China.

Zhu, C.  The Main Sources of Social Security for the Aged Under the New Circumstances of Rural China.  Pp. 312-15 in J. Schulz and D.  Davis-Friedmann (eds).  Aging China: Family, Economics, and Government Policies in Transition. Washington, DC:  The Gerontological Society of America, 1987.

Discusses consequences of post-1978 economic reforms with emphasis on migration of young out of villages and their unavailability to carry out their responsibilities to their parents.  Argues that as areas differ in their ability to take advantage of new opportunities it is neither possible nor desirable to offer a single prescription for the care of the rural elderly.


**JAPAN**

Ariyoshi, W.  Man in Ecstacy.  Tokyo:  Shinchosha, 1972.

Ariyoshi, W.  The Twilight Years.  Tanslated by M. Tahara. New York, NY:  Kodansha International, 1984.

Broberg, M., D. Melching, and D. Maeda.  Planning for the Elderly in Japan.  Gerontologist.  15:242-47, 1975.

Brown, T. R.  Long-Term Care for the Elderly in Kyoto, Japan.

Journal of Cross-Cultural Gerontology. 3(4):349-60, 1988.

Campbell, J. Problems, Solutions, Non-solutions, and Free Medical Care for the Elderly in Japan. Pacific Affairs. 57:53-64, 1984.

Campbell, R. Nursing Homes and Long Term Care in Japan. Pacific Affairs. 57:78-89, 1984.

Campbell, R. and E. Brody. Women's Changing Roles and Help to the Elderly: Attitudes of Women in the United States and Japan. Gerontologist. 25(6):854-92, 1985.

Caudill, W. and H. Scarr. Japanese Value Orientations and Culture Change. Ethnology. 1:53-91, 1962.

Hayashida, C. T. and H. Sasaki. The Musashino Plan: Japan's Home Equity Conversion Program for Social, Health and Financial Services. Journal of Cross-Cultural Gerontology. 1(3):255-76, 1986.

_____ Family Care in Japan. Gerontologist. 23:579-83, 1983.

Fumio, N. The Hateful Age. In Modern Japanese Stories, An Anthology. Rutland, VT: Charles Tuttle, 1962.

Hayashi, C. Time, Age and Ways of Thinking: From the Kokuminsei Surveys. Journal of Asian and African Studies. 10(1-2):75-85, 1974.

Holloway, N. Taxing Times: Japan Faces Increasing Bill for Care of Elderly. Far Eastern Economic Review. 145:85-86, 1989.

Ikegami, N. Institutionalized and the Non-Institutionalized Elderly. Social Science and Medicine. 16:2001-08, 1982.

Imamura, A. Urban Japanese Housewives: At Home and in the Community. Honolulu, Hawaii: University of Hawaii Press, 1987.

Inouye, Y. Chronicle of My Mother. Translated by J. O. Moy. New York, NY: Kodansha International, 1982.

Kiefer, C. Loneliness in Japan. In R. Audy, Y. Cohen, and J. Hartog (eds). The Anatomy of Loneliness. New York, NY: International University Press, 1980.

_____ Care of the Aged in Japan. In E. Norbeck and M. Lock (eds). Health, Illness and Medical Care in Japan. Honolulu, Hawaii: University of Hawaii Press, 1987.

_____ The Elderly in Modern Japan: Elite, Victims, or Plural Players. Pp. 181-96 in J. Sokolovsky (ed) The Cultural Context Aging: Worldwide Perspectives. Westport, CT: Bergin and Garvey, 1990.

Kii, T. Recent Extension of Retirement Age in Japan.

Gerontologist. 19:481-86, 1979.

Kii, T.  Status Changes of the Elderly in Japan's Legal, Family, and Economic Institutions.  Pp. 66-84 in C. Nusberg and M. Osako (eds).  The Situation of the Asian/Pacific Elderly.  Washington, DC:  International Federation on Ageing, 1980.

Koyama, T.  Changing Famliy Composition and the Position of the Aged in the Japanese Family.  International Journal of Comparative Sociology.  7:7-17, 1971.

Koyano, W.  Japanese Attitudes Toward the Elderly:  A Review of Research Findings.  Journal of Cross-Cultural Gerontology.  4(4):335-46, 1989.

Koyano, W., et al.  Co-Residence with Married Children and Health of the Elderly (in Japanese).  Shakai Ronengaky. 23:28-35, 1986.

Koyano, W., K. Inoue, and H. Sibata.  Negative Misconceptions About Aging in Japanese Adults.  Journal of Cross-Cultural Gerontology.  2(2):131-38, 1987.

Koyano, W., et al.  Mortality in Relation to Instrumental Activities of Daily Living:  One-Year Follow-up in a Japanese Urban Community.  Journal of Gerontology. 44:107-09, 1989.

Kumagai, F.  Satisfaction Among Rural and Urban Japanese Elderly in Three-Generation Families.  Journal of Cross-Cultural Gerontology .  2(3):225-40, 1987,

Lebra, T.  Japanese Women:  Constraint and Fulfillment. Honolulu, Hawaii:  University of Hawaii Press, 1984.

Maeda, D.  Growth of Old People's Clubs in Japan. Gerontologist.  15:254-56, 1975.

_____  Ageing in Eastern Society.  Pp. 45-72 in D. Hobman (ed).  The Social Challenge of Ageing.  London:  Croom Helm, 1978.

_____  The Japanese Situation.  Pp. 9-12 in C. Nusberg and M. Osako (eds).  The Situation of the Asian/Pacific Elderly. Washington, D.C.:  International Federation on Ageing, 1980.

_____  Family Care in Japan.  Gerontologist.  23:578-83, 1982.

Maeda, D., et al.  Ageing and Health in Japan.  Journal of Cross-Cultural Gerontology.  4(2):1989.

Maeda, N.  Health Schemes for the Aged in Japan.  Scientific Session Papers.  Tokyo:  Ninth Joint Tokyo/New York Medical Congress, 1983.

Martin, L. G.  The Graying of Japan.  Population Bulletin.

44:3-42, 1989.

Matsubara, T.  Mental Health in Diminishing Population Areas.
    Australian and New Zealand Journal of Psychiatry.
    10:111-13, 1976.

Ministry of Health and Welfare, Japan.  Health and Welfare
    Statistics in Japan.  Tokyo:  Health and Welfare Statistics
    Association, 1987.

Miyajima, S.  Combatting Elderly Disability (in Japanese).
    Kosei no Shihyo.  10:31-39, 1986.

Nakajima, K., K. Saito, and Y. Tsukihashi.  Actual Conditions
    of the Demented Elderly and Their Families.  Hokenfu
    Zasshi.  38:10-47, 1982.

Naoi, M.  Work Career and Earnings of the Young Old (in
    Japanese).  Shakai Ronengaku.  25:6-18, 1987.

Niwa, F.  The Hateful Age.  In I. Morris (ed).  Modern
    Japanese Stories:  An Anthology.  Rutland, VT:  C. T.
    Tuttle, 1962.

Noguchi, P. H.  Shiranai Station:  Not A Destination But a
    Journey.  Pp. 74-95 in D. W. Plath (ed).  Work and
    Lifecourse in Japan.  Albany, NY:  State University of New
    York Press, 1983.

Norbeck, E.  Age Grading in Japan.  American Anthropologist.
    55:373-83, 1953.

O'Brien, J. and D. Lind.  Book review of, The Honorable Elders
    by E. Palmore.  Gerontologist.  19:560-61 1936.

Okada, Y.  The Aged in Rural and Urban Japan.  Pp. 526-28 in
    C. Tibbits and W. Donahue (eds).  Social and Psychological
    Aspects of Aging.  New York, NY:  Columbia University
    Press, 1962a.

_____  Changing Family Relationships of Older People in Japan
    During the Last Fifty Years.  Pp. 454-58 in C. Tibbitts and
    W. Donahue (eds).  Aging Around the World.  New York, NY:
    Columbia University Press, 1962b.

Okamura, K.  The Employment of Fixed-Year Retirees:  The
    Unemployed Situation and Its Main Regulating Factors (in
    Japanese).  Shakai Ronengaku.  26:3-17, 1987.

Osako, M.  Social Changes and Public Policies for the Aged in
    Japan:  The Influence of Local Political Processes and
    Women's Roles on Welfare Programs.  Pp. 85-97 in C. Nusberg
    and M. Osako (eds).  The Situation of the Asian/Pacific
    Elderly.  Washington, DC:  International Federation on
    Ageing, 1980.

Pacific Affairs.  Medical Care for the Japanese Elderly:  A
    Symposium.  57:45-89, 1984.

Palmore, E.  The Honorable Elders:  A Cross-Cultural Analysis of Aging in Japan.  Durham, NC:  Duke University Press, 1975a.

In this study of the aged in Japan, the author espouses the view that the Japanese government is more supportive of the elders than is true in the United States.

_____ The Status and Integration of the Aged in Japanese Society.  Journal of Gerontology.  30:199-208, 1975b.

_____ What Can the USA Learn from Japan About Aging? Gerontologist.  15:64-67, 1975c.

Palmore, E. and D. Maeda.  The Honorable Elders Revisited. Durham, NC:  Duke University Press, 1985.

This study of 31 modernizing countries proposes that status of the aged declines during early stages of modernization but bottoms out and begins to improve in later stages.

Plath, D.  Where the Family of God is the Family:  The Role of the Dead in Japanese Households.  American Anthropologist. 66:300-17, 1964.

_____ Japan:  The After Years.  Pp. 133-50 in D. Cowgill and L. Holmes (eds).  Aging and Modernization.  New York, NY: Appleton-Century Crofts, 1972.

_____ Contours of Consociation:  Lessons from a Japanese Narrative.  In P. Baltes and O. Brim (eds).  Life-Span Development and Behavior.  New York, NY:  Academic Press, 1980a.

_____ Long Engagements:  Maturity in Modern Japan.  Stanford, CA:  Stanford University Press, 1980b.

_____ Ecstacy Years:  Old Age in Japan.  Pp. 147-53 in J. Sokolovsky (ed).  Growing Old in Different Cultures:  Aging in Cross-Cultural Perspective.  Acton, MA:  Copley Press, 1987.

Prime Minister's Office, Bureau of Aging.  The Present State of the Elderly (in Japanese).  Tokyo:  Ministry of Finance Printing Office, 1980.

_____ Lives and Opinions of Old People:  Report of a Cross-National Survey (in Japanese).  Tokyo:  Ministry of Finance Printing Office, 1982.

Shimonaka, Y. and K. Nakazato.  Personality Development Among the Japanese Elderly:  A Ten-Year Longitutinal Study on a Sentence Completion Test.  Journal of Cross-Cultural Gerontology.  4(4):347-56, 1989.

Shinmer, M.  Aging of the Population and its Influence Upon Society.  Japanese Journal of Geriatrics.  Supplement. 3:73, 1966.

Smith, R.  Japan:  The Later Years of Life and the Concept of
    Time.  Pp. 95-99 in R. Kleemeir (ed).  Aging and Leisure.
    New York, NY:  Oxford University Press, 1961.

Sparks, D.  The Still Rebirth:  Retirement and Role
    Discontinuity.  Journal of Asian and African Studies.
    10(1-2):64-74, 1975.

Stewart, C.  The Older Worker in Japan:  Realities and
    Possibilities.  Industrial Gerontology.  Winter:60-75,
    1974.

Sussman, M., J. Romeis, and D. Maeda.  Age Bias in Japan:
    Implications for Normative Conflict.  International Review
    of Modern Sociology.  10:243-54,1980.

Tobin, J. J.  The American Idealization of Old Age in Japan.
    Gerontologist.  27:53-58, 1987.

Tokyo Metropolitan Institute of Gerontology.  Ageing in Japan.
    Tokyo:  Tokyo Metropolitan Institute of Gerontology, 1978.

Tozawa, G.  Present and Future Problems of the Health Care
    System for the Elderly (in Japanese).  Kosei no Shihyo.
    10:4-12, 1986a.

_____ Trends in Medical Costs of the Aged (in Japanese).
    Kosei no Shihyo.  10:13-18, 1986b.

Watanabe, S.  Old People in Transitional Japan.  Tokyo:
    Gerontological Association of Japan, 1963.

## INDIA AND OTHER SOUTH ASIAN COUNTRIES

Beall, C. M. and M. C. Goldstein.  Work, Aging and Dependency
    in a Sherpa Population in Nepal.  Social Science and
    Medicine.  16:141-47, 1982.

Bhatia, H. S.  Aging and Society:  A Sociological Study of
    Retired Public Servants.  Udaipur, India:  The Arya's Book
    Center Publishers, 1983.

    Based largely on open-ended interviews with 200 male
    retired civil servants in the city of Udaipur, this study
    is among the more useful of its genre for its suggestive
    insights into the realities of life for a certain category
    of elderly people in urban India.  Though not particularly
    well-written or carefully edited, the book has the virtue
    of going beyond the usual mechanical tabulation of answers
    to a structured questionnaire to quote informants directly
    and at some length.  "Case studies" are also provided and
    are followed up by some insightful interpretations and
    generalizations.

Biswas, S. K. (ed).  Aging in Contemporary India.  Calcutta:
    Indian Anthropological Society, 1987.

Though published by the Indian Anthropological Society, and
consisting in part of papers originally prepared for the
Eleventh Congress of the IUAES (held in Vancouver in 1983),
few of the seven contributions are based upon research
employing anthropological field methods, and most are
highly general in focus and are based upon secondary
sources.  Topics include dependency and family care for the
elderly in rural India, the demographics of aging in India,
and psychological research on the the aged in India (a
review of the literature).  The most interesting paper, and
the one most solidly based in original research, is by
Ramesh Kanbargi on the relationship between fertility
behavior and the need for old age security in a south
Indian village.

Bose, A. B. and K. D. Gangrade (eds).  The Aging in India:
    Problems and Potentialities.  New Delhi:  Abhinav
    Publications, 1988.

    A very general overview of some of the problems facing the
    elderly in contemporary India, and some suggested
    solutions, many in the U.S.A., rather than from a close
    personal or research familiarity with the realities of
    Indian society.  It is apparently directed largely at an
    audience of social work professionals, and lacks such
    scholarly appurtenances as footnotes or bibliography.

Cain, M.  The Consequences of Reproductive Failure:
    Dependence, Mobility, and Mortality Among the Elderly of
    Rural South Asia.  Population Studies.  40:375-88, 1986.

Desai, K. G. (ed).  Aging in India.  Bombay, India:  Tata
    Institute of Social Sciences, 1982.

    A collection of 17 papers by Indian social and biological
    scientists, presented at a National Seminar on Aging in
    India at the Tata Institute of Social Sciences in Bombay in
    1981. Most papers provide general summaries or overviews of
    their chosen topic, rather than being reports of particular
    research investigations.  The emphasis is upon policy
    implications for the welfare of the Indian elderly.  The
    volume is divided into sections dealing respectively with
    demographic, economic, health, biological, psychological,
    social, and social welfare issues.  Some of the papers are
    extremely brief.  The book contains some useful
    information, but there is little of conceptual or
    theoretical interest for one who is already familiar with
    the basic background facts.

Desai, K. G. and R. G. Naik.  Problems of Retired People in
    Greater Bombay.  Bombay, India:  Tata Institute of Social
    Sciences (N. d.).

    As the title suggests, this book reports results of a
    questionnaire survey, conducted by two members of the
    social work faculty of the Tata Institute, on health,
    financial, and social-psychological adjustment to
    retirement among 600 urban male recipients of government

pensions.  Retirees who had been employed in non-white-collar jobs were excluded from the sample, on the grounds that the main problems of these older people would be economic, while their low educational level would prevent them from conceptualizing their problems clearly and prove a barrier to the establishment of rapport by the interviewers!  One of the first published sociological studies of the elderly in India.

de Souza, A.  The Social Organization of Aging Among the Urban Poor.  New Delhi:  Indian Social Institute, 1982.

A brief report of a sample survey conducted among 304 elderly male and female residents of eight slum settlements in metropolitan Delhi; it is the only published work of which I am aware that deals with this stratum of the population.  The questions asked seem to be the standard ones used in such investigations and the analysis is not particularly sophisticated but some of the findings provide a useful point of comparison to those from the more plentiful studies of middle-class pension recipients or rural agriculturalists and artisans.

D'Souza, V.  Changes in Social Structure and Changing Roles of Older People in India.  Sociology and Social Research. 55:297-304, 1971.

Ellickson, J.  Never the Twain Shall Meet:  Aging Men and Women in Bangladesh.  Journal of Cross-Cultural Gerontology.  3(1):53-70, 1988.

Goldstein, M. C. and C. M. Beall.  Modernization and Aging in the Third and Fourth World:  Views from the Rural Hinterland in Nepal.  Human Organization.  40:48-55, 1981.

_____  Indirect Modenization and the Status of the Elderly in a Rural Third World Setting.  Journal of Gerontology. 37:743-48, 1982.

_____  Family Change, Caste, and the Elderly in a Rural Locale in Nepal.  Journal of Cross-Cultural Gerontology. 1(3):305-16, 1986.

Goldstein, M. C., S. Schuler and J. Ross.  Social and Economic Forces Affecting Intergeneratinal Relations in Extended Families in a ThirdWorld Country:  A Cautionary Tale from South Asia.  Journal of Gerontology.  38:716-24, 1983.

A thoughtful, well-researched, and theoretically insightful article dealing with the impact of contemporary economic and social change upon the position of old people within the family in Kathmandu, Nepal.  The authors report that their elderly Nepali informants see themselves as able to cope in old age only by holding on to material resources as leverage against neglect by their adult offspring.  They suggest that this situation arises out of the growing impoverishment of the rapidly expanding urban Nepali population, with its rising consumption needs and aspiratins.  Elderly parents thus come to represent an insupportable economic burden for their employed children, particularly when the needs of the next generation are simultaneously pressing to be met.

Harlan, W.  Social Status of the Aged in Three Indian Villages.  Pp.  469-75 in B. Neugarten (ed).  Middle Age and Aging.  Chicago, IL:  University of Chicago Press, 1963.

An early and widely cited article that was probably the first to question the popular stereotpye of Indian society and its joint family system as providing an ideal setting for the aged person.  Based on sociological studies of rural men and women carried out by Indian graduate students.

Hiebert, P.  Old Age in a South Indian Village.  Pp. 211-26 in P. Amoss and S. Harrell (eds).  Other Ways of Growing Old: Anthropolgical Perspectives.  Stanford, CA:  Stanford University Press, 1981.

A descriptive account of the religious, cultural and social context of aging in the Andhra Pradesh village where the author had carried out ethnographic field research in the 1960s.  Gives attention to differences between men's and women's experiences of aging and provides some brief vignettes of individual old people and their varying modes of adaptation to the aging process.

Maduro, R.  Artistic Creativity and Aging in India.  Aging and Human Development.  5(4):303-29, 1974.

Deals with the relationship between the creative process and aging among a community of traditional painters in Rajasthan.

Martin, L. G.  The Status of South Asia's Growing Elderly Population Journal of Cross-Cultural Gerontology.  5(2):93-17, 1990.

A good review of recent published and unpublished sources, including both aggregate statistical and sample survey data, on recent trends in the situation of the aged in India, Nepal, Pakistan, Bangladesh and Sri Lanka.  Focus is on issues of living arrangements and family support for the elderly and an attempt is made to make some projections for the future in terms of well-being for the older population in these countries.

Marulasiddaiah, H. M.  Old People of Makunti.  Dharwar, India: Karnatak University, 1969.

The only published book-length anthropological study of old age in India.  The author conducted field research in a Karnataka village, focussing on its elderly residents, but examining their lives within the entire multigenerational family, caste, and community context.

Mines, M.  Indian Transitions:  A Comparative Analysis of
    Adult Stages of Development.  Ethos.  9:95-121, 1981.

_____    Conceptualizing the Person:  Hierarchical Society and
Individual Autonomy in India.  American Anthropologist.
90:568-79, 1988.

Both articles by Mines (1981 and 1988) are based on lengthy
life-history interviews with a  limited number of Indian
eldelry and middle-aged individuals, most of them male.
The focus of the research is on the entire process of adult
development rather than on old age per se, and raises some
important and interesting issues for cross-cultural
gerontological study.

Raj, B., et al.  A Study of Rural Aged Persons in Profile.
    Indian Journal of Social Work.  32:155-62, 1971.

Rowe, W.  The Middle and Later Years in Indian Society.  Pp.
    104-12 in R. Kleemeier (ed).  Aging and Leisure.  New York,
    NY:  Oxford University Press, 1961.

Sharma, M. L. and T. M. Dak.  Aging in India:  Challenge for
    the Society.  Delhi:  Ajanta Publications, 1987.

A collection of 23 papers presented at a 1986 conference
sponsored by the HelpAge India, to deal with social-
psychological and health aspects of aging in contemporary
India.  Includes findings from a number of sociological and
medical surveys of rural elderly carried out by students
and faculty of Haryana Agricutlrual University, as well as
a number of more general articles about aging issues in the
Indian context.

Soodan, K. S.  Changing Roles of the Aged.  Indian Journal of
    Gerontology.  1972.

_____    Aging in India.  Calcutta, India:  Minerva Associates,
1975.

Another sociological investigation of retirees, this time
in the city of Lucknow, based on responses to a structured
questionnaire.

Tilak, S.  Religion and Aging in the Indian Tradition.
    Albany, NY:  State University of New York Press, 1989.

A fascinating study of the ways in which the phenomenon of
aging within the ancient Indian textual literature.  The
author examines in detail a wide variety of original
Sanskrit and Pali sources to provide a picture of the
principal approaches and ideas about old age that are
represented in them.  He traces distinct patterns of change
over time and shows the differences between Hindu and
Buddhist treatments of the subject.  This book takes us far
beyond the obligatory references to Manusmriti and the four
ideal stages of human life that have by now become
commonplace in discussions of the religious and

philosophical foundations of the Indian perspective on old age.

Vatuk, S.  The Aging Woman in India:  Self-Perceptions and Changing Roles.  Pp. 142-63 in A. de Souza (ed).  Women in Contemporary India.  New Delhi, India:  Manohar, 1975.

Based on an anthropological field study of the social and cultural context of aging in an "urbanized village," a former agricultural community now encapsulated, due to the expansion of the metropolis, within a middle-class area of the city of Delhi.  Deals primarily with the women of the former landowning caste of the village.

_____ Withdrawal and Disengagement as a Cultural Response to Aging in India.  Pp. 126-48 in C. Fry (ed).  Aging in Culture and Society:  Comparative Viewpoints and Strategies.  Brooklyn, NY:  J. F. Bergin, 1980.

An examination of the applicability of "disengagement theory" to the Indian cultural context, drawing upon parallels between their theory and the classical Indian notion of the four stages of life, as the latter is understood by the uneducated lay villager in the Delhi community described above (Vatuk 1975).

_____ Cultural Perspectives on Social Services for the Aged in India.  Pp. 98-109 in C. Nusberg and M. Osako (eds).  The Situation of the Asian/Pacific Elderly.  Washington, DC:  International Federation of Ageing, 1981.

A summary discussion of the government-provided social services available in India to elderly persons, pointing out the paucity of such benefits and the limited population eligible to receive them, and stressing the role of the family as the only effective source of economic and social support for the vast majority of Indian old people.

_____ Old Age in India.  Pp. 70-103 in P. N. Stearns (ed).  Old Age in Preindustrial Society.  New York, NY:  Holmes and Meier, 1982a.

Using census and other published quantitative data, this article addresses the problem of trying to determine what the actual situation of the elderly in India used to be, and what evidence there may be for assessing the impact of various forces of social change-- industrialization, urbanization, modernization--during the period of the past 100 years.  Emphasis is placed upon trying to trace changes in family structure and living arrangements of older persons over time.

_____ The Family Life of Older People in a Changing Society: India.  Pp. 57-82 in J. Sokolovsky and J. Sokolovsky (eds).  Aging and the Aged in the Third World:  Part 2.  Studies in Third World Societies.  1982b.

Based upon the same research described for the Vatuk (1975)

article, this paper discusses sources and modes of
resolution of intergenerational tensions and conflict in a
community in which almost all old people live with their
adult offspring in extended family households.  It is
suggested that while some of the problems facing the
elderly in this community can be traced to its socio-
economic transformation over the past 30 years, others are
probably inherent in the structure of the Indian family
system.

_____ South Asian Cultural Conceptions of Sexuality.  Pp.
137-54 in J. Brown and V. Kerns (eds).  In Her Prime:  A
New View of Middle-Aged Women.  South Hadley, MA:  Bergin
and Garvey, 1984.

Deals with Indian cultural conceptions about the nature of
female sexuality and about how her sexuality is transformed
as a woman ages.  Based upn secondary sources and field
research data.

_____ Authority, Power and Autonomy in the Life Cycle of
North Indian Women.  Pp. 23-44 in P. Hockings (ed).
Dimensions of Social Life.  Berlin:  Mouton de Gruyter,
1987.

Traces the path of an Indian woman's changing degree of
access to legitimated authority and unofficial power over
others, and of autonomy to determine and control her own
activities as she progresses from childhood through
adolescnece, early married life, maturity, and old age.
Based upon field research in northern India, especially in
the Delhi area.

Vatuk, S.  "To Be a Burden on Others":  Dependency Anxiety
   Among the Elderly in India.  Pp. 64-88 in O. M. Lynch (ed).
   Divine Passions:  The Social Construction of Emotion in
   India.  Berkeley, CA:  University of California Press,
   1989.

Describes and interprets, within the Indian cultural
context, the widely expressed anxiety of older persons (in
the Delhi community described above) about becoming
physically helpless and dependent upon others in later
life.  Contrasts Indian and American cultural definitions
of, and emotional reactions, dependency in old age.


**UNITED STATES**

Achenbaum, W.  The Obsolescence of Old Age in America,
   1965-1914.  Journal of Social History.  8:48-62, 1974.

_____ Images of Old Age in America:  1790 to the Present.
   Ann Arbor, MI:  Institute of Gerontology, 1978.

Historical-pictorial images of the elderly in art.

_____ Old Age in the New Land.  Baltimore, MD:  Johns Hopkins

University Press, 1978.

Historically the meaning of old age has changed.  Achenbaum examines the change in the last stages of life and documents how old age has emerged as a social problem in the 20th century.

Anderson, B. G.  Stress and Psychopathology Among Aged Americans.  Southwestern Journal of Anthropology. 20:190-217, 1964.

_____  Deculturation Among the Aged.  Anthropological Quarterly.  45:209-16, 1972.

This is a description of a system of conscious and unconscious conditioning whereby older Americans are gradually groomed by their society for total cultural withdrawal.

_____  The Aging Game:  Success, Sanity, and Sex After Sixty. New York, NY:  McGraw Hill, 1979.

This book offers down-to-earth advice on how to prepare for and win the battle of aging in America.

Arth, M.  American Culture and the Phenomenon of Friendship in the Aged.  Gerontologist.  1(4):168-70, 1961.

Bahr, S. J. and E. T. Peterson.  Aging and the Family. Lexington, MA:  Lexington Books, 1989.

Barker, R. and L. Barker.  The Psychological Ecology of Old People in Midwest, Kansas and Yorkdale, Yorkshire.  Pp. 453-60 in B. Neugarten (ed).  Middle Age and Aging. Chicago, IL:  University of Chicago Press, 1968.

Berrien, F., A. Arkoff, and S. Iwahara.  Generational Difference in Values:  Americans, Japanese-Americans, and Japanese.  Journal of Social Psychology.  71:169-75, 1967.

Bould, S.  Eighty-five Plus:  The Oldest Old.  Belmont, CA: Wadsworth, 1989.

Boyer, E.  Health Perception in the Elderly:  Its Cultural and and Social Aspects.  Pp. 198-216 in C. Fry (ed).  Aging in Culture and Society:  Comparative Viewpoints and Strategies.  New York, NY:  J. F. Bergin, 1980.

This study shows that age-homogeneous housing can have a positive influence on mental and physical health of residents.

Butler, Robert.  Why Survive?  Being Old in America.  New York, NY:  Harper and Row, 1974.

This Pulitzer Prize-winning book is an indictment of American society in terms of its attitudes toward and treatment of the aged.  Readers should keep in mind that statistical data may be a bit dated now, but the book remains a very effective statement about American elders.

Chudacoff, H. P.  How Old Are You:  Age Consciousness in American Culture.  Princeton, NJ:  Princeton University Press, 1989.

Age has not always been a variable essential to identify and place others on the social map.  Chudacoff doeuments the rise of age consciousness which he attributes to universal education, medicine and the emergence of a peer society.

Clark, M.  Cultural Values and Dependency in Later Life.  Pp. 263-74 in D. Cowgill and L. D. Holmes, (eds).  Aging and Modernization.  New York, NY:  Appleton-Century-Crofts, 1972.

In this chapter, Clark discusses acceptable vs. unacceptable types of dependency for the aged as defined by the American value system.

Clark, M. and B. Anderson.  Culture and Aging.  Springfield, IL:  C. C. Thomas, 1967.

This is an excellent study of aging in America.  The investigators describe the search for relevant variables which influence successful adaptation to aging or development of mental illness in late life.  They conclude that differences in adaptation between mentally healthy and mentally ill elders seem related to differential orientation to American values.

Cowgill, D.  Aging in American Society.  Pp. 243-62 in D. Cowgill and L. Holmes (eds).  Aging and Modernization.  New York, NY:  Appleton-Century-Crofts, 1972.

This profile of the elderly in American culture stresses demographic, social, ideological and ritual aspects as well as the nature of service delivery.

Davis, R. H.  TV's Image of the Elderly.  Lexington, MA:  Lexington Books, 1985.

de Beauvoir, S.  The Harsh Arithmetic of Old Age in America.  Saturday Review of Society.  April 8:262-64, 1972.

Demos, J.  Past, Present and Personal:  The Family and the Life Course in American History.  New York, NY:  Oxford, 1988.

Detzner, D.  Growing Old Together:  A Social History of Aging in America, 1930-1977.  Ann Arbor, MI:  University Microfilms, 1977.

The characteristics and lifestyle of elderly residents of single room occupancy hotels in an area of San Diego targeted for urban renewal are the focus of this book.

Eckert, J. K., K. H. Namazi, and E. Kahana.  Unlicensed Board
    and Care Homes:  An Extra-Familial Living Arrangement for
    the Elderly.  Journal of Cross-Cultural Gerontology.
    2(4):377-94, 1987.

Fischer, D.  Growing Old in America.  New York, NY:  Oxford
    University Press, 1977.

    This volume presents a social historical analysis of age
    relationships since colonial times in the United States.
    Changes in attitudes toward and status of the old from
    venerated elders to "social problem" are documented.

    _____ Growing Old in America.  Pp. 34-49 in J. Quadagno (ed).
    Aging, the Individual and Society.  New York, NY:  St.
    Martin's Press, 1980.

Francher, J.  American Values and the Disenfranchisement of
    the Aged.  The Eastern Anthropologist.  22(1):29-36, 1969.

    _____ It's the Pepsi Generation:  Accelerated Aging and the
    Television Commercial.  Aging and Human Development.
    4(3):245-55, 1973.

Fry, C.  Cultural Dimensions of Age:  A Multidimensional
    Scaling Analysis.  Pp. 42-64 in C. L. Fry (ed).  Aging in
    Culture and Society:  Comparative Viewpoints and
    Strategies.  New York, NY:  J. F. Bergin, 1980.

Gutmann, D.  The Premature Gerontocracy:  Themes of Aging and
    Death in the Youth Culture.  Social Research.
    39(3):416-48, 1972.

Haber, C.  Beyond Sixty-Five:  The Dilemma of Old Age in
    America's Past.  New York, NY:  Cambridge University Press,
    1975.

    Haber examines the meaning of old age from the Colonial era
    to the rise of bureaucratic society.  Throughout the 19th
    century, old age became increasingly defined through the
    eyes of professionals who interpreted it through medical
    and institutional models.  In a bureaucratic society, the
    category of old age is increasingly defined by specialists.

Harris, L. and Associates.  The Myth and Reality of Aging in
    America.  Washington, DC:  National Council on Aging, 1975.

    _____ Aging in the Eighties:  America in Transition.
    Washington, DC:  National Council on Aging, 1981.

Henry, J.  Culture Against Man.  New York, NY:  Vintage Books,
    3.  1963.

    In an analysis of how culture may be "against" human
    beings, Henry describes three nursing homes--one for
    paupers, which is public-supported, and two private,
    profit-making facillities for the middle class.

Hochschild, A. R.  The Unexpected Community.  Berkeley, CA:
University of California Press, 1973

Holmes, L. D.  Pp. 102-11 in L. Holmes.  Other Cultures, Elder
Years:  An Introduction to Cultural Gerontology.
Minneapolis, MN:  Burgess, 1983.

Holmes, L. D. and J. W. Thomson.  Jazz Greats:  Getting Better
with Age.  New York, NY:  Holmes and Meier, 1986.

This book focuses on creativity, adaptability, and coping
strategies of elderly jazz musicians in America.

Holtzman, J. M. and H. Akiyama.  What Children See:  The Aged
on Television in Japan and the United States.  The
Gerontologist.  25:62-68, 1985.

Hornum, B.  Dependency Fears and Selection of Living
Arrangements:  A Study of One Life Care Community in
America.  Compendium Series:  Cultural Gerontology.  Jersey
City, NJ:  Brunswick Institute on Aging, 1986.

An in-depth study of the lives of the elderly in one Life
Care Community outside of Philadelphia.  The motivations
for entering this type of community are examined as are the
feelings of the well residents towards those in the skilled
nursing facility.

Jacobs, J.  An Ethnographic Study of a Retirement Setting.
Gerontologist.  14:483-87, 1974a.

This article considers the extent to which residents of
"Fun City," a retirement community, fit the disengagement
model.

_____  Fun City.  New York, NY:  Holt, Rinehart, and Winston,
1974b.

This is an ethnographic study of an American retirement
community which calls into question the active and secure
life espoused by its residents.

_____  Old Persons and Retirement Communities.  Springfield,
IL:  C, C. Thomas, 1975.

Johnson, S. K.  Idle Haven:  Community Building Among the
Working Class Retired.  Berkeley, CA:  University of
California Press, 1971.

Kaufman, S.  The Ageless Self:  Sources of Meaning in Late
Life.  Madison, WI:  University of Wisconsin Press, 1986.

Kayser-Jones, J. S.  Old, Alone and Neglected:  Care of the
Aged in Scotland and the United States.  Berkeley, CA:
University of California Press, 1981.

This book is a comparison of old people residing in a
nursing institution in Scotland with a similar group in the

U.S.  Provides interesting contrasts regarding developments in geriatric medicine, staff attitudes, status of residents and influence of differential value systems.  The book concludes with an effective analysis of the two settings according to exchange theory.

Keith, P. M.  The Unmarried in Later Life.  New York, NY: Praeger, 1989.

Kendig, H. L. and D. T. Rowland.  Family Support of the Australian Aged:  A Comparison with the United States.  The Gerontologist.  23:643-49, 1983.

Lasch, C.  The Culture of Narcissism:  American Life in an Age of Diminishing Expectations.  New York, NY:  Warner Books, 1979.

See especially pp. 351-67 for a discussion of planned obsolescence and age.

Lesnoff-Caravaglia, G. (ed).  Aging in a Technological Society.  New York, NY:  Human Sciences Press, 1988.

Longino, C.  Going Home:  Aged Return Migration in the U.S. 1965-1970.  Journal of Gerontology.  34(5):736-45, 1979.

Lozier, J.  Accommodating Old People in Society:  Examples from Appalachia and New Orleans.  Pp. 287-97 in N. Datan and L. Ginsberg (eds).  Life Span Developmental Psychology.  New York, NY:  Academic Press, 1975.

Lozier, J. and R. Althouse.  Retirement to the Porch in Rural Appalachia.  International Journal of Aging and Human Development.  6:7-16, 1975.

A phemenon peculiar to Appalachia, where a form of idleness is permitted people who have "paid their dues," is described.

Matthews, S. H.  Friendships Through the Life Course:  Oral Biographies in Old Age.  Beverly Hills, CA:  Sage, 1986.

Mead, M.  Cultural Contexts of Aging.  In No Time to Grow Old. Albany, NY:  Legislative Committee on the Problems of Aging, Legislative Document No. 12, 1951.

In this paper suggestions are offered about how America might profit from age desegregation.

_____  A New Style of Aging.  Christianity and Crisis. 31():240-43, 1971.

This article suggests that the elderly have shunned their responsibility to society by withdrawing and depriving the young of role models for aging.

Perkinson, M. A.  Alternate Roles for the Elderly:  An Example from a Midwestern Retirement Community.  Human

Organization. 39:219-26, 1980.

Pifer, A. and L. Bronte (eds). Our Aging Society. New York, NY: W. W. Norton, 1986.

Rathbone-McCuan, B. and B. Havens. North American Elders: United States and Canadian Perspectives. New York, NY: Greenwood, 1988.

Riley, M. W. and J. W. Riley, Jr. The Quality of Aging: Strategies for Interventions. Annals of the American Academy of Political and Social Science. Vol. 503. Newbury Park, CA: Sage, 1989.

Rosow, I. Old Age: One Moral Dilemma of an Affluent Society. Gerontologist. 2(4):182-91, 1962.

_____ Social Integration of the Aged. New York, NY: The Free Press, 1965.

_____ Socialization to Old Age. Berkeley, CA: University of California Press, 1974.

Rubinstein, R. L. Singular Paths, Old Men Living Alone. New York, MY: Columbia University Press, 1986.

Schulz, C. M. Age, Sex, and Death Anxiety in a Middle-Class American Community. Pp. 239-52 in C. Fry (ed). Aging in Culture and Society: Comparative Viewpoints and Strategies. New York, NY: J. F. Bergin, 1980.

Secunda, V. By Youth Possessed: The Denial of Age in America. New York, NY: Bobbs-Merrill, 1984.

Simic, A. Aging in the United States: Achieving New Understandings Through Foreign Eyes. In A. Kolker and P. Ahmed (eds). Coping With Aging. New York, NY: Elsevier, 1982.

Sontag, S. The Double Standard of Aging. Saturday Review. September 23, 1972.

    This article describes the American equation of youth with beauty and the way in which women are viewed more negatively than men as they age.

Sussman, M. B. and J. C. Romies. Willingness to Assist One's Elderly Parents: Responses from United States and Japanese Families. Human Organization. 41(3):256-59, 1982.

Teski, M., et al. A City Revitalized: The Elderly Lose at Monopoly. Lanham, MD: University Press of America, 1983.

    An exploration of the effects of economic revitalization in Atlantic City, New Jersey, on the elderly residents of areas surrounding the casinos.

Van Tassel, D. and P. N. Stearns. Old Age in a Bureaucratic

Society:  The Elderly, the Experts, and the State in American History.  New York, NY:  Greenwood Press, 1986.

Vesperi, M.  City of Green Benches:  Growing Old in a New Downtown.  Ithaca, NY:  Cornell University Press, 1985.

This is a study of the low-income elderly of St. Petersburg, Florida, a city long noted as a retirement haven but now trying to change its image.

Williamson, J. B.  Old Age Relief Policy Prior to 1900:  The Trend Toward Restrictiveness.  American Journal of Economic Sociology.  43:369-84, 1984.

Zube, M.  Outlook on Being Old:  Working Class Elderly in North Hampton, Massachusetts.  Gerontologist. 20(4):427-31, 1980.


**GREAT BRITAIN**

Abrams, M.  Time and the Elderly.  New Society.  33:685-86. 1978.

_____  Beyond Three-Score and Ten:  A First Report on a Survey of the Elderly.  London:  Age Concern, 1979.

_____  Beyond Three-Score and Ten:  A Second Report on a Survey of the Elderly.  London:  Age Concern, 1980.

The two Abrams reports (1979 and 1980) are based on a comparative study of elderly people living in selected towns in England.  The studies compare the 65-74's with the over 75's in terms of health, social contact, activities and use of time.

_____  People in Their Late Sixties:  A Longitudinal Survey of Ageing:  Part 1.  Survivors and Non-Survivors.  London: Age Concern, 1983.

A follow-up study re-interviewed 171 persons from the original 432 interviewees aged 65-69.  This report looks at the correlates of survival.

Allan, G. A.  A Sociology of Friendship and Kinship.  London: George Allen and Unwin, 1979.

A general and useful study of friendship which also pays attention to the role of friendship in England.

_____  Friendship and Care for Elderly People.  Ageing and Society.  6(1):1-12, 1986.

Andrews, C. T.  Early Days in Rural England.  Modern Geriatrics.  1(2):117-22, 1971.

A physician's account of the conditions under which the aged lived before 1948, focussing principally on institutional care.

Bell, C. Middle Class Families. London: Routledge & Kegan
Paul, 1968.

A general study of middle-class families in England of
interest to gerontologists in terms of its treatment of
expectations, obligations and responsibilities of middle
class kin.

Blythe, R. The View in Winter: Reflections on Old Age.
London: Penguin Books, 1981.

A philosophical exploration of attitudes towards old age,
illustrated by verbatim comments of a cross-section of old
people living in a rural part of south-east England.

Bott, E. Family and Social Network: Roles, Norms and
External Relationships in Ordinary Urban Families (2nd ed).
New York, NY: Free Press, 1957.

Bowling, A. and A. Cartwright. Life After a Death: A Study
of the Elderly Widowed. London: Tavistock, 1982.

A study of re-adjustment after bereavement.

Briggs, A. and J. Oliver. Caring: Experiences of Looking
After Disabled Relatives. London: Routledge & Kegan Paul,
1985.

Bulmer, M. Neighbours: The Work of Philip Abrams.
Cambridge: Cambridge University Press, 1986.

A general study of neighbouring, focussing on work
conducted in England. Of interest to gerontologists in
terms of its analysis and assessment of a variety of good
neighbour schemes.

Cartwright, A., L. Hockey, and J. Anderson. Life Before
Death. London: Routledge & Kegan Paul, 1973.

A study of the experiences of carers in the year before the
person they were caring for died. Focusses primarily on
experiences of stress and the caring professions.

Challis, D. and B. Davies. A New Approach to Community Care
of the Elderly. British Journal of Social Work. 10:1-18,
1980.

Clarke, L. Domiciliary Services for the Elderly. London:
Croom Helm, 1984.

Coleman, P. Social Gerontology in England, Scotland, and
Wales: A Review of Recent and Current Research.
Gerontologist. 15:219-29, 1975.

_____ Ageing and Reminiscence Processes: Social and Clinical
Implications. New York, NY: John Wiley, 1986.

Department of Health and Social Security. Growing Older.
    Government White Paper. London: Her Majesty's Stationery
    Office, 1981.

Davies, L. Three Score Years.... And Then? A Study of the
    Nutrition and Well-Being of Elderly People at Home.
    London: Heinemann, 1981.

    An empirical study of the content and usefulness of the
    meals-on-wheels service.

Dundee School of Social Administration. The Elderly in
    Tannadice: A Study of Some Aspects of the Daily Life of
    the Older People in a Rural Parish. Dundee, Scotland:
    Dundee School of Social Administration, 1972.

Equal Opportunities Commission. The Experience of Caring for
    Elderly and Handicapped Dependents: Survey Report.
    Manchester, England: Equal Opportunities Commission, 1980.

_____ Caring for the Elderly and Handicapped: Community Care
    Policies and Women's Lives. Research Report. Manchester,
    England: Equal Opportunities Commission, 1982a.

_____ Who Cares for the Carers? Opportunities for Those
    Caring for the Elderly and Handicapped. Manchester,
    England: Equal Opportunities Commission, 1982b.

Ever, H. Elderly Women and Disadvantages: Perceptions of
    Daily Life and Support Relationships. Pp. 25-43 in D.
    Jerrome (ed). Ageing in Modern Societies. London: Croom
    Helm, 1983.

Finch, J. and D. Groves (eds). A Labour of Love: Women, Work
    and Caring. London: Routledge & Kegan Paul, 1983.

    A collection of papers from a feminist conference on social
    policy and women's caring roles including children, the
    disabled and the elderly.

Fisk, M. J. Independence and the Elderly. London: Croom
    Helm, 1986.

    A detailed discussion and analysis of housing, housing
    policy and the elderly.

Firth, R., et al. Families and Their Relatives. London:
    Routledge & Kegan Paul, 1969.

    An ethnographic study of two metropolitan suburban middle-
    class samples aimed at an understanding of values.
    Discusses the nature of relationships with the wider family
    and intimacy at a distance.

Francis, D. Will You Still Need Me, Will You Still Feed Me,
    When I'm 84? Bloomington, IN: Indiana Univerwsity Press,
    1984.

Comparative ethnographic study of old parents in Leeds,
England, and Cleveland, Ohio.  Demonstrates convincingly
how early experiences affect adaptation to ageing.  Of
particular interest to those using biographical methods.

Ginsberg, Y.  Fear of Crime Among Elderly Jews in Boston and
London.  International Journal of Aging and Human
Development.  20(4):257-68, 1984-85.

Goldberg, E. M.  Helping the Aged.  London:  Allen & Unwin,
1970.

_____  Some Current and Future Issues in the Social Care of
Elderly People.  Pp.  195-207 in Elderly People in the
Community:  Their Service Needs.  London:  Her Majesty's
Stationery Office., 1983.

Grant G.  Older Carers, Interdependence and the Care of
Mentally Handicapped Adults.  Ageing and Society.
6(3):333-51, 1986.

Grant, G. and G. C. Wenger.  Patterns of Partnership:  Three
Models of Care for the Elderly.  Pp. 27-51 in D. Pancoast
(ed).  Rediscovering Self-Help:  Its Role in Social Care.
Beverly Hills, CA:  Sage, 1983.

Grant W.  Old People's Towns.  New Society.  13:817-18, 1971.

A descriptive account of life in a Devon seaside resort,
based on interviews.

Hadley, R. and A. Webb.  Loneliness, Social Isolation and Old
People:  Some Implications for Social Policy.  London:  Age
Concern, 1974.

_____  Across the Generations:  Old People and Young
Volunteers.  London:  George Allen and Unwin, 1975.

A description and analysis of an innovation using young
people to overcome loneliness in the city.

Harper, S.  The Kinship Network of the Rural Aged:  A
Comparison of the Indigenous Elderly and the Retired
Immigrant.  Ageing Society.  7:303-27, 1987.

Hazan, H.  The Limbo People:  A Study of the Constitution of
the Time Universe Among the Aged.  London:  Routledge and
Kegan Paul, 1980.

An ethnographic study of elderly Jews in a north London day
centre, dealing primarily with how they come to terms with
their relationships with the younger generation,
discontinuities in their lives and the passage of time.

_____  Continuity and Transformation Among the Aged:  A Study
in the Anthropology of Time.  Current Anthropology.
25:567-76, 1984.  Discussion.  25:576-78, 1984 and 26:281,
1985.

Hodes, C.  Care of the Elderly in General Practice.  British
Medical Journal.  4:41-42, 1974.

A policy paper stressing such topics as the importance of
prevention, early diagnosis, and health education, etc.

Hornum, B.  Aspects of Aging in Planned Communities.  Topics
in Clinical Nursing.  3(1):85-97, 1981.

_____  The Elderly and Alternative Options for Long-Term
Care.  In C. Babbitt (ed).  Sociology Toward the Year 2000.
Boston, MA:  Beacon, 1983.

An overview of the options available for the elderly for
long-term care in the United States with some comparable
material from Great Britain.

_____  The Elderly in British New Towns:  New Roles, New
Networks.  Pp. 211-24 in J. Sokolovsky (ed).  Growing Old
in Different Societies:  Cross-Cultural Perspectives.
Acton, MA:  Copley, 1987.

In-depth material on selected British New Towns.  The lives
of the elderly are examined in these planned communities
with a discussion of how these vary by region and age of
the New Town.  Different categories of elderly residents
are identified.

Hornum, B. and F. Hornum.  Problems in New Town Research.
Sociological Symposium.  Spring, 1975.

A review of some of the difficulties in doing research in
the British New Towns.

Hudson, B.  Helping the Helpers.  Health and Social Services
Journal.  12:826, 1984.

Outlines an approach for those caring for elderly
relatives.

Hunt, A.  The Elderly At Home:  A Study of People Aged Sixty-
five and Over Living in the Community in England in 1976.
Social Survey Division, Office of Population Censuses and
Surveys.  London:  Her Majesty's Stationery Office, 1978.

A statistical study of a large sample of elderly people.
The standard statistical reference in the United Kingdom.

Hunter, D. J., et al.  Survey of the Elderly Living at Home in
North Grampian:  A Minimum Data Set.  Unit for the Study of
the Elderly, Department of Community Medicine.  Aberdeen,
Scotland:  University of Aberdeen, 1984a.

_____  Survey of the Elderly Living at Home in Dundee:  A
Minimum Data Set.  Unit for the Study of the Elderly,
Department of Community Medicine.  Aberdeen, Scotland:
University of Aberdeen, 1984b.

Isaacs, B.   Treatment of the "Irremediable" Elderly Patient. British Medical Journal.  3:526-28, 1973.

A paper by a geriatrician, urging a more humane approach to incurable conditons of old age.

Isaacs, B., M. Livingstone, and Y. Neville.  Survival of the Unfittest:  A Study of Geriatic Patients in Glasgow. London:  Routledge & Kegan Paul, 1972

A watershed study of elderly people in the last year of their lives which demonstrated convincingly the commitment of the younger generation to provide care for old people.

Jenkins, D.   The Agricultural Community in South West Wales at The Turn of the Twentieth Century.  Cardiff, England: University of Wales Press, 1971.

A historical and descriptive study which includes interesting data on the role of the elderly.

Jerrome, D.   The Significance of Friendship for Women in Later Life.  Ageing and Society.  1(2):175-97, 1981.

An ethnographic study of the development and role of friendship in the lives of elderly women in Brighton.

_____ (ed).  Ageing in Modern society.  London:  Croom Helm, 1983.

A series of articles analyzing various aspects of aging in England from sociological and anthropological perspectives. Includes such topics as:  women, social support, urban aged, and residential living.

_____ "Me Darby, You Joan!"  Pp. 348-55 in C. Phillipson, M. Bernard, and P. Strang (eds).  Dependency and Interdependency in Old Age--Theoretical Perspectives and Policy Statements.  London:  Croom Helm, 1986.

An ethnographic study of role negotiation in an old people's club.

Jerrome, D.  Frailty and Friendship.  Journal of Cross-Cultural Gerontology.  5(1):51-64, 1990.

Johnson, M.  Self-Perception of Needs Amongst the Elderly. Sociological Review.  20(4):521-31, 1972.

Johnson, M., S. Di Gregorio, and B. Harrison.  Ageing, Needs and Nutrition:  A Study of Voluntary and Statutory Collaboration in Community Care for Elderly People. Research Paper 82-1.  London:  Policy Studies Institute, 1981.

Jones, R.  Cut Off From Society by the Curtain of Old Age. Social Work Today.  12(35):10-12, 1981.

A discussion  of the social forces which predisposed
towards loneliness, withdrawal and mental disorder.

Karn, V.  Retiring to the Seaside.  London:  Routledge & Kegan
Paul, 1977.

An empirical study of old people retiring to the South
Coast in terms of expectations and outcomes.

Klein, J. F.  Samples from English Culture.  London:
Routledge & Kegan Paul, 1965.

A synthesis of community studies.  Does not focus on the
elderly but provides useful background material on values
and patterns of culture.

Law, C. M. and A. M. Warnes.  The Movement of Retired People
to Seaside Resorts:  A Study of Morecombe and Llandudno.
Town Planning Review.  44(4):372-90, 1973.

An empirical study of retirement migration including the
problems of widowhood.

Lemon, A.  Retirement and Its Effect on Small Towns:  The
Example of Norfolk and Suffolk.  Town Planning Review.
44(3):254-62,1973.

Means, R. and R. Smith.  The Development of Welfare Services
for Elderly People.  London:  Croom Helm, 1985.

Discussion of retirement migrations.

Middleton, L.  Friendship and Isolation:  Two Sides of
Sheltered Housing.  Pp. 255-68 in D. Jerrome (ed).  Ageing
in Modern Society.  London:  Croom Helm, 1983.

Nissel, M. and L. Bonnerjea.  Family Care of the Handicapped
Elderly:  Who Pays?  Report No. 602.  London:  Policy
Studies Institute, 1982.

An account of the problems of carers based on a sample of
twenty-two individuals.

Oliver, J.  The Caring Wife.  Pp. 72-88 in J. Finch and D.
Groves (eds).  A Labour of Love:  Women, Work and Caring.
London:  Routledge & Kegan Paul, 1983.

Parker, S.  Work and Retirement.  London:  George Allen &
Unwin, 1982.

An inquiry into retirement practices and the experiences
and attitudes of people approaching retirement or recently
retired.

Perkins, A.  Being Old in Britain.  The Christian Century.
94:540-41, 1977.

Phillipson, C.  Capitalism and the Construction of Old Age.

London:  Macmillan, 1982.

An analysis of the social contruction of images of old age.
Includes analysis of interview material with old people.

Phillipson, C., M. Bernard, and P. Strang (eds).  Dependency
and Interdependency in Old Age--Theoretical Perspectives
and Policy Alternatives.  London:  Croom Helm, 1986.

Edited collection of papers from the 1985 Annual Conference
of the British Society of Gerontology.

Qureshi, H.  Responses to Dependency:  Reciprocity, Affect and
Power in Family Relationships.  Pp. 167-79 in C.
Phillipson, M. Bernard, and P.  Strang (eds).  Dependency
and Interdependency in Old Age:  Theoretical Perspectives
and Policy Alternatives.  London:  Croom Helm, 1986.

Rees, A. D.  Life in a Welsh Countryside.  Cardiff, Wales:
University of Wales Press, 1950.

Ethnographic community study of a Welsh village containing
data on the role and position of the elderly.

Richardson, J.  Age and Need, A Study of Older People in North
East Scotland.  Edinburg, Scotland:  Livingstone, 1964.

Shaw, J.  On Our Conscience:  The Plight of the Elderly.
London:  Penguin Books, 1971.

Sheldon, J. H.  The Social Medicine of Old Age:  Report of an
Inquiry in Wolverhampton.  London:  Oxford University
Press, 1948.

One of the earliest empirical studies of old age conducted
in the U.K. with useful statistics.

Stevenson, O.  A Special Relationship?  New Age.
Summer:18-22, 1980.

A discussion of the role of grandparenthood.

Strathern, M.  Kinship at the Core:  An Anthropoology of
Elmdon, A Village in North-west Essex in the Nineteen-
sixties.  London:  Cambridge University Press, 1981.

An ethnographic community study which stresses kinship
obligations.

Tinker, A.  The Elderly in Modern Society.  London:  Longman,
1981.

A text book for student practitioners, outlining the
services and benefits for elderly people.

Townsend, P.  The Family Life of Old People, An Inquiry in
East London.  London:  Routledge and Kegan Paul, 1957.

The now classic ethnographic study of old people which was part of the well-known Bethnal Green series.

_____ The Effects of Family Structure on the Likelihood of Admission to an Institution in Old Age:  The Application of a General Theory.  In E. Shanas and E. Streib (eds). Social Structure and the Family:  Generational Relations. Englewood Cliffs, NJ:  Prentice Hall, 1965.

Tunstall, J.  Old and Alone.  London:  Routledge and Kegan Paul, 1968.

Study of the elderly living alone which makes the important distinction between living alone, isolation, loneliness and anomie.

Ungerson, C.  Policy is Personal:  Sex, Gender and Informal Care.  London:  Tavistock, 1988.

A qualitative study of twenty-one carers of elderly dependents, which explores the policy issues.

Walker, A.  Community Care and the Elderly in Great Britain: Theory and Practice.  International Journal of Health Services.  11(4):541-57, 1981.

_____ Care for Elderly People:  A Conflict Between Women and the State.  Pp. 106-28 in J. Finch and D. Groves (eds).  A Labour of Love:  Women, Work and Caring.  London: Routledge & Kegan Paul, 1983.

Wedderburn, D.  Old People in Britain.  American Behavioral Scientist.  14:97-109, 1970.

Welsh Office.  A Good Old Age:  An Initiative on the Care of the Elderly in Wales.  Cardiff, Wales:  Welsh Office, 1985.

Wenger, C. G.  Ethnicity and Social Organization in North-east Wales.  Pp. 120-32 in G. Williams (ed).  Social and Cultural Change in Contemporary Wales.  London:  Routledge & Kegan Paul, 1978.

An anthropological study which focusses on sub-groupings and boundaries within village organization, looking at age and sex divisions.

_____ Ageing in Rural Communities:  Family Contacts and Community Integration.  Ageing and Society.  2(2):211-29, 1982.

_____ Loneliness:  A Problem of Measurement.  Pp. 145-67 in D. Jerrome (ed).  Ageing in Modern Society.  London:  Croom Helm, 1983.

A review of studies of loneliness in old age, including findings from an empirical study and the development of aggregate measures.

_____ The Supportive Network: Coping with Old Age. London: George Allen & Unwin, 1984a.

An empirical study of the support networks of elderly people in rural North Wales.

_____ Adapting to Old Age in Rural Britain. International Journal of Ageing and Human Development. 19(4):289-301, 1984b.

_____ Care in the Community: Changes in Dependency and Use of Domiciliary Services, A Longitudinal Perspective. Ageing and Society. 5(Pt. 2):143-59, 1985a.

Presentation of data from a follow-up study of old people living in the community in Wales, showing that policy provision has not kept pace with increased levels of dependency.

_____ Surtout des Meres et des Filles: des Vieux Parents Vivant avec Leurs Enfants Adultes au Pays de Galles. Special Edition: Vieillesses des Femmes. Paris. Penelope. 13:111-15, 1985b.

A discussion of shared households in rural Wales, showing that most such households are based on the needs of the younger generations.

_____ A longitudinal Study of Changes and Adaptations in the Support Networks of Welsh Elderly Over 75. Journal of Cross-Cultural Gerontology. 1(3):277-304, 1986a.

_____ What Do Dependency Measures Measure: Challenging Assumptions. Pp. 69-84 in C. Phillipson, M. Bernard, and P. Strang (eds). Dependency and Interdependency in Old Age: Theoretical Perspectives and Policy Alternatives. London: Croom Helm, 1986b.

Chapter suggests that many dependency measures are used as though measuring impairment but are primarily measuring the availability of help.

_____ Dependence, Interdependence and Reciprocity After 80. Journal of Aging Studies. 1(4):355-77, 1987.

A paper presenting empirical data about the development of caring relationships, comparing the experience of spouses with that of adult children.

_____ Old People's Health and Experiences of the Caring Services: Accounts from Rural Communities in North Wales. Occasional Paper No. 4. The Institute of Human Ageing. Liverpool, England: Liverpool University Press, 1988.

_____ Support Networks in Old Age--Constructing a Typology. Pp. 166-85 in M. Jefferys (ed). Ageing in the 20th Century. London, Routledge, Kegan Paul, 1989.

The author identifies five distinct types of support networks, describing the characteristics of each of them and comparing the resulting network typology with those of other authors and drawing attention to the importance of network type for coping behaviour.

_____ The Special Role of Friends and Neighbours. Journal of Ageing Studies. 4(2), 1990a.

A study based on quantitative and qualitative data exploring what the author considers the often under-valued contributions of friends and neighbours to the lives of old people. Relationships with friends are shown to be primarily expressive, while those with neighbours primarily instrumental.

_____ Elderly Carers:  The Need for Appropriate Intervention. Ageing and Society. 10(2), 1990b.

A study of caring after retirement age, which suggests that at least a third of people become carers in retirement. The paper draws attention to the different nature of caring in old age and notes that most intervention designed to support carers are based on the needs of middle-aged women rather than older, frailer people, typically caring for a terminally ill spouse.

_____ The Impact on the Family of Chronic Mental Illness in Old Age.  In R. F. W. Dieckstra and E. A. Sand. Mental Health and the Family. Copenhagen, Denmark:  World Health Organization, 1990c.

A paper based primarily on qualitative data, describing the way in which different types of support networks can be expected to cope with dementia.

_____ Change and Adaptation in Informal Support Networks. Process, Change and Social Support. Special Issue. Journal of Ageing Studies. 4(4):, 1990d.

Wenger, G. C. and S. Shahtahmasebi. Variations in Support Networks: Some Policy Implications. Chapter 15 in J. Mogey, P. Somlai, and J. Trost (eds). Aiding and Ageing: The Coming Crisis. Westport, CT: Greenwood Press, 1990a.

A description of five different types of support networks showing the different makeup of network membership, the different strengths and weaknesses and differential use of services.


**IRELAND**

Arensberg, C. M.  Irish Rural Social Organization. New York, NY: New York Academy of Science, Transactions. 4:202-07, 1941-42.

A historical sketch of the development of the stem family

after 1852 in response to the cessation of subdivision as well as the growth of non-farm employment opportunities after 1870.

Arensberg, C. and S. Kimball. Family and Community in Ireland. Cambridge, MA: Harvard University Press, 1940.

Aughey, H. Aged Solitary Rural Dwellers in County Wexford--A Survey of Fifty Rural Dwellers. British Journal of Geriatric Practice. 2:105-11, 1963.

A brief synopsis of a limited survey of fifty old people living alone in County Wexford. Covers housing conditions, health, nutrition and community support.

Brody, H. Iniskillane: Change and Decline in the West of Ireland. New York, NY: Schocken, 1974.

An analysis of rural demoralization in the west of Ireland, and the changing nature of community kin relationships that have important implications for the elderly.

Compton, P. A. and R. C. Murray. The Elderly in Northern Ireland with Special Reference to the City of Belfast. Pp. 83-109 in A. M. Warnes (ed). Geographical Perspectives on the Elderly. New York, NY: John Wiley, 1092.

A brief study of the demography and distribution of the elderly in Northern Ireland set in the context of a distinctive demography that features high emigration and birth rates. It also considers the position of the elderly in Belfast with respect to special distribution, social composition and housing.

Fleetwood, J. F. Ireland. Pp. 195-207 in E. Palmore (ed). The International Handbook on Aging. Westport, CT: Greenwood, 1980.

A survey of the status of geriatric and gerontological services in the 26-county Irish Republic.

Gordon, M., R. Vaughan, and B. Whelan. The Irish Elderly Who Live Alone: Patterns of Contact and Aid. Journal of Comparative Family Studies. 12:493-508, 1981.

A study of variation in recency of contact with children and siblings, and the incidence of aid in crises of elderly persons living alone.

Gordon, M., B. Whelan, and R. Vaughan. Old Age and Loss of Household Headship: A National Irish Study. Journal of Marriage and Family. 43(3):741-47, 1981.

An attempt to explain why some of the Irish 65 and over residing with children head the household while others do not. Preliminary findings seem to indicate that economic independence of both parents and children contribute strongly to headship.

Hannan, D.  Kinship, Neighbourhood and Social Change in Irish Rural Communities.  Economic and Social Review. 3(2):163-88, 1972.

Preliminary exploration of changes in rural social organization emphasizing:  the neighbour group, kinship systems, and local institutions.  Not directly covering elderly but significant because of age structure effects and impact on informal help.

Harrison, E., M. McKeown, and T. O'Shea.  Old Age in Northern Ireland-- A Study of the Elderly in a Sea-side Town. Economic and Social Review.  Autumn:53-72, 1971.

Survey of 113 old people in seaside town near Belfast. Describes relationships with family, friends and neighbours, and the role of voluntary associations.

James, A., W. L. James, and H. L. Smith.  Reciprocity as a Coping Strategy of the Elderly:  A Rural Irish Perspective. Gerontologist.  24(5):483-89, 1984.

A consideration of reciprocity as one of the strategies to maintain independence among the elderly in rural western Ireland.  The use of reciprocity in public policy formation is briefly addressed.

Kane, E.  The Changing Role of the Family in the Rural Irish Community.  Journal of Comparative Family Studies. 10:141-62, 1979.

An ethnographic description of family life in a county Galway community that is part of a larger study which includes six Irish-speaking communities.

Leyton, E. H.  Spheres of Inheritance in Aughnaboy.  American Anthropologist.  72(6):1378-88, 1970.

An examination of the transmission of fixed capital, houses and money from one generation to the next in a village in northeastern Ireland.

Power, B.  Old and Alone in Ireland.  Dublin, Ireland:  St. Vincent de Paul Society, 1979.

Survey covering both the Republic of Ireland and Northern Ireland.  Based on a total sample of 1,578 elderly people living alone.  Covers mainly housing, social contact, security and attitudes towards living alone.

Scheper-Hughes, N.  Saints, Scholars and Schizophrenics. Berkeley, CA:  University of California Press, 1979.

_____ Deposed Kings:  The Demise of the Rural Irish Gerontocracy.  Pp. 130-46 in J. Sokolovsky (ed).  Growing Old in Different Societies:  Cross-Cultural Perspectives. Acton, MA:  Copley Press, 1987.

Streib, G.  Farmers and Urbanites:  Attitudes Toward
   Intergenerational Relations in Ireland.  Rural Sociology.
   35(1):26-39, 1970.

   A comparative study of 50 Dublin males and 50 West Cork
   farmers that examined the idea that urbanism is associated
   with a less familistic orientation towards
   intergenerational relations.  Urbanites were less
   traditional but urbanization does not necessarily lead to
   the sudden abandonment of familistic attitudes.

_____  Old Age in Ireland:  Demographic and Sociological
   Aspects.  Pp. 167-82 in D. Cowgill and L. Holmes (eds).
   Aging and Modernization.  New York, NY:  Appleton-Century-
   Crofts, 1972.


## USSR

Acharkan, V. A.  State Pensions in the USSR.  International
   Social Science Review.  29(3):258-66, 1976.

Chebotarev, D. F. and N. N. Sachuk.  A Social Policy Directed
   Toward the Health and Welfare of the Aged in the Soviet
   Union.  Journal of the American Geriatric Society.
   26(2):49-57, 1979.

   A discussion of the factors which determined the
   characteristics and peculiarities of medical and social
   care of the aged in the USSR.  The importance of the UN-
   and WHO- sponsored international programs in this field is
   emphasized.  See bibliography for sources in Russian.

Chekalin, V.  The Family and Family Relationships Under
   Socialism.  Societ Law and Government.  Spring:75-88, 1974.

Current Digest of the Soviet Press.  American Association for
   the Advancement of Slavic Studies.  34:December 29, 1982;
   36:May 16, 1984; 36:December 12, 1984; 37:February 27,
   1985.

   Articles on various aspects of aging in the USSR appear in
   the issues listed.

Greenbaum, R. W.  Political Socialization of Children in the
   USSR.  Political Science Quarterly.  58:684-712, 1973.

Juviler, P. H.  The Family in the Soviet Union.  Carl Beck
   Papers in Russian and East European Studies.  Paper No.
   306.  Pittsburgh, PA:  Russian and East European Studies
   Program, University of Pittsburgh, 1984.

Lantsev, M. S. and L. Shchennikova.  Social Security and
   Social Services for the Aged in the USSR.  International
   Social Security Review.  35:541-53, 1982.

   An overview of the care of the elderly in the USSR.  Topics
   covered include demographics, pensions and pension policy,

employment of retirees, and medical services.

Lapidus, G. W. (ed). Women, Work and Family in the Soviet Union. Translated by Vladimir Talmy. Armonk, NY:  M. E. Sharpe, 1982.

McKain, W.  The Aged in the USSR.  Pp. 151-66 in D. Cowgill and L.  Holmes (eds).  Aging and Modernization.  New York, NY:  Appleton-Century-Crofts, 1972.

Medvedev, Z. A.  Negative Trends in Life Expectancy in the USSR, 1964-1983.  Gerontologist.  25:201-08, 1985.

Mitchell, N. J.  Ideology or the Iron Laws of Industrialism: the Case of Pension Policy in Britain and the Soviet Union. Comparative Politics.  15:177-201, 1983.

A detailed discussion of the history and operation of the Soviet pension system.

Peet, E. L.  Anxiety-free Old Age in the Soviet Union.  New World Review.  Winter:77-81, 1972.

This anecdotal account of the author's impressions of aging during a visit to the USSR is based on encounters arranged for him by the Soviet Intourist Office during the summer of 1971.

Rowland, R.  Withdrawal from the Work Force Among Persons of Retirement Age in the USSR: 1959-1970.  Industrial Gerontology.  2:144-45, 1975.

Ryan, M.  USSR Letter:  Care of the Elderly.  British Medical Journal.  284:1861-62, 1982.

A brief overview of geriatric medicine in the USSR.

Shapiro, V. D.  Life After Retirement--Social Problems and Life Styles.  Societ Sociology.  22:3-168, 1983.

This translation of a major Soviet study discusses retirement in the USSR, demographics, pension policy, public concern and services for the elderly.  The results of a field survey conducted among retirees in one section of Moscow deal with expectations of retirement, satisfactions/dissatisfactions, family involvement, daily and civic activism, employment.  See bibliography for sources in Russian.

Shimkin, D. B.  Aging in the Soviet Union:  A West Siberian Perspective.  International Journal of Aging and Human Development.  29(3):185-89, 1989.

Smirnov, S.  The Employment of Old-Age Pensioners in the USSR. International Labour Review.  116:87, 1977.

Soloviev, A. G.  The Employment of Pensioners in the National Economy of the USSR.  International Social Security Review.

33:159, 1976.

Talchuk, A., et al.  Social Conditions, Health and Heredity as Factors of Longevity in the Byelorussian Population.  The Impact of Science on Society.  153:81-91, 1989.

Ucko, L. G.  Perceptions of Aging East and West:  Soviet Refugees See Two Worlds.  Journal of Cross-Cultural Gerontology.  1(4):411-28, 1986.

Judgments made by members of refugee families about government policies, pensions, old age homes, families and public and private attitudes toward the elderly reveal both criticism anb praise of Soviet as well as American and Israeli practices.

Wheat, M. E., et al.  Aspects of Medical Care of Soviet Jewish Emigres.  Western Journal of Medicine.  139(6):900-04, 1983.

Attitudes of elderly refugee medical patients are traced to earlier responses to the Soviet system of medical care.

Yakushev, L.  Old Peoples' Rights in the USSR and Other European Socialist Countries.  International Labour Review.  113:253-54, 1976.


OTHER EUROPEAN NATIONS/CANADA

Almind, G.  Risk Factors in Eighty-plus Year-olds Living at Home:  An Investigation of a Danish Community.  Intergenerational Journal of Aging and Human Development.  21(3):227-34, 1985.

Baars, J. and K. Knipscheer.  Ageing in the Netherlands: Structural and Cultural Characteristics.  Journal of Cross-Cultural Gerontology.  4(2):129-42, 1989.

Bacon, W. E., et al.  Hospital Use by the Elderly in Poland and the United States.  American Journal of Public Health.  74:1220-26, 1984.

Barker, J. C.  Health and Functional Status of the Elderly in a Polynesian Population.  Journal of Cross-Cultural Gerontology.  4(2):162-94, 1989.

Bienvenue, R. M. and B. Havens.  Structural Inequalitites, Informal Networks:  A Comparison of Native and Non-Native Elderly.  Canadian Journal on Aging.  5(4):241-48, 1986.

Bjelland, A. K.  Aging and Identity Management in a Norwegian Elderly Home.  Human Relations.  38:151-66, 1985.

Bozzetti, L.  The Aged in Sweden II:  A Systems Approach--The Swedish Model.  Psychiatric Annals.  7:63-81, 1977.

Canadian Ethnic Studies.  Special Issue.  Ethnicity and Aging.

15(3), 1983.

Coleman, P.  Social Gerontology in the Netherlands:  A Review of Recent Current Research. Gerontologist.  15:155-59, 1975.

_____ The Netherlands:  Poverty and Disability in Old Age. Pp. 266-82 in R. Walker, R. Lawson, and P. Townsend (eds). Responses to Poverty:  Lessons from Europe.  London: Heinemann, 1984a.

_____ Asessing Self Esteem and Its Sources in Elderly People. Ageing and Society.  4(2):117-35, 1984b.

Cool, L.  Ethnicity and Aging:  Continuity through Change for Elderly Corsicans.  Pp. 149-69 in C. Fry (ed).  Aging in Culture and Society:  Comparative Viewpoints and Strategies.  Brooklyn, NY:  J. F. Bergin, 1980.

Driest, F.  Social Services and the Elderly in the Netherlands. Journal of Gerontological Social Work. 12(1-2):153-66, 1988.

Gerritsen, J. C., E. W. Wolffensperger, and W. J. A. Van den Heuvel.  Rural-Urban Differences in the Utilization of Care by the Elderly.  Journal of Cross-Cultural Gerontology. 5(2):131-48, 1990.

Gibson, R., et al.  The Zinc, Copper, and Selenium Status of a Selected Sample of Canadian Elderly Women.  Journal of Gerontology.  40:296-302, 1985.

Gothoni, R.  From Chaos to Cosmos:  The Telling of a Life Story Reconsidered.  Journal of Cross-Cultural Gerontology. 5(1):65-76, 1990.

Guillemard, A. M.  State, Society and Old-Age Policy in France:  From 1945 to the Current Crisis.  Social Science and Medicine.  23(12):1319-26, 1986.

Gustafson, B.  Macroeconomic Performance, Old Age Security and the Rate of Social Assistance Recipients in Sweden. European Economic Review.  26:319-38, 1984.

Haavisto, M., et al.  A Health Survey of the Very Aged in Tampere, Finland.  Age and Ageing.  13:266-72, 1984.

Haavisto, M., et al.  Living Conditions and Health of a Population Aged 85 Years or Over:  A Five-Year Follow-up Study.  Age and Ageing.  14:202-08, 1985.

Horl, J.  Looking Back to Caregiving:  Findings from Case Studies in Vienna, Austria.  Journal of Cross-Cultural Gerontology.  4(3):245-56, 1989.

Huseby-Darvas, E. V.  Elderly Women in a Hungarian Village: Childlessness, Generativity, and Social Control.  Journal of Cross-Cultural Gerontology.  2(1):15-42, 1987.

Kadar, R.  Social Status of the Aged in Hungary.  Pp. 553-57 in A.  Balazs (ed).  Proceedings of the Conference on Gerontology.  Budapest, Hungary:  Akademiai Kiado, 1965.

Kivela, S. L.  Prevalence of Depressive and Other Symptoms in Elderly Finnish Men.  Acta Psychiatrica Scandinavica. 73(1):93-100, 1986.

Kivela, S. L., et al.  Age and Regional Differences in Reliability and Factor of Zung Self-Rating Scale in Elderly Finnish Men.  Journal of Clinical Psychology.  43:318-27, 1987.

Kooy, G.  The Aged in Rural Netherlands.  Pp. 501-09 in C. Tibbits and W.  Donahue (eds).  Aging Around the World. New York, NY:  Columbia University Press, 1962.

Kooy, G. and C. van't Klooster-van Wingerden.  The Aged in an Urban Community in the Netherlands.  Human Development. 11:64-77, 1968.

Ledent, J. and K.-L. Liaw.  Provincial Out-Migration Patterns of Canadian Elderly:  Characterization and Explanation. Environment and Planning A.  21:1093-111, 1989.

Lipman, A.  Prestige of the Aged in Portugal:  Realistic Appraisal and Ritualistic Deference.  Aging and Human Development.  1(2):  127-36, 1970.

Marshall, V. (ed).  Aging in Canada: Social Perspectives. Post Mills, VT:Chelsea Green, Fitzhenry and Whiteside, 1980.

Mertens, F. and M. Wimmers.  Life-style of Older People: Improvement or Threat to Their Health?  Ageing and Sociology.  7:329-43, 1987.

Moller, I. H.  Early Retirement in Denmark.  Ageing and Society.  7:427-43, 1987.

Morabia, A., et al.  Medical Care and Social Support for the Elderly in Switzerland:  Imbalance and Mix.  Social Science and Medicine.  23(12):1327-32, 1986.

Morris, D. E.  Sante Service Bayonee:  A French Approach to Home Care.  Age and Ageing.  12:323-28, 1983.

Munnichs, J.  Linkages of Old People with Their Families and Bureaucracy in a Welfare State, the Netherlands.  Pp. 92-116 in E. Shanas and M. Sussman (eds).  Family, Bureaucracy, and the Family.  Durham, NC:  Duke University Press, 1977.

Pihlblad, C., E. Beverfelt, and H. Hellend.  Status and Role of the Aged in Norwegian Society.  Pp. 227-42 in D. Cowgill and L. Holmes (eds).  Aging and Modernization.  New York, NY:  Appleton-Century-Crofts, 1972.

Piotrowski, J.  Old People, Bureaucracy, and the Family in
    Poland.  Pp.  158-71 in E. Shanas and M. Sussman (eds).
    Family, Bureaucracy, and the Elderly.  Durham, NC:  Duke
    University Press, 1977.

Pflanczer, S. I. and B. J. Bognar.  Care of Elderly People in
    Hungary Today.  Gerontologist.  29:546-50, 1989.

Reis, W., et al.  Objectives, Organization, and Results of the
    Leipzig Longitudinal Study.  Age and Ageing.  14:30-36,
    1985.

Rosenberg, M. W., et al.  Components of Change in the Spatial
    Distribution of the Elderly Population in Ontario.  The
    Canadian Geographer.  33:218-29, 1989.

Rosenmayr, L.  The Elderly in Austrian Society.  Pp. 183-96 in
    D.  Cowgill and L. Holmes (eds).  Aging and Modernization.
    New York, NY:  Appleton-Century-Crofts, 1972.

Rubenstein, J. M.  Leisure Participation and Satisfaction in
    Two European Communities.  Journal of Cross-Cultural
    Gerontology.  2(2):151-70, 1987.

Schumann, J.  Social Services and Social Work Practice with
    the Elderly in the Federal Republic of Germany.  Journal of
    Gerontological Social Work.  12(1-2):61-76, 1988.

Shapiro, E. and L. Webster.  Nursing Home Utilization for All
    Manitoba Admissions, 1974-1981.  Gerontologist.  24:610-15,
    1984.

Simic, A.  Winners and Losers:  Aging Yugoslavs in a Changing
    World.  Pp. 77-105 in B. Myerhoff and A. Simic (eds).
    Life's Career-- Aging:  Cultural Variations on Growing Old.
    Beverly Hills, CA:  Sage, 1978.

    The theme of aging as a "kind of career" is thoughtfully
    exemplified in this chapter.  During this "career," self-
    evaluation is carried out, with gains and losses of a
    lifetime being appraised.  Most of the information is drawn
    from two Serbian family case studies conducted by Simic.
    The impact of culture change is included in adjunct
    fashion.  Photographs accompany the chapter.

Sterns, P.  Old Age in European Society:  The Case of France.
    New York, NY:  Holmes and Meier, 1976.

Sundstrom, G.  Intergenerational Mobility and the Relationship
    Between Adults and Their Aging Parents in Sweden.
    Gerontologist.  26:367-71, 1986.

Synak, B.  The Elderly in Poland:  An Overview of Selected
    Problems and Changes.  Ageing and Sociology.  7:19-35,
    1987.

_____ Formal Care for Elderly People in Poland.  Journal of
    Cross-Cultural Gerontology.  4(2):107-28, 1989.

Thomas, K. and A. Wister.  Living Arrangements of Older Women: The Ethnic Dimension.  Journal of Marriage and the Family. 46:301-11, 1984.

Thorslund, M. and L. Johanson.  Elderly People in Sweden: Current Realities and Future Plans.  Ageing and Sociology. 7:345-55, 1987.

Tornstam, L.  Formal and Informal Support for the Elderly:  An Analysis of Present Patterns and Future Options in Sweden. The Impact of Science on Society.  153:57-63, 1989.

Warnes, K.  A Feminist Perspective on the New Ideology of Community Care for the Elderly.  Acta Sociologica. 30(2):133-50, 1987.

Weatherford, J. M.  Labor and Domestic Life Cycles in a German Community.  Pp. 145-61 in C. Fry (ed).  Dimensions:  Aging, Culture, and Health.  Brooklyn, NY:  J. F. Bergin, 1981.

The life cycle approach is taken to examine aging in a holistic context in West Germany.  Broad but effective treatment is given to (1) the working cycle, (2) the domestic/family life cycle, and (3) the transitions within these life cycles.  The latter are of particular interest since Weatherford is able to avoid the standard litany of "rites of passage" while nonetheless highlighting significant transitions--such as that to retiree.  He concludes with a brief review of the relatively flexible German social policies regarding care of the elderly.

Worach-Kardas, H.  The Polish Family Tradition. Gerontologist.  23:593-96, 1983.

The author discusses the Polish family as it relates to the support of the aged.

Zelkovitz, B. M.  Transforming the "Middle Way":  A Political Economy of Aging Policy in Sweden.  Pp. 163-80 in J. Sokolovsky (ed).  The Cultural Context of Aging:  Worldwide Perspectives.  Westport, CT:  Bergin and Garvey, 1990.

## ISRAEL, JEWS OUTSIDE OF ISRAEL

Anson, O., et al.  Family, Gender, and Attitudes Toward Retirement.  Sex Roles.  20:355-69, 1989.

Atar, S.  Aging in Kibbutz Society.  Gerontology.  1(4):51-57, 1975.

Berman, Y.  Some Problems of the Aged in the Rural Milieu in Israel.  International Journal of Aging and Human Development.  5(3):257-63, 1974.

Cohen-Mansfield, J.  Employment and Volunteering Roles for the Elderly:  Characteristics, Attributions, and Strategies. Journal of Leisure Research.  21(3):214-27, 1989.

Feder, S.  Aging in the Kibbutz in Israel.  Pp. 211-26 in D.
   Cowgill and L. Holmes (eds).  Aging and Modernization.
   New York, NY: Appleton-Century-Crofts, 1972.

Fried, H. and H. M. Waxman.  Stockholm's Cafe 84:  A Unique
   Day Program for Jewish Survivors of Concentration Camps.
   Gerontologist.  28:253-55, 1988.

Greenbaum (Ucko), L.  Two Families, Three Generations, One
   Story.  Pp. 69-89 in R. J. Simon (ed).  New Lives:  The
   Adjustment of Soviet Jewish Immigrants in the United States
   and Israel.  Lexington, MA:  Lexington Books, 1985.

   First person accounts of life in and emigration from the
   Soviet Union by members of three generations in two
   different refugee families.  The author points to the
   variations in outlook and perceptions revealed at different
   stages in the life cycle.

Handelman, D.  Work and Play Among the Aged.  Assen, Holland:
   Royal Vangoreum, 1977.

Hazan, H.  Adjustment and Control in an Old Age Home.  Pp.
   239-56 in E. Marx (ed).  A Composite Portrait of Israel.
   London:  Academic Press, 1980a.

_____  Continuity and Change in a Tea-Cup:  On the Symbolic
   Nature of Tea-Related Behaviour Among the Aged.
   Sociological Review.  28(3):497-516, 1980b.

   Tea-related behavior is viewed as a nonreciprocal timeless
   event constituting a flexible and manipulable cultural
   symbol.  Such properties render a transitory quality to
   tea-related conduct, enabling it to serve as a vehicle for
   social transformation.  A case study of the manifestations
   of tea-related behavior in a day-care center for elderly
   Jewish inhabitants of a poor district of London is
   presented.  The members, having gone through a series of
   socio-economic changes in later life, reconstruct a new
   existential reality where change is arrested and present-
   bound society emerges.  Tea drinking is employed as a
   temporal symbol to delineate external boundaries between
   the center and its social surroundings, and internal
   boundaries between groups of members and between members
   and staff.  Both the structure and the content of that
   symbol are examined and construed as encapsulating and
   representing the dialectics of continuity and change in the
   last phase of the members' lives.

_____  The Limbo People:  A Study of the Constitution of the
   Time Universe Among the Aged.  London:  Routledge and Kegan
   Paul, 1980c.

   Based on fieldwork carried out in a day center for elderly
   Jewish people in London, this study explores some of the
   ways employed by old people to constitute their conception
   of time.  It demonstrates that the life histories of the
   members of the center, coupled with their current social,

economic and physical conditions, created a discrepancy
between social definition of time and personal experience.
Within the center, certain parts of the past were
obliterated, some were renounced, whereas others were
cherished. Alternative realities to the center and future
prospects were cognitively forestalled, and the possibility
of death was invalidated. This repatterning of time took
place against the background of a social system of interpersonal relationships characterized mainly by the
exclusion of mutuality and personal exchange; in this way,
relations between events would involve neither planning for
the future nor leaning on the past, and would therefore
take the form of a repetitive duration of time, thus
indicating the arrest of change and the negation of the
outside, changeable world. The manipulation of time is
thus revealed as a socially constructed response to an
existential dilemma experienced in the later years of life.

_____ Totality as an Adaptive Strategy:  Two Case Studies of
the Management of Powerlessness.  Social Analysis.
9:63-76, 1981.

_____ Discontinuity and Identity:  A Case Study of Social
Reintegration Among the Aged.  Research on Aging.
5(4):473-89, 1983.

This article discusses the dilemma of continuity versus
discontinuity in the life of the aged. The contradiction
that seems to exist between structural discontinutiy and
personal continuity may be resolved by suggesting that the
need for continuity is neither a universal nor a necessary
characteristic of identity formation in the elderly.  An
ethnographic study of the social reality of an English day
center for Jewish residents of an impoverished neighborhood
provides a case study wherein discontinuity of ties and
past involvements serves as a viable resource in the
construction of new identities.

_____ Religion in an Old Age Home:  Symbolic Adaptation as a
Survival Strategy.  Ageing and Society.  4:137-56, 1984a.

_____ Continuity and Transformation Among the Aged:  A Study
in the Anthropology of Time.  Current Anthropology.
25(5):567-78, 1984b.

Properties of social time developed among members of a
London day-care center for the aged at two points of
chronological time are compared.  In the first study,
members' temporal universe was found to be anchored in a
change-arresting conception of reality constructed and
sustained by an isolated, egalitarian, present-bound social
structure.  The re-study, conducted seven years later,
revealed that although the center was no longer an
isolated, egalitarian society, veteran members still
adhered to temporal principles of the former structure.
Thus the first period could be regarded as a formative
phase for a mode of structured continuity with enduring
elements of liminality.  It is therefore suggested that

time is not a mere reflection of social processes but their generator and hence a subject of anthropological investigation in its own right.

_____ Existential Boundaries in an Institutional Setting: The Care of the Aged. Pp. 239-56 in Y. Kashti and M. Arieli (eds). People in Institutions: The Israeli Case. London: Freund, 1986a.

_____ Body Image and Temporality Among the Aged: A Case Study of an Ambivalent Symbol. Study in Symbolic Interaction. 7(A):305-29, 1986b.

This paper interrelates socially constructed conceptions of the body among the elderly to temporal perspectives in old age. Based on an ethnography of a London day center, the study explores the ambivalent nature of the body as a spatial symbol of a stable social order on the one hand, and as a marker for physical and mental uncontrollable deterioration on the other. This inexorable cleavage is manifested in a number of seemingly behavioral contradictions which are explained in terms of the relationship between the participants' management of body image, i. e., elimination and diminishment of perceived somatic attributes, and the temporal universe of the center which became a change-arresting environment. The case study draws upon theoretical themes concerning the grid/group paradigm and the concepts of liminality and communitas.

_____ Victim into Sacrifice: The Construction of the Old As a Symbolic Type. Journal of Cross-Cultural Gerontology. 5(1):77-84, 1990a.

_____ The Construction of Personhood Among the Aged: A Comparative Study of Aging in Israel and England. Pp. 263-76 in J. Sokolovsky (ed). The Cultural Context of Aging: Worldwide Perspectives. Westport, CT: Bergin and Garvey, 1990b.

Holmes, D., et al. Informal Versus Formal Supports for Impaired Elderly People: Determinants of Choice on Israeli Kibbutzim. Gerontologist. 29:195-202, 1989.

Kahana, E., et al. Motivators, Resources and Barriers in Voluntary International Migration of the Elderly: The Case of Israel-Bound Aged. Journal of Cross-Cultural Gerontology. 1(2):191-208, 1986.

Litwin, H. and G. K. Auslander. Ageing and Society. 8:269-85, 1988.

Prager, E. H. Organizational Involvement as a Correlate of Relocation Adjustment Amongst Elderly Movers to Israel. Journal of Cross-Cultural Gerontology. 1(1):91-102, 1986.

_____ Observations of Simulated Data Accrual with Aged Clients. Social Casework. 68:345-51, 1987.

Schneider, R. L. and A. Lowenstein.  Outreach to the Elderly in Israel:  Service Delivery Issues.  Journal of Gerontological Social Work.  13(3-4):95-113, 1989.

Sered, S. S.  The Liberation of Widowhood.  Journal of Cross-Cultural Gerontology.  2(2)139-50, 1987.

_____ Women, Religion, and Modernization:  Tradition and Transformation Among Elderly Jews in Israel.  American Anthropologist.  92(2):306-18, 1990.

Shlesinger, B.  Family Life in the Kibbutz of Israel:  Utopia Gained or Paradise Lost.  International Journal of Comparative Sociology.  11:251-71, 1970.

Shomaker, D.  Economic Pressures Resulting From Aging of Kibbutz Society.  Gerontologist.  24:313-17, 1984.

Simos, B. and M. Kohls.  Migration, Relocation and Intergenerational Relations:  Jews of Quito, Ecuador.  Gerontologist.  15(3):206-11, 1975.

Talmon-Garber, Y.  Aging in Collective Settlements in Israel.  Pp.  426-41 in C. Tibbits and W. Donahue (eds).  Aging Around the World.  New York, NY:  Columbia University Press, 1962.

_____ Aging in Israel, A Planned Society.  Pp. 191-210 in B. Neugarten (ed).  Middle Age and Aging.  Chicago, IL:  University of Chicago Press, 1968.

Teresi, J., et al.  Factors Relating to Institutional Risk Among Elderly Members of Israeli Kibbutzim.  Gerontologist.  29:203-08, 1989.

Weihl, H.  Aging in Israel.  American Behavioral Scientist.  14:110-20, 1970a.

_____ Jewish Aged of Different Cultural Origin in Israel.  Gerontologist.  10:146-50, 1970b.

_____ Selected Aspects of Aging in Israel:  1969.  Pp. 197-209 in D. Cowgill and L. Holmes (eds).  Aging and Modernization.  New York, NY:  Appleton-Century-Crofts, 1982.

_____ Three Issues from the Israeli Scene.  Gerontologist.  23:576-78, 1983.

Weihl discusses three issues concerning the family support of the aged.

Wershow, H.  Aging with the Israel Kibbutz.  Gerontologist  9:300-04, 1969.

_____ Aging in the Israeli Kibbutz:  Growing Old in a Mini-Socialist Society.  Jewish Social Studies.  35:141-48, 1973a.

_____ Aging in the Israeli Kibbutz: Some Further Investigation. _Aging and Human Development_ 4(3):211-27, 1973b.


## OTHER NATIONAL/REGIONAL CULTURES

Andrews, G. R., et al. _Aging in the Western Pacific_. Manilla, Philippines: World Health Organization, 1986.

_____ Cross-Cultural Studies: An Important Development in Aging Research. _Journal of Geriatrics Society_. 37(5):483-85, 1989.

Barker, J. Between Humans and Ghosts: The Decrepit Elderly in a Polynesian Society. Pp. 295-314 in J. Sokolovsky, ed. _The Cultural Context of Aging: Worldwide Perspectives_. Westport, CT: Bergin & Garvey, 1990.

Chen, P. C. Y. Family Support and the Health of the Elderly Malaysian. _Journal of Cross-Cultural Gerontology_. 2(2):187-93, 1987.

This study was part of a larger, four-country comparative project sponsored by the World Health Organization. It is noteworthy in terms of its use of a purposive sample of 1,001 elderly Malaysians. Family structure, economic and familial social support, and social contacts were emphasized. Adherence to tradition was confirmed in that 62% of those surveyed depended upon the family for income, while 95% could turn to an immediate relative should they fall ill. Only 1% indicated that they would be unable to find support of any sort in the event of illness. The renewed institutionalization of extended familial support networks is recommended.

Chow, N. W. S. _Caregiving in Developing East and Southeast Asian Countries_. Tampa, FL: International Exchange Center on Gerontology, 1988.

Collette, J. Sex Differences in Life Satisfaction: Australian Data. _Journal of Gerontology_. 39:243-45, 1984.

Cowgill, D. The Social Life of the Aging in Thailand. _Gerontologist_. 8:159-63, 1968.

_____ The Role and Status of the Aged in Thailand. Pp. 91-102 in D. Cowgill and L. Holmes (eds). _Aging and Modernization_. New York, NY: Appleton-Century-Crofts, 1972.

Domino, G. Sleep Habits in the Elderly: A Study of Three Hispanic Cultures. _Journal of Cross-Cultural Gerontology_. 17(1):109-20, 1986.

Donner, W. W. Compassion, Kinship and Fosterage: Contexts for the Care of the Childless Elderly in a Polynesian Community. _Journal of Cross-Cultural Gerontology_.

2(1):43-60, 1987.

Evans, J.  The Economic Status of Older Men and Women in the
    Javanese Household and the Influence of This Upon Their
    Nutritional Level.  Journal of Cross-Cultural Gerontology.
    5(3):217-42, 1990.

Fadel-Girgis, M.  Family Support for the Elderly in Egypt.
    Gerontologist.  23:589-92, 1983.

Finaus, S. A., I. A. M. Prior, and J. G. Evans.  Ageing in the
    South Pacific.  Social Science and Medicine.  16:1539-49,
    1982.

Fink, A.  The Australian Situation.  Pp. 16-22 in C. Nusberg
    and M.  Osako.  The Situation of the Asian/Pacific Elderly.
    Washington, DC:  International Federation on Ageing, 1981.

_____  The Very Old of Palau:  Health and Mental State.  Age
    and Ageing.  17:220-26, 1988.

Gibson, D. M. and D. T. Rowland.  Community vs Institutional
    Care:  The Case of the Australian Aged.  Social Science
    Medicine.  18(11):997-1004, 1984.

Gilleard, C. J. and A. A. Gurkan.  Socioeconomic Development
    and the Status of Elderly Men in Turkey:  A Text of
    Modernization Theory.  Journal of Gerontology.  42:353-57,
    1987.

Griffiths, S. L.  Coping with Old Age in a Philippine Emigrant
    Community.  Journal of Cross-Cultural Gerontology.
    1(2):177-190, 1986.

Gutierrez-Robledo, L. M.  The Ageing Situation in Latin
    America.  Impact of Science on Society.  153:65-80, 1989.

Holmes, E. R. and L. D. Holmes.  Western Polynesia's First
    Home for the Aged:  Are Concept and Culture Compatible?
    Journal of Cross-Cultural Gerontology.  2(4):359-76, 1987.

Jensen, G. D. and A. H. Polloi.  Health and Life-Style of
    Longevous Palauans:  Implications for Developmental Theory.
    International Journal of Aging and Human Development.
    19(4):271-85, 1984.

Kalab, M.  Buddhism and Emotional Support for Elderly People.
    Journal of Cross-Cultural Gerontology.  5(1):7-20, 1990.

Kendig, H. L. and D. T. Rowland.  Family Support of the
    Australian Aged:  A Comparison with the United States.
    Gerontologist.  23:643-49, 1983.

Kivnick, H. Q.  Adulthood and Old Age Under Apartheid:  A
    Psychosocial Consideration.  Ageing and Society.  8:425-40,
    1988.

Koo, J. and D. O. Cowgill.  Health Care for Aged in Korea.

*Social Science Medicine*.  23(12):1347-52, 1986.

Levine, S. E.  Widowhood in Los Robles:  Parent-Child Relations and Economic Survival in Old Age in Urban Mexico. *Journal of Cross-Cultural Gerontology*.  1(3):223-38, 1986.

Manton, K. G., J. E. Dowd, and M. A. Woodbury.  Conceptual and Measurement Issues in Assessing Disability Cross-Nationally:  Analysis of a Who-Sponsored Survey of the Disablement Process in Indonesia.  *Journal of Cross-Cultural Gerontology*.  1(4):339-62, 1986.

Manton, K. G., G. C. Myers, and G. R. Andrews.  Morbidity and Disability Patterns in Four Developing Nations:  Their Implications for Social and Economic Integration of the Elderly.  *Journal of Cross-Cultural Gerontology*. 2(2):115-30, 1987.

Martin, L. G.  Living Arrangements of the Elderly in Fiji, Korea, Malaysia, and the Philippines.  *Demography*. 26:627-43, 1989.

_____  The Status of South Asia's Growing Elderly Population. *Journal of Cross-Cultural Gerontology*.  5(2):93-118, 1990.

McCallum, J.  Noncontributory Pensions for Less Developed Countries:  Rehabilitating an Old Idea.  *Journal of Cross-Cultural Gerontology*.  5(3):255-76, 1990.

Mitchell, J., J. Bort, and J. Sabella.  Children's Perceptions of Aging Adults:  An Exploration of Differences in Caribbean Panama.  *Journal of Cross-Cultural Gerontology*. 2(4):297-320, 1987.

Munro-Ashman, J.  Geriatric Assessment--An Australian Idea. *Social Science and Medicine*.  29(8):939-42, 1989.

Nusberg, C. and M. Osako (eds).  *The Situation of the Asian/ Pacific Elderly*.  Washington, DC:  International Federation on Ageing, 1981.

Osgood, C.  *The Koreans and Their Culture*.  New York, NY: Ronald Press, 1951.

Pyun, C-H.  The Korean Situation.  Pp. 13-16 in C. Nusberg and M. Osako (eds).  *The Situation of the Asian/Pacific Elderly*.  Washington, DC:  International Federation on Ageing, 1981.

Rosenman, L. S. and S. Winocur.  Australian Women and Income Security for Old Age:  A Cohort Study.  *Journal of Cross-Cultural Gerontology*.  5(3):277-92, 1990.

Rubinstein, R. L.  What Is 'Social Integraton of the Elderly' in Small-Scale Society?  *Journal of Cross-Cultural Gerontology*.  1(4):391-410, 1986.

_____  Childless Elderly:  Theoretical Perspectives and

Practical Concerns. _Journal of Cross-Cultural Gerontology_. 2(1):1-14, 1987.

Russell, C. and H. Oxley. Health and Ageing in Australia: Is There Culture After Sixty? _Journal of Cross-Cultural Gerontology_. 5(1):35-50, 1990.

Rustom, C. The Later Years of Life and the Use of Time Among the Burmans. Pp. 100-03 in R. Kleemeir (ed). _Aging and Leisure_. New York, NY: Oxford University Press, 1961.

Shebani, B. L., et al. Correlates of Life Satisfaction for Old Libyans Compared with the Judgments of Libyan Youth. _International Journal of Aging and Human Development_. 24(1):19-28, 1986-87.

Sorensen, C. Migration, the Family, and the Care of the Aged in Rural Korea: An Investihgation of a Village in the Yongso Region of Kangwon Province 1918-1983. _Journal of Cross-Cultural Gerontology_. 1(2):139-62, 1986.

Stokes, E. M. Ethnography of a Social Border: The Case of an American Retirement Community in Mexico. _Journal of Cross-Cultural Gerontology_. 5(2):169-82, 1990.

Sunar, D. G. Attitudes of Turkish Students Toward Elderly Relatives. _Journal of Cross-Cultural Gerontology_. 3(1):41-52, 1988.

Syryani, L. K., et al. The Physical and Mental Health of Elderly in a Balinese Village. _Journal of Cross-Cultural Gerontology_. 3(2):105-20, 1988.

Trevino-Richard, T. and M. A. Krain. A Factorial Analysis of Age-Related Changes in the Spatial Structure of Three Puerto Rican Cities. _Journal of Cross-Cultural Gerontology_. 1(4):363-90, 1986.

Warnes, A. M. Comparative Studies of Ageing and Elderly People: Review Article. _Ageing and Society_. 8:441-48, 1988.

Watson, W. H. and R. J. Maxwell. The Changing Status of Elders in a Polynesian Society. Pp. 46-58 in W. H. Watson and R. J. Maxwell (eds). _Human Aging and Dying: A Study in Sociocultural Gerontology_. New York, NY: St. Martin's Press, 1977.

A brief prelude covering the aged in other non-Western societies is followed by a balanced presentation on the elders of Samoa. The focus is on the changing roles of chiefs, with concomitant changes in prestige and upon the associated changes affecting their wives. An historical summary of Samoan-Western contacts since 1722 is included.

Webber, I., et al. Variations in Value Orientations by Age in a Developing Society. _Journal of Gerontology_. 29(6):676-83, 1974.

Yap, P.  Aging in Underdeveloped Asian Countries.  <u>Aging Around the World</u>.  New York, NY:  Columbia University Press, 1962.

# 6

# Modernization

Achenbaum, W. A. and P. N. Stearns. Essay: Old Age and
    Modernization. Gerontologist. 18(3):307-12, 1978.

This article provides a critique of modernization theory
from a historical point of view.

Adamchak, D. J. Population Aging in Sub-Saharan Africa: The
    Effects of Development on the Elderly. Population and
    Environment. 10(3):162-76, 1989.

Bengtson, V. and D. Simon. Social Modernity and Attitudes
    Toward Aging. Gerontologist. 8(3):26, 1968.

Bengtson, V., et al. Modernization, Modernity, and
    Perceptions of Aging: A Cross-Cultural Study. Journal of
    Gerontology. 30:688-95, 1975.

Report on a study of attitudes toward aging and the aged in
six developing countries. The investigators suggest the
usefulness of distinguishing between modernity and
modernization; their data indicate support for the
modernization theory.

Cherry, R. L. and S. Magnuson-Martinson. Modernization and
    the Status of the Aged in China : Decline or Equalization?
    Sociological Quarterly. 22(2):253-61, 1981.

These authors present an analysis of old age in China prior
to and following the revolution and propose that status of
the aged may be affected by political ideology as well as
other aspects of modernization.

Cole, T. R. Thoughts on Old Age and the Welfare State:
    Political Economy, History, and Health Policy. Journal of
    the American Geriatrics Society. 33(12):869-73, 1985.

Cowgill, D. The Aging of Populations and Societies. Annals,
    American Academy of Poltical and Social Sciences.
    415:1-18, 1974a.

_____ Aging and Modernization:  A Revision of the Theory.
Pp.  123-46 in J. Gubrium (ed).  Late Life:  Communities
and Environmental Policy.  Springfield, IL:  C. C. Thomas,
1974b.

This important article presents a revision of the aging and
modernization theory in terms of four modernization
variables most relevant to the status of the aged--health
technology, economic technology, urbanization, and
education.  Cowgill also offers a new definition of
modernization.

_____ Demographic Aging and Economic Dependency.  Pp. 303-05
in H. Orimo, et al. (eds).  Recent Advances in Gerontology:
Proceedings of the 11th International Congress of
Gerontology.  Amsterdam, Holland:  Excerpta Medica, 1979.

_____ Aging in Comparative Cultural Perspective.  Mid-
American Review of Sociology.  6(2):1-28, 1981.

Cowgill, D. O. and L. D. Holmes.  Aging and Modernization.
New York, NY:  Appleton-Century Crofts, 1972.

This volume presents data on aging in fourteen societies
differentially located along a traditional-modern
continuum.  These data provide the basis for the
development of the aging and modernization theory, which
postulates an inverse relationship between increased
societal modernization and status of the aged.

Cox, F. M. and N. Mberia.  Aging in a Changing Village
Society:  A Kenyan Experience.  Washington, DC:
International Federation on Ageing, 1977.

Dlugokinski, E. and S. Rest.  Facilitating Mutually Supportive
Linkages Between Generations:  GIFT after Two Years.
Lifelong Learning.  5(6):12-14, 1982.

This report on an intergenerational program finds that
modernization has led to isolation and compartmentalization
of generations.

Donner, W. W.  Compassion, Kinship, and Fosterage:  Contexts
for the Care of the Childless Elderly in a Polynesian
Community.  Journal of Cross-Cultural Gerontology.
2:43-59, 1987.

Dowd, J. J.  Industrialization and the Decline of the Aged.
Sociological Focus.  14(4):255-69, 1981.

This article provides a critique of modernization theory
and suggests that status of the aged is better explained in
terms of exchange theory.

_____ Beneficence and the Aged.  Journal of Gerontology.
39:102-08, 1984.

Dowd utilizes "the norms of beneficence and reciprocity" to

assess the status of the aged in industrialized societies.

Dressler, W. W.  Psychosomatic Symptoms, Stress, and
    Modernization:  A Model.  Culture, Medicine and Psychiatry.
    9(3):257-86, 1985.

Finley, G.  Modernization and Aging.  Pp. 511-23 in T. Field,
    et al.  Review of Human Development.  New York, NY:  Wiley-
    Interscience, 1982.

Foner, N.  Age and Social Change.  Pp. 195-216 in D. Kertzer
    and J.  Keith (eds).  Age and Anthropological Theory.
    Ithaca, NY:  Cornell University Press, 1984.

Fulgraff, B.  Social Gerontology in West Germany:  A Review of
    Recent and Current Research.  Gerontologist.  18:42-58,
    1978.

Gibson, M. J.  Family Support for the Elderly in International
    Perspective:  Part 1.  Ageing International.  7(3):12-17,
    1980a.

_____  Family Support for the Elderly in International
    Perspective:  Part 2.  Policies and Programs.  Ageing
    International.  7(4):13-19, 1980b.

_____  Older Women:  An Overlooked Resource in Development.
    Ageing International.  12(4):12-15, 1985-86.

    Gibson examines the effects of modernization on the roles
    and status of women in third world countries.

Gilleard, J. G. and A. A. Gurkan.  Socioeconomic Development
    and the Status of Elderly Men in Turkey:  A Test of
    Modernization Theory.  Journal of Gerontology.  42:353,
    1987.

Goldstein, M. and C. Beall.  Modernization and Aging in the
    Third and Fourth World:  Views from the Rural Hinterland in
    Nepal.  Human Organization.  40:48-55, 1981.

_____  Indirect Modernization and the Status of the Elderly in
    a Rural Third World Setting.  Journal of Gerontology.
    37:743-48, 1982.

    Research among rural elders in Nepal finds that migration
    of the young to India has affected the old people in an
    indirect way which the modernization theory has not taken
    into consideration.

_____  Family Change, Caste and the Elderly in a Rural Locale
    in Nepal.  Journal of Cross-Cultural Gerontology.
    1:277-304, 1986.

Goldstein, M. C., S. Schuler, and J. L. Ross.  Social and
    Economic Forces Affecting Intergenerational Relations in
    Extended Families in a Third World Country:  A Cautionary
    Tale from South Asia.  Journal of Gerontology.  38:716-24,

1983.

Goody, J.  Aging in Nonindustrial Societies.  In R. H.
    Binstock and E. Shanas (eds).  Handbook of Aging and Social
    Sciences.  New York, NY:  Van Nostrand Reinhold, 1976.

Green, B.  Internal Colonialism Versus the Elderly:  Renewal
    and Critique for Gerontological Theory.  Berkeley Journal
    of Sociology.  23:129-50, 1978-9.

Harris, R. J.  Recent Trends in the Relative Economic Status
    of Older Adults.  Journal of Gerontology.  41:401-07, 1986.

Hendricks, J.  The Elderly in Society:  Beyond Modernization.
    Social Science History.  6(3):321-45, 1982.

Holmes, L. and E. Rhoads.  Aging and Change in Samoa.  Pp.
    119-29 in J.  Sokolovsky (ed).  Growing Old in Different
    Societies:  Cross-Cultural Perspectives.  Acton, MA:
    Copley Press, 1987.

Kart, C. S. and C. Engler.  Family Relations of Aged Colonial
    Jews:  A Testamentary Analysis.  Ageing and Society.
    5(3):289-304, 1985.

Laslett, P.  The World We Have Lost (2nd ed).  New York, NY:
    Scribner, 1971.

_____  Societal Development and Aging.  Pp. 87-116 in R.
    Binstock and E. Shanas (eds).  Handbook of Aging and the
    Social Sciences.  New York, NY:  Van Nostrand Reinhold,
    1976.

Logue, B. J.  Modernization and the Status of the Frail
    Elderly:  Perspectives on Continuity and Change.  Journal
    of Cross-Cultural Gerontology.  5(4):345-74, 1990.

Maddox, G. L.  Sociology of Later Life.  Annual Review of
    Sociology.  5:113-35, 1979.

Maxwell, R. J.  The Changing Status of the Elders in
    Polynesia.  International Journal of Aging and Human
    Development.  1:137-46, 1970.

Maxwell, R. J. and P. Silverman.  Information and Esteem:
    Cultural Considerations in the Treatment of the Aged.
    International Journal of Aging and Human Development.
    1:361-92, 1970.

    This article explores the control of useful information as
    a determinant of status for the aged.

Meleis, A. I.  Effect of Modernization on Kuwaiti Women.
    Social Science and Medicine.  16(9):965-70, 1982.

    Women in modern Kuwait experience conflict between new
    opportunities and traditional restrictions on their roles.
    This article includes a comparison of findings with other

investigators' research on men in developing countries.

Morgenstern, H.   The Changing Association Between Social
    Status and Coronary Heart Disease in a Rural Population.
    Social Science and Medicine.   14A(3):191-201, 1980.

Myles, J.   The Aged, the State, and the Structure of
    Inequality.   Pp. 317-42 in J. Harp and J. Hofley (eds).
    Structural Inequality in Canada.   Toronto, Canada:
    Prentice-Hall, 1980.

Nevadomsky, J. J.   Changes in Hindu Institutions in an Alien
    Environment.   The Eastern Anthropologist.   33(1): 39-53,
    1980.

Nahemow, N. and B. Adams.   Old Age Among the Baganda:
    Continuity and Change.   Pp. 147-66 in J. Gubrium (ed).
    Late Life:   Communities and Environmental Policy.
    Springfield, IL:   C. C.   Thomas, 1974.

    This essay examines how individualism and personal
    achievement influence status among the modernized Baganda.

Neysmith, S. and J. Edwardh.   Economic Dependency in the
    1980's:   Its Impact on Third World Elderly.   Ageing and
    Society.   4:21-44, 1984.

Olson, P.   A Model of Eldercare in the People's Republic of
    China.   International Journal of Aging and Human
    Development.   24(4):279-300, 1986-87.

_____   Modernization in the People's Republic of China:   The
    Politicization of the Elderly.   Sociological Quarterly.
    29:241-62, 1988.

_____   The Future Status of the Aged.   Gerontologist.
    16(4):297-302, 1976.

Palmore, E. and K. Manton.   Modernization and Status of the
    Aged:   International Correlation.   Journal of Gerontology.
    29(2):205-10, 1974.

    This study of 31 modernizing countries proposes that status
    of the the aged declines during early stages of
    modernization but bottoms out and begins to improve in
    later stages.

Palmore, E. and F. Whittington.   Trends in the Relative Status
    of the Aged.   Social Forces.   50:84-91, 1971.

Pawson, I. G. and C. Janes.   Biocultural Risks in Longevity:
    Samoans in California.   Social Science and Medicine.
    16(2):183-90, 1982.

    Examines the biocultural ramifications of modernization
    among a migrant population.

Phillips, D. R.   Accommodation for Elderly Persons in Newly

Industrialized Countries:  The Hong Kong Experience.
*International Journal of Health Services*.  18(2):255-79,
1988.

Plath, D.  Ecstasy Years--Old Age in Japan.  *Pacific Affairs*.
46(3):421-29, 1973.

In this article a somewhat negative effect of modernization
on the Japanese elderly is presented.  Plath's view differs
from that of Palmore.

Press, I. and M. McKool.  Social Structure and Status of the
Aged:  Toward Some Valid Cross-cultural Generalizations.
*International Journal of Aging and Human Development*.
3:297-306, 1972.

Presents an analysis of four prestige-generating factors
formulated from research among Meso-American aged.

Quadagno, J. S.  *Aging in Early Industrial Society*.  New York,
NY:  Academic Press, 1982.

Focuses on British aged in the 19th century and attacks the
modernization theory.

Rhoads, E. C.  Reevaluation of the Aging and Modernization
Theory:  The Samoan Evidence.  *Gerontologist*.  24:243-50,
1984a.

Research testing the modernization theory in American Samoa
reveals little decline in status of the aged and suggests
that cultural values can be intervening variables in the
effects of modernization.

_____  The Impact of Modernization on the Aged in American
Samoa.  *Pacific Studies*.  7(2):15-33, 1984b.

Rhoads, E. C. and L. D. Holmes.  Mapuifagalele, Western
Samoa's Home for the Aged:  A Cultural Enigma.
*International Journal of Aging and Human Development*.
13:121-35, 1981.

Roebuck, J.  Grandma as Revolutionary:  Elderly Women and Some
Modern Patterns of Social Change.  *International Journal of
Aging and Human Development*.  17:249-66, 1983.

Rosenmayr, L.  On Freedom and Aging:  An Interpretation.
*Journal of Aging Studies*.  1(4):299-316, 1987.

_____  More Than Wisdom:  A Field Study of the Old in an
African Village.  *Journal of Cross-Cultural Gerontology*.
3(1):21-40, 1988.

Rosenthal, C. J.  Aging, Ethnicity and the Family:  Beyond the
Modernization Thesis.  *Canadian Ethnic Studies*.
15(3):1-16, 1983.

Rosow, I.  And Then We Were Old:  Did Primitive Man Treat His

Aged Better Than Modern Man?  Transaction/Society.
2(2):20-26, 1965.

   The author assesses cross-cultural factors that seem to
   contribute positively to the treatment of the aged.

Sando, R. A.  Doing the Work of Two Generations:  The Impact
   of Out-Migration on the Elderly in Rural Taiwan.  Journal
   of Cross-Cultural Gerontology.  1:117-39, 1986.

Sangree, W. H.  Role Flexibility and Status Continuity:
   Tiriki (Kenya) Age Groups Today.  Journal of Cross-Cultural
   Gerontology.  1:117-39, 1986.

Sharma, K.  A Cross-Cultural Comparison of Stereotypes Towards
   Older Persons.  Indian Journal of Social Work.
   32(3):315-20, 1971.

Simmons, L.  Aging in Modern Society.  Pp. 1-8 in Toward
   Better Understanding of the Aging.  Seminar on the Aging,
   Aspen, Colorado, September 8-13, 1958.  New York, NY:
   Council on Social Work Education, 1959.

Stack, S.  Suicide:  A Decade Review of Sociological
   Literature.  Deviant Behavior.  4(1):41-66, 1982.

   Considers theoretical emphases, including modernization, in
   works on suicide.  Also discusses current trends in suicide
   rates among both young and old.

Stearns, P. N.  The Modernization of Old Age in France:
   Approaches Through History.  International Journal of Aging
   and Human Development.  13:297-315, 1981.

Sternheimer, S.  The Vanishing Babushka:  A Roleless Role for
   Older Soviet Women?  Current Perspectives of Aging and the
   Life Cycle.  1:315-33, 1985.

Treas, J. and B. Logue.  Economic Development and the Older
   Population.  Population and Development Review.
   12(4):645-73, 1986.

Ulin, R. O.  Aging Education in the Public Schools:  A Global
   Perspective.  Educational Gerontology.  8(6):537-44, 1982.

Ward, R. A.  Aging, the Use of Time, and Social Change.
   International Journal of Aging and Human Development.
   14(3):177-87, 1982.

Yamanaka, K., H. C. Chang, and F. O. Lorenz.  Modernity and
   Fertility Preference in Taiwan.  Sociological Quarterly.
   23:539-51, 1982.

# 7

# Ethnic & Rural Segments
## of the United States

**GENERAL**

Abu-Laban, S. and B. Abu-Laban. Women and the Aged as
   Minority Groups: A Critique. Canadian Review of Sociology
   and Anthropology. 14(1):103-16, 1977.

Agee, E. M. A Portrait of Older Minorities. Washington, DC:
   American Association of Retired Persons, 1989.

Barg, S. and C. Hirsch. A Successor Model for Community
   Support of Low-Income Minority Group Aged. Aging and Human
   Development. 3:243-51, 1972.

Barron, M. Minority Group Characteristics of the Aged in
   American Society. Journal of Gerontology. 8:477-82, 1953.

Bechell, W. Politics of Aging and Ethnicity. Pp. 137-48 in
   D. Gelfand and A. Kutzik (eds). Ethnicity and Aging:
   Theory, Research and Policy. New York, NY: Springer,
   1979.

Bell, D., P. Kasschau, and G. Zellman. Delivering Services to
   Elderly Members of Minority Groups: A Critical Review of
   the Literature. Santa Monica, CA: Rand Corporation, 1976.

Bengtson, V. Ethnicity and Perceptions of Aging. Pp. 145-57
   in M. Mariot (ed). Aging: Challenges to Science and
   Social Policy. Assen, Holland: Royal Van Gorkum Press,
   1978.

_____ Ethnicity and Aging: Problems and Issues in Current
   Social Science Inquiry. Pp. 9-31 in D. Gelfand and A.
   Kutzik (eds). Ethnicity and Aging: Theory, Research and
   Policy. New York, NY: Springer, 1979.

Bengtson, V., J. Cuellar, and P. Ragan. Contrasts and
   Similarities in Attitudes Toward Death. Journal of
   Gerontology. 32:76-88, 1977.

Bengtson, V. and L. Morgan. Ethnicity and Aging: A

Comparison of Three Ethnic Groups.    Pp. 157-67 in J.
Sokolovsky (ed).  Growing Old in Different Societies:
Cross-Cultural Perspectives.  Acton, MA:  Copley Press,
1987.

Benitez, R.  Ethnicity, Social Policy and Aging.  Pp. 164-77
in R. Davis (ed).  Aging:  Prospects and Issues (rev ed).
Los Angeles, CA:  University of Southern California Press,
1975.

Berkanovic, E. and C. Telesky.  Mexican-American, Black-
American and White-American Differences in Reporting
Illnesses, Disability and Physician Visits for Illnesses.
Social Science and Medicine.  20:39-45, 1985.

Berrien, F., A. Arkoff, and S. Iwahara.  Generational
Difference in Values:  Americans, Japanese-Americans, and
Japanese.  Journal of Social Psychology.  71:169-75, 1967.

Biegel, D. and W. Sherman.  Neighborhood Capacity Building and
the Ethnic Aged.  Pp. 320-40 in D. Gelfand and A. Kutzik
(eds).  Ethnicity and Aging:  Theory, Research and Policy.
New York, NY:  Springer, 1979.

Blau, D. and M. Berezin.  Some Ethnic and Cultural
Considerations in Aging.  Journal of Geriatric Psychiatry.
2:3-5, 1968.

Blau, Z., G. Oser, and R. Stephens.  Aging, Social Class and
Ethnicity:  A Comparison of Anglo, Black and Mexican-
American Texans.  Pacific Sociological Review.
22(4):501-25, 1979.

Bourg, C.  Elderly in a Southern Metropolitan Area.
Gerontologist.  15:15-22, 1975.

Brog, S. and C. Hersch.  A Successful Model for Community
Support of Low-Income Minority Group Aged.  Aging and Human
Development.  3:243-52, 1976.

Browne, C. T.  An Anguished Relationship:  The White Aged
Institutionalized Client and the Non-White Paraprofessional
Worker.  Special Issue:  Ethnicity and Gerontological
Social Work.  Journal of Gerontological Social Work.
9(4):3-12, 1986.

Butler, R.  Old Age in Our Nation's Capital.  Aging and Human
Development.  2:197-201, 1971.

Canadian Ethnic Studies.  Special Issue.  15(3), 1983.

This special issue on aging and ethnicity includes papers
on:  theory, Japanese-Canadians, Chinese, long-term care
and counseling.

Cantor, M. H.  The Informal Support System of New York's
Inner-City Elderly:  Is Ethnicity a Factor?  Pp. 153-74 in
D. E. Gelfand and A. J.  Kutzik (eds).  Ethnicity and

*Aging:  Theory, Research and Policy*.  New York, NY:
Springer, 1979.

Cohen, E., et al.  *Minority Aged in America*.  Occasional
Papers in Gerontology.  Ann Arbor, MI:  Institute of
Gerontology, University of Michigan, 1973.

Cohler, B. and M. Lieberman.  Personality Change Across the
Second Half of Life:  Findings from a Study of Irish,
Italian and Polish American Men and Women.  Pp. 227-45 in
E. Gelfand and A. J. Kutzik (eds).  *Ethnicity and Aging:
Theory, Research and Policy*.  New York, NY:  Springer,
1979.

Cool, L. E.  The Effects of Social Class and Ethnicity on the
Aging Process.  Pp. 263-311 in P. Silverman (ed).  *The
Elderly as Pioneers*.  Bloomington, IN:  Indiana University
Press, 1987.

Cox, C. and D. E. Gelfand.  Familial Assistance, Exchange and
Satisfaction Among Hispanic, Portuguese, and Vietnamese
Ethnic Elderly.  *Journal of Cross-Cultural Gerontology*.
2(3):241-56, 1987.

Cuellar, J. and J. Weeks.  *Minority Elderly Americans:  A
Prototype for Area Agencies on Aging*.  San Diego, CA:
Allied Home Health Association, 1980.

Cuellar, J. B., E. P. Stanford, and D. I. Miller-Soule.
*Understanding Minority Aging:  Perspectives and Sources*.
San Diego, CA:  Center on Aging, San Diego University,
1982.

   A comprehensive discussion of minority aging including
   history, trends, and gaps.  There are chapters on Native
   Americans, Pacific/Asian Americans, Hispanics and Blacks.
   Also significant is the comprehensive bibliography on
   minority aging.

Dobrof, R. (ed).  *Ethnicity and Gerontological Social Work*.
New York, NY:  Haworth, 1987.

Dovenmuehle, R. and W. McGough.  Aging, Culture and Affect:
Predisposing Factors.  *Journal of Social Psychiatry*.
11:138-46, 1965.

Dowd, J. and V. Bengtson.  Aging in Minority Populations:  An
Examination of the Double Jeopardy Hypothesis.  *Journal of
Gerontology*.  33(3):427-36, 1978.

Driedger, L. and N. L. Chappell.  *Aging and Ethnicity:  Toward
An Interface*.  Toronto, Ontario:  Butterworths, 1986.

Federal Council on the Aging.  *Policy Issues Concerning the
Elderly Minorities*.  A Staff Report.  Washington, DC:
USDHHS Publication No. (OHDS)80-20670.  U.S. Government
Printing Office, 1980.

Fellin, P. A. and T. J. Powell. Mental Health Services and Older Adult Minorities: An Assessment. _Gerontologist_. 28(4):442-47, 1988.

Gelfand, D. Ethnicity, Aging and Mental Health. _Aging and Human Development_. 10(3):289-98, 1979-80.

_____ _Aging: The Ethnic Factor_. Boston, MA: Little, Brown, 1982.

A first-rate, brief introduction to ethnicity and aging. It focuses on concepts and definitions of ethnicity, the history of immigration, ethnic aged in the U.S., and service issues including family assistance. Includes materials on both minorities and Euro-American ethnic groups.

Gelfand, D. and A. Kutzik (eds). _Ethnicity and Aging: Theory, Research and Policy_. New York, NY: Springer, 1979.

Gelfand, D. and C. M. Barresi (eds). _Ethnic Dimensions of Aging_. New York, NY: Springer, 1987.

Gozdziak, E. _Older Refugees in the United States: From Dignity to Despair_. Washington, DC: Refugee Policy Group, 1988.

Greene, V. L. and D. J. Monahan. Comparative Utilization of Community-Based Long-Term Care Services by Hispanic and Anglo Elderly in a Case Management System. _Journal of Gerontology_.

Groger, B. L. Growing Old With or Without It: The Meaning of Land in a Southern Rural Community. _Research on Aging_. 5(4)511-16, 1983.

Harris, M. B., C. Begay, and P. Page. Activities, Family Relationships and Feelings About Aging in a Multicultural Elderly Sample. _International Journal of Aging and Human Development_. 29(2):103-17, 1989.

Hendricks, J. and C. Hendricks. Minority Groups in Later Years. Pp. 400-49 in _Aging in Mass Society: Myths and Realities_ (2nd ed). Cambridge, MA: Winthrop Publishers, 1981.

Holmes, D., et al. The Use of Community-based Services in Long-Term Care by Older Minority Persons. _Gerontologist_. 19(4):389-97, 1979.

Holzberg, C. S. Ethnicity and Aging: Anthropological Perspectives on More Than Just the Minority Aging. _Gerontologist_. 22:249-57, 1982a.

The two papers by Holzberg and the 1982 _Gerontologist_ paper by Markides cited below are an important set of writings on ethnicity and aging. Holzberg argues that a focus on

minority status among the aged leads to a conceptual muddle
in defining ethnicity.  She suggests that ethnicity is more
than just minority aging and that research should focus on
ethnicity as culture in understanding adjustment to later
life.

_____ Ethnicity and Aging:  A Rejoinder to a Comment by
Markides.  Gerontologist.  22:471-73, 1982b.

Hough, E. L.  Utilization of Health and Mental Health Services
by Los Angeles Mexican-American and Non-Hispanic Whites.
Archives of General Psychiatry.  44:702-09, 1987.

Hoyt, D. R. and N. Babchuk.  Ethnicity and Voluntary
Associations of the Aged.  Ethnicity.  8:67-81, 1981.

Hunter, K., M. Linn, and T. Pratt.  Minority Women's Attitudes
About Aging.  Experimental Aging Research.  5:95-108, 1979.

Institute of Gerontology.  Minority Aged in America.
Occasional Papers in Gerontology, No. 10.  Ann Arbor, MI:
University of Michigan, 1971.

Jackson, J.  Minorities and Aging.  Belmont, CA:  Wadsworth,
1980.

Jackson, M. and Z. Harel.  Ethnic Differences in Social
Support Networks.  Urban Health.  9:35-38, 1983.

Johnson, F. L., et al.  Life Satisfaction in the Minority
Elderly.  Issues in Mental Health Nursing.  6(1-2),
189-207, 1984.

Kail, B. L.  Drugs, Gender and Ethnicity:  Is the Older
Minority Woman at Risk?  Introduction to Drug Use and
Minority Older Women.  Journal of Drug Issues.
19(2):171-89, 1989.

Kalish, R.  A Gerontological Look at Ethnicity, Human
Capacities and Individual Adjustment.  Gerontologist.
11:78-87, 1971.

Kandel, R. F. and M. Heider.  Friendship and Factionalism in a
Tri-Ethnic Housing Complex for the Elderly in Northern
Miami.  Anthropological Quarterly.  52:49-59, 1979.

Kent, D.  The Elderly in Minority Groups:  Variant Patterns of
Aging.  Gerontologist.  11:26-29, 1971.

Kiefer, C.  Notes on Anthropology and the Minority Elderly.
Gerontologist.  11:94-98, 1971.

Kobata, F., S. Lockery, and S. Moriwaki.  Minority Issues in
Mental Health and Aging.  Pp. 448-67 in J. Birren and W.
Sloan (eds).  Handbook of Mental Health and Aging.  New
York, NY:  Van Nostrand Reinhold, 1980.

Levkoff, S., et al.  Minority Elderly:  A Historical and

Cultural Perspective. Corvallis, OR: Oregon State University, 1979.

Logue, B. J.  Race Differences in Long-Term Disability: Middle-Aged and Older American Indians, Blacks and Whites in Oklahoma. Social Science Journal. 27(3):253-72, 1990.

Lubben, J. E. and R. M. Becerra.  Social Support Among Black, Mexican, and Chinese elderly.  Pp. 130-44 in D. E. Gelfand and C. Barresi (eds).  Ethnic Dimensions of Aging.  New York, NY:  Springer, 1987.

The source of the data was the California Senior Survey (CSS) conducted in 1982 and 1983.  CSS respondents were all over 65 years of age and Medical recipients.  By controlling for socioeconomic status, this study allows for the exploration of ethnicity as a variable affecting the nature of social supports.

Luborsky, M. and R. L. Rubinstein.  Ethnic Identity and Bereavement in Later Life:  The Case of Older Widowers. Pp. 229-40 in J. Sokolovsky (ed).  The Cultural Context of Aging:  Worldwide Perspectives.  Westport, CT:  Bergin and Garvey, 1990.

Maclean, M. J., et al.  Institutional Racism in Old Age: Theoretical Perspectives and a Case Study About Access to Social Services.  Canadian Journal on Aging.  6(2):128-40, 1987.

A study of 3 community and social service centers in Montreal, Quebec.  One neighborhood consisted primarily of French and English Canadians; One contained many elderly Portuguese, and one had a large concentration of elderly Chinese.  Serious problems of access were perceived for the elderly Chinese, but not for the elderly of the other groups.

Manuel, R.  Minority Aging:  Sociological and Social Psychological Issues.  Westport, CT:  Greenwood Press, 1982.

This is a major work on minority aging.  Encyclopedic in scope, it includes 25 chapters in six sections: introduction, demography, sociology and social psychology, public policy, theory and research.

Manuel, R., et al.  Guidelines in Minority Aging.  Washington, DC:  National Center on Black Aged, 1979.

Markides, K. S.  Ethnicity and Aging:  A Comment. Gerontologist.  22:467-70, 1982.

The author defends an interest in minority aging per se, in contrast to studying all ethnic groups.  He notes, however, that less is known about the cultural aspects of aging.

_____ Minority Aging.  In M. W. Riley, B. B. Hess, and K.

Bond (eds). Aging in Society: Selected Reviews of Recent Research. Hillsdale, NJ:  L. Erlbaum, 1983a.

_____ Aging, Religiosity, and Adjustment:  A Longitudinal Analysis. Journal of Gerontology. 38:621-25, 1983b.

_____ Minority Status, Aging, and Mental Health. International Journal of Aging and Human Development. 23(4):285-300, 1986.

Markides, K. S. and R. Machalek.  Selective Survival, Aging and Society. Archives of Gerontology and Geriatrics. 3(3):207-22, 1984.

Markides, K. S. and J. S. Levin.  The Changing Economy and the Future of the Minority Aged. Gerontologist. 27:273-74, 1987.

The authors predict little improvement in the economic status of elderly Blacks and Hispanics who are concentrated in large cities.

Markides, K. W. and C. H. Mindel. Aging and Ethnicity. Newbury, Park, CA:  1987.

McIntosh, J. and J. Santos.  Suicide Among Minority Elderly: A Preliminary Investigation. Suicide and Life-Threatening Behavior. 11(3):151-66, 1981.

An investigation of official 1976 suicide statistics among minority elderly revealed that, as among the White population, rates peak in old age for Chinese-, Japanese-, and Filipino-Americans.  Among Blacks and Native Americans, however, suicide rates are extremely low for the aged.

McNeely, R. L. and J. N. Colen (eds). Aging in Minority Groups. Beverly Hills, CA:  Sage, 1983.

Meyers, A.  Ethnicity and Aging:  Public Policy and Differences in Aging and Old Age.  Pp. 61-80 in E. Markson and G. Batra (eds). Public Policies for an Aging Population. Lexington, MA:  Lexington Books, 1980.

Mindel, C. H. and R. W. Habenstein. Ethnic Families in America. New York, NY:  Elsevier, 1976.

Moore, J.  Situational Factors Affecting Minority Aging. Gerontologist. 11:88-93, 1971.

Moriwaki, S.  Ethnicity and Aging.  In I. Burnside, (ed). Nursing and the Aged. New York, NY:  McGraw Hill, 1976.

_____ Minority Curriculum:  Disappointing. Generations. Summer:29-30, 1978.

Myers, J. E., H. Wass, and M. Murphy.  Ethnic Differences in Death Anxiety Among the Elderly. Death Education. 4:237-44, 1980.

Newsome,B.  Insights on Minority Elderly.  Washington, DC:
     National Center on Black Aged, 1977.

Petrowsky, M.  Marital Status, Sex, and the Social Networks of
     the Elderly.  Journal of Marriage and the Family.
     38:749-56, 1976.

Pierce, R., M. Clark, and S. Kaufman.  Generation and Ethnic
     Identity:  A Typological Analysis.  International Journal
     of Aging and Human Development.  9(1):19-29, 1978/9.

Place, L.  The Ethnic Factor.  Pp. 195-226 in F. Berghorn and
     D.  Schafer (eds).  Dynamics of Aging.  Boulder, CO:
     Westview Press, 1981.

Poppy, M.  Needs Assessment in Minority Aging Research.  Pp.
     79-88 in E. Stanford (ed).  Minority Aging Research, Old
     Issues--New Approaches.  San Diego, CA:  Campanile Press,
     1979.

Ragan, P.  Crime Against the Elderly:  Findings From
     Interviews With Blacks, Mexican-Americans and Whites.  Pp.
     324-26 in M. Rifai (ed).  Justice and Older Americans.
     Lexington, MA:  D. C. Heath, 1977.

Reynolds, D. and R. Kalish.  Anticipation of Futurity As a
     Function of Ethnicity and Age.  Journal of Gerontology.
     29:224-31, 1974.

Rubinstein, R. and M. Luborsky.  Ethnic Identity in Life
     Course Perspective:  Older Widowers in Three Ethnic Groups.
     Pp. 229-40 in J.  Sokolovsky (ed).  The Cultural Context of
     Aging:  Worldwide Perspectives.  Westport, CT:  Bergin and
     Garvey, 1990.

Sherman, G. (ed).  Research and Training in Minority Aging.
     Washington, DC:  National Center on Black Aging, 1978.

_____   Curriculum Guidelines in Minority Aging.  Washington,
     DC:  National Center on Black Aging, 1980.

Sokolovsky, J.  Ethnicity, Culture and Aging:  Do Ethnic
     Differences Really Make A Difference?  Journal of Applied
     Gerontology.  4:6-17, 1985.

_____   Bringing Culture Back Home:  Aging, Ethnicity and
     Family Support.  Pp. 201-12 in J. Sokolovsky (ed).  The
     Cultural Context of Aging:  Worldwide Perspectives.
     Westport, CT:  Bergin and Garvey, 1990.

Stanford, E. P.  Minority Aging:  Institute on Minority Aging,
     Proceedings.  San Diego, CA:  San Diego State University,
     1974.

_____   Minority Aging:  Second Institute on Minority Aging,
     Proceedings.  San Diego, CA:  San Diego State University,
     1975.

_____ Minority Aging and the Legislative Process. San Diego, CA:  The Campanile Press, 1976.

_____ Comprehensive Service Delivery Systems for Minority Aged. San Diego, CA:  The Campanile Press, 1977.

_____ Retirement:  Concepts and Realities. San Diego, CA: The Campanile Press, 1978.

_____ Minority Aging Research:  Old Issues--New Approaches. San Diego, CA:  The Campanile Press, 1979.

_____ Minority Aging:  Policy Issues for the '80's. San Diego, CA:  The Campanile Press, 1981.

   This report from the Proceedings of the Seventh Institute
   on Minority Aging contains 29 articles on economics,
   health, social support, research and training.  Appendices
   contain policy recommendations.

Streib, G.  Are the Aged a Minority Group?  Pp. 311-28 in A.
   Gouldner and S. Miller (eds).  Applied Sociology.  Glencoe,
   IL:  Free Press, 1965.

Strong, L.  Stress and Caring for Elderly Relatives:
   Interpretations and Coping Strategies in an American Indian
   and White Sample.  Gerontologist.  24:251-56, 1984.

Swartz, J. and J. Bastien.  Off the Shelf and Into the
   Mainstream:  Public Policy Planning Workshops for Anglo,
   Black and Mexican-American Senior Citizens.  South Texas
   Journal of Research and the Humanities.  2(2):140-52, 1978.

Taylor, S.  Simple Models of Complexity:  Pragmatic
   Considerations in Providing Services for Minority Elderly.
   Pp. 91-94 in E. P. Stanford (ed).  Proceedings of Seventh
   National Institute on Minority Aging.  San Diego, CA:
   Campanile Press, 1981.

Thorson, J.  Attitudes Toward the Aged As a Function of Race
   and Social Class.  Gerontologist.  15:343-44, 1975.

Trela, J. and J. Sokolovsky.  Culture, Ethnicity and Policy
   for the Aged.  Pp. 117-36 in D. Gelfand and A. Kutzik
   (eds).  Ethnicity and Aging:  Theory, Research and Policy.
   New York, NY:  Springer, 1979.

US Congress.  House.  Select Committee on Aging.  Mental
   Health and the Elderly:  Issues in Service Delivery to the
   Hispanic and . Black Community.  Part 1.  Hearing Before
   the Select Committee on Aging.  Washington, DC:  Government
   Printing Office, 1988a.

US Congress.  House.  Select Committee on Aging.  Mental
   Health and the Elderly:  Issues in Service Delivery to the
   American Indian and the Hispanic Communities.  Part 2.
   Hearing Before the Select Committee on Aging.  Washington,
   DC:  Government Printing Office, 1988b.

Varghese, R. and F. Medinger.  Fatalism in Response to Stress
    Among the Minority Aged.  Pp. 96-116 in D. Gelfand and A.
    Kutzik (eds).  Ethnicity and Aging:  Theory, Research and
    Policy.  New York, NY:  Springer, 1979.

Vontress, C.  Counseling Middle-Aged and Aging Cultural
    Minorities.  The Personnel and Guidance Journal.
    55:132-36, 1976.

White House Conference on Aging.  Special Concerns Session
    Reports:  Asian American Elderly, Aging and Aged Blacks,
    The Elderly Indian, Spanish Speaking Elderly.  Washington,
    DC:  US Government Printing Office, 1971.

Woehrer, C.  Cultural Pluralism in American Families:  The
    Influences of Ethnicity on Social Aspects of the Aged.  The
    Family Coordinator.  27:329-40, 1978.

Woolf, L.  Serving Minority Persons in a Senior Center.  Pp.
    146-52 in A. Wolfson (ed).  Challenges Facing Senior
    Centers in the Nineteen Seventies.  New York, NY:  National
    Council on Aging, 1969.

Zola, I.  Oh Where, Oh Where Has Ethnicity Gone?  Pp. 66-80 in
    D. Gelfand and A. Kutzik (eds).  Ethnicity and Aging:
    Theory, Research and Policy.  New York, NY:  Springer,
    1979.


## BLACK AMERICANS

Anderson, A.  Excerpts on Black Aged From the Urban League
    News.  Pp. 298-310 in B. Hess (ed).  Growing Old in
    America.  New Brunswick, NJ:  Transaction Books, 1936.

Anderson, P.  Support Services and Aged Blacks.  Black Aging.
    3:53-59, 1978.

Bardo, H.  Attitudes of the Black Aging.  In J. Dorsett-
    Robinson (ed).  Proceedings of the Workshop Series on the
    Black Aged and Aging and the Conference on the Black Aged
    and Aging.  Carbondale, IL:  Southern Illinois University.

Beattie, W.  The Aging Negro:  Some Implications for Social
    Welfare Services.  Phylon.  21:131-35, 1960.

Bowman, P. J.  Research Perspectives on Black Men:  Role
    Strain and Adaptation Across the Adult Life Cycle.  Pp.
    117-50 in R. L. Jones (ed).  Black Adult Development and
    Aging.  Berkeley, CA:  Cobb and Henry, 1989.

    This chapter focuses on the classification, analysis and
    synthesis of research perspectives which characterize our
    current knowledge on Black men in America.  Four approaches
    to research--pathology, oppression, ethnicity and
    coping--are examined according to how they differ in
    emphasis on maladaptive-adaptive and internal-external
    dimensions of the Black male experience.

Burton, L. M. and V. L. Bengtson.  Black Grandmothers:  Issues
of Timing and Continuity of Roles.  Pp. 61-77 in V. L.
Bengtson and J. F.  Robertson (eds).  Grandparenthood.
Beverly Hills, Sage, 1985.

Cantor, M., K. Rosenthal, and L. Wilker.  Social and Family
Relationships of Black Aged Women in New York City.  The
Journal of Minority Aging.  4:50-61, 1979.

Chatters, L. M.  Subjective Well-Being Evaluations Among Older
Black Americans.  Psychology and Aging.  3(2):184-90, 1988.

The causal relationships among social status and resource,
health and stress factors, and a single-item measure of
subjective well-being (i.e. happiness) were examined among
a national sample of 581 Blacks aged 55 years and older.
Social status and resource factors had limited impact on
happiness ratings but were important in predicting
immediate factors related to health status and satisfaction
and stress.  Happiness was directly influenced by stress
and reported satisfaction with health, while the effect of
health disability was mediated by health satisfaction.

Chatters, L. M. and J. S. Jackson.  Health and Older Blacks.
Quarterly Contact, Ntional Center on Black Aged.  5(1):1,
7-8, 1982.

A preliminary, descriptive analysis provides a profile of
the self-reported physical and mental health status of
older Black adults.  Older Blacks were generally positive
in making overall evaluations of their life situations.

Chatters, L. M. and R. J. Taylor.  Age Differences in
Religious Participation Among Black Adults.  Journal of
Gerontology:  Social Sciences.  44S:183-89, 1989.

The present analysis investigates age differences in
religious involvement among Black adults and provides the
opportunity to assess current models of aging and
religiosity within a group who are highly involved in
religious concerns.  Among the indicators examined were
organizationl, non-organizational and attitudinal measures
(age status was positively associated with these three
measures).  The age relationships persisted in the presence
of controls for demographic and health factors.

_____  Life Problems and Coping Strategies of Older Black
Adults.  Social Work.  34:313-19, 1989.

This study examines the distribution and attitudes of self-
reported personal life problems (e.g., health, money,
family) in 581 Blacks 55 and older.  The results suggest
that life problems are a significant concern to older Black
adults and highlight the use of different coping strategies
in response to these difficulties.

Chatters, L. M., R. J. Taylor, and J. S. Jackson.  Size and
Composition of the Informal Helper Networks of Elderly

Blacks.  Journal of Gerontology.  40(5):605-14, 1985.

_____ Aged Blacks' Choices for an Informal Helper Network.
Journal of Gerontology.  41(1):94-100, 1986.

Chatters, L. M. and R. J. Taylor.  Age Differences in
Religious Participation Among Black Adults.  Journals of
Gerontology.  44(5):S183-89, 1989.

Chunn, J.  The Black Aged and Social Policy.  Aging Numbers.
287-88:10-14, 1978.

Clemente, F., P. Rexroad, and C. Hirsch.  The Participation of
Black Aged in Voluntary Associations.  Journal of
Gerontology.  30:469-78, 1975.

Coleman, L. M., et al.  Social Roles in the Lives of Middle-
Aged and Older Black Women.  Journal of Marriage and the
Family.  49(4):761-71, 1987.

This study explores participation in, and the effect of
social roles on the psychological and physical health of
middle-aged and older Black women.  Few of these women
participated in the three roles of parent, spouse and
employee simultaneously.  Employed women had higher self-
esteem and better heatlh.  The importance of the employment
role and other sociodemograhic factors in understanding the
well-being of middle-aged and older Black women is
discussed.

Dancy, J.  The Black Elderly:  A Manual for Practitioners.
Ann Arbor, MI:  The Institute of Gerontology, University of
Michigan, Wayne State University, 1977.

Davis, D.  Growing Old Black.  In Employment Prospects of Aged
Blacks, Chicanos and Indians.  Washington, DC:  National
Council on the Aging, 1971.

Ehrlich, J.  Toward a Social Profile of the Aged Black
Population in the United States:  An Exploratory Study.
Aging and Human Development.  4:271-76, 1973.

_____ The Aged Black in America:  The Forgotten Person.
Journal of Negro Education.  44:12-23, 1975.

Faulkner, A. O. and M. A. Heisel.  Giving, Receiving and
Exchanging:  Social Transactions Among Inner-City Black
Aged.  Pp. 117-30 in H. Strange and M. Teitelbaum (eds).
Aging and Cultural Diversity:  New Directions and Annotated
Bibliography.  South Hadley, MA:  Bergin and Garvey, 1987.

Gerber, D., et al.  Interorganizational and Political
Obstacles to Providing Low Cost Supportive Services to the
Elderly Poor.  Black Aging.  3:142-46, 1978.

Gibson, R.  Blacks at Middle and Late Life:  Resources and
Coping.  Annals of the American Academy of Political and
Social Sciences.  464:79-90, 1982a.

_____ Race and Sex Differences in Retirement Patterns. Quarterly Contact. 5(2), 1982b.

_____ Work Patterns of Older Black Female Heads of Household. Journal of MInority Aging. 8(2):1-16, 1983.

_____ Older Black Americans. Generations. 10(4):35-39, 1986a.

_____ Blacks in an Aging Society. New York, NY:  The Carnegie Corporation, 1986b.

This monograph contains a report of the proceedings of the conference "Blacks in an Aging Society."  The social problems of Blacks brought about by the aging of society have many dimensions which were defined with a multidisciplinary approach.

_____ Reconceptualizing Retirement for Black Americans. Gerontologist. 27(6):691-98, 1987a.

_____ Defining Retirement for Black Americans.  Pp. 224-38 in D. E. Gelfand and C. Barresi (eds).  Ethnicity and Aging. New York, NY:  Springer, 1987b.

_____ Minority Aging Research:  Opportunity and Challenge. Gerontologist. 28(4):559-60, 1988.

_____ Black Adults in an Aging Society.  Pp. 389-406 in R. L. Jones (ed).  Black Adult Development and Aging.  Berkeley, CA:  Cobb and Henry, 1989a.

_____ Minority Aging Research:  Opportunity and Challenge. Gerontologist. 28(4):559-60, 1989b.

Gibson, R. C. and J. S. Jackson.  The Health, Physical Functioning, and Informal Supports of the Black Elderly. In R. Willis (ed).  Currents of Health Policy and Impact on Black Americans.  The Milbank Quarterly (Supplement). 65(2):1-34, 1987.

_____ The Black American Oldest Old.  In R. Suzman, D. Willis and K. Manton (eds).  The Oldest Old.  New York, NY: Oxford University Press, 1990.

Gillespie, B.  Elderly Blacks and the Economy.  The Journal of Afro-American Issues.  3:324-35, 1975.

Golden, H.  The Myth of Homogeneity Among Black Elderly. Black Aging.  1,2,3:1-11, 1975-6.

_____ Black Ageism.  Social Policy.  7:40-42, 1976.

_____ Life Satisfastion Among Black Elderly in the Inner City. Black Aging.  2:21-43, 1977.

Gordon, J.  Use of Aging Services by Elderly Blacks in Douglas County, Kansas.  The Journal of Minority Aging.  4:88-91,

1979.

Green, V.  Underlying Issues of Diversity in the Study of
    Aging Blacks.  Pp. 101-16 in H. Strange and M. Teitelbaum
    (eds).  Aging and Cultural Diversity:  New Directions and
    Annotated Bibliography.  South Hadley, MA:  Bergin and
    Garvey, 1987.

Haber, D.  Health Promotion to Reduce Blood Pressure Level
    Among Older Blacks.  Gerontologist.  26(2):119-21, 1986.

Heisel, M.  Assessment of Learning Activity Level in a Group
    of Black Aged.  Adult Education Quarterly.  36(1):1-14,
    1985.

Heisel, M. and G. Larson.  Literacy and Social Milieu:
    Reading Behavior of the Black Elderly.  Adult Education
    Quarterly.  34(2):63-70, 1983.

Heisel, M. and M. Moore.  Social Interaction and Isolation of
    Elderly Blacks.  Gerontologist.  3:100, 1973.

Hill, R., et al.  The Black Old.  Pp. 273-83 in M. Seltzer, S.
    Corbett, and R. Atchley (eds).  Social Problems of the
    Aging:  Readings.  Belmont, CA:  Wadsworth, 1978.

Hippler, A.  Hunter's Point:  A Black Ghetto.  New York,  NY:
    Basic Books 1974.

Hudson, G. H.  Some Special Problems of Older Black Americans.
    Crisis.  83:88-90, 1976.

Huling, W.  Evolving Family Roles for the Black Elderly.
    Aging Numbers.  287-88:21-27, 1978.

Jackson, J. J.  Social Gerontology and the Negro:  A Review.
    Gerontologist.  7:168-7B, 1967.

_____ Negro Aged and Social Gerontology:  A Critical
    Evaluation.  Journal of Social and Behavioral Sciences.
    13:42-47, 1968.

_____ Negro Aged Parents and Adult Children:  Their Affective
    Relationships.  Varia.  2:1-14, 1969.

_____ Aged Negroes:  Their Cultural Departures From
    Statistical Stereotypes and Selected Rural-Urban
    Differences.  Gerontologist.  10:140-45, 1970.

_____ Compensatory Care for the Black Aged.  Pp. 15-23 in
    Minority Aged in America.  Occasional Paper No. 10.  Ann
    Arbor, MI:  Institute of Gerontology, University of
    Michigan--Wayne State University, 1971a.

_____ Sex and Social Class Variations in Negro Older Parent-
    Adult Child Relationships.  Aging and Human Development.
    2:96-107, 1971b.

_____ Negro Aged:  Toward Needed Research in Social Gerontology.  Gerontologist.  11:52-57, 1971c.

_____ Comparative Life Styles and Family and Friend Relationships Among Older Black Women.  The Family Coordinator.  21:477-85, 1972a.

_____ Marital Life Among Aging Blacks.  The Family Coordinator.  21:21-27, 1972b.

_____ Social Impacts of Housing Relocation Upon Urban, Low-Income Black Aged.  Gerontologist.  12(1):32-37, 1972c.

_____ Help Me Somebody, I'se an Old Black Standing in the Need of Institutionalizing.  Psychiatric Opinion.  10:6-16, 1973.

_____ NCBA, Black Aged, and Politics.  The Annals of Political and Social Science.  415:138-59, 1974.

_____ The Black Aging:  A Demographic Overview.  Pp. 25-31 in R. Kalish (ed).  The Later Years, Social Application of Gerontology.  Monterey, CA: Brooks/Cole, 1977.

_____ Black Grandparents in the South.  Pp. 207-14 in R. Staples (ed).  The Black Family:  Essays and Studies. Belmont, CA:  Wadsworth, 1978.

_____ Aging Patterns in Black Families.  Pp. 145-54 in A. Lichtman and J. Challinor (eds).  Kin and Communities, Families in America.  Washington, DC:  Smithsonian Institution Press, 1979.

Jackson, J. J. and M. Ball.  A Comparison of Rural and Urban Georgia Aged Negros.  Association of Social Science Teachers.  12:30-37, 1966.

Jackson, J. J. and B. Walls.  Myths and Realities About Aged Blacks.  Pp. 95-113 in M. Brown (ed).  Readings in Gerontology.  New Haven, CT:  Yale University Press, 1978.

Jackson, J. S.  Social Gerontology and the Black Aged.  In G. Maddox (ed).  The Encyclopedia of Aging.  New York, NY: Springer, 1987.

_____ Aging Black Women and Public Policies.  The Black Scholar.  May/June:31-43, 1988a.

_____ (ed).  The Black American Elderly:  Research on Physical and Psychosocial Health.  New York, NY:  Springer, 1988b.

The book derives from a workshop "Research on Aging Black Populations" held at the National Institutes of Health in 1986 and co-sponsored by NIA, AARP and DHHS.  The 16 chapters examine various facets of aging among older blacks, including comparisons/contrasts with the elderly in other racial and ethnic groups.  Topics explored include:

subjective well-being (especially impact of social status
position on aging, cultural values and traits, and life-
span conceptions of adaptation); summary of work,
retirement and disability research based on the National
Survey of Black Americans; demographic and health status
data (these data suggest that older blacks are at a
disadvantaged position relative to older whites but there
is great variability among blacks on these same
dimensions).  The book also explores possible sources of
error in planning and conducting survey research on aging
black population groups.

Jackson, J. S., L. M. Chatters, and H. W. Neighbors.  The
    Mental Health Status of Older Black Americans:  A National
    Study.  Black Scholar.  13(1):21-35, 1982.

Jackson, J. S. and R. C. Gibson.  Work and Retirement Among
    the Black Elderly.  Pp. 193-222 in Z. Blau (ed).  Current
    Perspectives on Aging and the Life Cycle.  Greenwich, CT:
    JAI Press, 1985.

Jackson, M. and J. Wood.  Aging in America:  Implications for
    the Black Aged.  Washington, DC:  National Council on the
    Aging, 1976.

James, N.  Cultural Differences.  In J. Dorsett Robinson (ed).
    Proceedings of the Workshop Series on the Black Aged and
    Aging and the Conference on the Black Aged and Aging.
    Carbondale, IL:  Illinois University, 1974.

Jenkins, A.  The Aged Black:  Some Reflections on the
    Literature.  Afro-American Studies.  3:217-21, 1972.

Jerome, N. W.  Dietary Intake and Nutritional Status of Older
    U. S. Blacks:  An Overview.  In J. S. Jackson (ed).  The
    Black American Elderly:  Research on Physical and
    Psychosocial Health.  New York, NY:  Springer, 1988.

Jones, F.  The Lofty Role of the Black Grandmother.  The
    Crisis.  80:19-21, 1973.

Kamara, J.  The Bio-Social Paradox in the Black Community.
    Omega.  9:301-12, 1978.

Kent, D.  The Negro Aged.  Gerontologist.  11(1):48-51, 1971.

Kivett, V.  Loneliness and the Rural Black Elderly:
    Perspectives on Intervention.  Black Aging.  3:160-66,
    1978.

Lasklen, C.  Aged, Black and Poor:  Three Case Studies.  Aging
    and Human Development.  2:202-07, 1971.

Krause, N. and T. Van Tran.  Stress and Religious Involvement
    Among Older Blacks.  Journal of Gerontology.  44(1):S4-13,
    1989.

Lambing, M.  Social Class Living Patterns of Retired Negroes.

Gerontologist. 1(1):285-88, 1972.

Lieberman, L. S.  Diabetes and Obesity in Elderly Black
Americans.  In J. S. Jackson (ed).  The Black American
Elderly:  Research on Physical and Psychosocial Health.
New York, NY:  Springer, 1988.

Lieberson, S.  Generational Differences Among Blacks in the
North.  American Journal of Sociology.  79:550-67, 1972.

I. B. Lindsay.  The Multiple Hazards of Age and Race:  The
Situation of Aged Blacks in the United States.  Washington,
DC:  U. S. Senate, Special Committee on Aging, 1971.

_____ Coping Capacities of the Black Aged.  Pp. 89-94 in No
Longer Young, The Older Woman in America.  Occasional
Papers in Gerontology No. 11.  Ann Arbor, MI:  Institute of
Gerontology, University of Michigan, 1975.

Martin, E. and J. Martin.  The Black Extended Families.
Chicago, IL:  University of Chicago Press, 1977.

McAdoo, J.  Well-Being and Fear of Crime Among the Black
Elderly.  Pp. 277-90 in D. Gelfand and A. Kutzik (eds).
Ethnicity and Aging:  Theory, Research and Policy.  New
York, NY:  Springer, 1979.

McCaslin, R. and W. Calvert.  Social Indicators in Black and
White:  Some Ethnic Considerations in Delivery of Service
to the Elderly. ·Journal of Gerontology.  50:60-66, 1975.

Morse, D.  Aging in the Ghetto:  Themes Expressed by Older
Black Men and Women Living in a Northern Industrial City.
Industrial Gerontology.  3:1-10, 1976.

Mosley, J.  Problems of the Black Aged.  Journal of Non-White
Concerns.  6:11-16B, 1977.

National Center on the Black Aged.  The Black Aged:  Facts and
Figures.  NCBA Technical Bulletin Series.  1:8, 1973.

National Dairy Council.  Diet and Nutrition-related Concerns
of Blacks and Other Ethnic Minorities.  Dairy Council
Digest.  Rosemont, IL:  National Dairy Council, 1988.

National Urban League.  Double Jeopardy:  The Older Negro in
America Today.  New York, NY:  National Urban League, 1964.

Oliver, M.  Elderly Blacks and the Economy.  The Journal of
Afro-American Issues.  3:316-23, 1975.

Parks, A. G.  Black Elderly in Rural America:  A Comprehensive
Study.  Bristol, IN:  Wyndham, 1988.

Peterson, J.  Age of Wisdom:  Elderly Black Women in Family
and Church.  Pp. 213-28 in J. Sokolovsky (ed).  The
Cultural Context of Aging:  Worldwide Perspectives.
Westport, CT:  Bergin and Garvey, 1990.

Pletchers, M. K. and S. E. Milligan.  Access to Health Care in a Black Urban Elderly Population.  Gerontologist. 28(2):213-17, 1988.

Primm, B. J.  Poverty, Folk Remedies, and Drug Misuse Among the Black Elderly.  In W. Watson (ed).  Black Folk Medicine.  New Brunswick, NJ:  Transaction Books, 1984.

Ralston, P.  Learning Needs and Efforts of the Black Elderly. International Journal of Aging and Human Development. 7(1):75-88,

_____ Senior Center Utilization by Black Elderly Adults: Social, Attitudinal and Knowledge Correlates.  Journal of Gerontology.  39(2):224-29, 1984.

Rice, C.  Old and Black.  Harvest Years.  8:38-47, 1968.

Rosen, C.  A Comparison of Black and White Rural Elderly. Black Aging.  3:60-65, 1978.

Rubenstein, D.  An Examination of Social Participation Found Among a National Sample of Black and White Elderly.  Aging and Human Development.  2:172-88, 1971.

Sheppard, N.  A Federal Perspective on the Black Aged:  From Concern to Action.  Aging Numbers.  287-88:28-32, 1978.

Shimkin, D. B., E. M. Shimkin, and D. A. Frate (eds).  The Extended Family in Black Societies.  Chicago, IL:  Aldine, 1978.

Smith, D., M. Dahlin, and M. Friedberger.  The Family Structure of the Older Black Population in the American South in 1880 and 1900.  Sociology and Social Research. 63:(3):544-65, 1979.

Smith, S.  The Older Rural Negro.  Pp. 262-80 in E. Youmans (ed).  Older Rural Americans:  A Sociological Perspective. Lexington, KY:  University of Kentucky Press, 1967.

Stanford, E.  The Elder Black.  San Diego, CA:  Campanile Press, 1978.

Synder, D.  Future Pension Status of the Black Elderly.  Pp. 291-307 in D. Gelfand and A. Kutzik (eds).  Ethnicity and Aging:  Theory, Research and Policy.  New York, NY: Springer, 1979.

Stretch, J.  Are Aged Blacks Who Manifest Differences in Community Security also Different in Coping Reaction. Aging and Human Development.  7:171-84, 1976.

Swanson, W.  How Do Elderly Blacks Cope in New Orleans.  Aging and Human Development.  2:210-16, 1971.

Taylor, R. J.  The Impact of Federal Health Care Policy on the Elderly Poor:  The Special Case of the Black Elderly.  In

Policy Issues for the Elderly Poor. Washington, DC:
Community Services Administration, Government Printing
Office, 1981.

_____ The Extended Family as a Source of Support to Elderly
Blacks. Gerontologist. 25(5):488-95, 1985.

_____ Religious Participation Among Elderly Blacks.
Gerontologist. 26(6):630-36, 1986.

_____ Aging and Supportive Relationships Among Black
Americans. In J. S. Jackson (ed). The Black American
Elderly: Research on Physical and Psychosocial Health.
New York, NY: Springer, 1988.

This chapter reviews recent research on kin and non-kin
informal social support networks of elderly blacks.
Embedded in the theoretical model is a series of familial
relationships (living arrangements/household composition,
proximity of relatives and immediate family, and family
closeness) and socio-demographic predictors of assistance
(gender, age, marital status, socio-economic status,
urbanicity/region, and health factors). Specific attention
is paid to  1) general differences among the aged;  2)
racial differences across the life-course;  3) racial
differences among the elderly;  4) differences among the
general black population; and  5) differences evident among
elderly blacks.

Taylor, R. J. and L. M. Chatters. Patterns of Informal
   Support to Elderly Black Adults: Family, Friends and
   Church Members. Social Work. 31(6):432-38, 1986a.

_____ Church-based Informal Support Among Elderly Blacks.
Gerontologist. 26(6):637-42, 1986b.

_____ Correlates of Eduction, Income, and Poverty Among Aged
Blacks. Gerontologist. 28:435-41, 1988.

Taylor, R. J. and W. H. Taylor. The Social and Economic
   Status of the Black Elderly. Phylon. 43:295-306, 1982.

Taylor, S. Mental Health and Successful Coping Among Black
   Women. In R. Manuel (ed). Minority Aging: Sociological
   and Social Psychological Issues. Westport, CT: Greenwood
   Press, 1982.

U. S. Senate Special Committee on Aging. The Multiple Hazards
   of Age and Race: The Situation of Aged Blacks in the US.
   Washington DC: US Government Printing Office, 1971.

Watson, W. (ed). Health and the Black Aged. Washington, DC:
   National Center on Black Aged, 1977.

_____ The Concentration of Older Blacks in the Southeastern
United States. In R. L. McNeely and J. Cohen (eds). Aging
in Minority Groups. Beverly Hills, CA: Sage, 1983.

_____ Sitting Location as an Indicator of Older Blacks in the Church:  A Comparative Analysis of Protestants and Catholics in the Rural South.  Phylon.  47:264-75, 1986.

Wolf, J., et al.  Access of the Black Urban Elderly to Medical Care.  Journal of the National Medical Association. 75(1):41-46, 1983.

Wylie, F.  Attitudes Toward Aging and the Aged Among Black Americans:  Some Historical Perspectives.  Aging and Human Development.  2:66-70, 1971.

Yelder, J.  The Influence of Culture on Family Relations:  The Black American Experience.  Pp. 83-93 in P. Ragan (ed). Aging Parents.  Los Angeles, CA:  University of Southern California Press, 1979.

## HISPANIC AMERICANS

Adams, G. L., R. J. Dworkin, and S. D. Rosenberg.  Diagnosis and Pharmacotherapy Issues in the Care of Hispanics in the Public Sphere.  American Journal of Psychiatry. 141(8):970-74, 1984.

Compares the psychopharmacotherapy of Hispanic patients with those of Black-Americans and Anglo-Americans. Hispanics were less likely to be diagnosed schizophrenic but were more like to have other mental illnesses.  They were also less likely to be given medication.

Applewhite, S. R. (ed).  Hispanic Elderly in Transition: Theory, Research, Policy and Practice.  New York, NY: Greenwood Press, 1988.

Applewhite and the contributors to this edited volume discuss what they call the transitional nature of Hispanic elderly (while recognizing the extensive ethnic diversity of the "Hispanic" population) by suggesting that the elderly are links to the past, have adapted to the present, and help shape the future.

_____ Planning and Research for the Hispanic Elderly.  Report of the Second National Conference on Aging.  Washington, DC, 1977.

Aguirre, B. E. and A. Bigelow.  The Aged in Hispanic Groups: A Review.  International Journal of Aging and Human Development  17:177-201, 1983.

Reviews of reports on Hispanic elderly reveals that gerontologists have neglected Cuban and Puerto Rican groups.

Alston, L. L. and B. Aguirre.  Elderly Mexican Americans: Nativity and Health Access.  International Migration Review.  21:626-42, 1987.

Asociacion Nacional Pro Personas Mayores.  The First Western
Regional Hispanic Conference on Aging:  Search for Hispanic
Models.  Final Report and Recommendations.  Los Angeles,
CA:  Asociacion Nacional Pro Personas Mayores, 1976.

Bastida, E.  Family Integration in Later Life Among Hispanic
Americans.  The Journal of Minority Aging.  4:42-49, 1979.

_____  Reconstructing the Social World at 60:  Older Cubans in
the United States.  Gerontologist.  24:465-70, 1984.

_____  Sex-Typed Age Norms Among Older Hispanics.
Gerontologist.  27(1):59-65, 1987.

Cadena, M.  The Mexican American Family and the Mexican
American Nurse.  In D. Hymouich and M.  Barnard (eds).
Family Health Care.  New York:  McGraw-Hill Book Company,
1973.

Canino, G. and I. A. Canino.  Culturally Syntonic Family
Therapy for Migrant Puerto Ricans.  Hospital and Community
Psychiatry.  33:299-303, 1982.

The Hispanic family has traditionally been the main support
for persons in stress.  Researchers warn that practitioners
should, however, recognize the difficulty of distinguishing
between family patterns that are culturally sanctioned
rather than dysfunctinal.

Carp, F.  Factors in Utilization of Services by the Mexican-
American Elderly.  Palo Alto, CA:  American Institute for
Research, 1968.

_____  Housing and Minority-Group Elderly.  Gerontologist
9:20-34, 1969.

_____  Communications With Elderly Mexican-Americans.
Gerontologist.  10:126-34, 1970.

Cartwright, W., W. Steglich, and C. Crouch.  Use of Community
Resources Among Aged Mexican Americans.  Proceedings of the
Southwestern Sociological Association.  9:184-88, 1969.

Clark, M.  Mexican-American Aged in San Francisco:  A Case
Description.  Gerontologist.  9:90-95.

Coles, R.  The Old Ones of New Mexico.  Albuquerque, NM:
University of New Mexico Press, 1973.

_____  Una Anciana.  Pp. 105-29 in B. Hess (ed).  Growing Old
in America.  New Brunswick, Canada:  Transaction, 1976.

Crouch, B.  Age and Institutional Support:  Perceptions of
Older Mexican-Americans.  Journal of Gerontology.
27:524-29, 1977.

Cruz-Lopez, M. and R. E. Pearson.  The Support Needs and
Resources of Puerto Rican Elders.  Gerontologist.

25:483-87, 1985.

This study looks at the support system of Puerto Rican elderly and is used to train people to work within the natural support system.

Cubillos, H. L. and M. M. Prieto. The Hispanic Elderly: A Demographic Profile. Washington, DC: National Council of La Raza, 1987.

Cuellar, J.  On the Relevance of Ethnographic Methods: Studying Aging in a Mexican-American Community.  In V. Bengtson, (ed). Gerontological Research and Community Concern: A Case of a Multi-Disciplinary Concern.  Los Angeles, CA:  Ethel Andrus Gerontological Center, University of Southern California, 1974.

_____ El Senior Citizens Club:  The Older Mexican American in the Voluntary Association.  Pp. 207-30 in B. Myerhoff and A. Simic (eds).  Life's Career--Aging: Cultural Variations on Growing Old.  Beverly Hills, CA:  Sage, 1978.

Davis, R. (ed).  Health Services and Mexican-American Elderly.  Los Angeles, CA:  University of Southern California Press, 1973.

Delgado, M.  Hispanic Natural Support Systems:  Implications for Mental Health Services.  Journal of Psychosocial Nursing and Mental Health Services.  21:19-24, 1983.

del Valle, A. G. and M. Usher.  Group Therapy with Aged Latino Women:  A Pilot Project and Study.  Clinical Gerontologist. 1:51-58, 1982.

Doherty, R.  Mexican-Americans:  Growing Old in the Barrio. Pp. 4-16 in Employment Prospect of Aged Blacks, Chicanos and Indians.  Washington, DC:  National Council on the Aging, 1971.

Drew, B. and J. Waters.  Aging and Work:  Perceptions of Low Income Puerto Rican Adults and High School Seniors.  Pp. 131-52 in H. Strange and M. Teitelbaum (eds).  Aging and Cultural Diversity:  New Directions and Annotated Bibliography.  South Hadley, MA:  Bergin and Garvey, 1987.

Edgerton, R., M. Karno, and I. Fernandez.  Curanderismo in the Metropolis:  The Diminished Role of Folk Psychiatry Among Los Angeles Mexican-Americans.  American Journal of Psychotherapy.  24(1):124-34, 1970.

Espino, D. V., et al.  Hispanic and Non-Hispanic Elderly on Admission to the Nursing Home:  A Pilot Study. Gerontologist.  28(6):821-24, 1988.

Gaitz, C. and J. Scott.  Mental Health of Mexican Americans: Do Ethnic Factors Make a Difference?  Geriatrics. 29:103-10, 1974.

Gallegos, E.  A Community Centered Project for the Chicano
    Aged.  Denver, CO:  Interstate Research Associates, 1973.

Gratton, B.  Familism Among the Black and Mexican-American
    Elderly:  Myth or Reality.  Journal of Aging Studies.
    1(1):19-32, 1987.

Greenstein, R., et al.  Shortchanged:  Recent Developments in
    Hispanic Poverty, Income, and Employment.  Washington, DC:
    Center on Budget and Policy Priorities, 1988.

Gelfand, D. E.  Immigration, Aging and Intergenerational
    Relationships.  Gerontologist.  29(3):366-72, 1989.

Henderson, J. N.  Mental Disorders Among the Elderly:
    Dementia and Its Sociocultural Correlates.  Pp. 357-74 in
    P. Silverman (ed).  The Elderly as Modern Pioneers.
    Bloomington, IN:  Indiana University Press, 1987.

    Dementia is discussed in terms of epidemiology,
    sociomedical history, case ascertainment, diagnosis, and
    management.  Research is presented regarding caregiving of
    dementia patients in Latin families using an ethnic-
    specific support group.

    _____ Alzheimer's Disease in Cultural Context.  Pp. 315-30 in
    J. Sokolovsky (ed).  The Cultural Context of Aging:
    Worldwide Perspectives.  Westport, CT:  Bergin and Garvey,
    1990.

    The cultural context of dementia in Latin families is
    emphasized.  Four cases are presented and discussed.

Hernandez, A. and J. Mendoza (eds).  Proceedings of the
    National Conference on Spanish-Speaking Elderly.  Kansas
    City, KS:  National Chicano Social Planning Council, 1975.

    _____ Old, Alone and Forgotten.  Nuestro.  1:60, 1977.

Latin, R. W., et al.  Mexicans in the United
    States--Anthropometric Estimations of Body Composition of
    Older Men.  Journal of Gerontology.  42:24-28, 1987.

Leonard, O.  The Older Rural Spanish-Speaking People of the
    Southwest.  Pp. 239-61 in E. Youmans (ed).  Older Rural
    Americans.  Lexington, KY:  University of Kentucky Press,
    1967.

Lopez-Aqueres, W., et al.  Health Needs of the Hispanic
    Elderly.  Journal of the American Geriatrics Society.
    32:191-98, 1984.

Mahard, R. E.  The CES-D as a Measure of Depressive Mood in
    the Elderly Puerto Rican Population.  Journal of
    Gerontology.  43:24-25, 1988.

Maldonado, D.  The Chicano Aged.  Social Work.  20:213-16,
    1975.

_____ La Familia Mexico-Americana and the Elderly.  Aging: Research Utilization Report.  4:9-18, 1977a.

_____ The Mexican American Grows Old.  In R. Kalish (ed). The Later Years:  Social Applications of Gerontology. Belmont, CA:  Wadsworth Publishing Company, Inc., 1977b.

_____ Aging in the Chicano Context.  Pp. 175-83 in D. Gelfand and A. Kutzik (eds).  Ethnicity and Aging: Theory, Research and Policy.  New York, NY:  Springer, 1979.

_____ The Hispanic Elderly :  A Socio-Historical Framework for Public Policy.  Journal of Applied Gerontology. 4:18-27, 1985.

Markides, K. S. and N. Kause.  Intergenerational Solidarity and Psychological Well-Being Among Older Mexican Americans: A Three Generations Study.  Journal of Gerontology. 40:390-92, 1985.

    This three-generation study looked at the influence of relationships with children and grandchildren on the well-being of elderly Mexican Americans.

Markides, K. S. and S. Vernon.  Aging, Sex-Role Orientation and Adjustment:  A Three Generations Study of Mexican Americans.  Journal of Gerontology.  39(5):586-91, 1984.

Markides, K. S., et al.  Sources of Helping and Intergenerational Solidarity:  A Three Generations Study of Mexican Americans.  Journal of Gerontology.  41:506-11, 1986.

Markides, K. S. and J. S. Levin.  The Changing Economy and the Future of the Minority Aged.  Gerontologist.  27(3):273-74, 1987.

Markides, K. S., et al.  Religion, Aging and Life Satisfaction:  An Eight-Year Three-Wave Longitudinal Study. Gerontologist.  27:660-65, 1987.

Marks, G., et al.  Health Behavior of Elderly Hispanic Women: Does Cultural Assimilation Make a Difference:  American Journal of Public Health.  77(10):1315-19, 1987.

Marshall, C. E. and J. Richards.  Developing Culturally Based Patient Education Materials for Non-Reading, Elderly Hispanics.  Tech Trends.  34(1):27-30, 1989.

Martin, H. W., et al.  Folk Illnesses Reported to Physicians in the Lower Rio Grande Valley:  A Binational Comparison. Ethnology.  24:229-36, 1985.

Martinez, H.  The Mexican-American Elderly.  Washington, DC: National Council on the Aging, 1971.

Miranda, M.  Latin American Culture and American Society

Contrast.  Pp.  43-46 in A. Hernandez and J. Mendoza (eds).
Proceedings of National Conference on Spanish-Speaking
Elderly.  Kansas City, KS:  National Chicano Planning
Council, 1975.

Mohl, R. A.  An Ethnic "Boiling Pot":  Cubans and Haitians in
Miami.  The Journal of Ethnic Studies.  13:51-74, 1984.

Moore, J.  The Death Culture of Mexico and Mexican-Americans.
Omega.  1:271-91, 1970.

Morton, D. J., et al.  Use of the Ces-D Among a Community
Sample of Older Mexican-Americans.  Journal of Cross-
Cultural Gerontology.  4(4):289-306, 1989.

National Council of La Raza.  Los Ancianos:  The Aging of the
Hispanic Community:  A Preliminary Demographic Profile.
Washington, DC:  Government Printing Office, 1987.

Page, J. B. and L. Rio.  Use of Psychotropic Medication Among
Elderly Hispanic Women:  Symptoms and Poverty and Social
Isolation.  Florida Journal of Anthropology.  10:59-68,
1985.

Prieto, M. M.  Project Ancianos:  Survey of Projects for the
Hispanic Elderly.  Washington, DC:  National Council of La
Raza, 1987.

Reich, J., M. Stegman, and N. Stegman.  Relocating the
Dispossessed Elderly:  A Study of Mexican Americans.
Philadelphia, PA:  University of Pennsylvania Institute of
Environmental Studies, 1966.

Rodriguez, O.  Hispanics and Human Services:  Help-Seeking in
the Inner City.  Monograph No. 14.  Bronx, NY:  Hispanic
Research Center, Fordham University, 1987.

Solis, F.  Cultural Factors in Programming of Services for
Spanish-Speaking Elderly.  Pp. 30-33 in A. Hernandez and J.
Mendoza (eds).  Proceedings of National Conference on
Spanish-Speaking Elderly.  Kansas City, KS:  National
Chicano Planning Council, 1975.

Sotomayor, M.  The Hispanic Elderly and the Intergenerational
Family.  Journal of Children in Contemporary Society.
20(3-4):55-65, 1989.

Spitzer, J. B.  Planning for Elderly Refugees:  The Vietnamese
and Soviet Jews.  Migration Today.  12(3):25-27, 1984.

Stumphauzer, J. S. and L. C. Davis.  Training Mexican-American
Mental Health Personnel in Behavior Therapy.  Journal of
Behavior Therapy and Experimental Psychiatry.  14:215-17,
1983.

Torres-Gil, F.  Concerns of the Spanish-Speaking Elderly.  Pp.
2-4 in E. Stanford (ed).  Minority Aging: Second
Institute on Minority Aging Proceedings.  San Diego, CA:

Center on Aging, San Diego State University, 1977.

Torres-Gil, F. and R. Becerra.  The Political Behavior of the
    Mexican-American Elderly.  Gerontologist.  17:392-99, 1977.

Valle, R. and L. Mendoza.  The Elder Latino.  San Diego, CA:
    Campanile Press, 1978.

US Congress.  House.  Report by Chairman of the Select
    Committee on Aging.  Demographic Characteristics of the
    Older Hispanic Population.  Washington, DC:  Government
    Printing Office, 1988.

US Congress.  Senate.  Hearing Before the Special Committee on
    Aging.  The Older Americans Act and Its Application to
    Native Americans.  Washington, DC:  Government Printing
    Office, 1986.

Woerner, L.  The Hispanic Elderly:  Meeting the Needs of a
    Special Population.  Civil Rights Digest.  11:3-11, 1979.

Zambrana, R., R. Merino and S. Antana.  Health Services and
    the Puerto-Rican Elderly.  Pp. 309-19 in D. Gelfand and A.
    Kutzik (eds).  Ethnicity and Aging:  Theory, Research and
    Policy.  New York, NY:  Springer, 1979.

**AMERICAN INDIANS**

Amoss, P.  Coast Salish Elders.  Pp. 227-48 in P. Amoss and S.
    Harrell, (eds).  Other Ways of Growing Old:
    Anthropological Perspectives.  Stanford, CA:  Stanford
    University Press, 1981a.

    Contemporary Coast Salish Indian elders show that it is
    possible for old people to enjoy high prestige on the basis
    of strictly cultural contributions with a negligible
    economic component.

_____  Cultural Centrality and Prestige for the Elderly.  Pp.
    47-64 in C. Fry (ed).  Dimensions:  Aging, Culture and
    Health.  Brooklyn, NY:  J. F. Bergin, 1981b.

    This chapter restates the general themes of the chapter in
    Other Ways of Growing Old cited above, from which it was
    adapted.

Apple, D.  The Social Structure of Grandparenthood.  American
    Anthropologist.  58:656-63, 1956.

    This study offers a structural analysis which confirms and
    expands Nadel's hypothesis that friendly equality between
    grandparents and grandchildren appears only with certain
    patterns of authority in the family.  Six American Indian
    tribes are included in the twenty-four tribal group
    comparison.

Bachtold, L. M. and K. L. Eckvall.  Current Value Orientations

of American Indians in Northern California:  The Hupa.
Journal of Cross-Cultural Psychology.  9:367-75, 1978.

Cultural values as to the treatment of the elderly Hupa and
their ceremonial and economic importance are discussed.

Benedict, R.  A Profile of Indian Aged.  Pp. 51-58 in Minority
Aged in America.  Papers from a Symposium--Triple Jeopardy:
The Plight of Aged Minorities, April 17, 1971, Detroit,
Michigan.  Ann Arbor, MI:  Institute of Gerontology of
Michigan,  1972.

Bergman, R.  A School for Medicine Men.  American Journal of
Psychiatry.  130(6):663-66, 1973.

Block, M.  Exiled Americans:  The Plight of Indian Aged in the
United States.  Pp. 184-92 in D. Gelfand and A. Kutzik
(eds).  Ethnicity and Aging:  Theory, Research and Policy.
New York, NY:  Springer, 1979.

A rather politically motivated but nonetheless informative
article that outlines the double jeopardy of the elderly
Indian.

Boyer, L. B., et al.  Effects of Acculturation on the
Personality Traits of the Old People of the Mescalero and
Chiricahua Apaches.  International Journal of Social
Psychiatry.  2(4):264-71, 1965.

Brown, J. K.  Iroquois Women:  An Ethnohistoric Note.  Pp.
235-51 in Rayna Reiter (ed).  Toward an Anthropology of
Women.  New York, NY:  Monthly Review Press, 1975.

Discusses the power and authority of middle-aged and older
Iroquois women both in the private (hearth) and public
(village politics) sectors of Iroquois life.

Carpenter, E.  Eternal Life and Self Definition Among the
Aivilik Eskimos.  American Journal of Psychiatry.
110:840-43, 1954.

Chesley-Lang, G.  Diabetics and Health Care in a Sioux
Community.  Human Organization.  44(3):251-60, 1985.

Chovan, M. J. and W. Chovan.  Stressful Events and Coping
Responses Among Older Adults in Two Sociocultural Groups.
Journal of Psychology.  119(3):253-60, 1985.

Cooley, R., D. Ostendorf, and D. Bickerton.  Outreach Services
for Elderly Native Americans.  Social Work.  March:151-53,
1979.

Curley, L.  Retirement:  an Indian Perspective.  Pp. 43-47 in
E. P.  Stanford (ed).  Retirement:  Concepts and Realities
of Ethnic Minority Elders.  San Diego, CA:  San Diego State
University, 1978.

_____  Title VI of the Older Americans Act, 'Grants to Indian

Tribes.' Pp. 223-26 in E. P. Stanford (ed). <u>Minority Aging Research: Old Issues--New Approaches</u>. San Diego, CA: San Diego State University, 1979.

Deal, P. Cultural Heritage Valued by Navaho Foster Grandparents. <u>Generations</u>. 2(20):27, 1977.

Doherty, R. P. Growing Old in Indian Country. Pp. 17-26 in <u>Employment Prospects of Aged Blacks, Chicano and Indians</u>. The National Council on the Aging, 1971.

Dukepoo, F. <u>The Elder American Indian</u>. San Diego, CA: San Diego University, Capanile Press, 1978.

Dunn, J. A. Tsimshian Grandchildren: Redistributive Mechanisms in Personal Property Inheritance. <u>Papers in Anthropology</u>. 20(2):13-32, 1979.

Edwards, W. D. Native American Elders: Current Issues and Social Policy Implications. Pp. 74-82 in R. L. McNeely and J. N. Colen (eds). <u>Aging in Minority Groups</u>. Beverly Hills, CA: Sage, 1983.

Edwards, E. D., M. E. Edwards, and G. M. Daines. American Indian/Alaska Native Elderly: A Current and Vital Concern. <u>Journal of Gerontological Social Work</u>. 2:213-24, 1980.

Fowler, L. Colonial Context and Age Group Relations Among Plains Indians. <u>Journal of Cross-Cultural Gerontology</u>. 5(2):149-68, 1990.

French, J. and D. Schwartz. Terminal Care at Home in Two Cultures. <u>American Journal of Nursing</u>. 73(3):502-05, 1973.

Goldstine, T. and D. Gutmann. A TAT Study of Navajo Aging. <u>Psychiatry</u>. 35:373-84, 1972.

Guemple, D. The Concept and Use of Time in the Middle Years: The St. Lawrence Island Eskimos. Pp. 91-95 in R. Kleemeier (ed). <u>Aging and Leisure: A Research Perspective into the Meaningful Use of Time</u>. New York, NY: Oxford University Press, 1961.

_____ Human Resource Management: The Dilemma of the Aging Eskimo. <u>Sociological Symposium</u>. 2:59-74, 1969.

_____ The Dilemma of the Aging Eskimo. Pp. 194-203 in C. Beattie and S. Crysdale (eds). <u>Sociology Canada: Readings</u> (2nd ed). Toronto, Canada: Butterworth, 1977.

_____ Growing Old in Inuit Society. Pp. 24-28 in J. Sokolovsky (ed). <u>Growing Old in Dieerent Societies: Cross-Cultural Perspectives</u>. Acton, MA: Copley Press, 1987.

Gutmann, D. Navajo Dependency and Illness. Pp. 181-98 in E. Palmore (ed). <u>Prediction of Life Span</u>. Lexington, MA:

Heath Lexington Book, 1971a.

_____ The Hunger of Old Men.  Transaction.
November/December, 1971b.

_____ The Cross-Cultural Perspective:  Notes Toward a
Comparative Psychology of Aging.  Pp. 302-26 in J. E.
Birren and K. W. Schaie (eds).  Handbook of the Psychology
of Aging.  New York, NY:  Van Nostrand, 1977.

A comparative psychological study of middle-aged and older
individuals in a variety of non-industrialized societies,
including the Mexican Maya and the Navajo.

Hagey, R.  The Phenomenon, the Explanations and the Responses:
Metaphors Surrounding Diabetes in Urban Canadian Indians.
Social Science and Medicine.  18:265-72, 1984.

Hill,  C.  Measures of Longevity of American Indians.  Public
Health Reports.  95:233-39, 1970.

Hoebel, E. A.  The Law of Primitive Man.  Cambridge, MA:
Harvard University Press, 1954.

General discussion of senilicide across cultures.  Eskimo
attitudes and practices are discussed in some detail.

Hughes, C.  The Concept and Use of Time in the Middle Years:
The St. Lawrence Island Eskimos.  Pp. 91-95 in R. W.
Kleemeier (ed).  Aging and Leisure.  New York, NY:  Oxford
University Press, 1961.

Indian Health Services.  Physical and Mental Health of Elderly
American Indians.  Oklahoma City, OK:  Association of
American Indian Physicians, Inc., 1978.

Outlines the physical and mental health needs of elderly
American Indians.  Adequate housing, nutrition and in-home
health care are underscored.

Jeffries, W. R.  Our Aged Indians.  In Triple Jeopardy--Myth
or Reality?.  Washington, DC:  National Council on Aging,
1972.

John, R.  The Older Americans Act and the Elderly Native
American.  Journal of Minority Aging.  5(4):293-98, 1980.

_____ Service Needs and Support Networks of Elderly Native
Americans:  Family, Friends, and Social Service Agencies.
Pp. 229-47 in W. A. Peterson and J. S. Quadagno (eds).
Social Bonds in Later Life:  Aging and Interdependence.
Beverly Hills, CA:  Sage, 1985.

_____ Social Policy and Planning for Aging American Indians:
Provision of Services by Formal and Informal Support
Networks.  Pp. 111-13 in J. R. Joe (ed).  American Indian
Policy and Cultural Values:  Conflict and Accommodation.
Contemporary American Indian Issues Series, No. 6.  Los

202    ANTHROPOLOGY OF AGING

Angeles, CA:  American Indian Studies Center, University of
California, 1986.

_____ Use of Cluster Analysis in Social Service Planning:  A
Case Study of Laguna Pueblo Elders. Journal of Applied
Gerontology.  7(1), 1988.

_____ American Indian Aging.  Brief Bibliography:  A
Selective Annotated Bibliography for Gerontology
Instruction. Washington, DC:  Association for Gerontology
in Higher Education, 1988.

Johnson, F. L., et al.  Life Satisfaction of the Elderly
American Indian. White Cloud Journal.  3(3):1-13, 1984.

Joos, S. K. and S. Ewart.  A Health Survey of Klamath Indian
Elders 30 Years After the Loss of Tribal Status. Public
Health Reports.  103;166-73, 1988.

The authors compare the health status and needs of Klamath
Indians (whose tribal status with the federal government
terminated in 1954) with samples of other Indian and non-
Indian elders.  Health status of the Klamaths was no better
than the other Indian comparison group and worse than the
non-Indians.  Further, the Klamaths scored more poorly than
either comparison group in terms of perceived unmet medical
needs and health insurance coverage.

Kaplan, H. and B. Taylor. Economic and Social Problems of the
Elderly Urban Indian in Phoenix, Arizona.  Phoenix, AZ:
LEAP, City of Phoenix, 1972.

Kelleher, E., et al.  Life Satisfaction of the Elderly
American Indian. International Journal of Nursing Studies.
23(3):265-73, 1986.

Knowler, W. C., et al.  Diabetes Incidence in Pima Indians:  A
19-Fold Greater Incidence Than in Rochester, Minnesota.
American Journal of Epidemiology.  108:497-505, 1978.

Kramer, B. J., D. Polisar, and J. C. Hyde. Study of Urban
American Indian Aging.  City of Industry, CA:  The Public
Health Foundation, 1990.

Krohn, A. and D. Gutmann.  Changes in Mastery Style With Age:
A Study of Navajo Dreams. Psychiatry.  34:289-300, 1971.

Kunitz, S. J. and J. E. Levy.  The Prevalence of Hypertension
Among Elderly Navajos:  A Test of the Acculturative Stress
Hypothesis. Culture, Medicine and Psychiatry.
10(2):97-121, 1986.

_____ A Prospective Study of Isolation and Mortality in a
Cohort of Elderly Navajo Indians. Journal of Cross-
Cultural Gerontology.  3(1):71-85, 1988.

Leighton, A. and C. Hughes.  Notes on Eskimo Patterns of
Suicide. Southwestern Journal of Anthropology.  3:327-38,

1955.

Leonard, C. and B. Leonard.  Zuni Diabetes Project.  Indian
    Health Service. Primary Care Provider. 10(4):17-20, 1985.

Levy, J.  The Older American Indian.  Pp. 221-38 in E. Youmans
    (ed). Older Rural Americans. Lexington, KY: University
    of Kentucky Press, 1967.

Liberman, D. and J. Frank.  Individuals' Perceptions of
    Stressful Life Events:  A Comparison of Native American,
    Rural, and Urban Samples Using the Social Readjustment
    Rating Scale. White Cloud Journal. 1(4):15-19, 1980.

Locust-Pettit Poppy, M.  Needs Assessment in Minority Aging
    Research.  Pp. 769-88 in E. P. Stanford (ed). Minority
    Aging Research: Old Issues--New Approaches. San Diego,
    CA:  San Diego State University, 1979.

Lustig, J. The Needs of Elderly Indians in Phoenix, Arizona:
    Recommendations for Services. Phoenix, AZ: Affiliation of
    Arizona Indian Centers, Inc., 1979.

Lyman, A. J. and M. E. Edwards.  Poetry:  Life Review for
    Frail American Indian Elderly. Journal of Gerontological
    Social Work. 14(1-2):75-91, 1989a.

    American Indian elderly in nursing homes explore various
    topics through the use of poetry:  the stages of life
    (youth and old age); values, beliefs and religion; and
    challenges of the present.

_____Reminiscence Poetry Groups:  Sheepherding--A Navajo
    Cultural Tie That Binds. Activities, Adaptation and Aging.
    14(4):1-8, 1989b.

    Navajo elders assess, through poetry, the impact of their
    early sheepherding days (challenges faced and knowledge
    gained) on their lives now as older people.

Lyon, J. (ed). The Indian Elder, A Forgotten American.  Final
    Report on the First National Indian Conference on Aging,
    Phoenix, Arizona, June 15-17, 1976.  Washington, DC:
    National Tribal Chairmen's Association, 1978.

Manson, S. M.  Long-Term Care in American Indian Communities:
    Issues for Planning and Research. Gerontologist.
    29(1):38-44, 1989a.

    Planning and research related to long-term care for the
    American Indian elderly population lag far behind the state
    of the art.  IHS, the major health care provider for this
    special population, has actively resisted developing
    services specific to older tribal members.  Yet, despite
    this lack of leadership, many innovative efforts have
    emerged at the local level.  These efforts, the issues that
    face subsequent program advancement, and critical questions
    for future study are discussed.

_____ Provider Assumptions About Long-Term Care in American Indian Communities. Gerontologist. 29(3):355-58, 1989b.

A brief survey of 208 IHS providers and allied personnel revealed the extent to which they subscribed to a number of myths about long-term care. With some exceptions, long-term care is equated with the nursing home, perceived as involving essentially health care professionals, and service objectives are assumed to be primarily rehabilitative and protective in nature. Underscored is the importance of past recommendations of geriatric training for IHS and tribal human service providers.

Manson, S. M. and D. Callaway. Health and Aging Among American Indians: Issues and Challenges for the Biobehavioral Sciences. In S. M. Manson and N. G. Dinges (eds). Health and Behavior Among American Indians and Alaska Natives: A Research Agenda for the Biobehavioral Sciences. Boulder, CO: Westview Press, 1988.

Manson, S. M., C. B. Murray, and L. D. Cain. Ethnicity, Aging and Support Networks: An Evolving Methodological Strategy. Journal of Minority Aging. 6(2):11-37, 1981.

Discusses network data eliciting and analysis strategies that accurately depict contemporary American Indian social structure.

Manson, S. and A. Pembrun. Social and Psychological Status of the Indian Elderly: Past Research, Current Advocacy and Future Inquiry. Presented at the Second National Indian Conference on Aging, Billings, Montana, 1978.

Maxwell, R. J. and E. K. Maxwell. Cooperative Independence Among the Tlingit Elderly. Human Organization. 42:(2):178-80, 1983.

McCabe, M. L. Health Care Accessibility for the Elderly on the Navajo Reservation. Pride Institute Journal of Long-Term Home Health Care. 7(4):22-26, 1988.

Discusses the programs administered by the Navajo Nation: senior citizen centers, several home health care services and programs for foster grandparetns.

Medicine, B. Kunsheilei (Grandmothers). Plainswoman. 1(10-11):11-12, 1978.

Mick, C. A Profile of American Indian Nursing Homes. Long-Term Care Gerontology Center. Tucson, AZ: University of Arizona, 1983.

Munsell, M. Functions of the Aged Among Salt River Pima. Pp. 127-32 in Cowgill and Holmes (eds). Aging and Modernization. New York, NY: Appleton-Century-Crofts, 1972.

Murdock, S. and D. Schwartz. Family Structure and the Use of

Agency Services:   An Examination of Patterns Among Elderly
Native Americans.  Gerontologist.  18:475-82, 1978.

National Indian Council on Aging.  The Indian Elder:  A
Forgotten American.  Final Report on the First National
Indian Conference on Aging.  Albuquerque, NM:  National
Indian Council on Aging, 1976.

_____   The Continuum of Life:  Health Concerns of the Indian
Elderly.  Final Report on the Second National Indian
Conference on Aging, Billings, Montana, August 15-18, 1978.
Albuquerque, NM:  Adobe Press, 1979.

A general review of age profile of the national Indian
population and a list of the various social, economic and
health problems which continue to afflict the American
Indian elderly.  Policy recommendations are outlined.

_____   Indian Elderly and Entitlement Programs:  An Accessing
Demonstration Project.  Albuquerque, NM:  National Council
on Aging, 1981a.

_____   May the Circle Be Unbroken:  A New Decade.  Final
Report on the Third National Indian Conference on Aging.
Albuquerque, NM:  National Indian Council on Aging, 1981b.

_____   American Indian Elderly:  A National Profile.
Alburquerque, NM:  National Indian Council on Aging, 1981c.

A report in much the same style as the 1978 report
described above.  The continuing absence of innovative
programs and policy planning on behalf of the Indian
elderly is underscored.

_____   Access, A Demonstration Project:  Entitlement Programs
for Indian Elders.  Albuquerque, NM:  National Indian
Council on Aging, 1983a

_____   Indian Elders:  A Tribute.  Proceedings of The Fourth
National Indian Conference on Aging, Reno, Nevada, August
23-25, 1982.  Albuquerque, NM:  National Indian Council on
Aging, 1983b.

_____   Let Us Continue in Unity.  Proceedings of the Fifth
National Indian Conference on Aging.  Albuquerque, NM:
National Council on Aging, 1985.

Nixon, R. M.  Text of Indian Message.  Congressional Quarterly
Alamanac.  Pp. 101-15, 1970.

Red Horse, J. G.  American Indian Elders:  Unifiers of Indian
Families.  The Phoenix from the Flame:  The American Indian
Today.  Special Issue.  Social Casework:  The Journal of
Contemporary Social Work.  61(8):490-93, 1980a.

_____   American Indian Elders:  Needs and Aspirations in
Institutional and Home Health Care.  Pp. 61-68 in E. P.
Stanford (ed).  Minority Aging:  Policy Issues for the

80's.  San Diego, CA:  San Diego State University, 1980b.

_____ American Indian and Alaskan Native Elders:  A Policy
Critique.  Pp. 15-26 in E. P. Stanford and S. A. Lockery
(eds).  Trends and Status of Minority Aging.  San Diego,
CA:  San Diego State University, 1982.

Red Horse J., et al.  Family Behavior of Urban American
Indians.  Social Casework.  59(2):67-72, 1978.

Rhoades, E. R., et al.  Impact of Mental Disorders Upon
Elderly American Indians as Reflected in Visits to
Ambulatory Care Facilities.  Journal of the American
Geriatrics Society.  28:33-39, 1980.

Rickert, H., O. Chuculate, and D. Klinert.  Aging and
Ethnicity in Healthy Elderly Women.  Geriatrics.
26(5):146-52, 1971.

    This article includes comments about Indian views of aging
    and physical health as well as on aging among Indian women.

Rogers, C. and T. Gallion.  Characteristics of Elderly Pueblo
Indians in New Mexico.  Gerontologist.  18(5-1):482-87,
1978.

Schweitzer, M.  The Power and Prestige of the Elderly in Two
Indian Communities.  Ann Arbor, MI:  University of Michigan
Microfilms, 1978.

_____ The Elders:  Cultural Dimensions of Aging in Two
American Indian Communities.  Pp. 168-78 in J. Sokolovsky
(ed).  Growing Old in Different Societies:  Cross-Cultural
Perspectives.  Acton, MA:  Copley Press, 1987.

    Ethnicity makes a positive difference in linking elders to
    tribal functions and the extended family system.  The
    Indian aged have retained power in the public domain by
    remaining in demand as ritual specialists, information
    sources, and storytellers at tribal functions.  The family
    system is the most enduring source of esteem.  It
    facilitates intense intergenerational ties and a context in
    which grandparents, through sponsorship, enhance the
    prestige of younger family members.

Sharp, H.  Old Age Among the Chipewyan.  Pp. 99-110 in P.
Amoss and S. Harrell (eds).  Other Ways of Growing Old:
Anthropological Perspectives.  Satnford, CA:  Stanford
University Press, 1981.

Shomaker, D. J.  Transfer of Children and the Importance of
Grandmothers Among the Navajo Indians.  Journal of Cross-
Cultural Gerontology.  4(1):19-34, 1989.

_____ Health Care, Cultural Expectations and Frail Elderly
Navajo Grandmothers.  Journal of Cross-Cultural
Gerontology.  5(1):21-34, 1990.

Simmons, L. W.   The Role of the Aged in Primitive Society.
    Hamden, CT:  Shoe String Press, 1970..

    Still the best source for general discussion of the
    traditional roles of North Amerian Indian and Eskimo
    elderly, Simmons culled data from ethnographies for eleven
    different tribes representative of the major culture areas
    as well as Eskimo communities located in three different
    locales.  His analysis included data on availability of
    food; property rights; political and civil activities; use
    of knowledge, magic, and religion; the function of the
    family; and the aged's reactions to death.

Strong, C.  Stress and Caring for Elderly Relatives:
    Interpretations and Coping Strategies in an American Indian
    and White Sample.  Gerontologist.  24(3):251-56, 1984.

    This study explores how families who care for their elderly
    relatives view their caretaking situations.  The stressful
    event literature suggests that a variety of dimensions may
    influence a person's subsequent coping behavior.  In semi-
    structured interviews with ten Indian and ten White
    caretakers of ill elderly relatives in the rural Northwest,
    eleven dimensions were used to define caretaking, with a
    focus on control.  The results imply that cultural
    background influences the meaning of caretaking and that
    both variables affect the coping strategies selected.

Stuart, P. and E. Rathbone-McCuan.  Indian Elderly in the
    United States.  Pp. 235-54 in E. Rathbone-McCuan and B.
    Havens (eds).  North American Elders.  Contributions to the
    Study of Aging, No. 8.  Westport, CT:  Greenwood, 1988.

Taylor, B. and W. Peach.  Social and Economic Characteristics
    of Elderly Indians in Phoenix, Arizona.  Journal of
    Economics and Business.  26:151-55, 1974.

Taylor, T. L.  Health Problems and Use of Services at Two
    Urban American Indian Clinics.  Public Health Reports.
    103:88-95, 1988.

Tefft, S.  Intergenerational Value Differentials and Family
    Structure Among the Wind River Shoshone.  American
    Anthropologist.  70:330-33, 1968.

Tom-Orme, L.  Diabetes Intervention on the Uintah-Ouray
    Reservation.  Pp. 27-38 in J. Uhl (ed).  Proceedings of the
    Ninth Annual Transcultural Nursing Conference.  Salt Lake
    City, UT:  Transcultural Nursing Society, 1984.

_____  Health Beliefs About Diabetes Mellitus in an American
    Indian Tribe:  A Preliminary Formulation.  Pp. 125-34 in M.
    A. Carter (ed).  Proceedings of the Tenth Annual
    Transcultural Nursing Conference.  Salt Lake City, UT:
    Transcultural Nursing Society, 1985.

United States Senate (Special Committee on Aging).  The
    American Indian Elderly:  The Forgotten Population.  Serial

No. 100-25.  Washington, DC:  US Government Printing
Office, 1989.

Vanderburgh, A.  Coming Back Slow.  Parabola.  5(1):20-23,
1980.

Vanderburgh, R. M.  When Legends Fall Silent Our Ways Are
Lost:  Some Dimensions of the Study of Aging Among Native
Canadians.  Culture.  2(1):21-29, 1982.

_____  The Impact of Government Support for Indian Culture on
Canada's Aged Indians.  Pp. 221-33 in E. Rathbone-McCuan
and B. Havens, (eds).  North American Elders:  United
States and Canadian Perspectives.  Contributions to the
Study of Aging, No. 8.  Westport, CT:  Greenwood, 1988.

Weibel-Orlando, J.  Indians, Ethnicity As a Resource and
Aging:  You Can Go Home Again.  Journal of Cross-Cultural
Gerontology.  3(4):323-48, 1988.

_____  Elders and Elderlies:  Well-Being in Indian Old Age.
American Indian Culture and Research Journal.
13(3-4):149-70, 1989.

Ethnically-inflected community statuses and roles in
American Indian old age contribute positively to social and
psychological well-being.  Factors which support and
sustain good mental health and personal well-being include:
active involvement in Indian community life, enactment of
community recognized and valued political and spiritual
roles, regular interaction with family and co-ethnics,
continued community contribution and service, personal acts
of altruism, and community recognition of such good works.

_____  Grandparenting Styles:  American Indian Perspectives.
Pp. 109-26 in J. Sokolovsky (ed).  The Cultural Context of
Aging:  Worldwide Perspectives.  Westport, CT:  Bergin and
Garvey, 1990.

Grandparental roles among contemporary North American
Indians are expressed across a range of activities, purpose
and intensity.  The ways these behavioral and attitudinal
components of role fit together are so varied as to be
identified as distinct grandparenting styles.  Five
identified grandparenting styles include:  the cultural
conservator, custodian, ceremonial, distanced, and fictive.

White House Conference on Aging.  The American Indian and
Alaska Native Elderly.  Technical Report.  Washington, DC:
US Government Printing Office, 1981.

Williams, B. S.  The Older American Indian Population:
Geographic Distribution, 1970.  Administration on Aging.
Facts and Figures on Older Americans.  No. 9.  Washington,
DC:  GPO, 1974.

_____  American Indian Population 55 Years of Age and Older:
Geographic Distribution, 1970.  Administration on Aging.

Statistical Reports on Older Americans. No. 1.  Washington, DC:  GPO,1977.

_____ Social, Economic and Health Characteristics of Older American Indians.  Agency on Aging.  Statistical Reports on Older Americans.  No. 4.  Washington, DC:  National Clearinghouse on Aging, 1978.

Williams, G.  Warriors No More:  A Study of the American Indian Elderly.  Pp. 101-11 in C. Fry (ed).  Aging in Culture and Society:  Comparative Viewpoints and Strategies.  Brooklyn, NY:  J. F.  Bergin, 1980.


## JAPANESE AMERICANS

Arkoff, A.  Need Patterns in Two Generations of Japanese Americans in Hawaii.  Journal of Social Psychology. 50:75-79, 1959.

Connor, J.  Tradition and Change in Three Generations of Japanese Americans.  Chicago, IL:  Nelson-Hall, 1978.

Glick, C., et al.  Changing Attitudes Toward the Care of the Aged Japanese Parents in Hawaii.  Social Process in Hawaii. 22:9-20, 1958.

Ishizuka, K.  The Elder Japanese.  San Diego, CA:  Campanile Press, 1978.

Johnson, C.  The Principle of Generation Among the Japanese in Honolulu.  Ethnic Groups:  An International Periodical of Ethnic Studies.  1:13-35, 1976.

_____ Interdependence, Reciprocity and Indebtedness:  An Analysis of Japanese-American Kinship Relations.  Journal of Marriage and the Family.  39(5):351-62, 1977.

Kiefer, C.  Changing Cultures, Changing Lives:  An Ethnographic Study of Three Generations of Japanese Americans.  San Francisco, CA:  Jossey-Bass, 1974.

_____ Lessons From the Issei.  In J. Gubrium (ed).  Late Life:  Communities and Environmental Policy.  Springfield, IL:  CC Thomas, 1974.

Levine, G. and D. Montero. Socioeconomic Mobility Among Three Generations of Japanese Americans.  Journal of Social Issues.  29(2):33-48, 1973.

Lipman, A.  Conference on the Potential for Japanese-American Cross-National Research on Aging.  Gerontologist. 15:248-53, 1975.

Masuda, M., G. Matsumoto, and G. Meredith.  Ethnic Identity in Three Generations of Japanese Americans.  Journal of Social Psychology.  81:199-207, 1970.

Montero, O.  Disengagement and Aging Among the Issei.  Pp.
    193-205 in D.  Gelfand and A. Kutzik (eds).  Ethnicity and
    Aging:  Theory, Research and Policy.  New York, NY:
    Springer, 1979.

_____  The Elderly Japanese-American:  Aging Among the First
    Generation Immigrants.  Genetic Psychology Monographs,
    1980.


## CHINESE AMERICANS

Adler, S.  Seeking Stillness in Motion:  An Introduction to
    Tai Chi for Seniors.  Activities, Adaptation and Aging.
    3(4):1-14, 1983.

    Describes Tai Chi Chuan, a traditional Chinese exercise, in
    terms of its potential benefits for older people.  Two
    major philosophical principles underlying Tai Chi exercises
    are discussed, and adaptations of traditional forms are
    described.

Carp, F.  Health Care Problems of the Elderly in San
    Francisco's Chinatown.  Gerontologist.  16:30-38, 1976.

Chan, K. B.  Coping with Aging and Managing Self-Identity:
    The Social World of the Elderly Chinese Women.  Canadian
    Ethnic  Studies.  15(3):36-50, 1983.

    Using data generated by questionnaires with 26 elderly
    Chinese women in Montreal, the author seeks to sensitize
    research attention to how these women cope with "double
    jeopardy" and the impacts of old age and widowhood.  (The
    Chinese experience in Canada parallels that of the Chinese
    in the United States.)

Chang, B. L.  Care and Support of Elderly Family Members:
    Views of Ethnic Chinese Young People.  Pp. 79-93 in W.
    McCready (ed).  Culture, Ethnicity and Identity.  New York,
    NY:  Academic Press, 1983

    Sample consists of 80 young people interviewed in the US
    and divided into three subsamples:  American-born, Taiwan,
    and Hong Kong Chinese.  All three subsamples generally
    agreed in  principle that offspring should care for the
    elderly, but the majority also agreed that they would
    prefer not to have the elderly living with them.

Chang, B. L., A. F. Chang, and S. Yung.  Attitudes Towards
    Aging in the United States and Taiwan.  Journal of
    Comparative Family Studies.  15(1):109-30, 1984.

    Compares attitudes of 400 students of Chinese descent in
    the United States with those of 200 students in Taiwan.

Chen, P.-N.  A Study of Chinese Elderly Living in Hotels.
    Social Case Work.  59:343-51, 1978.

The site of this study is Chinatown, Los Angeles,
California.

Chen, S. and J. Chen.  Effects of Culture on the Success of
    Aging:  A Preliminary Study Comparing the Productivity of
    Two Aging Groups of Chinese and American Men.  Boston
    Medical Quarterly.  15:14-22, 1964.

Cheng, E.  The Elder Chinese.  San Diego, CA:  Campanile
    Press, 1978.

Cheung, L. Y., et al.  The Chinese Elderly and Family
    Structure:  Implications for Health Care.  Public Health
    Reports.  95(5):491-95, 1980.

    The sample population consisted of 60 Chinese persons aged
    60 or older who lived in three low-income housing projects
    in Sacramento, California.  Despite norms advocating care
    by children, the authors found that most of their sample
    lived apart from children and needed expanded bilingual and
    bicultural services to meet their health needs.

Ikels, C.  Aging and Adaptation:  Chinese in Hong Kong and the
    United States.  Hamden, CT:  Archon Books, 1983a.

    This work is an anthropological study based on four years
    of fieldwork equally divided between Hong Kong and the
    Chinese community in Greater Boston.  It explores the
    variation among the Chinese elderly in both sites and
    describes the unique dilemmas faced by this particular
    cohort.

    _____  The Process of Care-Taker Selection.  Research on
    Aging.  5(4):491-509, 1983b.

    Based on fieldwork in the Chinese and Irish communities of
    Greater Boston.  Despite major cultural differences between
    these two populations, the author finds that the same
    principles guide the selection of the primary caretaker of
    elderly family members.  These factors include family
    composition, antecedent events, and situational factors at
    the time caretaking becomes an issue.

    _____  Parental Perspectives on the Significance of Marriage.
    Journal of Marriage and the Family.  42:253-64, 1985.

    Based on fieldwork in the Chinese and Irish communities of
    Greater Boston.  Describes how caretaking expectations of
    parents shape their views of the marriages of their
    children.  Chinese parents look forward to their sons'
    marriages as daughters-in-law are designated caretakers,
    whereas Irish parents worry about their daughters'
    marriages because their removal from the community means
    their likely unavailability for caretaking later.

    _____  Older Immigrants and Natural Helpers.  Journal of
    Cross-Cultural Gerontology.  1(2):209-22, 1986.

Notes the high proportion of elderly immigrants who are of Asian ancestry, most of whom have arrived since 1970, and describes the role of natural helpers in one ethnic population, the Chinese in Boston, in facilitating the adaptation of the elderly to life in the United States.

Lum, D., et al. The Psychological Needs of the Chinese Elderly. Social Casework. 61(2):100-06, 1980.

Nagasawa, R., et al. The Elderly Chinese: A Forgotten Minority. Tempe, AZ: Arizona State University Press, 1980.

Serby, M., J. C. Y. Chou, and E. H. Franssen. Dementia in an American-Chinese Nursing Home Population. American Journal of Psychiatry. 144(6):811-12, 1987.

Of 58 demented residents in an American-Chinese nursing home, 44 (75.9%) had multi-infarct dementia, 7 (12.1%) had possible Alzheimer's disease, 4 (6.9%) had other dementias, and 3 (5.2%) had unknown disorders. Alzheimer's disease was relatively less prevalent than in U. S. nursing homes overall.

Suzuki, P. T. Social Work, Culture-Specific Mediators, and Delivering Services to Aged Turks in Germany and Aged Chinese in San Francisco. International Social Work. 21(3):1-7, 1978.

Tien-Hyatt, J. L. Self-Perceptions of Aging Across Cultures: Myth or Reality? International Journal of Aging and Human Development. 24(2):129-48, 1986-87.

This study uses semi-structured interviews to explore the differences and similarities of self-perceptions of aging and associated factors among Anglo-Americans, Chinese-Americans, and Chinese in Taiwan. Each of the three subgroups consists of 20 female community residents between 60 and 75 years of age.

Wong, P. and G. Reker. Stress, Coping, and Well-Being in Anglo and Chinese Elderly. Canadian Journal on Aging. 4(1):29-37, 1985.

Compared ethnic differences related to the coping behaviors of 40 elderly Chinese living in Canada and 40 Caucasian Canadians. Findings are interpreted as in support of the double jeopardy hypothesis of ethnic minority aging.

Wu, F. Mandarin-Speaking Aged Chinese in the Los Angeles Area. Gerontologist. 15:271-75, 1975.

Yan, A. Dietary Factors of Frail Elderly Chinese in Community Based Long-term Care. Journal of Nutrition for the Elderly. 5(1):37-46, 1985.

Notes that the On Lok Senior Health Services model of community-based long-term care is unique for its large

ethnic population and alternative service delivery system.
Discusses ways of adapting foods to the cultural
preferences of the population.

Yu, E. S. H.  Health of the Chinese Elderly in America.
Research on Aging.  8(1):84-109, 1986.

This article examines the mortality and morbidity patterns
of Chinese elderly in America by using two established data
sources:  (1) one maintained by the National Center for
Health Statistics and (2) the other, the cancer registry
program, maintained by the National Cancer Institute.
Detailed statistics on rates of suicide, heart disease,
neoplasms, and various forms of cancer are presented.

Yu, L. C. and S.-C. Wu.  Unemployment and Family Dynamics in
Meeting the Needs of Chinese Elderly in the United States.
Gerontologist.  25(5):472-76, 1985.

The effects of unemployment on the discomfort level of
providing financial support and housing for a group of
Midwestern Chinese American elderly were examined.


## OTHER ASIAN/PACIFIC AMERICANS

Browne, C. and R. Onzuka-Anderson.  Hale Pulama Mau:  Meeting
the Needs of Hawaii's Elderly.  Aging.  July-August:31-38,
1981.

This informative article describes a comprehensive
residential, medical and day care facility for the elderly
in Hawaii.

Cuellar, J. B., E. P. Stanford, and D. I. Miller-Soule (eds).
Pacific/Asian Bibliography.  Pp. 204-15 in J. B. Cuellar,
E. P.  Stanford, and D. I. Miller-Soule, (eds).
Understanding Minority Perspectives and Sources.  San
Diego, CA:  University Center on Aging, San Diego State
University, 1982.

This is one of several specialized bibliographies in this
volume on various U. S. minorities.  Includes entries on
all Asian and Pacific groups.

Die A. and W. C. Seelbach.  Problems, Sources of Assistance,
and Knowledge of Services Among Elderly Vietnamese
Immigrants.  Gerontologist.  28:448-52, 1988.

Fujii, S.  Elderly Asian Americans and the Use of Public
Service.  Social Casework.  57:202-07, 1976a.

_____  Older Asian American Victims of Double Jeopardy.  Civil
Rights Digest.  Fall:24-25, 1976b.

_____  Retirement As It Relates to the Pacific-Asian Elderly.
Pp. 27-31 in E. P. Stanford (ed).  Retirement:  Concepts
and Realities of Ethnic Minority Elders.  San Diego, CA:

Campanile Press, 1978.

Gardner, R. W., B. Robey, and P. C. Smith. Asian Americans: Growth, Change and Diversity. Population Bulletin. 40(4):1-43, 1985.

Special journal issue which includes extensive demographic data on six Asian-American groups with emphasis on heterogeneity.

Grognet, A. G. Elderly Refugees and Language Learning. Aging. 359:8-11, 1989.

Hayes, C. Two Worlds in Conflict: The Elderly Hmong in the United States. Pp. 79-95 in D. Gelfand and C. Barresi (eds). Ethnic Dimensions of Aging. New York, NY: Springer, 1987.

Holmes L. D. Aging and Modernization: The Samoan Aged of San Francisco. Pp. 205-13 in B. Shore and R. Franco (eds). New Neighbors: Islanders in Adaptation. Santa Cruz, CA: Center for Pacific Studies, University of California, 1978.

This article presents a profile of migrant Samoan families with emphasis on the effect of modernization on attitudes toward and services rendered to the aged by their families and the community.

Hurh, W. M. and K. C. Kim. Korean Immigrants in America: A Structural Analysis of Ethnic Confinement and Adhesive Adaptation. Cranbury, NJ: Associated University Presses, 1984.

Ishikawa, W. The Elder Samoan. San Diego, CA: Campanile Press, 1978a.

Part of the San Diego project on minority elders, this book examines the situation of the aged Samoans of San Diego, their lifestyle and problems.

_____ The Elder Guamanian. San Diego, CA: Campanile Press, 1978b.

This brief book focuses on language differences, residence patterns, needs and coping strategies of the aged Guamanians of San Diego.

Kalish, R. and S. Moriwaki. The World of the Elderly Asian American. Journal of Social Issues. 29:187-209, 1973.

Kalish, R. and S. Yuen. Americans of East Asian Ancestry: Aging and the Aged. Gerontologist. 11(1):36-47, 1971.

Kiefer, C., et al. Adjustment Problems of Korean American Elderly. Gerontologist. 25:477-82, 1985.

Interviews with elderly Korean immigrants are analyzed in terms of factors contributing to stress and adjustment.

Kii, T.  Asian American Elderly:  Conceptualization for
   Research in Ethnicity and Aging.  Journal of Minority
   Aging.  9(1-2):20-29, 1984.

   This article considers the issue of life-satisfaction
   research among Asian Americans.

Kim, I.  New Urban Immigrants:  The Korean Community in New
   York.  Englewood Cliffs, NJ:  Prentice-Hall, 1981.

Kim, P. K. H.  Demography of Asian-Pacific Elderly:  Selected
   Problems and Implications.  Pp. 29-41 in R. L. McNeely and
   J. L. Colen (eds).  Aging in Minority Groups.  Beverly
   Hills, CA:  Sage, 1983.

Kurzeja, P. L., et al.  Ethnic Attitudes of Asian American
   Elderly:  The Korean Immigrants and Japanese Niseis.
   Research on Aging.  8(1):110-27, 1986.

Kwon, P. H.  Korean Elderly People's Lifestyle, Old and New in
   the U. S. A.  Pp. 57-62 in E. P. Stanford (ed).
   Retirement:  Concepts and Realities of Ethnic Minority
   Elders.  San Diego, CA:  Campanile Press, 1978.

Lee, J. J.  Asian American Elderly:  A Neglected Minority
   Group.  Journal of Gerontological Social Work.
   9(4):103-16, 1986.

Liu, W. T.  Culture and Social Support.  Research on Aging.
   8(1):57-83, 1986a.

   This article explores the role of cultural and social
   factors in both defining and coping with mental illness
   among Asians.

_____  Health Services for Asian Elderly.  Research on Aging.
   8(1):156-75, 1986b.

   The aim of this article is to clarify issues surrounding
   the myth that elderly Asian Americans are, in general,
   healthy, adequately provided for by their families and
   adult children, and that ethnic institutions exist for
   older immigrant communities.  While dealing with Asian
   Americans in general, the article contains quite a bit on
   the Chinese.

Liu, W. T. and E. Yu.  Asian/Pacific American Elderly:
   Mortality Differentials, Health Status, and Use of Health
   Services.  Journal of Applied Gerontology.  4(1):35-64,
   1985.

Lum, D.  Asian-Americans and Their Aged.  Pp. 85-94 in R. L.
   McNeely and J. L. Colen (eds).  Aging in Minority Groups.
   Beverly Hills, CA:  Sage, 1983.

Lurie, E., et al.  On Lok Senior Day Health Center:  A Case
   Study.  Gerontologist.  16:39-46, 1976.

Moriwaki, S.   Update of Current Status of and Future
    Directions for Ethnic Minority Elderly Groups:   Pacific
    Asians.   Pp. 86-110 in J. B.  Cuellar, E. P. Stanford, and
    D. I. Miller-Soule (eds).   Understanding Minority Aging
    Perspectives and Sources.  San Diego, CA:  University
    Center on Aging, San Diego State University, 1982.

Nelson, G. and N. D. Liem.   International Conference on Cross-
    Cultural Sensitivity to the Needs of Asian and Pacific
    Elderly.  Honolulu, HA:  University of Hawaii School of
    Social Work, 1982.

    Summaries of papers presented at the conference include
    varied topics and different societies.  Contact information
    for authors is provided.

Netland, P. A. and H. Brownstein.   Acculturation and the Diet
    of Asian American Elderly.  Journal of Nutrition for the
    Elderly.  3(3):37-56, 1984.

    This article examines diets of Asian and Caucasian elderly
    in San Francisco in terms of meal frequency and nutrient
    differentials.

Nusberg, C. and M. M. Osako (eds).   The Situation of the
    Asian/Pacific Elderly.  Washington, DC:  International
    Federation on Aging, 1981.

Pacific/Asian Elderly Research Project.  Critical Factors in
    Service Delivery.  Los Angeles, CA:  Pacific/Asian Elderly
    Research Project, 1978a.

    _____  Unmet Research Needs in the Pacific/Asian Elderly
    Community.  Los Angeles, CA:  Pacific/Asian Elderly
    Research Project, 1978b.

Peterson, R.  The Elder Pilipino.  San Diego, CA:  Campanile
    Press, 1978.

    Language difficulties, service awareness, neighborhood
    support mechanisms and needs of the Pilipino elderly of San
    Diego are described in this book.

Powers, E. A., W. J. Goudy, and P. M. Keith.  Later Life
    Transitions:  Older Males in Rural America.  Hingham, MA:
    Kluwer Nijhoff, 1985.

Rhoads, E. C.  The Impact of Modernization on the Aged in
    American Samoa.  Pacific Studies.  7(2):15-33, 1984.

Schwitters, S. Y.  Elderly Pacific/Asians:  Emerging Research
    Issues.  Pp. 111-44 in J. B. Cuellar, E. P. Stanford, and
    D. I. Miller-Soule (eds).  Understanding Minority Aging
    Perspectives and Sources.  San Diego, CA:  University
    Center on Aging, San Diego State University, 1982.

    This paper is a consideration of the state of the art in
    Pacific/ Asian research, including problems contributing to

the situation and suggestions for future research.

Schwitters, S. Y. and I. Ashdown.  Elderly Hawaiians in a
Changing Society.  Aging.  July-August:10-19, 1981.

Examines the role of the aged in traditional Hawaiian
society, various forces for sociocultural change, and the
situation of contemporary native Hawaiian elders.

Seefeldt, C. and S. R. Keawkumgwal.  Children's Attitudes
Toward the Elderly in Thailand and the U.S.  The
International Journal of Comparative Sociology.  26:226-31,
1985-86.

Skinner, K. A.  Vietnamese in America:  Diversity and
Adaptation.  California Sociologist.  3:103-24, 1980.

Skye, W. C.  Practical Procedure to Establish a Client's Age
for Social Security:  A Contemporary Problem Confronting
Hmong Immigrants Over Age 65.  Clearinghouse Review.
20(8):927-34, 1986.

Snyder, P.  Health Service Implications of Folk Healing Among
Asian Americans and Hawaiians in Honolulu.  Gerontologist.
24:471-76, 1984.

This paper explores the role of folk healing in
contemporary Hawaii and provides insight into the elderly
who participate in this practice.

Yee, B.  Multidimensional Perceptions of Control in Caucasian,
Japanese, and Vietnamese Elderly Women.  Journal of
Minority Aging.  9(1-2):76-84, 1984.

Yu, E. S. H.  Philipino Migration and Community Organization
in the United States.  California Sociologist.  3:76-102,
1980.


## EUROPEAN AMERICANS

Brubaker, T. H. and C. M. Michael.  Amish Families in Later
Life.  Pp. 106-17 in D. E. Gelfand and C. M. Barresi (eds).
Ethnic Dimensions of Aging.  New York, NY:  Spring, 1987.

Center for the Study of Pre-Retirement and Aging.  Proceedings
of the National Conference on Euro-American Elderly.
Washington, DC:  The Catholic University of America.
October, 1985.

Cohler, B. J. and H. Grunebaum.  Mothers, Grandmothers, and
Daughters:  Personality and Child Care in Three-Generation
Families.  New York, NY:  John Wiley, 1981.

Takes the psychosocial perspective on intergenerational
relations.  Utilizing a heavy methodological reliance on
the case study approach, examines the modified, extended,
three-generational Italian-American family.

Cohler, B. and M. Lieberman.  Personality Changes Across the
    Second Half of Life:  Findings From a Study of Irish,
    Italian and Polish-American Men and Women.  Pp. 227-45 in
    D. Gelfand and A. Kutzik (eds).  Ethnicity and Aging:
    Theory, Research and Policy.  New York, NY:  Springer, 1979

Cool, L.  Ethnic Identity:  A Source of Community Esteem for
    the Elderly.  Anthropological Quarterly.  54(4):179-89,
    1981.

Cottle, T. J.  Hidden Survivors:  Portraits of Poor Jews in
    America.  Englewood Cliffs, NJ:  Prentice-Hall, 1981.

    Many of the individuals discussed are poor and old.

Dileonardo, M.  The Varieties of Ethnic Experience:  Kinship,
    Class, and Gender Among Californian Italian-Americans.
    Ithaca, NY:  Cornell University Press, 1984.

    In the context of the larger issues of modern American
    ethnic identity, dicusses women's roles in the care of the
    elderly and varying perceptions of the elderly.

Fandetti, D. and D. Gelfand.  Care of the Aged:  Attitudes of
    White Ethnic Families.  Gerontologist.  16(6):544-49 1976.

    The ethnic groups discussed are Italian and Polish.

Francis, D.  Adaptive Strategies of the Elderly in England and
    Ohio.  Pp. 85-107 in C. L. Fry (ed).  Dimensions:  Aging,
    Culture and Health.  Brooklyn, NY:  Bergin, 1981.

Frank, B.  The American Orthodox Jewish Grandmother:  Ethnic
    Change and Stability.  Pp. 96-108 in A. Bloom (ed).  Select
    Studies on Aging Research in the Social Sciences at the
    Graduate School and University Center of the City
    University of New York.  New York, NY:  ERIC Document
    Reproduction Service No. ED 194 854, 1980.

Gelfand, D. E.  Assistance to New Russian Elderly.
    Gerontologist.  26:444-48, 1986.

_____  Directions and Trends in Aging Services:  A German-
    American Comparison.  International Journal of Aging and
    Human Development.  27(1):57-68, 1988.

Gelfand, D. E. and D. V. Fandetti.  Suburban and Urban White
    Ethnics:  Attitudes Toward Care of the Elderly.
    Gerontologist.  27:588-94, 1987.

Gelfand, D. and J. Olsen.  Aging in the Jewish Family and in
    the Mormon Family.  Pp. 206-21 in D. Gelfand and A. Kutzik
    (eds).  Ethnicity and Aging:  Theory, Research and Policy.
    New York, NY:  Springer, 1979.

Gerber, L.  Ethnicity Still Matters:  Socio-Demographic
    Profiles of the Ethnic Elderly in Ontario.  Canadian Ethnic
    Studies.  15:60-80, 1983.

Ginsberg, Y.  Fear of Crime Among Elderly Jews in Boston and London.  International Journal of Aging and Human Development.  20:257-68, 1985.

Gutmann, D.  Leisure Time Activity Interests of Jewish Aged. Gerontologist.  13:2, 1973.

_____ Use of Informal and Formal Supports by White Ethnic Aged.  Pp. 246-62 in D. Gelfand and A. Kutzik (eds). Ethnicity and Aging:  Theory, Research and Policy.  New York, NY:  Springer, 1979.

Hayes, C. L., R. A. Kalish, and D. Guttmann (eds).  European-American Elderly:  A Guide for Practice.  New York, NY: Springer, 1986.

This is a major work on Euro-American elderly.  Especially important is the chapter on the demography of American elderly of European origins.  Other chapters focus on the meaning of ethnicity, language barriers, family assistance, neighborhoods, religion, service organizations, government support, resources, service collaboration, and service worker education and training.

Holzberg, C. A.  Anthropology, Life Histories and the Aged: The Toronto Baycrest Centre.  International Journal of Aging in Human Development.  18:255-75, 1984.

Ikels, C.  Delayed Reciprocity and the Support Networks of the Childless Elderly.  Journal of Comparative Family Studies. 21(1):99-112, 1988.

This paper considers the roles of cultural values and family history as predictors of the support networks of the childless elderly.  The data were gathered from 38 Irish-American families in the Greater Boston area.

Johnson, C.  Family Support Systems to Elderly Italian-Americans.  Journal of Minority Aging.  3(1):34-41, 1979.

_____ Growing Up and Growing Old in Italian-American Families.  New Brunswick, NJ:  Rutgers University Press, 1985.

An examination of social--including filial and marital--relations, social networks, and socialization over the life courses of Italian Americans.  Sixty-six older Italians were interviewed, of a total sample of 414 including Protestant controls.  Ways in which ethnicity continues to determine the form of Italian family life are discussed.  Continuities in ethnic social patterns are traced in the relations between elderly parents and middle-aged children.

_____ Interdependence and Aging in Italian Families.  Pp. 92-103 in J. Sokolovsky (ed).  Growing Old in Different Societies:  Cross-Cultural Perspectives.  Acton, MA: Copley, 1987.

Journal of Aging and Judaism.

   Volume 1 appeared in 1986.  Published 4 times a year, this
   journal features articles on many aspects of lives of
   American elderly Jews.

Kahana, E. and B. Felton.  Social Context and Personal Need:
   A Study of Polish and Jewish Aged.  Journal of Social
   Issues.  33:56-64, 1977.

Kart, Cary S.  Age and Religious Commitment in an American
   Jewish Community.  In D. E. Gelfand and C. M. Barresi
   (eds).  Ethnic Dimensions of Aging.  New York, NY:
   Springer, 1987.

Kozaitis, K. A.  Being Old and Greek in America.  Pp. 179-95
   in D. E. Gelfand and C. M. Barresi (eds).  Ethnic
   Dimensions of Aging.  New York, NY:  Springer, 1987.

Krammer, S. and J. Masur (eds).  Jewish Grandmothers.  Boston,
   MA:  Beacon Press, 1976.

Luborsky, M. and R. L. Rubinstein.  Ethnicity and Lifetimes:
   Self Concepts and Situational Contexts of Ethnic Identity
   in Late Life.  Pp. 35-50 in C. M. Baresi and D. E. Gelfand,
   (eds).  Ethnic Dimensions of Aging.  New York, NY:
   Springer, 1987.

   Discusses the meaning of ethnicity and its relationship to
   bereavement among older Italian, Irish and Jewish men.

McGoldrick, M., J. K. Pearce, and J. Giordano.  Ethnicity and
   Family Therapy.  New York, NY:  Guilford, 1982.

   While ostensibly for family therapists, this book reviews
   issues germane to intergenerational family relations and
   aging among many American ethnic groups including a large
   number of European groups.

Metress, S.  The History of Irish-American Care of the Aged.
   Social Service Review.  March:18-31, 1985.

Mostwin, D.  Emotional Needs of Elderly Americans of Central
   and Eastern European Background.  Pp. 263-76 in D. Gelfand
   and A. Kutzik (eds).  Ethnicity and Aging:  Theory,
   Research and Policy.  New York, NY:  Springer, 1979.

Myerhoff, B.  We Don't Wrap Herring in a Printed Page:
   Fusion, Fictions and Continuity in Secular Ritual.  Pp.
   199-224 in S. Moore and B.  Myerhoff (eds).  Secular
   Ritual.  Amsterdam, Netherlands:  Van Gorcum, 1977.

_____  Number Our Days.  New York, NY:  Dutton, 1978a.

_____  A Symbol Perfected in Death:  Continuity and Ritual in
   the Life and Death of an Elderly Jew.  Pp. 163-205 in B.
   Myerhoff and A.  Simic (eds).  Life's Career--Aging:
   Cultural Variations on Growing Old.  Beverly Hills, CA:

Sage, 1978b.

_____ Bobbes and Zeydes:  Old and New Roles for Elderly Jews. In J. Hoch-Smith and A. Springs (eds).  Women in Ritual and Symbolic Roles.  New York, NY:  Plenum, 1978c.

_____ Number Our Days.  Pp. 179-88 in J. Sokolovsky (ed). Growing Old in Different Societies:  Cross-Cultural Perspectives.  Littleton, MA:  Copley Press, 1987.

Rempusheski, V. F.  Caring for Self and Others:  Second Generation Polish American Elders in an Ethnic Club. Journal of Cross-Cultural Gerontology.  3(3):223-72, 1988.

Rubinstein, R. L. and M. Luborsky.  Ethnic Identity and Bereavement in Later Life:  The Case of Older Widowers. Pp. 229-40 in J. Sokolovsky (ed).  The Cultural Context of Aging:  Worldwide Perspectives.  Westport, CT:  Bergin and Garvey, 1990

Shenk, D.  Aging and Retirement in a Lebanese-American Community.  Immigrant Communities and Ethnic Minorities in the US and Canada Series No. 71.  New York, NY:  AMS Pr, 1990.

Siemaszko, M.  Kin Relations of the Aged:  Possible Consequences of Social Services Planning.  Pp. 253-91 in C. Fry (ed).  Aging in Culture and Society:  Comparative Viewpoints and Strategies.  Brooklyn, NY:  Bergin, 1980.

Stein, H.  Aging and Death Among Slovak-Americans:  An Essay in the Thematic Unity of the Life Cycle.  Journal of Psychological Anthropology.  1(3):297-320, 1978.

Stoller, E. P.  Ethnicity in the Informal Networks of Older Sunbelt Migrants:  A Case History of the Finns in Florida. Pp. 118-29 in C. M. Barresi and D. E. Gelfand (eds). Ethnic Dimensions of Aging.  New York, NY:  Springer, 1987.

Tripp-Reimer, T., et al.  To Be Different from the World: Patterns of Elder Care Among Iowa Old Order Amish.  Journal of Cross-Cultural Gerontology.  3(3):185-96, 1988.

Wagner, B. T.  Aging and the Aged in the Contemporary Jewish Community in America.  Pp. 259-70 in D. E. Flesner and E. D. Freed (eds).  Aging and the Aged:  Problems, Opportunities, Challenges.  Lanham, MD:  University Press of America, 1980.

Wershow, H.  The Older Jews of Albany Park:  Some Aspects of a Subculture of the Aged and Its Interaction With a Gerontological Research Project.  Gerontologist. 1:198-202, 1964.

Wood, P. A. D.  Aging in the Amish Community.  Pp. 247-58 in D. E.  Flesner and E. D. Freed (eds).  Aging and the Aged: Problems, Opportunities, Challenges.  Lanham, MD: University Press of America, 1980.

## RURAL/APPALACHIAN AMERICANS

Bainton, B.  Drinking Patterns of the Rural Aged.  Pp. 201-18
    in C. Fry (ed).  Dimensions:  Aging, Culture, and Health.
    Brooklyn, NY:  J. F. Bergin, 1981.

Coward, R.  Planning Community Services for the Rural Elderly:
    Implications from Research.  Gerontologist.  19(3):275-82,
    1979.

Coward, R. T. and G. R. Lee (eds).  The Elderly in Rural
    Society:  Every Fourth Elder.  New York,, NY:  Springer,
    1985.

DeHaney, W. T.  Romanticizing the Status of the Rural Elderly:
    Theory and Policy Implications.  Gerontologist.  27:321-29,
    1987.

Harbert, A. and C. Wilkinson.  Growing Old in Rural America.
    Aging.  291-92:36-40, 1979.

Krout, J. A.  The Aged in Rural America.  Westport, CT:
    Greenwood Press, 1986.

    Comprehensive review of the available literature on the
    aged in rural areas in the U. S.  Includes consideration of
    demographic characteristics, and issues such as physical
    and mental health, housing and transportation, informal
    support and formal services and service provision.

_____ Rural Elderly:  A Bibliography.  Revised and Updated.
    Kansas City, MO:  National Resource Center for Rural
    Elderly, University of Missouri-Kansas City, 1989.

Lee, G. R. and M. L. Lassey.  The Elderly.  Pp. 85-93 in D. A.
    Dillman and D. J. Hobbs (eds).  Rural Society in the US:
    Issues for the 1980s.  Boulder, CO:  Westview Press, 1982.

Lozier, J. and R. Althouse.  Social Enforcement of Behavior
    Toward Elders in an Appalachian Mountain Settlement.
    Gerontologist.  14:69-80, 1974.

_____ Retirement to the Porch in Rural Appalachia.  Aging and
    Human Development.  6:7-15, 1975.

Lubbern, J. W., et al.  Health Promotion for the Rural
    Elderly.  The Journal of Rural Health.  4(3):85-96, 1988.

McCay, B. J.  Old People and Social Relations in a
    Newfoundland "Outport."  Pp. 61-87 in H. Strange and M.
    Teitelbaum (eds).  Aging and Cultural Diversity:  New
    Directions and Annotated Bibliography.  South Hadley, MA:
    Bergin and Garvey, 1987.

Mercier, J. and E. Powers.  The Family and Friends of Rural
    Aged As A Natural Support System.  Journal of Community
    Psychology.  12:334-46, 1984.

Meyer, R. (ed).  Bend the Trend:  Meeting the Needs of the Rural Elderly.  Proceedings of a Conference on the Rural Elderly.  KS:  Kansas University, 1988.

Ralson, P.  Senior Centers in Rural Communities:  A Qualitative Study.  Journal of Applied Gerontology. 5(1):76-92, 1986.

Rowles, G.  Prisoners of Space?  Exploring the Geographical Experience of Older People.  Boulder, CO:  Westview Press, 1978.

_____ Growing Old 'Inside':  Aging and Attachment to Place in an Appalachian Community.  Pp. 153-70 in N. Datan and N. Lohmann (eds).  Transitions of Aging.  New York, NY: Academic Press, 1980.

_____ Aging in Rural Environments.  In J. Altman, M. Lawton, and J. Wohlwill (eds).  Elderly People and the Environment. New York, NY:  Plenum Press, 1984.

Shenk, D.  Someone to Lend a Helping Hand:  The Lives of Rural Older Women in Central Minnesota.  St. Cloud, MN:  St. Cloud State University, 1987.

Smith, L.  The Aged in Rural Society.  In M. Derber (ed).  The Aged and Society.  Champaign, IL:  Industrial Relations Research Association, 1950.

Storer, J. H., et al.  Adapting Relaxation Techniques to Rural Populations:  Implications for High Blood Pressure Therapy. The Journal of Rural Health.  5(1):13-18, 1989.

van Willigen, J.  Gettin' Some Age on Me:  Social Organization of Older People in a Rural American Community.  Lexington, KY:  University of Kentucky Press, 1989.

Willits, R., R. Bealer, and D. Crider.  Persistence of Rural/Urban Differences.  Pp. 69-76 in D. Dillman and D. Hobbes (eds).  Rural Society in the US:  Issues for the 1980s.  Boulder, CO:  Westview Press, 1982.

Youmans, E. (ed).  Older Rural Americans:  A Sociological Perspective.  Lexington, KY:  University of Kentucky Press, 1967.

# 8

# Social Structure

**LIFE CYCLE--LIFE COURSE**

Abeles, R. and M. Riley.  A Life-Course Perspective on the
    Later Years of Life:  Some Implications for Research.
    Social Science Research Council Annual Report.  New York,
    NY:  Social Science Research Council, 1976-77.

Aires, M.  Centuries of Childhood.  New York, NY:  Random
    House, 1962.

    This is a classic which documents the beginning of the
    differentiation of the life course into stages.  Here
    childhood is first differentiated as a product of a
    changing economic order.

Anderson, N.  The Significance of Age Categories for Older
    Persons.  Gerontologist.  7:164-67, 224, 1967.

Atchley, R.  The Life Course, Age Grading and Age Linked
    Demands for Decision Making.  Pp. 261-78 in N. Datan and L.
    Ginsberg (eds).  Life Span Developmental Psychology.  New
    York, NY:  Academic Press, 1980.

Atkin, S.  Old Age and Aging:  The Psychoanalytical Point of
    View.  American Journal of Orthopsychiatry.  10:79-83,
    1940.

Back, K.  Life Course:  Integrative Theories and Exemplary
    Populations.  Boulder, CO:  Westview Press, 1980.

Bates, P. and K. Schaie (eds).  Life-Span Developmental
    Psychology:  Personality and Socialization.  New York, NY:
    Academic Press, 1973.

Baty, C.  Variations in Subcultural Definitions of the Aged
    Status.  Proceedings of the Southwestern Sociological
    Association.  19:59-63, 1968.

Becker, H.  The Self and Adult Socialization.  Pp. 194-208 in
    E.  Norbeck, D. Price-Williams, and W. McCord (eds).  The

_Study of Personality:  An Interdisciplinary Appraisal_.  New
York, NY:  Holt, Rinehart and Winston, 1968.

Bertaux, D.  _Biography and Society_.  Beverly Hills, CA:  Sage,
1981.

As an edited volume, this addresses methodological issues
in life history research as well as some experimentation
with life histories.  It also considers lives as historical
data.

Brim, O.  Socialization Through the Life Cycle.  Pp. 1-49 in
O. Brim and S. Wheeler (eds).  _Socialization After
Childhood_.  New York, NY:  Wiley, 1966.

Buhler, C.  The Curve of Life as Studied in Biographies.
_Journal of Applied Psychology_.  19:405-09, 1935.

Buhler was among the first to look at lives, using
biographies in an attempt to abstract patterns using a
psychological perspective.

Burnside, I.  Transition to Later Life:  Developmental
Theories and Research.  Pp. 381-404 in I. Burnside, P.
Ebersole, and H. Monea (eds).  _Psychosocial Caring
Throughout the Life Span_.  New York, NY:  McGraw-Hill,
1979.

Butler, R.  The Life Review:  An Interpretation of
Reminiscence in the Aged.  Pp. 486-96 in B. Neugarten (ed).
_Middle Age and Aging_.  Chicago, IL:  University of Chicago
Press, 1968.

Cain, L.  Life Course and Social Structure.  Pp. 272-309 in R.
Faris (ed).  _Handbook of Modern Sociology_.   Chicago, IL:
Rand McNally, 1964.

Although now a classic, this chapter is among the first to
look at the way lives are integrated into social
structures.

_____  Age Status and Generational Phenomena:  The New Old
People in Contemporary America.  _Gerontologist_.  7:83-92,
1967.

Carou, R.  Self and Role Adjustment During Old Age.  Pp.
526-36 in M. Ross (ed).  _Human Behavior and Sociological
Processes:  An Interactionist Approach_.  Boston, MA:
Houghton Mifflin, 1962.

Cavan, R.  Role of the Old in Personal and Impersonal
Societies.  _Family Coordinator_.  27(4):315-20, 1978.

Chiriboga, D.  Personality in Later Life.  Pp. 133-57 in P.
Silverman (ed).  _The Elderly as Modern Pioneers_.
Bloomington, IN:  Indiana University Press, 1987.

Chiriboga, D. and L. Gigy.  Perspectives of Life Course.  Pp.

122-45 in M. Lowenthal, et al (eds). Four Stages of Life. San Francisco, CA: Jossey-Bass, 1975.

Clausen, J. The Life Course of Individuals. Pp. 457-514 in M. Riley and A. Foner (eds). Aging and Society. Vol. 3. A Sociology of Age Stratification. New York, NY: Russell Sage Foundation, 1972.

_____ The Life Course: A Sociological Perspective. Englewood Cliffs, NJ: Prentice Hall, 1986.

In a basic way, this volume summarizes the life course perspective and social issues from infancy to old age.

Elder, G. H., Jr. Children of the Great Depression. Chicago, IL: University of Chicago Press, 1974.

This volume examines the effect on the life chances of children who experienced the great depression at different ages. It is a classic on cohort analysis.

_____ Age Differentiation and the Life Course. Annual Review of Sociology. 1:165-90, 1975.

This is a review article which takes a sociological perspective on age norms and age stratification.

Erikson, E. Identity and the Life Cycle. Psycholological Issues. 1:18-164, 1959.

Featherman, D. L. The Life Span Perspective in Social Science Research. New York, NY: Social Science Research Council, 1981.

A review article which is an absolute must. It surveys psychological and sociological development of the life course perspective.

Foner, A. Age in Society, Structure and Change. American Behavioral Scientist. 19:144-68, 1975.

Foner, N. Some Consequences of Age Inequality in Non-Industrial Societies. Pp. 71-86 in M. Riley, R. Abeles, and M. Teitelbaum (eds). Aging From Birth to Death. Vol 2. Sociotemporal Perspectives. Boulder, CO: Westview Press, 1982.

Fortes, M. Age, Generation, and Social Structure. Pp. 99-122 in D. I. Kertzer and J. Keith (eds). Age and Anthropological Theory. Ithaca, NY: Cornell University Press, 1984.

Friedsham, H. The Coming of Years. Social Science Quarterly. 5:120-28, 1970.

Fry, C. The Ages of Adulthood: A Question of Numbers. Journal of Gerontology. 31(2):170-77, 1976.

_____    Cultural Dimensions of Age:  A Multidimensional Scaling
Analysis.  Pp. 42-64 in C. Fry (ed).  Aging in Culture and
Society:  Comparative Viewpoints and Strategies.  Brooklyn,
NY:  J. F. Bergin, 1980.

This chapter uses ethnosemantic strategies in examining the
emics of the life course and statistical strategies to
explore the dimensions of the life course.

Fry, C. and J. Keith.  The Life Course as a Cultural Unit.  In
M. W. Riley, R. Ables, and M. S. Teitelbaum (eds).  Aging
From Birth to Death.  Vol 2.  Sociotemporal Perspectives.
Boulder, CO:  Westview Press, 1982.

Comparative perspectives on the life course, the way time
is defined, the dimensions of lives, and the variability
across cultures is the focus of this chapter.

Gallagher, E. G.  The Life Review and Third World Contexts:
Toward A Sociological Understanding of Elderly Reminiscence
in Developing Societies.  Pp. 33-52 in J. Morgan (ed).
Aging in Developing Societies:  A Reader in Third World
Gerontology.  Bristol, IN:  Wyndham Hall Press, 1985.

Gordon, C.  Role and Value Development Across the Life Cycle.
Pp.  65-105 in J. Jackson (ed).  Role:  Sociological
Studies 4.  New York, NY:  Van Nostrand Reinhold, 1972.

Gould, R.  The Phases of Adult Life:  A Study in Developmental
Psychology.  American Journal of Psychiatry.  129:521-31,
1972.

Gutmann, D.  The Country of Old Men:  Cross-Cultural Studies
in the Psychology of Later Life.  Occasional Papers in
Gerontology.  Institute of Gerontology.  Ann Arbor, MI:
University of Michigan, 1969.

_____    The Cross-Cultural Perspective:  Notes Toward A
Comparative Psychology of Aging.  Pp. 302-26 in J. Birren
and K. Schaie (eds).  Handbook of the Psychology of Aging.
New York, NY:  Van Nostrand Reinhold, 1977.

_____    Observations on Culture and Mental Health in Later Life.
Pp. 429-44 in J. Birren and W. Sloan (eds).  Handbook of
Mental Health and Aging.  New York, NY:  Van Nostrand
Reinhold, 1980.

Hagestad, G. O. and B. L. Neugarten.  Age and the Life Course.
Pp. 35-61 in R. H. Binstock and E. Shanas (eds).  Handbook
of Aging and the Social Sciences.  New York, NY:  Van
Nostrand Reinhold, 1985.

A comprehensive review of work done on the life course from
multiple perspectives.  The authors consider the cultural
meanings and the problems with norms as well as issues
dealing with transitions and the timing of events.

Hammel, E.  Age in the Fortesian Coordinates.  Pp. 141-58 in

D. I. Kertzer and J. Keith (eds). Age and Anthropological Theory. Ithaca, NY: Cornell University Press, 1984.

Hareven, T. The Last Stage: Historical Adulthood and Old Age. Daedalus. 105:13-27, 1976.

_____ (ed). Transitions: The Family and the Life Course in Historical Perspective. New York, NY: Academic Press, 1978.

_____ The Life Course and Aging in Historical Perspective. Pp. 9-26 in K. Back (ed). Life Course: Integrative Theories and Exemplary Populations. Boulder, CO: Westview Press, 1980.

_____ Family Time and Industrial Time. Cambridge: Cambridge University Press, 1982.

The two volumes Transitions (1978) and Family Time (1982) are representative of using historical data to ascertain the effects of change on the life course. They are a must in looking at the effects of a major historical event on the life course.

Henry, W. Personality Change in Middle and Old Age. Pp. 209-17 in E. Norbeck, D. Price-Williams, and W. McCord (eds). The Study of Personality: An Interdisciplinary Appraisal. New York, NY: Holt, Rinehart and Winston, 1968.

Hogan, D. P. Transitions and Social Change: The Early Lives of American Men. New York, NY: Academic Press, 1981.

This volume innovatively looks at the changes in the timing of early life events.

Jung, C. The Stages of Life. The Collected Works of C. G. Jung. Vol 8. The Structure and Dynamics of the Psyche. New York, NY: Pantheon, 1960.

Kaufman, S. Cultural Components of Identity in Old Age. Ethos. 9(1):51-87, 1981.

Kertzer, D. and A. Foner. Cross-Cultural Perspectives on Life Course Transitions. Generation. 4(1):24-25, 1979a.

_____ Intrinsic and Extrinsic Sources of Change in Life-Course Transitions. Pp. 121-36 in M. Riley (ed). Aging from Birth to Death. Boulder, CO: Westview Press, 1979b.

Kimmel, D. Adulthood: Developmental Theory and Research. Pp. 1-41 in D. Kimmel. Adulthood and Aging. New York, NY: John Wiley, 1980.

Kleemeier, R. Aging and Leisure. New York, NY: Oxford University Press, 1961.

Kohli, M. The World We Forgot: A Historical Review of the

Life Course. Pp. 271-303 in V. W. Marshall (ed). <u>Later Life: The Social Psychology of Aging</u>. Beverly Hills, CA: Sage, 1986.

Historically the life course has only been very recently differentiated as a cognitive unit. This is a product of industrialization and the need of the state to rationalize the labor force.

Kramer, D. A.  Cognition and Aging:  The Emergence of a New Tradition.  Pp. 114-32 in P. Silverman (ed).  <u>The Elderly as Modern Pioneers</u>.  Bloomington, IN:  Indiana University Press, 1987.

LaFontaine, J. (ed).  <u>Age and Sex as Principles of Differentiation</u>.  New York, NY:  Academic Press, 1978.

Lansing, S.  Cycles of Time.  <u>Parabola</u>.  5(1):34-37, 1980.

Examines the cultural view of time on the island of Bali.

Levine, R.  Adulthood and Aging in Cross-Cultural Perspective. <u>Items</u>.  31-32:1-5, 1978a.

_____ Comparative Notes on the Life Course.  Pp. 287-96 in T. Haraven (ed).  <u>Transitions:  The Family and the Life Course in Historical Perspective</u>.  New York, NY:  Academic Press, 1978b.

Linden, M and D. Courtney.  The Human Life Cycle and Its Interpretations.  <u>American Journal of Psychiatry</u>. 109:906-15, 1953.

Linton, R.  Age and Sex Categories.  <u>American Sociological Review</u>.  7:589-603, 1942.

Lowenthal, M.  Toward a Socio-Psychological Theory of Change in Adulthood and Old Age.  Pp. 116-27 in J. Birren and K. Schaie (eds).  <u>Handbook of the Psychology of Aging</u>.  New York, NY:  Van Nostrand Reinhold, 1973.

Lowenthal, M., et al.  <u>Four Stages of Life</u>.  San Francisco, CA:  Jossey-Bass, 1975.

Mayer, K. U. and W. Muller.  The State and the Structure of the Life Course.  Pp. 217-46 in A. B. Soresen, F. W. Weinert, and L. F. Sherrod (eds).  <u>Human Development and the Life Course:  Multidisciplinary Perspectives</u>. Hillsdale, NJ:  Lawrence Erlbaum, 1986.

This article looks at the state and the way the state has penetrated lives as western democracies have individuated the people within their domains.  As a result, the life course is more predictable and institutionalized.

Meyer, J. W.  The Self and the Life Course: Institutionalization and Its Effects.  Pp. 199-218 in A. B. Soresen, F. W. Weinert, and L. R.  Sherrod (eds).  <u>Human</u>

Development and the Life Course: Multidisciplinary Perspectives. Hillsdale, NY: Lawrence Erlbaum, 1986.

Institutionalization and the life course is the theme of this article. The reasons for institutionalization and the consequences for individuals are explored.

Myerhoff, B. Remembered Lives. The Old Ones: Myth and the Quest for Meaning. Parabola. 5(1)74-77, 1980.

Myerhoff discusses memory and survival, emphasizing the importance of our own life stories.

Myerhoff, B. Rites and Signs of Ripening: The Intertwining of Ritual, Time, and Growing Older. Pp. 305-30 in D. I. Kertzer and J. Keith (eds). Age and Anthropological Theory. Ithaca, NY: Cornell University Press, 1984.

Needham, R. Age, Category and Descent. Pp. 72-108 in R. Needham (ed). Remarks and Inventions. London, UK: Tavistock, 1974.

Neugarten, B. Dynamics of Transition of Middle Age to Old Age. Journal of Geriatric Psychiatry. 4(1):71-87, 1970a.

_____ The Old and the Young in Modern Societies. American Behavioral Scientist. 14(1):13-24, 1970b.

_____ Personality and Aging. Pp. 629-49 in J. Birren and K. W. Schaie (eds). Handbook of the Psychology of Aging. New York, NY: Van Nostrand Reinhold, 1977.

Neugarten, B. and N. Datan. Sociological Perspectives on the Life Cycle. Pp. 53-69 in P. Baltes and K. Schaie (eds). Life-Span Developmental Psychology: Personality and Socialization. New York, NY: Academic Press, 1973.

This article looks at the ways in which the life course has been considered sociologically. The authors differentiate between life time, social time and historical time in integrating the age stratification perspective with the normative perspective.

Neugarten, B. and D. Gutmann. Age-Sex Roles and Personality in Middle Age. Pp. 58-71 in B. Neugarten (ed). Middle Age and Aging. Chicago, IL: University of Chicago Press, 1968.

Neugarten, B. and J. Moore. The Changing Age Status System. Pp. 5-21 in B. Neugarten (ed). Middle Age and Aging. Chicago, IL: University of Chicago Press, 1968.

Neugarten, B., J. Moore, and J. Lowie. Age Norms, Age Constraints, and Adult Socialization. American Journal of Sociology. 70:710-17, 1965.

Neugarten, B. and L. Peterson. A Study of the American Age-Grade System. Proceedings of the International Association of Gerontology.  3:497-502, 1957.

Nydegger, C.  Age and Life Course Transitions.  Pp. 131-61 in
    C. Fry and J. Keith (eds).  New Methods for Old Age
    Research.  South Hadley, MA:  Bergin and Garvey, 1986.

    Transitions are the markers which differentiate the life
    course.  This chapter addresses methodological issues in
    studying transitions and in conceptualizing the life
    course.

Parsons, T.  Age and Sex in the Social Structure of the United
    States.  American Sociological Review.  7:604-16, 1942.

Phillipson, C.  Capitalism and the Construction of Old Age.
    London:  MacMillan, 1982.

    In this work, Phillipson links the social construction of
    old age to the labor market.  He argues that in times of
    high unemployment, old age becomes defined as a well-
    bounded social category as older workers are encouraged to
    retire.  Conversely, when labor is needed, the
    chronological limits of old age are raised and the social
    category is more ambiguous.

Plath, D. and K. Ikeda.  After Coming of Age:  Adult Awareness
    of Age Norms.  Pp. 107-23 in T. Williams (ed).
    Socialization and Communication in Primary Groups.
    Chicago, IL:  Aldine, 1975.

    Presents a comparison of age norms in Japan and the United
    States.

Pollock, G.  Aging or Aged:  Development of Pathology.  Pp.
    549-85 in S. Greenspan and G. Pollock (eds).  The Courses
    of Life:  Psychoanalytic Contributions Toward Understanding
    Personality Development.  Vol 3.  Adulthood and the Aging
    Process.  Washington, DC:  National Institute of Mental
    Health, 1980.

Radcliffe-Brown, A.  Age:  Organization Terminology.  Man.
    29:21, 1929.

Ragan, P. and J. Wales.  Age Stratification and the Life
    Course.  Pp.  377-99 in J. Birren and W. Sloan (eds).
    Handbook of Mental Health and Aging.  New York, NY:  Van
    Nostrand Reinhold, 1980.

Riley, M. W., et al.  Socialization for the Middle and Later
    Years.  Pp.  951-82 in D. Goslin (ed).  Handbook of
    Socialization Theory and Research.  New York, NY:  Random
    House, 1969.

Riley, M. W., M. E. Johnson, and A. Foner (eds).  Aging and
    Society:  A Sociology of Age Stratification.  Vol 3.  New
    York, NY:  Russel Sage, 1972.

    This is one of the volumes which first defined the life

course as a sociological concept.  The age stratification
paradigm is fully explicated in this work.  Lives are seen
as cohorts moving through society, shaped by the historical
events which happen before or in their own time.

Rosow, I.  What is a Cohort and Why?  Human Development.
21:65-75, 1978.

The meaning of cohorts has been a problem.  Rosow attempts
to show they must have cultural as well as historical
meaning.

Rossi, A. (ed).  Gender and the Life Course.  New York, NY:
1985.

Sankar, A.  The Living Dead:  Cultural Constructions of the
Oldest Old.  Pp. 345-56 in P. Silverman (ed).  The Elderly
As Modern Pioneers.  Bloomington, IN:  Indiana University
Press, 1987.

Siegler, I.  The Psychology of Adult Development and Aging.
Pp. 169-221 in W. Busse and D. Blazer (eds).  Handbook of
Geriatric Psychiatry.  New York, NY:  Van Nostrand
Reinhold, 1980.

Silverman, P.  Introduction:  The Life Course Perspective.
Pp. 1-16 in P. Silverman (ed).  The Elderly as Modern
Pioneers.  Bloomington, IN:  Indiana University Press,
1987.

Silverman's chapter is a good review of recent and useful
publications dealing with the life course perspective.

Smith, R.  Cultural Difference in the Life Cycle and the
Concept of Time.  Pp. 83-112 in R. Kleemier.  Aging and
Leisure.  New York, NY:  Oxford University Press, 1961.

An introduction to a series of short reports about studies
among Andean peasants, the Eskimo, the Japanese and the
people of Burma and India.

Spierer, H.  Major Transitions in the Human Life Cycle.  New
York, NY:  Academy for Educational Development, 1977.

Spoehr, A.  Time Perspective in Micronesia and Polynesia.
Southwestern Journal of Anthropology.  8:457-65, 1952.

van den Berghe, P.  Age Differentiation in Human Societies.
Pp. 72-81 in J. Sokolovsky (ed).  Growing Old in Different
Societies:  Cross-Cultural Perspectives.  Acton, MA:
Copley Press, 1987.

Van Gennep, A.  The Rites of Passage.  Translated by M. B.
Vizedom and G. L. Caffee.  Chicago, IL:  University of
Chicago Press, 1960.

Webster, H.  Primitive Secret Societies.  New York, NY:
MacMillan, 1908.

234 ANTHROPOLOGY OF AGING

Williams, T.  Introduction to Socialization.  St. Louis, MO:
Mosby, 1972.


FAMILY--INTERGENERATIONAL RELATIONS--ANCESTORS

Abel, E. K.  Adult Daughters and Care for the Elderly.
Feminist Studies.  12:479-97, 1986.

Adams, B.  Isolation, Function and Beyond:  American Kinship
in the 1960's.  Pp. 163-85 in C. Broderick (ed).  A Decade
of Family Research and Action.  Minneapolis, MN:  National
Council on Family Relations, 1971.

_____  The Family:  A Sociological Interpretation.  Chicago,
IL:  Rand McNally, 1980.

Akiyama, H., T. Antonucci, and R. Campbell.  Exchange and
Reciprocity Among Two Generations of Japanese and American
Women.  Pp. 127-38 in J. Sokolovsky (eds).  The Cultural
Context of Aging:  Worldwide Perspectives.  Westport, CT:
Bergin and Garvey, 1990.

Albrecht, R.  The Parental Responsibilities of Grandparents.
Marriage and Family Living.  16:201-04, 1954.

_____  The Role of Older People in Family Rituals.  In C.
Tibbitts and W. Donahue (eds).  Aging Around the World.
New York; NY:  Columbia University, 1962.

Aldous, J.  The Consequences of Intergenerational Continuity.
Journal of Marriage and the Family.  27:462-68, 1965.

_____  New Views on the Family Life of the Elderly and the
Near-Elderly.  Journal of Marriage and the Family.
49:227-34, 1987.

Allan, G.  Kinship, Responsibility and Care for Elderly
People.  Ageing and Society.  8:249-68, 1988.

Anderson, T. B.  Widowhood as a Life Transition:  Its Impact
on Kinship Ties.  Journal of Marriage and the Family.
46:105-14, 1984.

Apple, D.  The Social Structure of Grandparenthood.  American
Anthropologist.  58:656-63, 1956.

Aronson, M. K., et al.  A Community Based-Family/Patient Group
Program for Alzheimer's Disease.  Gerontologist.
24:339-42, 1984.

Barranti, C. C. R.  The Grandparent/Grandchild Relationship:
Family Resource in an Era of Voluntary Bonds.  Family
Relations.  34:343-52, 1985.

Barusch, A. S. and W. M. Spaid.  Gender Differences in
Caregiving:  Why Do Wives Report Greater Burden?
Gerontologist.  29:667-76, 1989.

Bascom, W.  The Principle of Seniority in the Social Structure of the Yoruba. American Anthroplogist. 44:37-46, 1942.

Beck, S. H. and R. W. Beck.  The Formation of Extended Households During Middle Age.  Journal of Marriage and the Family.  46:277-87, 1984.

Beland, F.  The Family and Adults 65 Years of Age and Over: Coresidency and Availability of Help. Canadian Review of Sociology and Anthropology.  21:302-17, 1984.

_____  Multigenerational Households in a Contemporary Perspective.  International Journal of Aging and Human Development.  25(2):147-66, 1987.

Bengtson, V. and N. Cutler.  Generations and Intergenerational Relations.  Pp. 130-59 in R. Binstock and E. Shanas (eds). Handbook of Aging and the Social Sciences.  New York, NY: Van Nostrand, 1976.

Bengtson, V., M. Furlong, and R. Laufer.  Time, Aging and the Continuity of Social Structure:  Themes and Issues in Generational Analysis.  Journal of Social Issues. 30(2):1-30, 1974.

Bengtson, V. and R. Laufer (eds).  Youth, Generations and Social Change.  Special Issue.  Social Issues.  30:3, 1974.

Bengtson,V., P. Kasschau, and P. Ragan.  The Impact of Social Structure on Aging Individuals.  Pp. 327-53 in J. Birren and K. Schaie (eds).  Handbook of the Psychology of Aging. New York, NY:  Van Nostrand Reinhold, 1977.

Blieszner, R.  Trends in Family Gerontology Research. Family Research.  35:555-62, 1986.

Borke, H.  A Family Over Three Generations:  The Transmission of Interacting and Relating Patterns. Journal of Marriage and the Family.  29:639-55, 1967.

Boyd, R.  The Valued Grandparent:  A Changing Social Role. Pp. 90-112 in W. Donahue (ed).  Living in Multigeneration Family.  Ann Arbor, MI:  Institute of Gerontology, 1969.

Bradbury, R.  Fathers, Elders and Ghosts in Edo Religion.  In M. Banton Anthropological Approaches to the Study of Religion.  New York, NY:  Praeger, 1966.

Brain, J.  Ancestors as Elders in Africa:  Further Thoughts. Africa.  43(2):122-33, 1973.

Brody, E. M., et al.  Work Status and Parent Care:  A Comparison of Four Groups of Women.  Gerontologist. 27:201-08, 1987.

Brody, E. M., et al.  Caregiving Daughters and Their Local Siblings:  Perceptions, Strains and Interactions. Gerontologist.  29:529-38, 1989.

Brubaker, T. and L. Sneden, II.  Aging in a Changing Family
    Context.  Family Coordinator.  27(4):301-02, 1978.

Bulcroft, K., et al.  Filial Responsibility Laws:  Issues and
    State Statutes.  Research on Aging.  11:374-93, 1989.

Bultana, G.  Rural-Urban Differences in the Familial
    Interaction of the Aged.  Rural Sociology.  34:5-15, 1969.

Cantor, M. H.  Social Care:  Family and Community Support
    Systems.  The Annals of the American Academy of Political
    and Social Science.  503:99-112, 1989.

Cantor, M. H. and B. Hirshorn.  Intergenerational Transfers
    Within the Family Context:  Motivating Factors and Their
    Implications for Caregiving.  Women and Health.
    14(3-4):39-51, 1988.

Cheal, D. J.  Intergenerational Family Transfers.  Journal of
    Marriage and the Family.  45:805-13, 1983.

Chevan, A. and J. Korson.  Family Structure and Residential
    Patterns of the Widowed in Israel.  In J. Gubrium (ed).
    Time, Roles, and Self in Old Age.  New York, NY:  Human
    Sciences Press, 1976.

Chudacoff, H. and T. Hareven.  Family Transitions into Old
    Age.  In T. Hareven (ed).  Transitions.  New York, NY:
    Academic Press, 1978.

Cicirelli, V. G.  Adult Children's Attachment and Helping
    Behavior to Elderly Parents:  A Path Model.  Journal of
    Marriage and the Family.  45:815-24, 1983.

Coe, R. M., et al.  Complementary and Compensatory Functions
    in Social Network Relationships Among the Elderly.
    Gerontologist.  24:396-400, 1984.

Cole, T. R.  Generational Equity in America:  A Cultural
    Historian's Perspective.  Journal of Social Science and
    Medicine.  29(3):377-83, 1989.

    The author provides a cultural history of generational
    relations, analyzing present-day changes in the context of
    a decline in the social centrality of a life course or life
    span perspective.  The consequences of this decline for the
    distribution of social benefits are discussed.

Colson, E.  Ancestral Spirits and Social Structure Among the
    Plateau Tonga.  International Archives of Ethnography.
    47(1):21-68, 1954.

Dean, A., et al.  Measuring the Communication of Social
    Support from Adult Children.  Journal of Gerontology.
    44S:71-79, 1989.

Doka, K. J. and M. E. Mertz.  The Meaning and Significance of
    Great-Grandparenthood.  Gerontologist.  28:192-97, 1988.

Donner, W. W.  Compassion, Kinship and Fosterage:  Contexts
    for the Care of the Childless Elderly in a Polynesian
    Community.  Journal of Cross-Cultural Gerontology.
    2(1):43-60, 1987.

Doty, P.  Family Care of the Elderly:  The Role of Public
    Policy.  Milbank Memorial Fund Quarterly.  64:34-75, 1986.

Dunkle, R. E.  The Effect of Elders' Household Contributions
    on Their Depression.  Journal of Gerontology.  38:732-37,
    1983.

Ebersole, P. and S. DePacia.  Meaning in Life Categories of
    Later Life Couples.  Journal of Psychology.  121:185-91,
    1987.

Fiawoo, D.  Characteristic Features of Ewe Ancestor Worship.
    Pp.  263-82 in W. Newell (ed).  Ancestors.  Chicago, IL:
    Aldine, 1976.

Feuer, L.  The Conflict of Generations.  New York, NY:  Basic
    Books

Field, M.  The Aged, The Family, and the Community.  New York,
    NY:  Columbia University, 1972.

Flori, D. E.  The Prevalence of Later Life Family Concerns in
    the Marriage and Family Therapy Journal Literature
    (1976-1985).  Journal of Marital and Family Therapy.
    15:289-97, 1989.

Fortes, M.  Some Reflections on Ancestor Worship in Africa.
    Pp. 122-42 in M. Fortes and G. Dieterien (eds).  African
    Systems of Thought.  London:  Oxford University Press,
    1965.

Gelfand, D., J. Olsen, and M. Block.  Two Generations of
    Elderly in the Changing American Family:  Implications for
    Family Services.  Family Coordinator.  27(4):395-404, 1978.

Gordon, C.  Familial Support for the Elderly in the Past:  The
    Case of London's Working Class in the Early 1930s.  Ageing
    and Society.  8:287-320, 1988.

Greenbaum, J. and L. Rader.  Marital Problems of the "Old"
    Elderly As They Present to a Mental Health Clinic.  Journal
    of Gerontological Social Work.  14(1-2):111-26, 1989.

Greenberg, J. S. and M. Becker.  Aging Parents as Family
    Resources.  Gerontologist.  28:786-91, 1988.

Gutmann, D.  Parenthood:  Key to the Comparative Psychology of
    the Life Cycle.  Pp. 167-84 in N. Oatan and L. Ginsberg
    (eds).  Life Span Development Psychology.  New York, NY:
    Academic Press, 1975.

_____  A Cross-Cultural View of Adult Life in the Extended
    Family.  Pp. 364-73 in K. Riegel and J. Meachan (eds).  The

Developing Individualism in a Changing World.  Chicago, IL:
Aldine, 1976.

Hader, M.  The Importance of Grandparents in Family Life.
Family Process.  4:228-40, 1965.

Hagestad, G. O.  Able Elderly in the Family Context:  Changes,
Chances, and Challenges.  Gerontologist.  27:417-22, 1987.

Hagestad, G. O. and L. M. Burton.  Grandparenthood, Life
Context, and Family Development.  American Behavioral
Scientist.  29(4):471-84, 1986.

Harris, M. B., et al.  Activities, Family Relationships and
Feelings About Aging in a Multicultural Elderly Sample.
International Journal of Aging and Human Development.
29(2):103-17, 1989.

Harrison, S. and L. J. Waite.  Mature Women's Kin Availability
and Contact.  Sociology and Social Research.  71:266-70,
1987.

Hays, J. A.  Aging and Family Resources:  Availability and
Proximity of Kin.  Gerontologist.  24:149-53, 1984.

Hentig, H.  The Sociological Function of the Grandmother.
Social Forces.  24:389-92, 1946.

Hess, B. and J. Waring.  Changing Patterns of Aging and Family
Bonds in Later Life.  Family Coordinator.  27(4):303-14,
1978.

Hill, R.  Decision Making and the Family Life Cycle.  Pp.
113-39 in E. Shanas and G. Streib (eds).  Social Structure
and the Family:  Generational Relations.  Englewood Cliffs,
NJ:  Prentice Hall, 1965.

Houser, B. B. and S. L. Berkman.  Aging Parent/Mature Child
Relationships.  Journal of Marriage and the Family.
46:295-99, 1984.

Howe, A.  Family Support of the Aged:  Some Evidence and
Interpretation.  Australian Journal of Social Issues.
14:259-73, 1979.

Ikels, C.  Delayed Reciprocity and the Support Networks of the
Childless Elderly.  Journal of Comparative Family Studies.
19:99-112, 1988.

Inglehart, R.  The Silent Revolution in Europe:
Intergenerational Change in Post-Industrial Societies.
American Political Science Review.  65:991-1017, 1951.

Johnson, C. L.  A Cultural Analysis of the Grandmother.
Research on Aging.  5(4):547-68, 1983.

_____  In-law Relationships in the American Kinship System:
The Impact of Divorce and Remarriage.  American

_Ethnologist_.  16:87-99, 1989.

Johnson, C. L. and B. M. Barer.  Marital Instability and the
    Changing Kinship Networks of Grandparents.  _Gerontologist_.
    27:330-35, 1987.

Johnson, C. L. and D. J. Catalano.  A Longitudinal Study of
    Family Supports to Impaired Elderly.  _Gerontologist_.
    23:612-18, 1983.

Kahana, E. and B. Kahana.  Theoretical and Research
    Perspectives on Grandparenthood.  _Aging and Human
    Development_.  2:261-68, 1970.

Kahana, R. and S. Levin.  Aging and The Conflict of
    Generations.  _Journal of Geriatric Psychiatrist_.
    4(2):115-35, 1971.

Kalish, R.  Of Children and Grandfathers:  A Speculative Essay
    on Dependence.  _Gerontologist_ 7:65-69, 79, 1967.

Keesing, H.  Death, Property and the Ancestors:  A
    Reconsideration of Goody's Concepts.  _Africa_.  40(1):40-49,
    1970.

Kertzer, D.  Generation and Age in Cross-Cultural
    Perspectives.  Pp.  27-50 in M. Riley, R. Abeles, and M.
    Teitelbaum (eds).  _Aging from Birth to Death_.  Vol. 2.
    _Sociotemporal Perspectives_.  Boulder, CO:  Westview Press,
    1982.

Kivett, V. R.  Grandfathers and Grandchildren:  Patterns of
    Association, Helping, and Psychological Closeness.  _Family
    Relations_.  34:565-71, 1985.

Kivett, V. R. and M. P. Atkinson.  Filial Expectations,
    Associations, and Helping as a Function of Number of
    Children Among Older Rural-Transitional Parents.  _Journal
    of Gerontology_.  39:499-503, 1984.

Kivnick, H. Q.  Grandparenthood, Life Review, and Psychosocial
    Development.  _Journal of Gerontological Social Work_.
    12(3-4):63-81, 1988.

Kleban, M. H., et al.  Family Help to the Elderly:
    Perceptions of Sons-in-law Regarding Parent Care.  _Journal
    of Marriage and the Family_.  51:303-12, 1989.

Kopytoff, I.  Ancestors as Elders in Africa.  _Africa_
    41:129-42, 1971.

Kuypers, J. and Bengtson, V.  Generational Difference and the
    "Developmental" Stake.  _Aging and Human Development_.
    2(1):249-60, 1971.

Laufer, B. and V. Bengtson.  Aging, Generations and Social
    Stratification:  On the Creation of Generation Units.
    _Journal of Social Issues_.  30:181-205, 1974.

Levine, R.  Intergenerational Tensions and Extended Family
    Structure.  Pp. 188-204 in E. Shanas and G. Streib (eds).
    Social Structure and the Family:  Generational Relations.
    Englewood Cliffs, NJ:  Prentice Hall, 1965.

Luken, P. C.  Social Identity in Later Life:  A Situational
    Approach to Understanding Old Age Stigma.  International
    Journal of Aging and Human Development.  25(3):177-93,
    1987.

Mabuchi, T.  A Note on Ancestor Worship in 'Cognatic'
    Societies.  Pp.  105-18 in W. Newell (ed).  Ancestors.
    Chicago, IL:  Aldine, 1976.

Maeda, T.  Ancestor Worship in Japan:  Facts and History.  Pp.
    139-62 in W. Newell (ed).  Ancestors.  Chicago, IL:
    Aldine, 1976.

Maeda, D. and M. Sussman.  Japan-US Cross Cultural Study on
    the Knowledge of Aging:  The Attitude Toward Old People and
    the Sense of Responsibility for Aged Parents.  Social
    Gerontology.  12:40-79, 1980.

Mancini, J. A. and R. Blieszner.  Aging Parents and Adult
    Children:  Research Themes in Intergenerational Relations.
    Journal of Marriage and the Family.  51:275-90, 1989.

Mannheim, K.  The Problem of Generations.  Pp. 276-322 in P.
    Kecskemeti (ed).  Essay on the Sociology of Knowledge.
    London:  Routeledge and Kegan Paul, 1952.

Matthews, S. H.  Provision of Care to Old Parents:  Division
    of Responsibility Among Adult Children.  Research on Aging.
    9:45-60, 1987.

Matthews, S. H. and J. Sprey.  The Impact of Divorce on
    Grandparenthood:  An Exploratory Study.  Gerontologist.
    24:41-47, 1984.

Maybury-Lewis, D.  Age and Kinship:  A Structural View.  Pp.
    123-40 in D. I. Kertzer and J. Keith (eds).  Age and
    Anthropological Theory.  Ithaca, NY:  Cornell Press, 1984.

Mead, M.  Culture and Commitment:  A Study of the Generation
    Gap.  New York, NY:  Doubleday, 1969.

Mercier, J. M., et al.  Rural and Urban Elderly:  Differences
    in the Quality of the Parent-Child Relationship.  Family
    Relations.  37:68-72, 1988.

Messer, M.  Age Grouping and the Family Status of the Elderly.
    Sociology and Social Research.  52:271-79, 1968.

Minkler, M.  The Politics of Generational Equity.  Social
    Policy.  17-48-52, 1987.

Mitchell, J. and J. C. Register.  An Exploration of Family
    Interaction with the Elderly by Race, Socioeconomic Status,

and Residence. Gerontologist. 24:48-54, 1984.

Montgomery, R. J. V. Respite Care: Lessons from a Controlled Design Study. Health Care Financing Review. Supplement:133-38, 1988.

Morgan, L. A. Intergenerational Economic Assistance to Children: The Case of Widows and Widowers. Gerontologist. 38:725-31, 1983.

_____ Changes in Family Interaction Following Widowhood. Journal of Marriage and the Family. 46:323-31, 1984.

Morioka, K. Life Cycle Patterns in Japan, China and the United States. Journal of Marriage and the Family. 29:595-608, 1967.

Neugarten, B. and K. Weinstein. The Changing American Grandparent. Journal of Marriage and the Family. 26:199-204, 1964.

Newell, W. (ed). Ancestors. Chicago, IL: Aldine, 1976.

Nydegger, C. Family Ties of the Aged in Cross-Cultural Perspective. Gerontologist. 23:26-32, 1983.

Nydegger, C. and L. Mitteness. Transitions in Fatherhood. D. Chiriboga (ed). Transitions. Special Issue. Generations. 4:14-16, 1979.

_____ Strains in Father-Child Relations: A Double Perspective. Generations. 7, 1982.

Nydegger, C. N., L. S. Mitteness, and J. O'Neil. Experiencing Social Generations: Phenomenal Dimensions. Research on Aging. 5(4):527-46, 1983.

Okraku, I. O. Age and Attitudes Toward Multigenerational Residence. Journal of Gerontology. 42:280-87, 1987.

Ooms, H. A Structural Analysis of Japanese Ancestral Rites and Beliefs. Pp. 61-90 in W. Newell (ed). Ancestors. Chicago, IL: Aldine, 1976.

Parsons, R. J. and E. O. Cox. Family Mediation in Elder Caregiving Decisions: An Empowerment Intervention. Social Work. 34:122-26, 1989.

Pillemer, K. and D. Kinkelhor. Causes of Elderly Abuse: Caregiver Stress Versus Problem Relatives. American Journal of Orthopsychiatry. 59:179-87, 1989.

Poulshock, S. W. and G. T. Deimling. Families Caring for Elders in Residence: Issues in the Measurement of Burden. Journal of Gerontology. 39:230-39, 1984.

Pratt, C. C., et al. A Model Legal-Financial Education Workshop for Families Caring for Neurologically Impaired

Elders. _Gerontologist_. 29:258-62, 1989.

Riley, M., et al. _Aging and Society_. Vol. 3. _A Sociology of Age Stratification_. New York, NY: Russell Sage Foundation, 1972.

Roberts, W. All in the Family: The Older Person in Context. Pp. 177-91 in E. Bauwens (ed). _The Anthropology of Health_. St. Louis, MO: C. V. Mosby, 1978.

Robertson, J. Significance of Grandparents' Perceptions of Young Adult Grandchildren. _Gerontologist_. 16(2):137-40.

_____ Grandmotherhood: A Study of Role Conception. _Journal of Marriage and the Family_. 39(1):165-74, 1977

Rosenmayr, L. Family Relations of the Elderly. _Journal of Marriage and the Family_. 30:672-79, 1968.

Rosenmayr, L. and E. Kockeis. Family Relations and Social Contacts of the Aged in Vienna. Pp. 492-500 in C. Tibbitts and W. Donahue (eds). _Aging Around the World_. New York, NY: Columbia University Press, 1962.

_____ Propositions for a Sociological Theory of Aging and the Family. _International Social Science Journal_. 15:(3):410-26, 1963.

Rubinstein, R. L. Never Married Elderly as a Social Type: Re-evaluating Some Images. _Gerontologist_. 27:108-13, 1987.

Salamon, S. and S. O'Reilly. Family Land and Developmental Cycles Among Illinois Farmers. _Rural Sociology_. 44:525-42, 1979.

Salamon, S. and V. Lockhart. Land Ownership and the Position of Elderly in Farm Families. _Human Organization_. 39:324-31, 1980.

Sancier, B. A Model for Linking Families to Their Institutionalized Relatives. _Social Work_. 29:63-65, 1984.

Sanders, G. F. and D. W. Trygstad. Stepgrandparents and Grandparents: The View from Young Adults. _Family Relations_. 38:71-75, 1989.

Savishinsky, J. Ancestor Memorial: A Comparison of Jews and Japanese. Pp. 241-59 in W. Newell (ed). _Ancestors_. The Hague: Mouton, 1976.

Savitsky, E. and H. Sharkey. Study of Family Interaction in the Aged. _Journal of Geriatric Psychiatry_. 5(1):3-10, 1972.

Scott, J. P. and K. A. Roberto. Informal Supports of Older Adults: A Rural-Urban Comparison. _Family Relations_. 36:444-49, 1987.

Seccombe, K.  Children:  Their Impact on the Elderly in
   Declining Health.  Research on Aging.  9:312-26, 1987.

Seltzer, M. M., et al.  Families as Case Managers:  A
   Longitudinal Study.  Family Relations.  38:332-36, 1989.

Shanas, E.  Social Myth as Hypothesis:  The Case of the Family
   Relations of Old People.  Gerontologist.  19(1):3-9, 1979.

Shanas, E. and G. Streib (eds).  Social Structure and the
   Family:  Generational Relations.  Englewood Cliffs, NY:
   Prentice-Hall, 1965.

Shanas, E. and M. Sussman (eds).  Family, Bureaucracy and the
   Elderly.  Durham, NC:  Duke University Press, 1977.

Sheehan, N. W.  The Caregiver Information Project:  A
   Mechanism to Assist Religious Leaders to Help Family
   Caregivers.  Gerontologist.  29:703-06, 1989.

Shimkin, D., E. Shimkin, and D. Frate.  The Extended Family in
   Black Societies.  The Hague:  Morton, 1978:

Silverman, P.  Family Life.  Pp. 205-33 in P. Silverman (ed).
   The Elderly as Pioneers.  Bloomington, IN:  Indiana
   University Press, 1987.

Simic, A.  Aging in the United States and Yugoslavia:
   Contrasting Models of Intergenerational Relationships.  Pp.
   82-91 in J. Sokolovsky (ed).  Growing Old in Different
   Cultures:  Anthropological, Perspectives on Aging.  Acton,
   MA:  Copley Press, 1987.

_____  Aging, World View, and Intergenerational Relations in
   America and Yugoslavia.  Pp. 89-108 in J. Sokolovsky (ed).
   The Cultural Context of Aging:  Worldwide Perspectives.
   Westport, CT:  Bergin and Garvey, 1990.

Simmons, L.  Aging in Primitive Societies:  A Comparative
   Survey of Family Life and Relationships.  Law and
   Contemporary Problems.  27:36-51, 1962.

Skinner, E.  Intergenerational Conflict Among the Mossi:
   Father and Son.  Journal of Conflict Resolution.  5:
   55-60, 1961.

Smolic-Krkovic, N.  Aging, Bureaucracy, and the Family.  Pp.
   75-89 in E. Shanas and M. Sussman (eds).  Family
   Bureaucracy and the Elderly.  Durham, NC:  Duke University
   Press, 1977.

Stenning, O.  Household Viability Among the Pastoral Fulani.
   In J. Goody (ed).  The Developmental Cycle in Domestic
   Groups.  Cambridge:  Cambridge University Press, 1971.

Sterns, H. L., et al.  A Conceptual Approach to Counseling
   Older Adults and Their Families.  Counseling Psychology.
   12(2):55-61), 1984.

Steuve, A. and L. O'Donnell. Interactions Between Women and
    Their Elderly Parents: Constraints of Daughters'
    Employment. Research on Aging. 11:331-53, 1989.

Stoller, E. P. Parental Caregiving by Adult Children.
    Journal Marriage and the Family. 45:851-58, 1983.

Streib, G. An Alternative Family Form for Older Persons:
    Need and Social Context. Family Coordinator.
    27(4):413-20, 1978.

Streib, G. F. and R. W. Beck. Older Families: A Decade
    Review. Journal of Marriage and the Family.
    November:937-56, 1980.

Suggs, P. K. and V. R. Kivett. Rural/urban Elderly and
    Siblings: Their Value Consensus. International Journal of
    Aging and Human Development. 24(2):149-59, 1986-87.

Suitor, J. J. and K. Pillemer. The Presence of Adult
    Children: A Source of Stress for Elderly Couples'
    Marriages? Journal of Marriage and the Family. 49:717-25,
    1987.

Sussman, M. Relationships of Adult Children with Their
    Parents in the United States. Pp. 62-92 in E. Shanas and
    G. Streib (eds). Social Structure and the Family:
    Generational Relations. Englewood Cliffs, NJ: Prentice-
    Hall, 1965.

_____ The Family Life of Old People. In R. Binstock and E.
    Shanas (eds). Handbook of Aging and the Social Sciences.
    New York, NY: Van Nostrand, 1976.

_____ Family, Bureaucracy, and the Elderly Individual: An
    Organizational/Linkage Perspective. Pp. 2-20 in E. Shanas
    and M. Sussman (eds). Family, Bureaucracy and the
    Elderly. Durham, NC: Duke University Press, 1977.

Sussman, M. and L. Burchinal. Kin Family Network: Unheralded
    Structure in Current Conceptualizations of Family
    Functioning. Pp. 247-54 in B. Neugarten (ed). Middle
    Age and Aging. Chicago, IL: University of Chicago Press,
    1968.

Sweetser, D. Intergenerational Ties in Finnish Urban
    Families. American Sociological Review. 33:236-46, 1968.

Takeda, C. Family Religion in Japan: Ie and Its Religious
    Faith. Pp. 119-28 in W. Newell (ed). Ancestors. Chicago,
    IL: Aldine, 1976.

Tatje, T. and F. Hsu. Variations in Ancestor Worship Beliefs
    and Their Relation to Kinship. Southwestern Journal of
    Anthropology. (25);153-73, 1969.

Thurnher, M. Midlife Marriage: Sex Differences in
    Evaluations and Perspectives. International Journal of

_Aging and Human Development_.  7(2):129-35, 1976.

Thurnher, M. and B. Robinson.  Taking Care of Aged Parents:  A Family Cycle Transition.  _Gerontologist_.  19(6):586-93, 1979.

Titus, S., P. Rosenblatt, and R. Anderson.  Family Conflict over Inheritance of Property.  _Family Coordinator_.  28(3):337-46, 1979.

Treas, J.  Family Support Systems for the Aged. _Gerontologist_.  17(6):486-91, 1977.

Troll, L.  Issues in the Study of Generations. _Aging and Human Development_.  1(3):199-218, 1970.

_____ The Family of Later Life:  A Decade Review.  _Journal of Marriage and the Family_.  3:263-90, 1971.

_____ Intergenerational Relations in Later Life:  A Family System Approach.  Pp. 75-91 in N. Datan and N. Lohmann (eds).  _Transitions of Aging_.  New York, NY:  Academic Press, 1980.

Troll, L., S. Miller, and R. Atchley.  _Families in Later Life_. Belmont, CA:  Wadsworth, 1979.

Uchendu, V.  Ancestorcide.  Are African Ancestors Dead?  Pp. 283-96 in W. Newell (ed).  _Ancestors_.  Chicago, IL: Aldine, 1976

Walker, A. J. and L. Thompson.  Intimacy and Intergenerational Aid and Contact Among Mothers and Daughters.  _Journal of Marriage and the Family_.  45:841-49, 1983.

Ward, R.  Limitations of the Family as a Supportive Institution in the Lives of the Aged.  _Family Coordinator_. 27(4):365-74, 1978.

Weatherford, J.  Labor and Domestic Life Cycles in a German Community.  Pp. 145-161 in C. Fry (ed).  _Dimensions: Culture, Medicine and Aging_.  Brooklyn, NY:  J. F. Bergin, 1981.

Wimberley, H. and J. Savishinsky.  Ancestor Memorialism:  A Comparison of Jews and Japanese.  Pp. 115-31 in B. Misra and J. Preston (eds).  _Community, Self and Identity_.  The Hague, The Netherlands:  Mouton, 1978.

Wood, V. and J. Robertson.  The Significance of Grandparenthood.  Pp. 278-304 in J. Gubrium (ed).  _Time, Roles and Self in Old Age_.  New York, NY:  Human Science Press, 1976.

Youmans, E.  Generation and Perceptions of Old Age:  An Urban-Rural Comparison.  _Gerontologist_.  17:284-88, 1971.

Young, M. and P. Willmott.  _Family and Kinship in East London_.

London:    Routledge and Kegan Paul, 1957.

Young, R. F. and E. Kahana.  Specifying Caregiver Outcomes:
    Gender and Relationship Aspects of Caregiving Strain.
    Gerontologist.  29:660-66, 1989.

## AGE-SETS AND AGE GROUP SYSTEMS

Abrahams, R.  Aspects of Labwor Age and Generation Grouping
    and Related Systems.  Pp. 37-67 in P. Baxter and U. Almagor
    (eds).  Age, Generation and Time:  Some Features of East
    African Age Organization.  London:  Hurst, 1978.

Almagor, U.  Gerontocracy, Polygyny and Scarce Resources.  Pp.
    139-58 in J. LaFontaine (ed).  Sex and Age as Principles of
    Differentiation.  New York, NY:  Academic Press, 1978a.

_____  Pastoral Partners.  Manchester, England:  Manchester
    University Press, 1978b.

Baxter, P.  Boran Age-Sets and Generation Sets:  Gada, A
    Puzzle or a Maze?  Pp. 151-82 in P. Baxter and U. Almagor
    (eds).  Age, Generation and Time:  Some Features of East
    African Age Organization.  New York, NY:  St. Martin's
    Press, 1978.

_____  Boran Age Set and Warfare.  Senri Ethnological
    Studies.  Osaka, Japan:  National Museum of Ethnology.
    3:69-95, 1979.

Baxter, P. and U. Almagor (eds).  Age, Generation and Time:
    Some Features of East African Age Organization.  New York,
    NY:  St. Martin's Press, 1978.

Bernardi, B.  Age Class Systems:  Social Institutions and
    Polities Based on Age.  Translated by D. Kertzer.
    Cambridge:  Cambridge University Press, 1985.

Bischofberger, O.  The Generation Classes of the Zanaki
    (Tanzania).  Studia Ethnographica Friburgensia.  Vol 1.
    Fribourg, Switzerland:  University Press, 1972.

Dyson-Hudson, N.  The Karimojong Age System.  Ethnology.
    2:353-401, 1963.

Eisenstadt, S.  African Age Groups.  Africa.  24:100-13, 1954.

_____  From Generation to Generation:  Age Groups and Social
    Structure.  Glencoe, IL:  Free Press, 1956.

Evans-Pritchard, E.  The Nuer:  Age Sets.  Sudan Notes and
    Records.  29(2):233-69, 1936.

_____  The Nuer.  Clarendon, UK:  Oxford University Press,
    1940.

Foner, A. and D. Kertzer.  Transitions Over the Life Course:

Lessons From Age-Set Societies. *American Journal of Sociology*. 83:1081-1104, 1978.

_____ Intrinsic and Extrinsic Sources of Change in Life Course Transitions. Pp. 121-36 in M. W. Riley (ed). *Aging from Birth to Death*. Boulder, CO: Westview Press, 1979.

Gulliver, P. The Age Set Organization of the Jie Tribe. *Journal of the Royal Anthropological Institute of Great Britain and Ireland*. 83:147-68, 1953.

_____ The Turkana Age Organization. *American Anthropologist*. 60:900-12, 1958.

_____ *Social Control in an African Society: A Study of the Arusha*. London, UK: Routledge and Kegan Paul, 1963.

This monograph deals with agricultural Maasai (most Maasai are pastoralists) and emphasizes intergenerational relations and role transitions rather than the formal or structural properties of the agegroup system.

_____ The Jie of Uganda. Pp. 157-96 in J. Gibbs (ed). *People of Africa*. New York, NY: Holt, Rinehart and Winston, 1965.

_____ Age Differentiation. *International Encyclopedia of the Social Sciences*. Vol 1. 1969.

Hallpike, C. *The Konso of Ethiopia: A Study of the Values of A Cushitic People*. Oxford, UK: Clarendon, 1972.

Hamer, J. Sidamo Generational Class Cycles: A Political Gerontocracy. *Africa*. 40(1):50-70, 1970.

Hinnant, J. The Guji Gada as a Ritual System. Pp. 207-43 in P. Baxter and U. Almagor (eds). *Age, Generation and Time: Some Features of East African Age Organization*. New York, NY: St. Martin's Press, 1978.

_____ Age Grade Organization: An Explicit Model for the Aging Process. Pp. 146-54 in C. Fry and J. Keith (eds). *New Methods for Old Age Research: Anthropological Alternatives*. Chicago, IL: Center for Urban Policy, Loyola Unviersity of Chicago, 1980.

_____ Ritualization of the Life Cycle. Pp. 163-84 in C. Fry and J. Keith (eds). *New Methods for Old Age Research*. South Hadley, MA: Bergin and Garvey, 1986.

Holding, E. Some Preliminary Notes on Meru Age Grades. *Man*. 42(31):58-65, 1942.

Huntingford, G. *The Nandi of Kenya*. Clarendon, UK: Oxford University Press, 1953.

Jones, G. Ibo Age Organization, With Special Reference to the Cross River and Northeastern Ibo. *Journal of the Royal*

Anthropological Institute of Great Britain and Ireland.
92:191-211, 1962.

Kertzer, D.  Theoretical Developments in the Study of Age-
Group Systems.  American Ethnologist.  5:368-74, 1978.

A review of Fundamentals of Age Group Systems by F.
Stewart, 1977.

Kertzer, D. and O. Madison.  African Age-Set Systems and
Political Organization:  The Latuka of Southern Sudan.
L'Uomo.  4(1):85-109, 1980.

_____ Women's Age-Set Systems in Africa:  The Latuka of
Southern Sudan.  Pp. 109-30 in C. Fry (ed).  Dimensions:
Aging, Culture and Health.  Brooklyn, NY:  J. F. Bergin,
1981.

Kuper, H.  The Swazi of Swaziland.  Pp. 479-512 in J. Gibbs
(ed).  People of Africa.  New York, NY:  Holt, Rinehart and
Winston, 1965.

Laughlin, C. and E. Laughlin.  Age Generation and Political
Process in So.  Africa.  44(3):266-79, 1974.

Legesse, A.  Gada:  Three Approaches to African Society.  New
York, NY:  Free Press, 1973.

LeVine, R. and W. Sangree.  The Diffusion of the Age Group
Organization in East Africa:  A Controlled Comparison.
Africa.  32:97-110, 1962.

Lowie, R.  Plains Indians Age Societies.  New York, NY:
Anthropological Papers of the American Museum of Natural
History.  11:877-992, 1916.

Lowenthal, R.  Tharaka Age Organization and the Theory of Age
Set Systems.  Ann Arbor, MI:  University Microfilms, 1974.

Lowie, R.  Societies of the Hidatsa and Mandan Indians.
Anthropological Papers of the American Museum of Natural
History.  11:219-358, 1913.

Maybury-Lewis, D.  Akwe-Shavante Society.  Cambridge:  Oxford
University Press, 1967.

_____ Age and Kinship:  A Structural View.  Pp. 123-40 in D.
Kertzer and J. Keith (eds).  Age and Anthropological
Theory.  Ithaca, NY:  Cornell University Press, 1984.

One of the few treatments of age-class systems in Latin
America.

Ottenberg, S.  Leadership and Authority in an African Society:
The Afikpo Village-Group.  Seattle, WA:  University of
Washington Press, 1971.

Paulme, D. (ed).  Classes et Association d'Age en Afrique de l'Ouest.  Paris:  Plon, 1971.

Age organization in West Africa.

_____ Blood Pacts, Age Classes and Castes in Black Africa.
In P. Alexandre (ed).  French Perspectives in African
Studies.  Oxford:  Oxford University Press, 1973.

Peristiany, J.  The Social Institutions of the Kipsigis.
London:  Routledge and Sons, 1939.

_____ The Age Set System of the Pastoral Pokot.  Africa.
21:188-206, 1951.

Prins, A.  East African Age-Class Systems:  An Inquiry into
the Social Order of Galla, Kipsigis, and Kikuyu.
Groningen, The Netherlands:  J. B. Wolters, 1953.

Sangree, W.  The Bantu Tiriki of Western Kenya.  Pp. 69-72 in
J. Gibbs (ed).  Peoples of Africa.  New York, NY:  Holt,
Rinehart and Winston, 1965.

_____ Age, Prayer and Politics in Ritiki, Kenya.  New York,
NY:  Oxford University Press, 1966.

Spencer, P.  The Samburu:  A Study in Gerontocracy in a
Nomadic Tribe.  London, UK:  Routledge and Kegan Paul,
1965.

_____ Opposing Streams and the Gerontocratic Ladder.  Man.
2:153-74, 1976.

_____ The Jie Generation Paradox.  Pp. 133-49 in P. Baxter
and U. Almagor (eds).  Age, Generation and Time:  Some
Features of East African Age Organization.  New York, NY:
St. Martin's Press, 1978.

Stewart, F.  Fundamentals of Age-Group Systems.  New York, NY:
Academic Press, 1977.

Stewart utilized a rule-oriented approach to develop a
theoretical model of age-set systems.  He also provides an
extensive bibliography.

Torry, W.  Gabra Age Organization and Ecology.  Pp. 183-206 in
P.  Baxter and U. Almagor (eds).  Age, Generation and Time:
Some Features of East African Age Organizaton.  London:
Hurst, 1978.

Townsend, N.  Age, Descent and Elders Among the Pokomo.
Africa.  47(4):386-97, 1977.

Whyte, W.  Age-Grading of the Plains Indians.  Man.  Vol 56.
1944.

Wilson, M.  Nyakyusa Age Villages.  Journal of the Royal
Anthropological Institute.  79:21-25, 1951.

_____ Good Company:  A Study of Nyakyusa Age Villages.
Boston, MA:  Beacon Press, 1963.


RETIREMENT

Arroba, G.  The Financing of Social Security in Latin America.
Studies and Research.  15:61-82, 1979.

Assesses the volume of economic resources needed to support
social security programs in Latin America and the effect on
current national economies in developing Latin countries.

Atchley, R.  Adjustment to Loss of Job at Retirement.  Pp.
52-9 in M.  Seltzer, S. Corbett, and R. Atchley (eds).
Social Problems of the Aging.  Belmont, CA:  Wadsworth,
1978.

_____ The Sociology of Retirement.  New York,  NY:
Schenkman, 1976.

A still timely and comprehensive text detailing the
multiple cultural, social, and psychological influences on
the course of retirement and the nature of the transition.
Contains a useful introduction to the history and
institutional features of retirement.  Intended for college
level students, but with adequate detail and reference to
be a valuable resource to researchers.

Aves, G.  Aims and Achievements in the Provision of Welfare
Services for the Elderly in the United Kingdom.
Gerontologist.  1:171-77, 1961.

Back, K.  The Ambiguity of Retirement.  Pp. 78-98 in E. Busse
and E. Pfeiffer (eds).  Behavior and Adaptation in Late
Life.  Boston, MA:  Little, Brown & Co., 1977.

A description of the intersecting, sometimes conflicting,
definitions of retirement posed by cultural and social
structural factors in western society.  The author suggests
some of the difficulties retirees face in adjusting are the
result of the lack of clarity in the definition of the
construct and role of retirement.

Beeson, D.  Women in Aging Studies:  A Critique and
Suggestion.  Social Problems.  23:52-59, 1975.

Solid scholarly literature review and examination of the
social and cultural biases which prevent adequate treatment
of women in retirement studies.

Bell, D. and C. Patton.  Reaction to Induced Early Retirement.
Gerontologist.  18:173-79, 1978.

Bixby, L.  Retirement Patterns in the United States:  Research
and Policy Interaction.  Social Security Bulletin.
39:3-19, 1976.

Blau, Z. (ed). Current Perspectives on Aging and the Life Cycle: Work, Retirement, and Social Policy. Greenwich, CT: JAI Press, 1985.

Broadly conceived edited volume with each chapter building from social science empirical data studying planned and actual retirement patterns and occupational structures, and cross-national data on social security provisions. Other chapters focus on retirement of nonmarried women, and of women in Russia, and policies in China.

Bond, K. Retirement History Study's First Four Years: Work, Health, and Living Arrangements. Washington DC: US Government Printing Office, 1977.

Buhler, C. Meaningful Living in the Mature Years. Pp. 345-87 in R. Kleemeier (ed). Aging and Leisure: A Research Perspective into the Meaningful Use of Time. New York, NY: Oxford University Press, 1961.

Burkhauser, R. and J. Quinn. Barriers to Work in Old Age: A Review of the American Retirement System. Pp. 13-32 in C. Garbacz (ed). Economic Resources for the Elderly. Boulder, CO: Westview, 1983.

Carp, I. (ed). Retirement. New York, NY: Human Sciences Press, 1972.

Interdisciplinary volume with chapters presenting anthropological, sociological, psychological, economic, and policy views of retirement. Each chapter portrays retirement in theoretical perspective, outlines major research issues, and future directions. A major contribution which continues to be a useful resource; good bibliography.

Clark, M. An Anthropological View of Retirement. Pp. 117-56 in F. Carp (ed). Retirement. New York, NY: Behavioral Publications, 1972.

Clear discussion of the problems of constructing cross-cultural definitions of work and retirement, and of international variations in practices. The author describes the differing materials on retirement presented by social, psychological, and cultural anthropology, and concludes by presenting a model of the behavioral environment of the retiree including attention to the role of current public values and changes in institutional practices.

Crawford, M. Retirement: A Rite de Passage. Sociological Review. 21:255-78, 1973.

Ekerdt, D. The Busy Ethic: Moral Continuity Between Work and Retirement. Gerontologist. 26(2):239-44, 1986.

A study of meanings and beliefs underlying the practice and process of retirement which is a vital complement to the preponderance of survey-based analyses in the literature.

_____ Why the Notion Persists That Retirement Harms Health. Gerontologist. 27(4):454-57, 1987.

Fecher, V. Retirement, Religion and Aging. San Antonio, TX: Trinity University Press, 1982.

Annotated bibliography which includes articles on the ideology and practice of retirement of clergy and nuns with attention to the theological dimensions as well as personal adjustment of clergy.

Fitzgerald, F. Cities on a Hill: A Journey Through Contemporary American Cultures. New York, NY: Simon & Schuster, 1986.

Excellent narrative and finely detailed ethnography depicting retirement community case studies.

Foner, A and K. Schwab. Aging and Retirement. Monterey, CA: Brooks/Cole, 1981.

A review and interpretation of the literature on processes and impacts of retirement on individual lives and public institutions. Chapters include myths and old stereotypes of family and community, policy, and dilemmas and solutions to retirement problems. The conclusion examines wider implications of retirement for understanding the relationships between individual and society.

Friedman, E. The Meaning of Work and Retirement. Chicago, IL: University of Chicago, 1954.

Despite its age, this book remains a vital but neglected contribution due to the focus on meanings and individuals. Contains many chapters which refute common, but enduring, misconceptions about the relationship between the meaning of work and career for an individual and the nature of their adjustment to retirement.

George, L. Role Transitions in Later Life: The World of Work. Pp. 55-76 in L. George. Role Transitions in Later Life. Monterey, CA: Brooks/Cole, 1980.

Goudy, W. and C. Dobson. Work, Retirement and Financial Situations of the Rural Elderly. Pp. 57-78 in R. Coward and G. Lee (eds). The Elderly in Rural Society. New York, NY: Springer, 1985.

A study of retirement in rural settings which provides a needed counterbalance to the predominant focus on urban retirement. Provides data (largely survey and census) and extensive bibliography on farmers and also on rural elderly men. Three issues are addressed: work and retirement dynamics, orientation to retirement, financial situations, and future research issues.

Graebner, W.  A History of Retirement:  The Meaning and
    Function of an American Institution, 1885-1978.  New Haven,
    CT:  Yale, University Press, 1985.

Gratton, B and R. Haug.  Decision and Adaptation:  Research on
    Female Retirement.  Research on Aging.  5:59-76, 1983.

Green, L.  Retirement Options:  A Gerontological Simulation.
    Institute of Gerontology.  Ann Arbor, MI:  University of
    Michigan Press, 1979.

Guillemard, A. M. (ed).  Old Age and the Welfare State.
    London, UK:  Sage Studies in International Sociology, 1983.

Havighurst, R. et al (eds).  Adjustment to Retirement:  A
    Cross-National Study.  Assen, Holland:  Van Gorcum, 1969.

Havighurst, R., B. Neugarten, and V. Bengtson.  A Cross-
    National Study of Adjustment to Retirement.  Gerontologist.
    6:137-38, 1966.

Havighurst, R., et al (eds).  Adjustment to Retirement:  A
    Cross-National Study.  Assen, Holland:  Van Gorcum, 1969.

International Federation on Ageing.  Mandatory Retirement:
    Blessing or Curse?  Washington, DC:  International
    Federation on Ageing, 1978.

Laczko, F.  Phase Retirement in Western Europe.  Pp. 217-26 in
    C.  Phillipson, M. Bernard, and P. Strang (eds).
    Dependency and Interdependency in Old Age:  Theoretical
    Perspectives and Policy Alternatives.  London, UK:  Croom
    Helm, 1986.

Legesse, A.  Age Sets and Retirement Communities.
    Anthropological Quarterly.  52(1):61-69, 1979.

Liu, Y.  Retirees and Retirement Programs in The People's
    Republic of China.  Industrial Gerontology.  1:72-81, 1974.

Longino, C., et al.  The Retirement Migration Project:  A
    Final Report for the National Institute on Aging.  Center
    for Social Research in Aging.  Coral Gables, FL:
    University of Miami, 1984.

Luborsky, M.  Social and Cultural Foundations of the
    Retirement.  Transition.  Ann Arbor, MI:  University
    Microfilms, 1985.

    An in-depth longitudinal ethnography describing a study of
    forty-four workers starting one year prior to and ending
    one year after their retirements.  The chapters describe
    folk models and beliefs about retirement in American
    culture, social structural and situational contexts shaping
    retirement experiences and behavior both familial and
    worksite and a detailed presentation of three workers'
    retirement passages.  The final chapter proposes alternate
    definitions for retirement adjustment and life course

transitions.

Lyon, P.  Nearing Retirement:  A Study of Late Working Lives.
Brookfield, VT:  Gowen, 1987.

Miletich, J.  Retirement:  An Annotated Bibliography.
Westport, CT:  Greenwood, 1986.

Surveys 600+ current works from several perspectives
including policy and practice, scientific and popular
literature on retiring and retirement life.  Special
attention is given to women, professionals, adjustment and
counseling issues, but no anthropological studies are
included.

Milleti, M.  Voices of Experience:  1500 Retired People Talk
About Retirement.  New York, NY:  TIAA-CREF, 1984.

Results of a survey of annuitants are reported with the
goal of letting retirees use their own words to describe
concerns, needs, and acquired retirement wisdom.  Treats
customary topics regarding, health, finances, housing,
adjustment, family life, and single life.

Moller, V.  Quality of Life in Retirement:  A Case Study of
Zulu Return Migrants.  Social Indicators Research.
20:562-82, 1988.

_____  Personal Adjustment to Rural Retirement Among
Circulatory Migrants.  In M. Ferreira, L. S. Gillis, and V.
Moller (eds).  Aging in South Africa:  Social Research
Papers.  Human Sciences Research Council.  Pretoria, South
Africa:  V and R Printers, 1989.

Morris, R. and S. A. Bass (eds).  Retirement Reconsidered:
Economic and Social Roles for Older People.  New York, NY:
Springer, 1988.

Morse, D, A. Dutka, and S. Gray.  Life After Early Retirement:
The Experience of Lower-level Workers.  Totowa, NJ:
Allanheld, Osmun, 1983.

Monaban, D. and V. Greene.  Predictors of Early Retirement
Among University Faculty.  Gerontologist.  27(1):46-52,
1987.

Palmore, E.  Retirement:  Causes and Consequences.  New York,
NY:  Springer, 1985.

Exhaustive review and synthesis of the seven major
longitudinal surveys of retirement including demographic,
socioeconomic and psychometric data.  Based on interviews
with over 7000 subjects from seven separate long-term
studies by the Social Security Administration, Duke
University, Department of Labor and others.  Chapters
include summaries of findings regarding predictors of
retirement, consequences, determinants, reasons for, work
after, gender, race and socioeconomic differences.

Parnes, H., et al. Retirement Among American Men. Lexington, MA: Lexington Books, 1985.

Reports findings from sociologically- and psychologically-based longitudinal project. Bibliography.

Pendrell, J. Old Age Around the World. Social Policy. 7:3:107-10, 1976

Deals with retirement in industrialized nations.

Phillipson, C. The Transition to Retirement. In G. Cohan (ed). Social Change and the Life Course. New York, NY: Tavistock, 1987.

Powers, A, W. Goudy, and P. Keith. Later Life Transitions: Older Males in Rural America. Boston, MA: Kluwer-Nijhoff, 1985.

Longitudinal study of attitudes of aged men in Iowa. Sparse in data and analysis.

Quadagno, J. Work and Retirement. Pp. 139-72 (Chapter 4) in J. Quadagno. Aging in Early Industrial Society: Work, Family, and Social Policy in Nineteenth-century England. New York, NY: Academic, 1982.

Meticulous study of the economic, social, and political influences on conceptions of old age, retirement, and institutional practices shaping the conditions of the elderly. The author uses first-hand documents to trace the decline of the household as a productive unit and living arrangements for the elderly, the nature and impact of the transfer of financial support for the elderly to the state, and the rise of formal retirement.

Rhee, H. Human Aging and Retirement. Geneva, Switzerland: International Social Security Association, 1974.

Rosa, J-J. (ed). World Crisis in Social Security. Rutgers, NY: Transaction Books, 1982.

Reviews public retirement programs in France, Great Britain, Italy, Japan, Sweden, Switzerland, the United States and West Germany. Discusses the importance of social security programs and the crises they face in the future.

Schnore, M. Retirement: Bane or Blessing. Ontario, Canada: Wilfrid Laurier University Press, 1985.

Sheppard, H. Work and Retirement. Pp. 286-308 in R. Binstock and E. Shanas (eds). Handbook of the Social Sciences. New York, NY: Van Nostrand Reinhold, 1976

Simmons, L. Old Age Security in Other Societies. Geriatrics. 3:237-44, 1948.

Simpson, I., K. Back, and J. McKinney. Orientation to Work and Retirement. Pp. 106-19 in I. Simpson and J. McKinney (eds). Social Aspects of Aging. Durham, NC: Duke University, 1966.

Streib, G and C. Schneider. Retirement in American Society: Impact and Process. Ithaca, NY: Cornell University Press, 1972.

Reports findings from a seven-year longitudinal study of attitudes and behavior during the retirement process using statistical methods and illustrative case materials. Based on study of health, finances, behavior, and pscyhological well-being, the authors propose the theory of differential disengagement as an alternative to disengagement theories of aging. Chapters cover preparation, experiences, and outcomes of retirement and adjustment.

Szinovacz, M. (ed). Women's Retirement: Implications of Recent Research. Beverly Hills, CA: Sage, 1982.

Thorough review of current state of the art of retirement and women studies from sociological, psychological and policy viewpoints. The book provides a solid introductory overview, and works to develop theory from current literature. It offers sections on work history patterns and lives of older women, retirement preparation attitudes and plans, and womens' experiences in adjusting to retirement. It provides comparisons with men, and pays attention to subpopulations such as single and married women in retirement.

Tilak, S. Religion and Aging in the Indian Tradition. Albany, NY: State University of New York Press, 1989.

A scholarly study of aging, old age, and cultural precepts for later life as represented in the primary historical documents from traditional and ancient India. Includes many sections on "retirement" stage of life.

Tracy, M. and R. Ward. Trends in Old-age Pensions for Women: Benefit Levels in Ten Nations 1960-1980. Gerontologist. 26(2):286-91, 1986.

Wanner, R. and P. McDonald. The Vertical Mosaic in Later Life: Ethnicity and Retirement in Canada. Journal of Gerontology. 41(5):662-71, 1986.

## SEMIOTICS: AGING AND COMMUNICATION

Aronoff, C. Old Age in Prime Time. Journal of Communication. 24:86-87, 1974.

Bakdash, D. P. Communication with the Aged Patient: A Systems View. Journal of Gerontological Nursing. 3(5):29-32, 1977.

Banziger, G.  Intergenerational Communication in Prominent Western Drama. _Gerontologist_. 19(5):471-80, 1979.

Barker, R. G. and L. S. Barker.  The Psychological Ecology of Old People in Midwest, Kansas and Yoredale, Yorkshire.  In B. Neugarten (ed). _Middle Age and Aging_. Chicago, IL: University of Chicago Press, 1968.

Bayles, K. A. and A. W. Kaszniak.  _Communication and Cognition in Normal Aging and Dementia_. Boston, MA:  Little Brown, 1987.

A very comprehensive literature review which relates to current theoretical debates regarding the structure of mind.

Beasley, D. S. and G. A. Davis (eds).  _Aging:  Communication Processes and Disorders_. New York, NY:  Grune and Stratton, 1981.

A broad overview of aging and communication issues within a traditional fremework.

Beattie, A. and J. Curtis.  Hospital Corridors as a Case Study in Architectural Psychology. _Journal of Architectural Research_. 3:44-50, 1974.

Becker, G.  _Growing Old in Silence_. Berkeley, CA:  University of California Press, 1980.

Bollinger, R.  Geriatric Speech Pathology. _Gerontologist_. 14:217-20, 1974.

Carlson, S.  Communication and Social Interaction in the Aged. _Nursing Clinics of North America_. 7(2):270-77, 1972.

Clark, C. and G. C. Mills.  Communicating with Hearing Impaired Elderly Adults. _Journal of Gerontological Nursing_. 5(3):41-44, 1979.

Coleman, P. G.  Measuring Reminiscence Characteristics from Conversation as Adaptive Features of Old Age. _International Journal of Aging and Human Development_. 5(3):281-94, 1974.

Gubrium, J. F.  _Oldtimers and Alzheimer's:  The Descriptive Organization of Senility_. Greenwich, CT:  JAI Press, 1986.

This 1986 work is a logical extension of Gubrium's classic nursing home ethnography as it details the ways in which social actors construct, modify, and sustain the realities of old age and disease in social interaction.

Hardimann, C. J., A. Holbrook, and D. L. Hedrick.  Non-verbal Communication Systems for the Severely Handicapped Geriatric Patient. _Gerontologist_. 19(1):96-102, 1979.

Jones, D. C.  Social Isolation, Interaction, and Conflict in

Two Nursing Homes. <u>Gerontologist</u>. 12:230-34, 1972.

_____ Spatial Proximity, Interpersonal Conflict, and Friendship Formation in the Intermediate Care Facility. <u>Gerontologist</u>. 15:150-54, 1975.

Koncelik, J. A. <u>Designing the Open Nursing Home</u>. Stroundsburg, PA: Dowden, Hutchinson and Ross, 1976.

Lawton, M. P. The Impact of Environment on Aging and Behavior. Pp. 276-301 in J. E. Birren and K. W. Schaie (eds). <u>Handbook of the Psychology of Aging</u>. New York, NY: Nostrand, 1977.

Lawton, M. P., B. Liebowitz, and H. Charon. Physical Structure and the Behavior of Senile Patients Following Ward Remodeling. <u>International Journal of Aging and Human Development</u>. 1:231-39, 1970.

LeFevre, A. Speech Therapy for the Geriatric Patient. <u>Geriatrics</u>. 12:681-89, 1957.

Lipman, A. A Socio-Architectural View of Life in Three Homes for Old People. <u>Gerontologica Clinica</u>. 10:88-101, 1968.

Lubinski, R. B. Why So Little Interest in Whether or Not Old People Talk: A Review of Recent Research on Verbal Communication Among the Elderly. <u>International Journal of Aging and Human Development</u>. 9(3):237-45, 1978-79.

An early plea for attention to the subject with reference to researchers' tendency to neglect the everyday lives of older persons.

Marshall, V. Organizational Feature of Terminal Status Passage in Residential Facilities for the Aged. <u>Urban Life: A Journal of Analytic Ethnography</u>. 4(3):349-68, 1975a.

_____ Socialization for Impending Death in a Retirement Village. <u>American Journal of Sociology</u>. 80(5):1224-44, 1975b.

_____ No Exit: A Symbolic Interactionist Perspective on Aging. <u>International Journal of Aging and Human Development</u>. 9(4):345-58, 1978.

These three powerful essays by Marshall (1975a, 1975b and 1978) point out the "double-binding" nature of certain communication networks in which older people find themselves.

Oyer, H. J. and E. J. Oyer. <u>Aging and Communiction</u>. Baltimore, MD: University Park Press, 1976.

Pastalan, L. and D. H. Carson. <u>The Spatial Behavior of Older People</u>. Ann Arbor, MI: University of Michigan Press, 1970.

Posner, J.   Notes on the Negative Implications of Being
    Competent in a Home for the Aged.  International Journal of
    Aging and Human Development.  5(4):357-64, 1974.

    An effective analysis of the role of "signs of competence"
    in the everyday lives of the institutionalized aged.

Rubin, K. and I. O. R. Brown.  A Life-Span Look at Person
    Perception and Its Relationship to Communicative
    Interaction.  Journal of Gerontology.  30(4):461-68, 1975.

Schow, R. L., et al.  Communication Disorders of the Aged:  A
    Guide for Health Professionals.  Baltimore, MD:  University
    Park Press, 1978.

Schulz, R. and G. Brenner.  Relocation of the Aged:  A Review
    and Theoretical Analysis.  Journal of Gerontology.
    32:323-33, 1977.

Senn, B. and J. R. Steiner.  Don't Tread on Me:  Ethological
    Perspectives on Institutionalizaton.  International Journal
    of Aging and Human Development  9(2):177-85, 1978.

    An early study of communication in natural settings which
    points to differences in proxemic behaviors towards older
    persons.

Snyder, L. H.  An Exploratory Study of Patterns of Social
    Interaction, Organization, and Facility Design in Three
    Nursing Homes.  International Journal of Aging and Human
    Development.  4(4):319-33, 1973.

Sommer, R. and H. Ross.  Social Interaction on a Geriatrics
    Ward.  International Journal of Social Psychiatry.
    4:128-33, 1958.

Stafford, P.  The Semiotics of Old Age in a Small Midwestern
    Town:  An Interactionist Approach.  Ann Arbor, MI:
    University Microfilms, 1978.

Teski, M.  Social Structure and Reality Construction in a
    Retirement Hotel.  Ann Arbor, MI:  University Microfilms,
    1976.

    Based on dissertaton research, the monographs by Stafford
    (1978) and Teski (1976) discuss how networks of
    communication constitute/uphold structures of reality.

Ulatowska, H. K. (ed).  The Aging Brain:  Communication in the
    Elderly.  San Diego, CA:  College Hill, 1985.

Walle, E.  Communication Problems of the Chronically Ill and
    Aged in Institutional Setting.  Hearing and Speech News.
    39:16-17, 1971.

Watson, W.  Body Image and Staff-to-Resident Deportment in a
    Home for the Aged.  Journal of Aging and Human Development.
    1:345-59, 1970.

Weiss, C.  Communicative Needs of the Geriatric Population.
    Journal of the American Geriatrics Society.  19:640-45,
    1971.

Winogrond, I. R.  A Comparison of Interpersonal Distancing
    Behavior in Young and Elderly Adults.  International
    Journal of Aging and Human Development.  13(1):53-60, 1981.

# 9

# Community Organization
# and
# Age-Homogeneous Residences

Aldridge, G.  The Role of Older People in a Florida Retirement
    Community.  Geriatrics.  11:223-26, 1956.

Angrosino, M.  Anthropology and the Aged.  Gerontologist.
    152:174-80, 1976.

    A retirement mobile home park in Tampa, Florida.

Bultena, G.  Relationship of Occupational Status to Friendship
    Ties in Three Planned Retirement Communities.  Journal of
    Gerontology.  24(4):461-64, 1969.

Bultena, G. and V. Wood.  The American Retirement Community:
    Bane or Blessing?  Journal of Gerontology.  24:209-17,
    1969.

Byrne, S.  Arden, An Adult Community.  Pp. 123-52 in G. Foster
    and R. Kemper (eds).  Anthropologists in Cities.  Boston:
    Little Brown, 1974.

Carp, F.  A Future for the Aged:  Victoria Plaza and Its
    Residents.  Austin, TX:  University of Texas Press, 1966.

    A landmark study, exceptional because the researchers were
    able to interview all eligible applicants to a new public
    housing building, making possible systematic comparisons of
    the greatly improved lives of those who eventually moved
    into this age-homogeneous setting with the lives of those
    who did not.

_____  Relevance of Personality Traits to Adjustment in Group
    Living Situations.  Journal of Gerontology.  40:544-51,
    1985.

Coons, D. and J. Bykowski.  Brookside Manor--A Gerontological
    Simulation.  Institute of Gerontology.  Ann Arbor, MI:  The
    University of Michigan and Detroit, MI:  Wayne State
    University, 1975.

Deck, J.  Rancho Paradise:  Retired Americans in a Mobile Home
     Park.  Chicago, IL:  Harcourt, Brace and Javanovich, 1972.

Francis, D.  Adaptive Strategies of the Elderly in England and
     Ohio.  Pp. 85-107 in C. Fry (ed).  Dimensions:  Aging,
     Culture, and Health.  Brooklyn, NY:  J. F. Bergin, 1981.

Fry, C.  Community as Commodity:  The Age Graded Case.  Human
     Organization.  36:115-23, 1977.

_____ Structural Conditions Affecting Community Formation
     Among the Aged:  Two Examples from Arizona.  J. Keith (ed).
     The Ethnography of Old Age.  Special Issue.
     Anthropological Quarterly.  52(1):7-18, 1979.

Hendel-Sebestyen, G.  Role Diversity:  Toward the Development
     of Community in a Total Institutional Setting.  J. Keith
     (ed).  The Ethnography of Old Age.  Special Issue.
     Anthropological Quarterly.  52(1):19-28, 1979.

Hornum, B.  Aspects of Aging in Planned Communities.  Topics
     in Clinical Nursing.  3:1, 1981.

Hoyt, G.  The Life of the Retired in a Trailer Park.  American
     Journal of Sociology.  50(4-1):361-70, 1954(59).

Hunt, Michael E.  Retirement Communities:  An American
     Original.  New York, NY:  The Haworth Press, 1983.

Jacobs, J.  Fun City:  An Ethnographic Study of a Retirement
     Community.  New York, NY:  Holt, Rinehart and Winston,
     1974a.

_____ An Ethnographic Study of a Retirement Setting.
     Gerontologist.  14(5):483-87, 1974b.

_____ Older Persons and Retirement Communities:  Case Studies
     in Social Gerontology.  Springfield, IL:  C. C. Thomas,
     1975.

Jerrome, D.  That's What It's All About:  Old People's
     Organization As a Context for Aging.  Journal of Aging
     Studies.  2(1):71-82, 1988.

Johnson, S.  Idle Haven:  Community Building Among the Working
     Class Retired.  Berkeley, CA:  University of California
     Press, 1971.

Jonas, K.  Factors in Development of Community Among Elderly
     Persons in Age-Segregated Housing:  Relationships Between
     Involvement in Friendship Roles within the Community and
     External Social Roles.  J. Keith (ed).  The Ethnography of
     Old Age.  Special Issue.  Anthropological Quarterly.
     52(1):29-38, 1979.

Kandel, R. and M. Heider.  Friendship and Factionalism in a
     Tri-Ethnic Housing Complex for the Elderly in North Miami.
     J. Keith (ed).  The Ethnography of Old Age.  Special Issue.

_Anthropological Quarterly_.  52(1):49-59, 1979.

Keith, J.  _The Ethnography of Old Age_.  _Anthropological Quarterly_.  Special Issue. 52(1), 1979a.

_____  The Ethnography of Old Age:  An Introduction.  J. Keith (ed).  _The Ethnography of Old Age_.  Special Issue. _Anthropological Quarterly_.  52(1)1-6, 1979b.

_____  Old Age and Community Creation.  Pp. 170-97 in C. Fry (ed).  _Aging in Culture and Society:  Comparative Viewpoints and Strategies_.  Brooklyn, NY:  J. F. Bergin, 1980.

_____  _Old People, New Lives:  Community Creation in a Retirement Residence_.  Chicago, IL:  University of Chicago Press, 1982.  (Phoenix paperback edition of Ross, 1977, with new Preface).

Describes the process of community creation in a residence for retired construction workers in Paris, France.  Factors that promote community formation are identified through comparison with other settings, including utopias and squatter settlements, as well as retirement residences in the U. S.

Keith, J., C. L. Fry, and C. Ikels.  Community as Context for Successful Aging.  Pp. 245-62 in J. Sokolovsky (ed).  _The Cultural Context of Aging:  Worldwide Perspectives_. Westport, CT:  Bergin and Garvey, 1990.

Kleemeier, R.  Moosehaven:  Congregate Living in a Community of the Retired.  _American Journal of Sociology_.  59:347-51, 1954(59) .

La Greca, A. J., G. F. Streib, and W. E. Folts.  Retirement Communities and Their Life Stages.  _Journal of Gerontology_. 40:211-18, 1985.

Legesse, A.  Age Sets and Retirement Communities:  Comparison and Comment.  J. Keith (ed).  _The Ethnography of Old Age_. Special Issue.  _Anthropological Quarterly_.  52(1):61-69, 1979.

Longino, C.  Retirement Communitites.  In F. J. Berghorn and D. E. Schafer (eds).  _The Dynamics of Aging_.  Boulder, CO: Westview Press, 1981.

Reports on characteristics of individuals who move to three different types of retirement housing (planned full-service, planned public housing, de facto retirement communities) and their reasons for doing so.

Marshall, V.  Socialization for Impending Death in a Retirement Village.  _American Journal of Sociology_. 80:1124-44, 1935.

McMillan-Heintz, K.  _Retirement Communities_.  New York, NY:

Centre for Urban Policy Research, 1976.

Messer, M.  The Possibility of an Age-Concentrated Environment Becoming a Normative System.  Gerontologist.  7:247-51, 1967.

Osgood, Nancy J.  Senior Settlers:  Social Integration in Retirement Communities.  New York, NY:  Praeger, 1982.

Perkinson, M.  Alternate Roles for the Elderly:  An Example from a Midwestern Retirement Community.  Human Organization.  39:  219-26, 1980.

Quadagno, J., R. Kuhar, and W. Peterson.  Maintaining Social Distance in a Racially-Integrated Retirement Community.  Black Aging.  3:97-112, 1978.

Ross, J. K.  Learning to be Retired:  Socialization into a French Retirement Residence.  Journal of Gerontology.  29(2):211-23, 1974a.

_____  Life Goes On:  Social Organization in a French Retirement Residence.  Pp. 99-120 in J. Gubrium (ed).  Late Life.  Springfield, IL:  C. C. Thomas, 1974b.

_____  Old People, New Lives.  Chicago, IL:  University of Chicago Press, 1977.

Sherman, S. R.  Mutual Assistance and Support in Retirement Housing.  Journal of Gerontology  30:479-83, 1975a

_____  Patterns of Contacts for Residents of Age-Segregated and Age-Integrated Housing.  Journal of Gerontology.  30:103-07, 1975b.

Silverman, P.  Community Settings.  Pp. 234-62 in P. Silverman (ed).  The Elderly as Pioneers.  Bloomington, IN:  Indiana University Press, 1987.

Smithers J.  Determined Survivors:  Community Life Among the Urban Elderly.  New Brunswick, NJ:  Rutgers University Press, 1985.

Streib, G. F., W. E. Folts, and A. J. La Greca.  Autonomy, Power, and Decision-Making in Thirty-six Retirement Communities.  Gerontologist.  25:403-09, 1985.

Teski, M.  Living Together:  An Ethnography of a Retirement Hotel.  Washington, DC:  University Press of America, 1979.

Webber, I. and C. Osterbind.  Types of Retirement Villages.  Pp. 3-10 in E. Burgess (ed).  Retirement Villages.  Ann Arbor, MI:  University of Michigan Press, 1961.

Wellin, E. and E. Boyer.  Adjustments of Black and White Elderly to the Same Adaptive Niche.  J. Keith (ed).  The Ethnography of Old Age.  Special Issue.  Anthropological Quarterly.  52(1):39-48, 1979.

# 10

# Urban Aged, Social Networks, Support Systems

Antonucci, T. C. Personal Characteristics, Social Networks and Social Behavior. Pp. 94-174 in R. H. Binstock and E. Shanas (eds). Handbook of Aging and the Social Sciences (2nd ed). New York, NY: Van Nostrand Reinhold, 1985.

Antonucci, T. C. and C. Depner. Social Support and Informal Helping Relationships. In T. A. Willis (ed). Basic Process in Helping Relationships. New York, NY: Academic Press, 1982.

Antonucci, T. C. and J. S. Jackson. Social Support, Interpersonal Efficacy, and Health: A Life Course Perspective. Pp. 291-311 in L. L. Carstensen and B. A. Edelstein (eds). Handbook of Clinical Gerontology. New York, NY: Pergamon Press, 1987.

Arling, G. The Elderly Widow and Her Family, Neighbors, and Friends. Journal of Marriage and the Family. 38(3):757-68, 1976.

Atchley, R., L. Pignatiello, and E. Shaw. Interaction with Family and Friends. Research on Aging. 1:83-95, 1979.

Babchuk, N. Aging and Primary Relations. Aging and Human Development. 9(2):137-51, 1978-9.

Baxter, E. and K. Hopper. Private Lives/Public Spaces: Homeless Adults on the Streets of New York City. New York, NY: Community Service Society, 1981.

Berghorn, F., et al. The Urban Elderly: A Study of Life Satisfaction. New York, NY: Universe Books, 1978.

Berkman, L. and S. Syme. Social Networks, Host Resistance and Mortality: A Nine-Year Follow-Up Study of Alameda County Residents. American Journal of Epidemiology. 109:186-204, 1979.

Blau, Z. Structural Constraints on Friendship in Old Age.

266   ANTHROPOLOGY OF AGING

*American Sociological Review*.  26:429-39, 1961.

Bohannan, P.  Food of Old People in Center-City Hotels.  Pp.
185-200 in C. Fry (ed).  *Dimensions: Aging, Culture, and
Health*.  Brooklyn, NY:  J. F. Bergin, 1981.

Brown, A.  Satisfying Relationships for the Elderly and Their
Patterns of Disengagement.  *Gerontologist*.  14(3):258-62,
1974.

Byerts, T. (ed).  Symposium--The City:  A Viable Environment
for the Elderly?  Phase I.  *Gerontologist*.  15(1):13-45,
1975.

Candy, S.  Neighborhood Concerns in an Urban Area:  An
Analysis of Age Differences.  *The Journal of Minority
Aging*.  4:25-33, 1979.

Cantor, M.  Life Space and the Social Support System of the
Inner City Elderly of New York.  *Gerontologist*.  15:23-27,
1975.

_____Neighbors and Friends:  An Overlooked Resource in the
Informal Support System.  *Research on Aging*.  1:434-63,
1979a.

_____The Informal Support System of New York's Inner City
Elderly:  Is Ethnicity a Factor?  Pp. 153-74 in D. Gelfand
and A.  Kutzik (eds).  *Ethnicity and Aging:  Theory,
Research and Policy*.  New York, NY:  Springer, 1979b.

Clark, M.  Patterns of Aging Among the Elderly Poor of the
Inner City.  *Gerontologist*.  11(1):58-66, 1971.

Coalition for the Homeless.  *Crowded Out:  Homelessness and
the Elderly Poor in New York City*.  New York, NY:
Coalition for the Homeless, 1984.

Cohen, C., A. Alder, and J. Mintz.  Assessing Social Network
Interventions--Results of an Experimental Service Program
Conducted in a Single-Room Occupancy Hotel.  Pp. 67-88 in
P. Parker and D. Pancoast (eds).  *Rediscovering Self-Help:
Professionals and Informal Care*.  Beverly Hills CA:  Sage,
1983.

Cohen, C. and J. Sokolovsky.  Isolation of the Inner City
Aged:  Ending an Old Myth with a New Method.  *Black Aging*.
3:132-42, 1978.

_____Social Engagement Versus Isolation:  The Case of the
Aged in SRO Hotels.  *Gerontologist*.  20(1):36-44, 1980.

_____A Reassessment of the Sociability of Long-Term Skid Row
Residents--A Social Network Approach.  *Social Networks*.
3:93-105, 1981a.

_____Social Networks and the Elderly:  Clinical Techniques.
*International Journal of Family Therapy*.  3:281-94, 1981b.

_____ Toward A Concept of Homelessness Among the Elderly.
Journal of Gerontology. 38:81-89, 1983.

This article is a comparison of Skid-Row elderly and SRO
Hotel residents.

_____ Old Men of the Bowery. New York, NY:  Guilford, 1989.

Cohler, B.  Stress or Support:  Relations Between Older Women
from Three European Ethnic Groups and Their Relatives.  Pp.
115-20 in R. Manuel (ed). Minority Aging:  Sociological
and Social Psychological Issues. Westport, CT:  Greenwood
Press, 1983.

Cubbitt, T.  Friends, Neighbors and Kin:  Development of
Social Contacts with Special Reference to Stages in the
Life Cycle and Class Factors. Connections. 1:42, 1978.

Eckert, J. K.  The Unseen Community:  Understanding the Older
Hotel Dweller. Aging.  291-292:28-35, 1979a.

_____ The Social Ecology of SRO Living.  Generations.
Winter-Spring:22-23, 1979b.

_____ Urban Development and Renewal:  High Risk Factors for
the Elderly. Gerontologist.  19(5):496-502, 1979c.

_____ The Unseen Elderly:  A Study of Marginally Subsistent
Hotel Dwellers.  San Diego, CA:  San Diego University, The
Campanile Press, 1980.

_____ Dislocation and Relocation of the Urban Elderly:
Social Networks as Mediators of Relocation Stress. Human
Organization. 42(1):39-45, 1983.

Eckert, J. K. and R. E. Dunkle.  The Differential Use of
Health Services Among Two Groups of Older Hotel Dwellers.
Journal of Health and Social Workd. 7(2):123-30, 1982.

_____ Need for Services in the Elderly Experiencing Urban
Change. Gerontologist.  24:247-60, 1984.

Eckert, J. K., S. S. Galazka, and J. Carroll.  The Geriatric
Patient in Ecological Perspective. Journal of Family
Practice. 16(4):757-61, 1983.

Eckert, J. K. and M. C. Goldstein.  An Anthropological
Approach to the Study of Illness Behavior in the Urban
Community. Urban Anthropology.  12(2):125-39, 1985.

Eckert, J. K. and J. Haug.  The Impact of Forced Residential
Relocation on the Health of the Elderly Hotel Dweller.
Journal of Gerontology.  39(6):753-55, 1984.

Eckert, J. K. and J. Murrey.  Alternative Modes of Living for
the Elderly.  Pp. 95-128 in M. P. Lawton, J. F. Wohlwill,
and I. Altman (eds). Environments for the Elderly.  Vol.
7. Human Behavior and Environment.  New York, NY:  Plenum,

1984.

Erickson, R. and J. K. Eckert. The Elderly Poor in Downtown San Diego Hotels. Gerontologist. 17:440-46, 1977.

Evans, R. and L. Northwood. The Utility of Locality Based Social Networks. Journal of Minority Aging. 3:199-211, 1978.

Gibson, M. J. Family Support Patterns, Programs, and Policies. In C. Nusberg, M. J. Gibson, and S. Peace (eds). Innovative Aging Programs Abroad: Implications for the US. Westport, CT: Greenwood Press, 1984.

Graney, M. Happiness and Social Participation in Old Age. Journal of Gerontology. 30:701-06, 1975.

Granick, R. and L. Nahemow. Preadmission Isolation as a Factor in Adjustment to an Old Age Home. Pp. 285-92 in P. Hoch and J. Zubin (eds). Psychopathology of Aging. New York, NY: Grune and Stratton, 1961.

Gurland, G., et al. The Mind and Mood of Aging: Mental Health Problems of the Community Elderly in New York and London. New York, NY: Haworth Press, 1983.

This study based on the United States-United Kingdom Cross-National Geriatric Community Study of the health and social problems of the over 65 examines incidence of psychiatric problems in New York and London.

Hayse, G. and A. Blevine, Jr. Primary Group Interaction of Residents in a Retirement Hotel. International Journal of Aging and Human Development. 6(3):183-229, 1975.

Hess, B. Friendship. Pp. 357-93 in M. Riley, et al. (eds). Aging and Society. New York, NY: Russell Sage Foundation, 1972.

Ikels, C. The Process of Caretaker Selection. Research on Aging. 5(4):491-510, 1983.

_____ Older Immigrants and Natural Helpers. Journal of Cross-Cultural Gerontology. 1(2)209-22, 1986.

Johnson, C. and D. Catalano. Childless Elderly and Their Family Supports. Gerontologist. 21:610-18, 1981.

Jonas, K. and E. Wellin. Dependency and Reciprocity: Home Health Aid in an Elderly Population. Pp. 217-38 in C. Fry (ed). Aging in Culture and Society: Comparative Viewpoints and Strategies. Brooklyn, NY: J. F. Bergin, 1980.

Kahn, R. Aging and Social Support. Pp. 77-91 in M. Riley (ed). Aging From Birth to Death. AAAS Selected Symposia Series. Boulder, CO: Westview, 1979.

Kendig, H. (ed). Ageing and Families: A Support Networks Perspective. Sydney, Australia: Allen and Unwin, 1986.

Kent, D., C. Hirsch, and S. Barg. Indigenous Workers as a Crucial Link in the Total Support System for Low-Income, Minority Group Aged. Aging and Human Development. 2:189-96, 1971.

Lawton, M., M. Kleban, and M. Singer. The Aged Jewish Person and the Slum Environment. Journal of Gerontology. 26(2):231-39, 1971.

Lieberman, G. Children of the Elderly as Natural Helpers: Some Demographic Difference. American Journal of Community Psychology. 6:489-98, 1978.

Lopata, H. The Social Involvement of American Widows. Behavioral Scientist. 14(1):41-48, 1970.

_____ Support Systems of Elderly: Chicago of the 1970's. Gerontologist. 15:35-41, 1975.

_____ Support Systems of Urban Widows. Family Coordinator. 27(4):383-88, 1978a.

_____ The Absence of Community Resources in Support Systems of Urban Widows. Family Coordinator. 27(4):383-88, 1978b.

_____ Contributions of Extended Families and the Support System of Metropolitan-Area Widows. Limitations of the Modified Kin Network. Journal of Marriage and the Family. 40:355-64, 1978c.

Lowenthal, M. and B. Robinson. Social Networks and Isolation. In R. Binstock and E. Shanas (eds). Handbook of Aging and the Social Sciences. New York, NY: Van Nostrand, 1976.

Lowenthal, M., et al. Life Course Perspectives on Friendship. Pp. 48-71 in M. Lowenthal, et al. (eds). Four Stages of Life. San Francisco, CA: Jossey-Bass, 1975.

Mayer, P. (ed). Socialization: The Approach from Social Anthropology. London, UK: Tavistock, 1970.

Munnichs, J. Loneliness, Isolation and Social Relations in Old Age. Pp. 484-91 in Age With a Future. Proceedings of the 6th International Congress of Gerontology, Copenhagen 1963. Philadelphia, PA: F. A. Davis Company, 1964.

Pilsuk, M. and M. Minkler. Supportive Networks: Life Ties for the Elderly. Journal of Social Issues. 36:95-116, 1981.

Robertson, J. Women in Midlife: Crises, Reverberations, and Support Networks. Family Coordinator. 27(4):375-82, 1978.

Rooney, J. Friendship and Disaffiliation Among the Skid Row Population. Journal of Gerontology. 31(1):82-89, 1976.

Rosenberg, G.  Age, Poverty and Isolation from Friends in the
    Urban Working Class.  Journal of Gerontology.  23:533-39,
    1968.

Rosow, I.  Old People:  Their Friends and Neighbors.  American
    Behavioral Scientist.  14:59-69, 1970.

Ruffini, J. and H. Todd.  A Network Model for Leadership
    Development Among the Elderly.  Gerontologist.
    19(2):158-62, 1979a.

_____  Community Network Developing in Older Residential
    Areas.  Generations.  3(3):19, 1979b.

_____  Neighborhood Injustices:  Aging in a Changing
    Neighborhood Environment.  In M. Lawton (ed).  Community
    Housing Choices for Older Americans.  New York, NY:
    Springer, 1980.

Schmitz-Scherzer, R.  Interaction of Personality, SES, and
    Social Participation in Old Age.  Pp. 621-27 in K. Riegel
    and J. Meacham (eds).  The Developing Indvidual in a
    Changing World.  Chicago, IL:  Aldine, 1976.

Shanas, E.  Family Help Patterns and Social Class in Three
    Countries.  In B. Neugarten (ed).  Middle Age and Aging.
    Chicago, IL:  University of Chicago Press, 1968.

_____  Family-Kin Networks and Aging in a Cross-Cultural
    Perspective.  Journal of Marriage and the Family.
    35(3):505-11, 1973.

_____  The Family as a Social Support System in Old Age.
    Gerontologist.  192:169-74, 1979.

Siegal, H.  Outposts of the Forgotten, New York City's Welfare
    Hotels and Single Room Occupancy Tenements.  Edison, NJ:
    Transaction Books, 1977.

Sokolovsky, J. and C. Cohen.  Being Old in the Inner City:
    Support Systems of the SRO Aged.  Pp. 163-84 in C. Fry
    (ed).  Dimensions:  Aging, Culture, and Health.  Brooklyn,
    NY:  J. F. Bergin, 1981.

    Social network mapping reveals the support systems of SRO
    dwellers in New York.  Methodologically significant because
    the technique reveals support that is explicitly denied in
    response to more general questions, because many SRO
    residents place a high value on being "loners."

_____  Networks as Adaptation:  The Cultural Meaning of Being
    a "Loner" Among the Inner-City Elderly.  Pp. 189-201 in J.
    Sokolovsky (ed).  Growing Old in Different Societies:
    Cross-Cultural Perspectives.  Acton, MA:  Copley Press,
    1987.

_____  Uncle Ed, Super Runner and the Fry Cook:  Old Men in
    the Street in the 1980's.  Pp. 277-88 in J. Sokolovsky

(ed).  The Cultural Context of Aging:  Worldwide
Perspectives.  Westport CT:  Bergin and Garvey, 1990.

Stephens, J.  Society of the Alone:  Freedom, Privacy, and
Utilitarianism as Dominant Norms in the SRO.  Journal of
Gerontology.  30(2):230-35, 1975.

_____  Loners, Losers and Lovers:  A Sociological Study of the
Aged Tenants of a Slum Hotel.  Seattle, WA:  University of
Washington Press, 1976.

Stephens, R., et al.  Aging, Social Support Systems and Social
Policy.  Journal of Gerontological Social Work.  1:33-45,
1978.

Sterne, R., J. Phillips, and A. Rabushka.  The Urban Elderly
Poor:  Racial and Bureaucratic Conflict.  Lexington, MA:
Lexington Books, 1974.

Swenson, C.  Social Networks, Mutual Aid and the Life Model of
Practice.  Pp. 213-38 in C. Germain (ed).  Social Work
Practice:  People and Environments.  New York, NY:
Columbia University Press, 1979.

Tissue, T.  Old Age, Poverty, and the Central City.  Aging and
Human Development.  2:235-48, 1971.

Tobin, S. and B. Neugarten.  Life Satisfaction and Social
Interaction in the Aging.  Journal of Gerontology.
16:344-46, 1961.

U. S. Congress.  Senate.  Special Committee on Aging.  Single
Room Occupancy:  A Need for National Concern:  An
Information Paper.  Washington, DC:  US Government Printing
Office, 1978.

Vesperi, M.  City of Green Benches.  Ithaca, NY:  Cornell
Univesrity Press, 1985.

Wagner, D. and N. Chapman.  Informal Group Interaction,
Informal Supports and Neighborhood Environment:
Perspectives on the Frail, Urban Elderly.  Networks for
Helping:  Illustrations from Research And Practice.
Proceedings of the Conference on Networks.  Portland, OR:
Regional Research Institute for Human Services, 1980.

Weeks, J. and J. Cuellar.  The Role of Family Members in the
Helping Networks of Older People.  Gerontologist.
21(4):388-94, 1981.

Wenger, G. C.  The Supportive Network:  Coping with Old Age.
London, UK:  Allen and Unwin, 1984.

_____  A Longitudinal Study of Changes and Adaptation in the
Support Networks of Welsh Elderly Over 75.  Journal of
Cross-Cultural Gerontology.  1(3):277-304, 1986.

Wentowski, G.  Reciprocity and the Coping Strategies of Older

People:  Cultural Dimensions of Network Building.
Gerontologist.  21:600-09, 1982.

Worauch-Kardas, H.  Family and Neighbourly Relations--Their
Role for the Elderly.  In G. Dooghe and J. Helander (eds).
Family Life in Old Age.  The Hague, The Netherlands:
Martinus Nijhoff, 1979.

Zborowski, M. and L. Eyde.  Aging and Social Participation.
Journal of Gerontology.  17:4, 1962.

# 11

# Women

Akiyama, H., T. Antonucci, and R. Campbell. Exchange and Reciprocity Among Two Generations of Japanese and American Women. Pp. 127-38 in J. Sokolovsky (ed). The Cultural Context of Aging: Worldwide Perspectives. Westport, CT: Bergin and Garvey, 1990.

Albert, E. Women of Burundi: A Study of Social Values. Pp. 179-215 in B. Pauline (ed). Women in Tropical Africa. Translated by H. M. Wright. Berkeley and Los Angeles, CA: University of California Press, 1981.

Alter, G. Family and the Female Life Course: The Women of, Verviers, Belgium--1849-1880. Madison, WI: University of Wisconsin Press, 1988.

Barbee, E. L. Feeling Older and Wanting to Be Younger. Journal of Cross-Cultural Gerontology. 3(3):209-22, 1988.

Barrett, C. Women in Widowhood. Signs. 2:856-68, 1977.

Bart, P. Why Women's Status Changes in Middle Age. Sociological Symposium. 3:1-18, 1969.

_____ Depression in Middle-Aged Women. Pp. 3-21 in V. Gornick and B. Moran (eds). Woman in a Sexist Society. New York, NY: Signet New American Library, 1972.

_____ Emotional and Social Status of the Older Woman. Pp. 3-21 in No Longer Young: The Older Woman in America. Proceedings of the 26th Annual Conference on Aging. Ann Arbor, MI: Institute of Gerontology, University of Michigan, 1975.

Bastida, E. (ed). Older Women: Current Issues and Problems. Convergence in Aging. Mid-America Congress on Aging. Vol. 2. 1984.

Beeson, D. Women in Aging Studies: A Critique and Suggestion. Social Problems. 23:52-59, 1975

Bell, I.  The Double Standard.  Transaction.  8:75-88.  1970.

Bell, M.  (ed).  Women as Elders -- The Feminist Politics of Aging.  New York, NY:  Harrington Park Press, 1986.

Bever, E.  Old Age and Witchcraft in Early Modern Europe.  Pp. 150-90 in P. Stearns (ed).  Old Age in Preindustrial Society.  New York, NY:  Holmes and Meier, 1982.

Blau, Z.  Old Age in a Changing Society.  New York, NY:  New Viewpoints, 1973.

Block, M., J. Davidson, and J. Grambs.  Women Over Forty -- Visions and Realities.  New York, NY:  Springer, 1981.

Boellhoff, C. and N. Datan.  The Competent Older Woman.  Pp. 57-72 in N. Datan and N. Lohmann (eds).  Transitions of Aging.  New York, NY:  Academic Press, 1980.

Boyd, J. and M. Last.  The Role of Women as Agents Religieux in Sokoto.  Canadian Journal of African Studies. 19(2):283-300, 1985.

Brown, J. K.  Cross-Cultural Perspectives on Middle-Aged Women.  Current Anthropology.  23(2):143-56, 1982.

    Cross-cultural studies suggest that as women age beyond the childbearing years, they are freed from a variety of restrictions, are given authority over certain kin, and are provided with the opportunity for achievement and recognition beyond the household.  The article documents these positive changes, discusses theories that explain improvement in older women's status, and analyzes why these changes are more dramatic in some societies than others.

Brown, J. K. and V. Kerns (eds).  In Her Prime:  A New View of Middle-Aged Women.  South Hadley, MA:  Bergin and Garvey, 1985.

    This collection of papers arose from a 1982 session at the American Anthropological Association and provides description and analysis of the similarities and differences in the experiences of middle-aged women in eleven societies, six of which are small-scale traditional or intermediate societies (the !Kung San of Botswana, the Bakgalagadi of Botswana, the Mayotte of the Comoro Islands, the Garifuna of Belize and the people of rural northern Sudan).  The book also includes a chapter on an evolutionary perspective on menopause, a chapter analyzing development perspectives for the vital older woman as well as an introductory chapter that discusses the changes that middle-age brings in the lives of women.

Cain, M., S. Khanam, and S. Nahar.  Class, Patriarchy and Women's Work in Bangladesh.  Population and Development Review.  5:405-38, 1979.

Campbell, R. and E. Brody.  Women's Changing Roles and Help to

the Elderly:  Attitudes of Women in the United States and
Japan.  Gerontologist.  25(6):584-92, 1985.

Chevan, A. and J. Korson.  Living Arrangements of Widows in
the United States and Israel, 1960 and 1961.  Demography.
12:505-18, 1975.

Cohen, L.  Small Expectations -- Society's Betrayal of Older
Women.  Toronto, Canada:  McClelland and Stewart, 1984.

Cohler, B. J. and H. U. Grunebaum.  Mothers, Grandmothers, and
Daughters:  Personality and Childcare in Three-Generation
Families.  New York, NY:  John Wiley, 1981.

This book discusses personality and the concerns of
childcare in Italian-American families.

Coles, C.  The Older Woman in Hausa Society:  Power and
Authority in Urban Nigeria.  Pp. 57-82 in J. Sokolovsky
(ed).  The Cultural Context of Aging:  Worldwide
Perspectives.  Westport, CT:  Bergin and Garvey, 1990.

Cool, L.  Role Continuity or Crisis in Later Life?  A Corsican
Case.  Aging and Human Development.  13(3):169-81, 1981.

Cool, L. and J. McCabe.  The 'Scheming Hag' and the Dear Old
Thing:  The Anthropology of Aging Women.  Pp. 56-68 in J.
Sokolovsky (ed).  Growing Old in Different Societies:
Cross-Cultural Perspectives.  Acton, MA:  Copley Press,
1987.

This chapter is a cross-cultural exploration of the aging
process for women, with an emphasis on women's increased
power.  Contrasts are made between sex-role leveling of
women in the U. S. and role reversal for women in
nonindustrial societies.  Two case studies from
Mediterranean societies present the path to power and
dominance.

Daly, F.  To Be Black, Poor, Female and Old.  Freedomways.
16:222-29, 1976.

Datan, N., A. Antonovsky, and B. Maoz.  A Time To Reap:  The
Middle Age of Women in Five Israeli Sub-Cultures.
Baltimore, MD:  Johns Hopkins University Press, 1981.

Department of Aging, City of New York.  Older Women in the
City.  New York, NY:  Arno Press, 1979.

de Beauvoir, S.  The Second Sex.  New York, NY:  Random House,
1953.

Dougherty, M.  An Anthropological Perspective on Aging and
Women in the Middle Years.  Pp. 177-91 in E. Bauwens (ed).
The Anthropology of Health.  St. Louis, MO:  C. V. Mosby,
1978.

Ellickson, J.  Never the Twain Shall Meet:  Aging Men and

Women in Bangladesh. Journal of Cross-Cultural Gerontology. 3(1):53-70, 1988.

Faulkner, A. O. and M. Micchelli. The Aging, the Aged, and the Very Old: Women the Policy Makers Forgot. Journal of Women and Health. 14(3-4):5-19, 1988.

Fennell, V. Friendship and Kinship in Older Women's Organizations: Curlew Point, 1973. Pp. 131-43 in C. Fry (ed). Dimensions: Aging, Culture, and Health. Brooklyn, NY: Bergin, 1981.

Fuller, M. and C. Martin (eds). Older Woman: Lavendar Rose or Gray Panther. Springfield, IL: Charles C. Thomas, 1980.

Gee, E. Issei Women. Pp. 359-64 in E. Gee (ed). Counterpoint: Perspectives on Asian America. Los Angeles, CA: Asian American Studies Center, University of California, 1976.

Gee, E. M. Women and Aging. Toronto, Canada: Butterworths, 1987.

Gibson, M. J. Older Women Around the World. Washington, DC: International Federation on Ageing, 1985.

Heisel, M. A. Older Women in Developing Countries. Women and Health. 14(3-4):253-72, 1988.

Herzog, A. R., K. C. Holden, and M. M. Seltzer (eds), Health and Economic Status of Older Women. Amityville, NY: Baywood, 1989.

Hess, B. Old Women: Problems, Potentials, and Policy Implications. Pp. 39-60 in E. Markson and G. Batra (eds). Public Policies for an Aging Population. Lexington, MA: Lexington Books, 1980.

_____ Older Women in the City. Pp. 124-38 in C. Stimpson, et al (eds). Women and the American City. Chicago, IL: University of Chicago Press, 1981.

Himes, J. and M. Hamlett. The Assessment of Adjustment of Aged Negro Women in a Southern City. Phylon. 23:139-48, 1962.

Holley, M. R. Elderly Women in Developing Societies: An Examination of the Social Exchange Model. Pp. 15-32 in J. Morgan (ed). Aging in Developing Societies: A Reader in Third World Gerontology. Bristol, IN: Wyndham Hall Press, 1985.

Holloway, K. and S. Demetrakopoulos. Remembering Our Foremothers: Older Black Women, Politics of Age, Politics of Survival as Embodied in the Novels of Toni Morrison. Pp. 13-34 in M. Bell (ed). Women as Elders -- The Feminist Politics of Aging. New York, NY: Harrington Park Press,

1986.

Huseby-Darvas, E. V.  Elderly Women in a Hungarian Village:
   Childlessness, Generativity, and Social Control.  Journal
   of Cross-Cultural Gerontology.  2(1):15-42, 1987.

Jackson, J. J.  Comparative Lifestyles and Family and Friend
   Relationships Among Older Black Women.  Family Coordinator.
   21:477-85, 1972.

_____ Aging Black Women.  Washington, DC:  The National
   Caucus on the Black Aged, 1975.

_____ Plights of Older Black Women in the United States.
   Black Aging.  1:12-20, 1976.

_____ Older Black Women.  Pp. 182-86 in L. Troll, J. Israel,
   and  K. Israel (eds).  Looking Ahead, A Woman's Guide to
   the Problems and Joys of Growing Old.  Englewood Cliffs,
   NJ:  Prentice-Hall, 1977.

_____ Epidemiological Aspects of Mental Illness Among Aged
   Black Women and Men.  The Journal of Minority Aging.
   4:76-87, 1979.

Johansson, S.  Longevity in Women.  Cardiovascular Clinics.
   19:3-16, 1989.

Jones, F.  The Lofty Role of the Black Grandmother.  The
   Crisis.  80:19-21, 1973.

Kaberry, P.  Aboriginal Women:  Sacred and Profane.  New York,
   NY:  Gordon Press, 1973.

Kassel, V.  Polygyny After Sixty.  Geriatrics.  21:137-43,
   1966.

Kay, M., et al.  The Health and Symptom Care of Widows.
   Journal of Cross-Cultural Gerontology.  3(3):197-208, 1988.

Kerns, V.  Aging and Mutual Support Relations Among the Black
   Carib.  Pp. 112-25 in C. Fry (ed).  Aging in Culture and
   Society:  Comparative Viewpoints and Strategies.  Brooklyn,
   NY:  Bergin, 1980.

_____ Women and the Ancestors -- Black Carib Kinship and
   Ritual.  Champagne/Urbana, IL:  University of Illinois
   Press, 1983.

Kivett, V.  Loneliness and the Rural Widow.  Family
   Coordinator.  27(4):389-94, 1978.

Kline, D.  The Socialization Process of Women.  Gerontologist.
   15:486-92, 1975.

Langner, T.  Psychological Symptoms and the Status of Women in
   Two Mexican Communities.  Pp. 360-92 in J. Murphy and A.
   Leighton (eds).  Approaches to Cross-Cultural Psychiatry.

Ithaca, NY:  Cornell University Press, 1965.

Lesnoff-Caravaglia, G. (ed).  The World of the Older Woman --
     Conflicts and Resolutions.  New York, NY:  Human Sciences
     Press, 1984.

Lewis, M. and R. Butler.  Why is Women's Lib Ignoring the
     Older Woman.  Aging and Human Development.  3(3):223-31,
     1972.

Lopata, H.  Widows as a Minority Group.  Gerontologist.
     11(1):67-77, 1971.

_____  Role Changes in Widowhood:  A World Perspective.  Pp.
     275-304 in D. Cowgill and L. Holmes (eds).  Aging and
     Modernization.  New York, NY:  Appleton Century-Crofts,
     1972a.

_____  Social Relations of Widows in Urbanizing Societies.
     Sociological Quarterly.  13:259-71, 1972b.

_____  Widowhood in an American City.  Cambridge, MA:
     Schenkman, 1973.

_____  Women as Widows: Support Systems.  New York, NY:
     Elsevier, 1979.

     See especially the chapter entitled "Widowhood, Other
     Places, Other Times."

Makiesky-Barrow, S. and A. M. Lovell.  Homelessness and the
     Limited Options of Older Women.  Association for
     Anthropology and Gerontology Newsletter.  8(4):3-6, 1987.

Markson, E. W. (ed).  Older Women -- Issues and Prospects.
     Lexington, MA:  D. C. Heath, 1983.

Mathews, S.  The Social World of Old Women.  Beverly Hills,
     CA:  Sage, 1979.

Mathison, J.  A Cross-Cultural View of Widowhood.  Omega.
     1:201-18, 1970.

Matthews, S.  The Social World of Old Women:  Management of
     Self-Identity.  Beverly Hills, CA:  Sage, 1979.

Moss, Z.  It Hurts to Be Alive and Obsolete, or, The Aging
     Woman.  Pp. 170-75 in R. Morgan (ed).  Sisterhood is
     Powerful.  New York, NY:  Vintage Books, 1970.

Murphy, Y. and R. Murphy.  Women of the Forest.  New York, NY:
     Columbia University Press, 1974.

Myerhoff, B.  Bobbes and Zeddes:  Old and New Roles for
     Elderly Jews.  Pp. 207-41 in J. Hoch-Smith and A. Spring
     (eds).  Women in Ritual and Symbolic Roles.  New York, NY:
     Plenum Press, 1978.

Nelson, M.  Why Witches Were Women.  Pp. 335-56 in J. Freeman
    (ed).  Woman:  A Feminist Perspective (2nd ed).  Palo Alto,
    CA:  Mayfield, 1979.

Network News.

    A Newsletter of the Global Link for Midlife and Older
    Women.

Padgett, D.  Aging Minority Women:  Issues in Research and
    Health Policy.  Women and Health.  14(3-4):213-25, 1988.

Palmore, E.  Cross-Cultural Perspectives on Widowhood.
    2(1):93-105, 1987.

Pfeiffer, E.  Sexual Behavior in Old Age.  Pp. 130-41 E. Busse
    and E.  Pfeiffer (eds).  Behavior and Adaptation in Late
    Life.  Boston, MA:  Little, Brown and Company, 1969.

Pihlblad, C. and D. Adams.  Widowhood, Social Participation
    and Life Satisfaction.  Aging and Human Development.
    3:323-30, 1972.

Preston, C.  An Old Bag:  The Stereotype of the Older Woman.
    Pp. 41-45 in No Longer Young:  The Older Woman in America.
    Proceedings of 26th Annual Conference on Aging.  Ann Arbor,
    MI:  Institute of Gerontology, University of Michigan,
    1975.

Richeck, H., O. Chuculate, and D. Klinert.  Aging and
    Ethnicity in Healthy Elderly Women.  Geriatrics.
    26:146-52, 1971.

Roebuck, J.  Grandma as Revolutionary:  Elderly Women and Some
    Modern Patterns of Social Change.  International Journal on
    Aging and Human Development.  17(4):249-66, 1983.

Rossi, A.  Life-Span Theories and Women's Lives.  Signs:
    Journal of Women in Culture and Society.  6(1):432, 1980.

Roth, J.  Shopping Bag Ladies of New York.  New York, NY:
    Pilgrim Press, 1982.

Sanchez-Ayendez, M.  Puerto Rican Elderly Women:  The Cultural
    Dimension of Social Support Networks.  Women and Health.
    14(3-4):239-52, 1988.

Sankar, A.  The Conquest of Solitude:  Singlehood and Old Age
    in Traditional Chinese Society.  Pp. 85-107 in C. Fry (ed).
    Dimensions:  Aging, Culture and Health.  Brooklyn, NY:
    1981.

Seltzer, M.  Jewish-American Grandmothers.  Pp. 157-61 in L.
    Troll, J.  Israel, and K. Israel (eds).  Looking Ahead:  A
    Woman's Guide to Problems and Joys of Growing Old.
    Englewood Cliffs, NJ:  Prentice-Hall, 1977.

Sennott-Miller, L (ed).  Mid-Life and Older Women in Latin

America and the Caribbean. Washington, DC:   American
Association of Retired Persons, 1989.

Sheehan, N.  Planned Obsolesence:  Historical Perspectives on
Aging Women.  Pp. 59-68 in K. Riegel and J. Meacham (eds).
The Developing Individual in a Changing World.  Vol. 1.
Chicago, IL:  IL:  Aldine, 1976.

Sinnott, J.  Sex-Role Inconstancy, Biology and Successful
Aging.  Gerontologist.  17(5):459-63, 1977.

Sontag, S.  The Double Standard of Aging.  Pp. 31-39 in No
Longer Young:  The Older Woman in America.  Proceedings of
the 26th Conference on Aging.  Ann Arbor, MI:  Institute of
Gerontology, University of Michigan, 1975.

Sterling, N.  Black Foremothers--Three Lives.  Old Westbury,
NY:  The Feminist Press, 1979.

Troll, L.  Development of the Cognitively Complex Woman Over
the Generations.  Pp. 81-87 in No Longer Young:  The Older
Woman in America.  Proceedings of the 26th Annual
Conference on Aging.  Ann Arbor, MI:  Institute of
Gerontology, University of Michigan, 1975.

Vatuk, S.  The Aging Woman in India:  Self-Perceptions and
Changing Roles.  Pp. 142-63 in A. de Souza (ed).  Women in
Contemporary India.  New Delhi, India:  Manohar Press,
1975.

Ward, B.  Men, Women and Change:  An Essay in Understanding
Social Roles in South and Southeast Asia.  Pp. 25-99 in B.
Ward (ed).  Women of The New Asia.  Paris:  UNESCO, 1963.

Wentowski, G. J.  Older Women's Perceptions of Great-
Grandmotherhood:  A Research Note.  Gerontologist.
25:593-96, 1985.

Williams, H.  Social Isolation and the Elderly Immigrant
Woman.  Pp. 1-14 in J. Morgan (ed).  Aging in Developing
Societies:  A Reader in Third World Gerontology.  Bristol,
IN:  Wyndham Hall Press, 1985.

Youmans, E.  Family Disengagement Among Older Urban and Rural
Women.  Journal of Gerontology.  22:209-11, 1967.

## WOMEN AND MENOPAUSE

Abe, T. and T. Mortisuka.  A Case-Control Study of Climacteric
Symptoms and Complaints of Japanese Women by Somatic Type
for Psychosocial Variables.  Maturitas.  80(3):255-65,
1986.

Agoestina, T. and P. van Keep.  The Climacteric in Bamdung,
West Java Province, Indonesia:  A Survey of 1025 Women
Between 40-55 Years of Age.  Maturitas.  6(4):327-33, 1984.

Ballinger, S.  Psychosocial Stress and Symptoms of Menopause: A Comparative Study of Menopause Clinic Patients and Non-Patients. Maturitas. 7(4):315 -27, 1985.

Bharadwaj, J., S. Kendurkar, and P. Vaidya.  Age and Symptomatology of Menopause in Indian Women. Journal of Postgraduate Medicine. 29(4):218-22, 1983.

Brand, P. and P. Lehent.  A New Way of Looking at Environmental Variables that May Affect Age at Menopause. Maturitas. 1(2):121-32, 1978.

Bungay, G., M. Vessey, and C. McPherson.  Study of Symptoms in Middle Life with Special Reference to Menopause. British Medical Journal.  281(6234):181-83, 1980.

Butler, R. and M. Lewis. Sex After 60. New York, NY:  Harper and Row, 1976.

Campagnoli, C., et al.  Climacteric Symptoms According to Body Weight in Women of Different Socio-Economic Groups. Maturitas.  3(3-4):279-87, 1981.

Campbell, S. (ed).  The Management of the Menopause and Post-Menopause Years.  Baltimore, MD:  University Park Press, 1976.

Channon, L. and S. Ballinger.  Some Aspects of Sexuality and Vaginal Symptoms During Menopause and Their Relation to Anxiety and Depression. British Journal of Medical Psychology.  59:173-80, 1986.

Cutler, W. and C. Garcia.  The Medical Management of the Menopause and Pre-Menopause.  Philadelphia, PA:  J. P. Lippincott, 1984.

Dans, O.  Women's Status and Experience of the Menopause in a Newfoundland Fishing Village. Maturitas.  4(3):207-16, 1982.

_____  The Newfoundland Change of Life:  Insights into the Medicalization of Menopause. Journal of Cross-Cultural Gerontology.  4(1):49-74, 1989.

Dinnerstein, L. and G. Butrows.  A Review of Studies of the Psychological Symptoms Found at the Menopause. Maturitas. 1(1):55-64, 1978.

Doress, P. and D. Siegal, and the Mid-Life Older Women's Book Project. Ourselves Growing Older. New York, NY:  Simon and Schuster, 1987.

Dowty,N., et al.  Climacterium in Three Culture Contexts. Tropical and Geographical Medicine.  22:77-86, 1970.

du Toit, B. M. Aging and Menopause Among Indian South African Women. Ithaca, NY:  State University of New York Press, 1990.

Flint, M.  The Menopause:  Reward or Punishment?
Psychosomatics.  16:161-63, 1975.

_____  Transcultural Influences in Peri-Menopause.  Pp. 41-56
in A. Haspells and H. Musaph (eds).  Psychosomatics in
Peri-Menopause.  Lancaster, UK:  MTP Press Limited, 1976a.

_____  Cross-Cultural Factors that Affect Age of Menopause.
Pp. 73-83 in P. van Keep, R. Greenblatt, and M. Albeaux-
Fernet (eds).  Consensus on Menopause Research.  Lancaster,
UK:  MTP Press, 1976b.

_____  Is There a Secular Trend in Age of Menopause?
Maturitas.  1(2):133-39, 1978.

_____  Sociology and Anthropology of the Menopause.  In P. van
Keep, D. Seer, and R. Greenblatt (eds).  Female and Male
Climacteric.  Baltimore, MD:  University Park Press
1979a.

_____  Culture and the Climacteric.  Supplement 6.  Journal of
Biosocial Science.  1979b.

_____  Anthropological Perspectives of the Menopause and
Middle Age.  Maturitas.  4(3):173-80, 1982.

Flint, M. and M. Garcia.  Culture and the Climacteric.
Journal of Biosocial Science.  Supplement.  6:197-215,
1979.

Flint, M., F. Kronenberg, and W. Utian (eds).
Multidisciplinary Perspectives on the Menopause.  New York,
NY:  New York Academy of Sciences, 1990.

Gambrell, R. (ed).  The Menopause.  Philadelphia, PA:
Obstetrics and Gynecology Clinics of North America.  W. B.
Saunders, 1987.

Generations.  Gender and Aging.  14(3), 1990.

Goodman, M., J. Grove, and F. Gilbert.  Age At Menopause in
Relation to Reproductive History in Japanese, Caucasian,
Chinese, and Hawaiian Women Living in Hawaii.  Journal of
Gerontology.  33(5):668-94, 1978.

Goodman, M., C. Stewart, and F. Gilbert.  Patterns of
Menopause, A Study of Certain Medical and Physiological
Variables Among Caucasian and Japanese Women Living in
Hawaii.  Journal of Gerontology.  32:291-98, 1977.

Greenberg, G., S. Thompson, and T. Meade.  Relation Between
Cigarette Smoking and Use of Hormonal Replacement Therapy
for Menopausal Symptoms.  Journal of Epidemiological
Community Health.  4(1):26-29, 1987.

Greenblatt, R. (ed).  A Modern Approach to the Perimenopausal
Years.  New York, NY:  De Gruyter, 1986.

Greene, J.  The Social and Psychological Origins of the Climacteric Syndrome.  Brookfield, VT:  Gower, 1984.

Greenwood, S.  Menopause Naturally.  San Francisco, CA: Volcano Press, 1984.

Hagstad, A. and P. Janson.  The Epidemiology of Climacteric Symptoms.  Acta Obstretrics Gynecology Scandinavia. 134:59-65, 1986.

Haspels, A. and H. Musaph (eds).  Psychosomatics in Perimenopause.  Lancaster, UK:  MTP Press, 1979.

Hunter, M., R. Battersby, and M. Whitehead.  Relationships Between Psychological Symptoms, Somatic Complaints and Menopausal Status.  Maturitas.  8(3):217-28, 1986.

Jackson, J.  Menopausal Attitudes and Behaviors Among Senescent Black Women and Descriptions of Changing Attitudes and Activities Among Aged Blacks.  Black Aging. 1:8-18, 1976.

Journal of Women and Aging.

Judd, H.  Aging, Reproduction and the Climacteric.  New York, NY:  Plenum Press, 1983.

Kaufert, P. and J. Syrotuin.  Symptom Reporting at the Menopause.  Social Science Medicine.  Part E.  Psychology. 15(3):173-84, 1981.

Kaufman, D., et al.  Cigarette-Smoking and Age at Natural Menopause.  American Journal of Public Health. 70(4):420-22, 1980.

Kay, M, et al.  Ethnography of the Menopause-Related Hot Flash.  Marurits.  4(3):217-27, 1982.

Leiblum, S. R. and L. C. Swartzman.  Women's Attitudes Toward the Menopause:  An Update.  Maturitas.  8(1):47-56, 1986.

Lindquest, O., et al.  Effect of Age and Menopause on Osteoporosis.  Scandinavian Journal of Social Medicine. 14:80-84, 1980.

Locu, M.  Models and Practice in Medicine:  Menopause as Syndrome or Life Transition?  Culture, Medicine and Psychiatry.  6(3):261-80, 1982.

Maoz, B., et al.  Female Attitudes to Menopause.  Social Psychology.  5(1):35, 1970.

Maoz, B., et al.  The Effect of Outside Work on the Menopausal Woman.  Maturitas.  1(1):43-53, 1978.

Maturitas.

   Maturitas is the journal of the International Menopause

Society.  It covers topics in any discipline related to the menopause.

McKinley, S., N. Bifano, and J. McKinley.  Smoking and Age at Menopause in Women.  Annals of Internal Medicine. 103(3):350-56, 1985.

Moore, B.  Climacteric Symptoms in an African Community. Maturitas.  3(1):25-29, 1981.

Nachtigill, L. and J. Heilman.  Estrogen:  The Facts Can Change Your Life.  New York, NY:  Harper and Row, 1986.

Notelovitz, M, P. van Keep, and D. Serr (eds).  The Climacteric in Perspective.  Proceedings of the 4th International Congress on the Menopause.  Lancaster, UK: MTP Press, 1984.

Porcino, J.  Growing Older, Getting Better.  Reading, MA: Addison-Wesley, 1983.

Reitz, R.  Menopause:  A Positive Approach.  New York, NY: Penguin Books, 1977.

Rosenthal, M.  Psychological Aspects of Menopause.  Primary Care.  6(2):357-64, 1979.

Talukdar, S.  Age of Menopause in India.  Menopause Journal of India.  57(4):345-50, 1977.

Townsend, J.  Menopause Syndrome:  Illness of Social Role--A Transcultural Analysis.  Culture, Medicine and Psychiatry. 4(3):229-48, 1980.

Uphold, C. and E. Susman.  Childrearing, Marital, Recreational and Work Role Integration and Climacteric Symptoms in Midlife Women.  Research Nursing Health.  8(1):73-81, 1985.

Utian, W.  Your Middle Years:  A Doctor's Guide for Today's Women.  New York, NY:  Appleton-Century-Crofts, 1980.

van Keep, P., R. Greenblatt, and M. Albeaux-Fernet (eds).  The Management of the Menopause.  Proceedings of the 1st International Congress on the Menopause.  Lancaster, UK: MTP Press, 1976.

van Keep, P. and H. Prill.  Psycho-Sociology of Menopause and Post-Menopause.  Frontiers of Hormone Research.  3:32-39, 1975.

van Keep, P., D. Serr, and R. Greenblatt.  Female and Male Climacteric:  Current Opinions.  Baltimore, MD:  University Park Press, 1979.

van Keep, P., W. Utian, and A. Vermeulen (eds).  The Controversial Climacteric.  Proceedings of the 3rd International Congress on the Menopause.  Lancaster, UK: MTP Press, 1981.

Voda, A., M. Dinnerstein, and S. O'Donnell. Changing
    Perspectives on Menopause. Austin, TX:  University of
    Texas Press, 1982.

Waltisch, S., H. Antonovsky, and B. Maoz.  Relationship
    Between Biological Changes and Symptoms and Health
    Behaviour During the Climacteric.  Maturitas.  6(1):9-17,
    1984.

Weiderger, P.  Menstruation and Menopause.  New York, NY:
    Delta, 1977.

Wilbush, J.  Historical Perspectives, Climacteric Expression
    and Social Context.  Maturitas.  4(3):195-205, 1982.

_____ Surveys of Climacteric Semeiology in Nonwestern
    Populations:  A Critique.  Maturitas.  7(4):289-96, 1985.

# 12

# Death and Dying

Ablon, J.  The Samoan Funeral in Urban America.  Ethnology.
    9:209-27, 1970.

Anderson, B.  Bereavement as a Subject of Cross-Cultural
    Inquiry:  An American Sample.  Anthropological Quarterly.
    38:181-200, 1965.

Aries, P.  Western Attitudes Toward Death:  From The Middle
    Ages to the Present.  Baltimore, MD:  Johns Hopkins
    University Press, 1974.

_____  The Reversal of Death:  Changes in Attitudes Toward
    Death in Western Societies.  Pp. 134-58 in D. Stannard
    (ed).  Death in America.  Philadelphia, PA:  University of
    Pennsylvania Press, 1975.

_____  The Hour of Our Death.  New York, NY:  Knopf, 1981.

    One important point of this fascinating book is that the
    meaning of death is historically and culturally situated.
    Well worth reading, it is a detailed history and sociology
    of death from the Middle Ages through the 1970s.

Averill, R. C.  Grief:  Its Nature and Significance.
    Psychological Bulletin.  70:721-48, 1968.

Backer, B. A., N. Hannum, and N. A. Russell.  Death and Dying:
    Individuals and Institutions.  New York, NY:  Wiley, 1982.

    This is a general undergraduate text on death and dying.
    The focus is on American society, the dying process,
    medical and ethical issues, and funerals.  There is one
    chapter on death in cross-cultural perspective.

Ball, J.  Widow's Grief:  The Impact of Age and Mode of Death.
    Omega.  7(4):307-33, 1966/7.

Barker, J.  Voluntary Bereavement Counseling Schemes.
    Mitcham, Surrey, Britain:  Age Concern England, 1983.

Barrett, C. J. and K. M. Schneweis.  An Empirical Search for
    Stages of Widowhood.  Omega.  11:97-104, 1980.

Baston, David (ed).  Death and Dying:  A Clinical Guide for
    Caregivers.  Baltimore, MD:  Williams and Wilkins, 1977.

    A collection of 17 individually authored articles for
    doctors and other clinicians.  One chapter focuses on the
    elderly.

Beauchamp, T. L. and S. Perlin.  Ethical Issues in Death and
    Dying.  Englewood Cliffs, NJ:  Prentice Hall, 1978.

    A collection of 37 readings on ethical aspects of death and
    dying.  Included are coverage of brain death and coma,
    legal definitions, suicide, diagnosis and euthanasia.
    Abstracted articles include works by Tolstoy, Camus, and
    St. Thomas Aquinas.

Becker, H. and D. Bruner.  Attitude Toward Death and the Dead
    and Some Possible Causes of Ghost Fear.  Mental Hygiene.
    15:828-37, 1931.

Bengtson, V., J. Cuellar, and P. Ragan.  Stratum Contrasts and
    Similarities in Attitudes Toward Death.  Journal of
    Gerontology.  32(1):76-88, 1977.

Benohel, J.  Nurses and the Human Experience of Dying.  Pp.
    123-41 in H. Feifel (ed).  New Meanings of Death.  New
    York, NY:  McGraw-Hill, 1977.

Berardo, F. M.  Survivorship and Social Isolation:  The Case
    of the Aged Widower.  Family Coordinator.  19:11-25, 1970.

Berdes, C.  Social Services for the Aged Dying and Bereaved in
    International Perspective.  Washington, DC:  International
    Federation on Ageing, 1978.

Berman, A.  Belief in Afterlife, Religion, Religiosity and
    Life-Threatening Experiences.  Omega.  5(2):127-35, 1974.

Bettis, S. K. and F. G. Scott.  Bereavement and Grief.  Annual
    Review of Gerontology and Geriatrics.  2:144-59, 1981.

Blauner, R.  Death and Social Structure.  Psychiatry.
    29:378-94, 1966.

Bock, E. W. and I. L. Weber.  Suicide Among the Elderly:
    Isolating Widowhood and Mitigating Circumstances.  Journal
    of Marriage and the Family.  34:24-31, 1972.

Bogen, L.  Human Grief:  A Model for Prediction and
    Intervention.  American Journal of Orthopsychiatry.
    47:196-206, 1977.

Bowlby, J.  Attachment and Loss.  3 vols.  New York, NY:
    Basic Books, 1972, 1976, 1980.

Long after the twentieth century is gone, this will remain
as one of the great works of social and behavioral science.
The work presents a major conceptual framework to
understand loss.  Volume 3 (1980) deals with the mourning
experiences of adults and cross-culturally.

Bynum, J.  Social Status and Rites of Passage:  The Social
Context of Death.  Omega.  4(4):323-32, 1973.

Carpenter, J. and C. Wylie.  On Aging, Dying and Denying.
Public Health Reports.  89(5):403-07, 1974.

Carr, A. C. (ed).  Grief:  Selected Readings.  New York, NY:
Health Sciences Press, 75.

Carruthers, M.  The Western Way of Death:  Stress, Tension,
and Heart Attacks.  New York, NY:  Pantheon, 1974.

Carse, J. P.  Death and Existence:  A Conceptual History of
Human Mortality.  New York, NY:  Wiley, 1980.

A detailed account of death as a philosophical concept from
Platonism through Kierkegaard.  Text is organized both
historically and thematically, e.g., death as change, as
dispersion, as separation, as illusion, as fiction.  As
well as western notions, two chapters consider Hindu and
Buddhist views of death.

Carter, W.  Secular Reinforcement in Aymara Death Ritual.
American Anthropologist.  70:238-63, 1968.

Castles, M. R. and R. B. Murray.  Dying in an Institution:
Nurse/Patient Perspectives.  New York, NY:  Appleton
Century, 1979.

Charmaz, K.  The Social Reality of Death.  Reading, PA:
Addison Wesley, 1980.

Clayton P., J. A. Halikas, and W. Maurice.  The Depression of
Widowhood.  British Journal of Psychiatry.  120:71-78,
1972.

Cohen, K. P.  Hospice:  Prescription for Terminal Care.
Germantown, MD:  Aspen, 1979.

Copperman, H.  Dying at Home.  Chichester, UK:  J. Wiley,,
1983.

Corr, C. A. and D. M. Corr (eds).  Hospice Care:  Principles
and Practice.  New York, NY:  Springer, 1983.

The 25 individually-authored chapters cover the hospice
approach to dying:  pharmacological issues, caregiving,
bereavement, implementing hospice movement.

Counts, D.  The Good Death in Kaliai:  Preparation for Death
in Western New Britain.  Omega.  7(4):367-72, 1976/7.

Counts, D. A. and D. R. Counts (eds). Aging and Its Transformations: Moving Toward Death in Pacific Societies. ASAO Monograph No. 10. Lanham, MD: University Press of America, 1985.

Cox, P. R. and J. R. Ford. The Mortality of Widows Shortly After Widowhood. The Lancet. 1:163-64, 1964.

Davidson, G. W. (ed). The Hospice: Development and Administration (2nd ed). Washington, DC: Harper & Row, Hemisphere, 1985.

Contains 11 individually-authored chapters on, among other things, starting a community hospice, administrative issues, interdisciplinary teams, the physician's role, stress among staff, mourning, ethics, and spiritual help.

Dempsey, D. The Way We Die: An Inventory of Death and Dying in America. New York, NY: MacMillan, 1975.

This is a general sociology of death in modern America. Includes chapters on violent death, the search for longevity, medical treatment, the right to die, burial, and natural death.

Devos, G. and H. Wagatsuma. Psychocultural Significance of Concern over Death and Illness Among Rural Japanese. International Journal of Social Psychiatry. 5:5-19, 1959.

Doyle, P. Grief Counseling and Sudden Death: A Manual and Guide. Springfield, IL: C. C. Thomas, 1980.

The special focus of this book for counselors is sudden death such as accidents, homicide, suicide--including elderly suicide. Contains information on training.

DuBois, P. M. The Hospice Way of Death. New York, NY: Human Sciences Press, 1980.

A general account of hospice programs. The chapter on "the quality of dying" is excellent. Three case studies form the core of the book. Also covered is the history of the Hospice Movement.

Dumont, R. and D. Foss. The American View of Death: Acceptance or Denial? Cambridge, MA: Schenkman, 1972.

Elias, N. The Loneliness of Dying. Oxford, UK: Blackwell, 1985.

A general, philosophically-oriented discussion for individual's confrontations with the inevitibility of death. The book centers on the existential loneliness of dying. It features a postscript on aging and dying.

Fabian, J. How Others Die: Reflections on the Anthropology of Death. Social Research. 39(3):543-67, 1972.

Feifel, H. (ed). New Meanings of Death. New York, NY: McGraw Hill, 1977.

   Nineteen individually-authored chapters. Sections are on development, clinical management of dying, the survivors, and responses to death.

Ferraro, K. F. and C. M. Baressi. The Impact of Widowhood on the Social Relations of Older Persons. Research on Aging. 4:227-47, 1982.

Friedsham, H. The Coming On of Years: Social Science Perspectives on Aging and Death. Social Science Quarterly. 5:120-28, 1970.

Fulton, R. (ed). Death and Identity (rev ed). Bowie, MD: Charles Press, 1976.

   There are 27 chapters in this edited volume on issues in the sociology of death. Sections are on attitudes and responses, grief and mourning, and social organization and society.

Gallagher, D. E., et al. Effects of Bereavement on Indicators of Mental Health in Elderly Widows and Widowers. Journal of Gerontology. 38:565-71, 1983.

Garfield, C. A. (ed). Psychosocial Care of the Dying Patient. New York, NY: McGraw Hill, 1978.

Garrity, T. and J. Wyss. Death, Funeral and Bereavement Practices in Appalachian and Non-Appalachian Kentucky. Omega. 7(3):209-28, 1976.

Glaser, B. G. and A. Strauss. Awareness of Dying. Chicago, IL: Aldine 1965.

   Treats the question, do people die socially before they die biologically? Deciding yes, it asks, what is the meaning of this for human relationships? The research, undertaken in a hospital, documents the extensive unwillingness to talk about the process of death, the closed awareness.

_____ Temporal Aspects of Dying as a Non-Scheduled Status Passage. Pp. 520-30 in B. Neugarten (ed). Middle Age and Aging. Chicago, IL: University of Chicago Press, 1968.

Glick, I. O., R. D. Weiss, and C. M. Parkes. The First Year of Bereavement. New York, NY: Wiley, 1974.

Goin, M. K., R. W. Burgoyne, and J. M. Goin. Timeless Attachment to a Dead Relative. American Journal of Psychiatry. 136:988-89, 1979.

Goldschmidt, W. Freud, Durkheim and Death Among the Sebei. Omega. 3(3):227-31, 1972.

Goody, J. Death, Property and the Ancestors. Palo Alto, CA:

Stanford University Press, 1962.

Gorer, G.  Death, Grief and Mourning.  Garden City, NY: Doubleday Anchor, 1965.

Green, J.  The Days of the Dead in Oaxaca, Mexico:  An Historical Inquiry.  Omega.  3(3):245-61, 1972.

Grollman, E. A.  Concerning Death:  A Practical Guide for the Living.  Boston, MA:  Beacon, 1974.

Hagglund, T.-B.  Death:  A Psychoanalytic Study With Special Reference to Individual Creativity and Defense Organization.  New York, NY:  International University Press, 1978.

Hardt, Dale V.  An Investigation of the Stages of Bereavement. Omega.  9:279-85, 1978.

_____ Death:  The Final Frontier.  Englewood Cliffs, NJ: Prentice Hall, 1979.

A general account of death and dying.  Covers attitudes, what is death, aging, the right to die, burial customs and cultural variation, grief, the funeral, longevity, and wills.

Harper, B. C.  Death:  The Coping Mechanism of the Health Professional.  Greenville, SC:  Southeastern University Press, 1977.

Haug, H.  Aging and the Right to Terminate Medical Treatment. Journal of Gerontology.  33:586-91, 1978.

Heidegger, M.  Being and Time.  Translated by J. McQuarrie and E. Robinson.  New York, NY:  Harper and Row, 1962.

Henderson, D.  Death as a Fact of Life.  New York, NY: Norton, 1977.

Heyman, D. K. and D. T. Gianturco.  Long-term Adaptation by the Elderly to Bereavement.  Journal of Gerontology. 28:350-53, 1973.

Hinton, J.  Dying.  Baltimore, MD:  Penguin, 1967.

A general, first-rate introduction to the death and dying field.  Contains 14 chapters in four sections covering attitudes to the dying, their care, and mourning.  While by now somewhat dated, it continues to be a useful work.

Hippler, A.  Fusion and Frustration: Dimensions in the Cross-Cultural Ethnopsychology of Suicide.  American Anthropologist.  71:1074-87, 1969.

Howard, A and R. Scott.  Cultural Values and Attitudes Toward Death.  The Journal of Existentialism.  6(22):161-74, 1965/6.

Huber, P.  Death and Society Among the Anggor of New Guinea.
     _Omega_.  3(3):233-43, 1972.

Huntington, R. and P. Metcalf.  _Celebrations of Death:  The
     Anthropology of Mortuary Ritual_.  Cambridge, MA:  Cambridge
     University Press, 1979.

Hyman, H. H.  _Of Time and Widowhood:  Nationwide Studies of
     Enduring Affects_.  Durham, NC:  Duke University Press,
     1983.

Jones, R.  Religious Symbolism in Limbu Death-by-Violence.
     _Omega_.  5(3):257-66, 1974.

Jury, M. and D. Jury.  _Gramp_.  New York, NY:  Grossman, 1976.

     The moving account of the death of a senile, 81-year-old
     man through pictures and words.  A classic.  Throughout his
     total deterioration, Gramp was cared for by his family at
     home.  Besides the experience of the death, the book
     describes way in which family members learned about
     themselves through the caregiving experience.

Kalish, R.  Death and Dying in a Social Context.  Pp. 483-507
     in R.  Binstock and E. Shanas (eds).  _Handbook of Aging and
     the Social Sciences_.  New York, NY:  Van Nostrand Reinhold,
     1976.

_____  _Between Living and Dying_.  New York, NY:  Springer,
     1979.

_____  _Death and Dying:  Views from Many Cultures_.
     Farmingdale, NY:  Baywood, 1980.

_____  _Death, Grief, and Caring Relationships_.  Monterey, CA:
     Brooks/Cole, 1981.

_____  (ed).  _Midlife Loss:  Coping Strategies_.  Newbury Park,
     CA:  Sage, 1989.

Kalish, R. and D. Reynolds.  _Death and Ethnicity--A
     Psychocultural Study_.  Los Angeles, CA:  University of
     Southern California Press, 1976.

     Results of a California study of death and dying attitudes,
     beliefs and behaviors among Afro-, Japanese-, Anglo-, and
     Mexican-Americans, age 20 and up.  A significant work in
     its treatment of cultural variables.  Includes the research
     schedule as an appendix.

Kastenbaum, R.  Death and Development Through the Lifespan.
     Pp. 18-45 in H. Feifel (ed).  _New Meanings of Death_.  New
     York, NY:  McGraw-Hill, 1977a.

_____  _Death, Society, and Human Experience_.  St. Louis, MO:
     C. V. Mosby, 1977b.

_____  _Between Life and Death_.  New York, NY:  Springer,

1979a.

_____ Reflections on Old Age, Ethnicity, and Death.  Pp. 81-95
in D. Gelfand and A. Kutzik (eds).  Ethnicity and Aging:
Theory, Research and Policy.  New York, NY:  Springer,
1979b.

Kastenbaum, R. and R. Aisenberg.  The Psychology of Death.
New York, NY:  Springer, 1977.

This is one of the most important books in the death and
dying field:  a comprehensive and significant treatment of
the psychology and philosophy of dying.  Two chapters (of
16) are on the cultural milieu of death.

Keleman, S. I.  Living Your Dying.  New York, NY:  Random
House, 1974.

A discussion of the experience of death, including styles
of dying, emotions surrounding the experience, and key
turning points.  By focusing on living during the time of
dying, the book teaches acceptance of changing perceptions
as essential to living while dying.

Kennedy, P. H.  Dying at Home with Cancer.  Springfield, IL:
C. C. Thomas, 1982.

Krant, M. J.  Dying and Dignity:  The Meaning and Control of a
Personal Death.  Springfield, IL:  C. C. Thomas, 1974.

Krupp, G. R.  The Bereavement Reaction:  A Special Case of
Separation Anxiety With Sociocultural Considerations.
Psychoanalytic Study of Society.  2:42-74, 1962.

Krupp, G. R. and B. Kligfeld.  The Bereavement Reaction:  A
Cross-cultural Evaluation.  Journal of Religion and Health.
1:222-46, 1962.

Kubler-Ross, E.  On Death and Dying.  New York, NY:
MacMillan, 1979.

_____ Living with Death and Dying.  New York, NY:  MacMillan,
1981.

Teaches the importance of listening to "our dying
patients."  We should listen not only to words, but also to
other symbolic representations of affect such as behavior
and drawings.

Kubler-Ross, E. and M. Warshaw.  To Live Until We Say Goodbye.
Englewood Cliffs, NJ:  Prentice Hall, 1978.

Personal accounts and moving photos of three dying
individuals.  Discussion of alternatives to hospital care
for the dying.

Lamerton, R.  Care of the Dying.  Westport, CT:  Technomic,
1976.

Lee, J.  Death and Beyond in the Eastern Perspective.  New
    York, NY:  Interface Books, 1974.

Levine, S.  Who Dies?:  An Investigation of Conscious Living
    and Conscious Dying.  Garden City, NY:  Anchor Press, 1982.

Lieberman, M. A. and S. S. Tobin.  The Experience of Old Age:
    Stress, Coping, Survival.  New York, NY:  Basic Books,
    1983.

Lofland, L. H.  Toward a Sociology of Death and Dying.
    Beverly Hills, CA:  Sage, 1976.

_____  The Craft of Dying:  The Modern Face of Death.  Beverly
    Hills, CA:  Sage, 1978.

    This brief sociology of dying considers the secularization
    of dying, role problems, and the prolongation of the dying
    period.  A focus, too, is on the individual and the
    collective constructions of death; the Happy Death Movement
    is discussed.

Lopata, H.  Grief Work and Identity Reconstruction.  Journal
    of Geriatric Psychiatry.  8(1):41-57, 1975.

Margolis, O. S., et al.  Acute Grief:  Counseling the
    Bereaved.  New York, NY:  Columbia University Press, 1981.

    A general overview of bereavement issues, with a special
    emphasis on counseling.

Marshall, V.  Last Chapters:  A Sociology of Aging and Dying.
    Monterey, CA:  Brooks/Cole, 1980.

Masamba, J. and R. A. Kalish.  Death and Bereavement:  The
    Role of the Black Church.  Omega.  7:23-34, 1976.

McDonnell, A.  Quality Hospice Care.  Owings Mills, MD:
    National Health Pulbications, 1986.

McNulty, E. G. and R. A. Holderby.  Hospice:  A Caring
    Challenge.  Springfield, IL:  C. C. Thomas, 1983.

Miller, S. I. and L. Schoenfeld.  Grief in the Navajo:
    Psychodynamics and Culture.  International Journal of
    Social Psychiatry.  19:187-91, 1973.

Moore, J.  The Death Culture of Mexico and Mexican Americans.
    Omega.  1:271-91, 1970.

Moriarity, D. M. (ed).  The Loss of Loved Ones:  The Effect of
    a Death in the Family on Personality Development.
    Springfield IL:  C. C. Thomas, 1967.

Moss, M. S. and S. Z. Moss.  The Image of the Deceased Spouse
    in Remarriage of Elderly Widow(er)s.  Journal of
    Gerontological Social Work.  3:59-70, 1980.

Munley, Anne. The Hospice Alternative: A New Context for Death and Dying. New York, NY: Basic Books, 1983.

An excellent account of dying and the hospice. Contains a general overview of dying as a social problem and "the hospice solution." Describes life in a hospice. Also, includes discussions of pain and the dynamics of dying.

Munnichs, J. Old Age and Finitude. Basel, Switzerland: Karger, 1966.

A summary of a research project on attitudes towards death among the elderly. It contains a review of the literature and a discussion of research findings. Significant is the treatment of finality as a human theme.

Myers, J. E., H. Wass, and M. Murphy. Ethnic Differences in Death Anxiety Among the Elderly. Death Education. 4:237-44, 1980.

Ogg, E. Facing Death and Loss. Lancaster, PA: Technomic, 1985.

Omega: The Journal of Death and Dying.

Osterweis, M., F. Solomon, and M. Green (eds). Bereavement: Reactions, Consequences, and Care. Washington, DC: National Academy Press, 1984.

Contains 11 chapters on bereavement, including epidemiological perspectives and types of bereavement. One chapter focuses on sociocultural influences and the cultural backdrop to bereavement. Also discussed are intervention programs.

Parkes, C. M. The Effects of Bereavement on Physical and Mental Health: A Study of the Case Records of Widows. British Medical Journal. 2:274-79, 1964.

_____ 'Seeking' and 'Finding' a Lost Object: Evidence from Recent Studies of Reaction to Bereavement. Social Science and Medicine. 4:187-201, 1970.

_____ Bereavement: Studies of Grief in Adult Life. New York, NY: International Universities Press, 1972.

This classic book reviews a great deal of work by Parkes, his colleagues, and others. Well written, it is an easily accessible overview of the survivor's life.

_____ Determinants of Outcome Following Bereavement. Omega. 6:303-23, 1975.

Parkes, C. M., B. Benjamin, and R. G. Fitzgerald. Broken Heart: A Statistical Study of Increased Mortality Among Widowers. British Medical Journal. 1:740-43, 1969.

Parkes, C. M. and R. S. Weiss. Recovery from Bereavement.

New York, NY:  Basic Books, 1983.

Parsons, T. (ed).  Death in American Experience.  Social
Research.  39:367-567, 1972.

Pegg, P. F. and E. Metze.  Death and Dying: A Quality of
Life.  London, UK:  Pitman, 1981.

Pine, V.  Comparative Funeral Practices.  Practical
Anthropology.  16:49-62, 1969.

_____ Social Organization and Death.  Omega.  3(2):149-53,
1972.

_____ Dying, Death and Social Behavior.  Pp. 31-47 in B.
Schoenberg (ed).  Anticipatory Grief.  New York, NY:
Columbia University Press, 1974.

_____ Caretaker of the Dead: The American Funeral Director.
New York, NY:  Irvington Publishers, 1975.

Pollock, G. H.  On Mourning and Anniversaries: The
Relationship of Culturally Constituted Defense Systems to
Intrapsychic Adaptive Processes.  Israel Annals of
Psychiatry.  10:9-40, 1972.

Preston, C. and R. Williams.  Views of the Aged on the Timing
of Death.  Gerontologist.  11(4):300-04, 1971.

Rando, T. A. (ed).  Loss and Anticipatory Grief.  Lexington,
MA:  Lexington Books, 1986.

    Fifteen individually-authored chapters on general
    perspective, the principles involved, clinical
    interventions and developmental issues.  One chapter
    concerns anticipating the death of an elderly parent.

Rees, W. D.  The Hallucinations of Widowhood.  British Medical
Journal.  4:37-41, 1971.

Rehfisch, F.  Death, Dreams and the Ancestors in Mambila
Culture.  Pp. 306-14 in M. Douglas and P. Kaberry (eds).
Man in Africa.  Garden City, NY:  Anchor Books, 1971.

Reynolds, D. and R. Kalish.  Anticipation of Futurity as a
Function of Ethnicity and Age.  Journal of Gerontology.
29(2):224-31, 1974.

Rosenblatt, P., R. Walsh and D. Jackson.  Grief and Mourning
in Cross-Cultural Perspective.  New Haven, CT:  HRAF Press,
1976.

Rosenblatt, P. C.  Bitter, Bitter Tears: Nineteenth-Century
Diarists and Twentieth-Century Grief Theories.
Minneapolis, MN:  University of Minnesota Press, 1983.

Rowe, D.  The Construction of Life and Death.  Chichester, UK:
Wiley, 1982.

Russell, O. R.  Freedom to Die:  Moral and Legal Aspects of
    Euthanasia. New York, NY:  Human Sciences Press, 1974.

Savishinsky, J. S.  Common Fate, Difficult Decision:  A
    Comparison of Euthanasia in People and in Animals.  Pp. 3-8
    in W. J. Kay, et al (eds).  Euthanasia of the Companion
    Animal:  The Impact on Pet Owners, Veterinarians, and
    Society.  Philadelphia, PA:  The Charles Press, 1988.

    Examines several parallel issues raised by euthanasia with
    people and with animals:  moral ambiguity, the roles of
    medical professionals' images of caretaking and
    callousness, the use of language and metaphor, and the role
    of ritual are explored.

Schoenberg, B. (ed).  Anticipatory Grief.  New York, NY:
    Columbia University Press, 1974.

    A major compendium--41 chapters--of research and findings
    on this important aspect of the bereavement experience.
    Includes a cogent discussion of the concepts involved,
    clinical aspects of this grief, of childhood illness, and
    of the management of anticipatory grief.

Schoenberg, B., et al.  Psychosocial Aspects of Terminal Care.
    New York, NY:  Columbia University Press, 1972.

    This edited volume treats an important topic in the death
    and dying field.  Of interest are chapters on mourning
    ritual in Western culture and grief in cross-cultural and
    historic perspective.

Schulz, C.  Age, Sex and Death Anxiety in a Middle-Class
    American Community.  Pp. 239-52 in C. Fry (ed).  Aging in
    Culture and Society.  Brooklyn, NY:  J. F. Bergin, 1980.

Shibles, W.  Death:  An Interdisciplinary Analysis.
    Whitewater, WI:  Language Press, 1974.

Shneidman, E. S.  Voices of Death.  New York, NY:  Harper and
    Row, 1980.

    This book has some unusual windows into the death
    experience:  interviews with survivors of suicide attempts
    and discussion of the contents of suicide notes.  It also
    discusses self-mourning and mourning by survivors

Shuchter, S. R.  Dimensions of Grief:  Adjustment to the Death
    of a Spouse.  San Francisco, CA:  Jossey-Bass, 1986.

Sinick, D.  Counseling Older Persons:  Cancer, Retirement,
    Dying.  New York, NY:  Human Sciences Press, 1977.

Sourkes, B. M.  The Deepening Shade:  Psychological Aspects of
    Life-Threatening Illness.  Pittsburgh, PA:  University of
    Pittsburgh Press, 1982.

Stannard, D. E.  Death in America.  Philadelphia, PA:

University of Pennsylvania Press, 1975.

Stephenson, J. S.  Death, Grief, and Mourning:  Individual and Social Realities.  New York, NY:  The Free Press, 1985.

Tallmer, M. (ed).  The Life-Threatened Elderly.  New York, NY: Columbia University Press, 1984.

Trelease, M.  Dying Among Alaskan Indians:  A Matter of Choice.  Pp. 33-7 in E. Kubler-Ross.  Death the Final State of Growth.  Englewood Cliffs, NJ:  Prentice Hall, 1975.

Vallee, F.  Burial and Mourning Customs in a Hebritean Community.  Journal of the Royal Anthropological Institute. 85:119-30, 1955.

Van Tassel, D, (ed).  Aging, Dying and the Completion of Being.  Philadelphia, PA:  University of Pennsylvania Press, 1979.

Veatch, R.  Death, Dying and the Biological Revolution.  New Haven, CT:  Yale University Press, 1956.

A discussion of moral and ethical issues surrounding life-sustaining technologies.  Thorough-going coverage of the definition of death, euthanasia, right-to-refuse treatment, organ banks, and public policy.

Vernon, G.  Sociology of Death.  New York, NY:  Ronald, 1970.

Wass, H.  Death and the Elderly.  Pp. 182-207 in H. Wass (ed). Dying:  Facing the Facts.  New York, NY:  Hemisphere, 1979.

Weisman, A. D.  On Dying and Denying:  A Psychiatric Study of Terminality.  New York, NY:  Behavioral Publications, 1972.

_____  The Coping Capacity:  On the Nature of Being Mortal. New York, NY:  Human Sciences Press, 1984.

Weizman, S. G. and P. Kanin.  About Mourning:  Support and Guidance.  New York, NY:  Human Sciences Press, 1985.

A counseling-oriented treatment of survivorship, from death through the funeral and the emotional work thereafter. There is a chapter on the death of an adult's parent.

Yamamoto, J., et al.  Mourning in Japan.  American Journal of Psychiatry.  125:1660-65, 1969.

Zarit, S. H.  Readings in Aging and Death:  Contemporary Perspectives, 1977-8.  New York, NY:  Harper and Row, 1978.

Zimmerman, J. M.  Hospice:  Complete Care for the Terminally Ill (2nd ed).  Baltimore, MD:  Urban and Schwarzenberg, 1986.

# 13

# Methods

Agar, M. The Professional Stranger. New York, NY: Academic Press, 1980.

This volume is billed as an informal introduction to ethnography. It leads one from preparing for ethnographic research through getting started, moving to more formal methods, the development of research applications, and evaluation of cultural theory.

Angrosino, M. The Use of Autobiography as "Life History." Ethos 4:133-54, 1976.

Avrer, U. and H. Weihl. A Cross-Cultural Study in a Single Country. Pp. 14-17 in E. Shanas and J. Madge (eds). Interdisciplinary Topics in Gerontology Methodology: Problems in Cross-National Studies in Aging. Vol 2. New York, NY: Karger, 1968.

Beall, C. M. and J. K. Eckert. Measuring Functional Status Cross-Culturally. Pp. 21-56 in C. Fry and J. Keith (eds). New Methods for Old Age Research. South Hadley, MA: Bergin & Garvey, 1986.

Bengtson, V., et al. Relating Academic Research to Community Concerns: A Case Study in Collaborative Effort. Journal of Social Issues. 33(4):75-92, 1977.

Bohannon, P. The Unseen Community: The Natural History of a Research Project. Pp. 29-45 in D. Messerschmidt (ed). Anthropologists at Home: Toward an Anthropology of Issues in America. New York, NY: Cambridge University Press, 1981.

Buros, O. (ed). The Eighth Mental Measurements Yearbook. Vol 1. Highland Park, NJ: Gryphon Press, 1978.

Cohen, D. The Twin: Twin-Family Approach to Cross-Cultural Aging Research. Gerontologist. 16:82-85, 1976.

Cook, T. D. and C. S. Reichardt (eds). Qualitative and Quantitative Methods in Evaluation Research. Beverly Hills, CA: Sage, 1979.

Important because the editors try to bridge the supposed gap in the false dichotomy between qualitative and quantitative methods. They are effective in demonstrating the complementarity and effectiveness of both.

Crapanzano, V. The Life History in Anthropological Field Work. Anthropology and Humanism Quarterly. 2(2/3):3-7, 1977.

Eckert, J. K. Anthropological Community Studies in Aging Research: A Method to the Madness. Research on Aging. 5(4):455-72, 1983.

_____. Ethnographic Research on Aging. Pp. 241-55 in S. Reinharz and G. D. Rowles (eds). Qualitative Gerontology. New York, NY: Springer, 1987.

Ellen, R. F. Ethnographic Research: A Guide to General Conduct. New York, NY: Academic Press, 1984.

This is the first in a series of volumes on research methods in social anthropology to be produced by the Association of Social Anthropologists. Like others of its kind, it covers the spectrum of the research process from a variety of approaches, the experience, ethics, producing data, to the production of texts.

Fry, C. and J. Keith (eds). New Methods for Old Age Research. South Hadley, MA: Bergin and Garvey, 1986.

The new methods in this edited volume look at specific ethnographic techniques such as perticipant observation, ethnosemantic research, historical demography, holocultural research, and life histories as strategies in comparative research. Also variables which have dominated gerontological research (functionality, the measurement of age, transitions, well-being, social networks, rituals and ethnicity) are examined with emphasis on comparative measurement. The introduction also makes useful comments on present methods for peer review.

Georges, R. and M. Jones. People Studying People. Berkeley, CA: University of California Press, 1980.

Langness, L. and G. Frank. Lives: An Anthropological Approach to Biography. Novato, CA: Chandler and Sharp, 1981.

The authors examine the historical development of life histories in anthropological research. A real contribution of this volume is a discussion of the specifics of obtaining life histories, analyzing life histories, and ethical and moral issues in reporting this kind of data.

Luborsky, M.   Analysis of Multiple Life History Narratives.
    Ethos:  Journal of Psychological Anthropology.
    15(4):366-81, 1987.

    Analysis of cultural and personalized meanings of
    retirement in thirty-seven life histories from subjects in
    a three-year retirement transition study.  Variations in
    beliefs and in narratives are linked to systematic
    differences in the process of retirement.

Manuel, R.   Social Research Among the Minority Aged:
    Providing a Perspective for a Select Number of Issues.  Pp.
    16-30 in G.  Sherman (ed).  Research and Training in
    Minority Aged.  Washington, DC:  National Center on Black
    Aging, 1978.

Matthews, S. H.   Analyzing Topical Oral Biographies of Old
    People.  Research on Aging.  5(4):569-89, 1983.

Maxwell, R., E. Krassen-Maxwell, and P. Silverman.  The Cross-
    Cultural Study of Aging:  A Manual for Coders.  New Haven,
    CT:  HRAF Press, 1978.

McTavish, D.  Perceptions of Old People:  A Review of Research
    Methodologies.  Gerontologist.  11:90-101, 1971.

Messerschmidt, D. A. (ed).  Anthropologists at Home in North
    America.  Cambridge:  Cambridge University Press, 1981.

    Since anthropologists have worked in their own society,
    this is a timely volume showing both the experiences and
    problems of working at home and indicating the differences
    in the fieldwork experience in comparison with working
    abroad.

Miles, M. B. and A. M. Huberman.  Qualitative Data Analysis:
    A Sourcebook of New Methods.  Beverly Hills, CA:  Sage,
    1984.

    A major question is how to manage the descriptive data that
    are obtained from qualitative research.  This volume
    provides suggestions and strategies using different
    research designs.  The majority of the case examples are
    from education research.

Mintz, S.  The Anthropological Interview and the Life History.
    The Oral History Review.  18-26, 1979.

Myerhoff, B.  Remembered Lives.  Parabola.  5(1):74-77, 1980a.

_____ Telling One's Story.  The Center Magazine.  3:22-40,
    1980b.

Myerhoff, B. and V. Tufte.  Life History as Integration:  An
    Essay on an Experimental Model.  Gerontologist.  15:541-43,
    1975.

Naroll, R. and R. Cohen (eds).  A Handbook of Method in

<u>Cultural Anthropology</u>.  New York, NY:  Columbia University Press, 1973.

This compendium is now a classic and a real treasure trove of issues and problems faced in ethnographic and comparative research.  The contributors examine general problems:  the fieldwork process, models of ethnographic analysis, categorization, comparative approaches, and special problems in comparative research.

Neugarten, B. and V. Bengtson.  Cross-National Studies of Adulthood and Aging.  Pp. 18-3 in H. Blumenthal (ed). <u>Interdisciplinary Topics in Gerontology</u>.  Vol 2.  New York, NY:  S. Karger, 1968.

Nydegger, C. (ed).  Anthropoogical Approaches to Ageing Research:  Applications to Modern Societies.  Special Issue. <u>Research on Aging</u>.  5(4), 1983.

Pelto, J. and G. Pelto. <u>Anthropological Research:  The Structure of Inquiry</u> (2nd ed).  New York, NY:  Harper and Row, 1978.

The Peltos have produced what has become a classic in texts for anthropological research.  The strength of this volume is that it integrates both qualitative and quantitative research strategies and is explicit on the structure of scientific inquiry.

Pitt, N. <u>Using Historical Sources in Anthropology and Sociology</u>.  New York, NY:  Holt, Rinehart and Winston, 1972.

Powdermaker, H. <u>Stranger and Friend</u>.  New York, NY:  Morrow, 1966.

Reichard, S., F. Livson, and P. Peterson. <u>Aging and Personality</u>.  New York, NY:  John Wiley, 1962.

Reinharz, S. and G. D. Rowles (eds). <u>Qualitative Gerontology</u>. New York, NY:  Springer, 1987.

Qualitative methods in gerontological research have increased in use and sophistication.  The editors have assembled a collection of essays which demonstrate the diversity of research problems and projects which have employed qualitative methods.

Romanucci-Ross, L.  With Margaret Mead in the Field: Observations on the Logic of Discovery. <u>Ethos</u>.  4:439-48, 1976.

Shanas, E.  Some Observations on Cross-National Surveys of Aging. <u>Gerontologist</u>.  3:7-9, 1963.

Shanas, E. and J. Madge (eds).  Methodological Problems in Cross-National Studies in Aging.  Pp. 1-17 in H. Blumenthal (ed). <u>Interdisciplinary Topics in Gerontology</u>.  Vol 2.

New York, NY:  Karger, 1968.

Sherman, E.  Working with Older Persons:  Cognitive and Phenomenological Methods.  Hingham, MA:  Kluwer Nijhoff, 1984.

Simmons, L.  A Prospectus for Field Research in the Position and Treatment of the Aged in Primitive and Other Societies. American Anthropologist.  47:433-48, 1945.

Sokolovsky, J. and C. Cohen.  Measuring Social Interaction of the Urban Elderly:  A Methodological Synthesis.  Aging and Human Development.  13(3):233-44, 1981.

Spradley, J.  Participant Observation.  New York, NY:  Holt, Rinehart and Winston, 1979a.

_____  The Ethnographic Interview.  New York, NY:  Holt, Rinehart and Winston, 1979b.

   These two volumes by Spradley are full of good ideas and strategies.  The first, Participant Observation, focuses on observational techniques.  The second, The Ethnographic Interview, emphasizes interviewing techniques with some emphasis on ethnosemantics.

Watson, L.  Understanding a Life History as a Subjective Document.  Ethos.  4:95-131, 1976.

Welch, S., J. Cromer, and M. Steinman.  Interviewing in a Mexican-American Community:  An Investigation of Some Potential Sources of Response Bias.  Public Opinion Quarterly.  37:115-16, 1973.

Werner, O. and G. M. Schoepfle.  Systematic Fieldwork.  2 vols.  Beverly Hills, CA:  Sage, 1987.

   These two volumes address the issues of doing ethnography and the analysis and management of ethnographic data.  In places these are a little tedious for detail, but the authors are systematic and do provide an abundance of ideas.

Whyte, W.  On Making the Most of Participant Observation.  The American Sociologist.  14:56-66, 1979.

Wright, N.  Golden Age Apartments:  Ethnography of Older People.  Pp. 121-36 in J. Spradley and D. McCurdy.  The Cultural Experience.  Chicago, IL:  Science Research Association, 1972.

# 14

# Bibliographies

Bailey, W. G.  Human Longevity from Antiquity to the Modern
  Laboratory:  A Selected Annotated Bibliography.  Westport,
  CT:  Greenwood Press, 1987.

Bagwell, D.  Gerontology and Geriatrics Collections.  Special
  Collections Series.  1(3), 1982.

Balkema, J.  The Aged in Minority Groups:  A Bibliography.
  Washington, DC:  National Council on Aging, 1973.

_____.  The Creative Spirit:  An Annotated Bibliography on the
  Arts, the Humanities, and Aging.  Washington, DC:  National
  Council on Aging, 1986.

Barnes, G. M., E. L. Abel, and C. A. Ernst.  Alcohol and the
  Elderly:  A Comprehensive Bibliography.  Westport, CT:
  Greenwood Press, 1980.

Barnes, N.  Black Aging:  An Annotated Bibliography.
  Monticello, IL:  Vance Bibliographies, 1979.

Bengtson, V., K. Edwards, and G. Baffa.  Intergenerational
  Relations and Aging:  A Selected Bibliography.  Technical
  Bibliographies on Aging.  Los Angeles, CA:  E. Percy Andrus
  Gerontology Center, 1975.

Bieulac, M.  Bibliographie International de Gerontologie
  Social.  2 vols.  Paris:  Centre International de
  Gerontologie Social, 1982.

Boston, H. S.  Housing and Living Arrangements for the
  Elderly:  A Selected Bibliography.  Washington, DC:
  National Council on Aging, 1985.

Brady, M. L.  Growing Old in Today's Society:  A Selective
  Bibliography.  San Luis Obispo, CA:  California Polytechnic
  State University, 1987.

Brearly, C. P.  A Bibliography on Social Work and Ageing.

Mitcham, Surrey, England:  Age Concern England, 1979.

Cassel, C. K., D. E. Meier, and M. L. Traines.  Selected
Bibliography of Recent Articles in Ethics and Geriatrics.
Journal of the American Geriatrics Society.  34(5):399-409,
1986.

Central Mortgage and Housing Corporation.  The Seventh Age:  A
Bibliography of Canadian Sources in Gerontology and
Geriatrics 1964-1972.  Ottawa, Canada:  Environmics Group,
1972.

Choquet, M.  Indications Bibliographiques Sur Les Loisirs.
Paris, France:  Centre International de Gerontologie, 1972.

Cox, E. and J. Sandberg.  Nutrition and the Elderly:  A
Selected Annotated Bibliography for Nutrition and Health
Professionals.  Bibliographies on Literature and
Agriculture, No. 34.  Washington, D.C.:  Government
Printing Office, 1985.

Cuellar, J. B., E. P. Stanford, and D. I. Miller Soule.  The
Minority Aging Bibliographies.  Pp. 186-379 in
Understanding Minority Aging.  San Diego State University,
CA:  University Center on Aging, 1982.

Davis, L.  Black Aged in the US:  An Annotated Bibliography.
London, UK:  Greenwood Press, 1980.

Delgado, M. and G. Finley.  The Spanish-Speaking Elderly:  A
Bibliography.  Gerontologist.  18(4):387-94, 1978.

Dinan, J. and L. Bowker.  Selected Annotated Bibliography of
the Humanistic Needs of Nursing Home Residents.  Milwaukee,
WI:  Center for Advanced Studies in Human Services,
University of Wisconsin, 1982.

Dolan, E. and D. M. Gropp.  The Mature Woman in America:  A
Selected Annotated Bibliography, 1972-82.  Washington, DC:
National Council on Aging, 1984.

Fecher, V. J.  Religion and Aging:  An Annotated Bibliography.
San Antonio, TX:  Trinity University Press, 1984.

Garen, W.  Alternatives to Institutionalization:  An Annotated
Research Bibliography on Housing and Services for the Aged.
Urbana, IL:  Housing Research and Development, University
of Illinois, 1976.

Gibson, M. J., A. Heath, and C. Nusberg.  International Survey
of Periodicals in Gerontology (2nd ed).  Washington, DC:
International Federation on Aging, 1982.

Hagerty, K.  Retirement:  A Bibliography Through 1972.
Chicago, IL:  Bush Library, Industrial Relations Center,
University of Chicago, 1974.

Harris, D. K.  The Sociology of Aging:  An Annotated

*Bibliography and Sourcebook*.  New York, NY:  Garland, 1985.

Hawley, D. L.  *Women and Aging:  A Comprehensive Bibliography*.
Bibliographical Series, 85-1.  Burnaby, British Columbia:
Gerontological Research Centre, Simon Fraser University,
1985.

Hesslein, S. B.  *Serials on Aging:  An Annotated Guide*.
Westport, CT:  Greenwood Press, 1986.

Interface Bibliographies.  *Age Is Becoming:  An Annotated
Bibliography on Women and Aging*.  Berkeley, CA:  Interface
Bibliographies, 1977.

Jackson, J. S.  Partial Bibliography of Gerontological and
Related Literature About Minorities:  Part 1.  *Black Aging*.
1:41-55, 1976.

_____  Partial Bibliography of Gerontological and Related
Literature About Minorities:  Part 2.  *Black Aging*.
2:50-65, 1976-77.

Johnson, T. F., J. G. O'Brien, and M. F. Hudson.  *Elder
Neglect and Abuse:  An Annotated Bibliography*.  Westport,
CT:  Greenwood Press, 1985.

Kagan, D. and A. Keown.  *Aging and the Aged in Non-Industrial
Societies:  A Selected Bibliography*.  Riverside, CA:
Department of Anthropology, University of California, 1973.

Kim, P. and H. Lamprey.  *A Bibliography on Rural Aging*.
Lexington, KY:  College of Social Professions, Mental
Health and Rural Gerontology, Rural Gerontology Project,
1979.

Krout, John A.  *The Rural Elderly:  An Annotated Bibliography
of Social Science Research*.  Westport CT:  Greenwood Press,
1983.

McIlvaine, B.  *Old Age:  A Register of Social Research 1972
Onwards*.  Nuffield Lodge, Regents Park, London, UK:  The
National Corporation for the Care of Old People, 1975.

McIlvaine, B. and M. Mundkur.  *Aging:  A Guide to Reference
Sources*.  Storrs, CT:  University of Connecticut, 1978.

Miletich, J. J.  *Retirement:  An Annotated Bibliography*.
Westport CT:  Greenwood Press, 1986.

Missine, L. and B. Seem.  *Comparative Gerontologist:  A
Selected Annotated Bibliography*.  Washington, DC:
International Federation on Aging, 1979.

Molina, A.  *Minority Aged*.  Bibliography No. 49 in Urban
Diversity Series.  New York, NY:  Teachers College
Institute for Urban and Minority Education, Columbia
University, 1979.

Monroe, M. E. and R. J. Rubin.  The Challenge of Aging:  A
    Bibliography.  Littleton, CO:  Libraries Unlimited, 1983.

Moss, W.  Humanistic Perspectives on Aging:  An Annotated
    Bibliography and Essay.  Ann Arbor, MI:  Institute of
    Gerontology, University of Michigan, 1976.

Murguia, E.  Ethnicity and Aging:  A Bibliography.  San
    Antonio, TX:  Trinity University Press, 1984.

Natress, W. K.  Gerontology and Mental Retardation:  A
    Functional Bibliography.  Harrisburg, PA:  Institute for
    Research and Development in Retardation, 1980.

Osako, M.  Bibliography:  Social Participation of Rural
    Elderly in Developing Nations, With Special Emphasis on
    Their Roles in Family, Community and Economy.  New York,
    NY:  Center for Social Development, United Nations, 1982.

Osgood, N. J. and J. L. McIntosh.  Suicide and the Elderly:
    An Annotated Bibliography.  Westport CT:  Greenwood Press,
    1986.

Place, L. F., L. Parker, and F. J. Berghorn.  Aging and the
    Aged:  An Annotated Bibliography and Library Research
    Guide.  Boulder, CO:  Westview Press, 1981.

Polisar, D., et al.  Where Do We Come From?  What Are We?
    Where Are We Going?  An Annotated Bibliography of Aging and
    the Humanities.  Washington, DC:  The Gerontological
    Society of America, 1988.

Ragan, P. and M. Simonin.  Blacks and Mexican American Aging:
    A Selected Bibliography.  Technical Bibliographies on
    Aging, Series 2.  Los Angeles, CA:  Ethel Percy Andrus
    Gerontology Center, 1977.

Rooke, M. L. and C. Wingrove.  Gerontology:  An Annotated
    Bibliography, 1966-1977.  Washington, DC:  University Press
    of America, 1977.

Rosenthal, M. J.  Geriatrics:  An Updated Bibliography.
    Journal of the American Geriatrics Society.  35(6):560-86,
    1987.

Ryan, N.  Rural Aging in Canada:  An Annotated Bibliography.
    Guelph, Ontario:  Gerontological Research Centre, The
    University of Guelph, 1985.

Sell, I. L.  Death and Dying:  An Annotated Bibliography.  New
    York, NY:  Tiresias Press, 1977.

St. Clair, B. E. and S. A. Wong.  Nutrition and Aging:  A
    Selected Bibliography.  Toronto, Ontario:  Nutritional
    Information Service, Ryerson Polytechnical Institute, 1982.

Strange, H. and V. Green.  Cultural Perspectives on Aging:  An
    Annotated Bibliography.  New Brunswick, NJ:  Institute on

Aging, Rutgers University, 1980.

Strange, H. and M. Teitelbaum (eds). Aging and Cultural Diversity:  New Directions and Annotated Bibliography. South Hadley, MA:  Bergin and Garvey, 1987.

Suzuki, P.  Minority Group Aged in America:  A Comprehensive Bibliography of Recent Publications on Blacks, Mexican Americans, Native Americans, Chinese and Japanese.  No. 816:1-25.  Monticello, IL:  Council of Planning Librarians, 1975.

United States Department of Housing and Urban Development. The Built Environment for the Elderly and the Handicapped: A Selective Bibliography.  Washington, DC:  U. S. Government Printing Office, 1979.

U. S. Human Resources Corporation.  The Spanish-Speaking Elderly:  A Bibliography, 1983.

Webber, I.  Aging and Retirement:  A Bibliographic Review of Recent and Current Research at Seven University Centers. Chicago, IL:  University of Chicago, 1954.

Wharton, G. F.  Sexuality and Aging:  An Annotated Bibliography.  Metuchen, NJ:  The Scarecrow Press, 1981.

Wilkinson, C.  The Rural Aged in America, (1975-1978):  An Annotated Bibliography.  Occasional Papers on the Rural Aged, No.1.  Morgantown, WV:  Gerontology Center, West Virginia University, 1978.

# Index

Abe, T., 280
Abel, E. K., 234
Abel, E. L., 307
Abeles, R., 225
Ablon, J., 287
Abrahams, R., 246
Abrams, M., 135
Abu-Laban, B., 173
Abu-Laban, S., 173
Acharkan, V. A., 148
Achenbaum, W. A., 128, 165
Acsadi, G., 31
Adamchak, D. J., 165
Adams, B., 83, 169, 234
Adams, D., 279
Adams, F., 94
Adams, G. L., 192
Adams, M., 68
Adelman, R. C., 31
Adeokun, L., 79, 84, 87
Adler, S., 210
Agar, M., 301
Agee, E. M., 173
Ageing International, 99
Agoestina, T., 280
Aguirre, B. E., 192
Ahern, E., 104
Aimei, J., 104
Aires, M., 225
Aisenberg, R., 294
Akinnawo, E. O., 29
Akiyama, H., 132, 234, 273
Albeaux-Fernet, M., 284
Albert, E., 273
Albert, S. M., 51
Albrecht, R., 234
Alder, A., 266
Aldous, J., 234

Aldridge, G., 261
Alexander, L., 51
Allan, G. A., 135, 234
Almagor, U., 246
Almind, G., 150
Alston, L. L., 192
Alter, G., 273
Altergott, D., 18
Althouse, R., 133, 222
Altman, I., 51
Amann, A., 99
Ammundsen, E., 51
Amoss, P., 3, 18, 198
Anderson, A., 31, 182
Anderson, B. G., 51, 129, 130, 287
Anderson, J., 136
Anderson, N., 225
Anderson, P., 182
Anderson, R., 245
Anderson, T. B., 234
Andres, R., 31
Andretta, E. H., 80
Andrews, C. T., 135
Andrews, G. R., 101, 159, 161
Angrosino, M., 261, 301
Anisimov, V. N., 31
Anson, O., 154
Antana, S., 198
Antonovsky, A., 275, 285
Antonucci, T., 234, 265, 273
Apple, D., 198, 234
Applewhite, S. R., 192
Apt, N., 84
Araki, S., 31
Arensberg, C. M., 145, 146
Arie, T., 70

Siegal, H., 270
Siegel, J. B., 100
Siegel, J. S., 46
Siegler, I., 233
Siemaszko, M., 65, 221
Sigman, S. J., 76
Silberstein, J., 76
Siler, W., 46
Sill, J., 17
Silverman, P., 4, 25, 26,
27, 90, 168, 233, 243, 264,
303
Simic, A., 4, 27, 134, 153,
243
Simmons, L., 27, 28, 171,
207, 243, 255, 305
Simms, P., 55
Simon, D., 165
Simon, R. J., 65
Simonin, M., 310
Simons, R. L., 65
Simopoules, A., 46
Simos, B., 158
Simpson, I., 256
Sinclair, D., 46
Singer, M., 269
Sinick, D., 298
Sinnott, J., 280
Skinner, E., 243
Skinner, J., 67
Skinner, K. A., 217
Skye, W. C., 217
Slater, P., 28
Slivinske, L. R., 65
Smircina, M. T., 33
Smirnov, S., 149
Smith, D., 46, 47, 190
Smith, H. L., 147
Smith, J. R., 47
Smith, L., 223
Smith, M. J., 56
Smith, P. C., 214
Smith, R., 122, 141, 233
Smith, S., 190
Smithers, J., 264
Smolic-Krkovic, N., 243
Sneden, L., II, 236
Snider, E., 65
Snyder, D., 190
Snyder, L. H., 259
Snyder, P., 217
Sokolovsky, J., 3, 5, 29,
54, 95, 180, 181, 266, 267,
270, 271, 305

Soldo, B. J., 61
Solis, F., 197
Solomon, B., 65
Solomon, F. 0, 296
Soloviev, A. G., 149
Sommer, R., 259
Sontag, S., 134, 280
Soodan, K. S., 126
Sorensen, C., 162
Soto, D., 54
Sotomayor, M., 197
Soules, M. R., 47
Sourkes, B. M., 298
Spaid, W. M., 234
Sparks, D., 122
Spector, S., 97
Speigelman, M., 36
Spencer, P., 249
Spicker, S., 11
Spierer, H., 233
Spiering, A. L., 47
Spitzer, J. B., 197
Spoehr, A., 233
Spradley, J., 305
Sprey, J., 240
Ssenkoloto, G., 83
St. Clair, B. E., 310
Stack, S., 171
Stafford, P., 259
Stall, R., 65
Stanford, E. P., 175, 180,
181, 190, 213, 308
Stannard, C., 76
Stannard, D. E., 298
Stearns, P. N., 5, 76, 134,
165, 171
Steen, B., 47
Steglich, W., 193
Stegman, M., 197
Stegman, N., 197
Stein, H., 65, 221
Steiner, J. R., 259
Steiner, R. A., 37
Steinman, M., 305
Stennett, R., 17
Stenning, O., 243
Stephenson, J. S., 299
Stephens, J., 271
Stephens, R., 174, 271
Sterling, N., 280
Sterne, R., 271
Sternheimer, S., 171
Sterns, H. L., 243
Sterns, P., 153

Welch, G. J., 88
Woehrer, C., 182
Woerner, L., 198
Wofford, S., 45
Wohwill, J., 51
Wolanski, N., 49
Wolf, J., 192
Wolffensperger, E. W., 151
Wolk, R. L., 94
Wolk, R. B., 94
Women of Mutira, 82
Wong, P., 212
Wong, S. A., 310
Wood, J., 188
Wood, P., 221
Wood, V., 245, 261
Woodbury, M. A., 61, 101, 161
Woodhead, A. D., 50
Woodruff, D. S., 11
Woolf, L., 182
Woolfson, P., 104
Woon, Y-F., 115
Worach-Kardas, H., 154, 272
World Health Organization, 68
Wright, N., 305
Wright, R., Jr., 68
Wu, C., 115
Wu, C-I., 115
Wu, F., 212
Wu, S-C, 213
Wu, Y., 115
Wylie, C., 289
Wylie, F., 192
Wyss, J., 291

Xi, H., 50
Xu, Q., 115

Yakushev, L., 150
Yamamoto, J., 299
Yamanaka, K., 171
Yan, A., 212
Yang, C., 116
Yang, Q., 116
Yap, P., 163
Yee, B., 217
Yelder, J., 192
Yin, P., 116
Yoels, W. C., 8
York, J., 77
Youmans, E., 18, 223, 245, 280

Young, M., 104, 245
Young, R. F., 246
Yu, E., 215
Yu, E. S. H,., 68, 116, 213, 217
Yu, L. C., 213
Yuan, F., 116
Yuan, J., 116
Yuen, S., 214
Yung, S., 210

Zambrana, R., 68, 198
Zarit, S. H., 299
Zborowski, M., 272
Zelkovitz, B. M., 154
Zellman, G., 52, 173
Zhang, C., 117
Zhang, K., 117
Zhang, Y., 109
Zhu, C., 117
Zimmer, L., 93
Zimmerman, J. M., 299
Zola, I., 182
Zube, M., 135
Zubrow, E. B. W., 50

**About the General Editor**

MARJORIE M. SCHWEITZER is Professor Emeritus in the Department of Sociology at Oklahoma State University. She received her Ph.D. in Anthropology from the University of Oklahoma. She is the immediate past president and a charter member of the Association for Anthropology and Gerontology.